The Art of Sex T
Supervision

MW00805793

The Art of Sex Therapy Supervision is a collection of scholarly writings and case narratives that sheds light on issues that sex therapists face as supervisors or supervisees, and provides techniques that can be adapted to fit clients' specific needs. Written by several sexuality supervisor experts in the field, this book covers a wide range of perspectives and methodologies for assisting diverse populations, including conservative Christians, LGBTQ clients, and those who exhibit out of control sexual behavior. It addresses individual, relational, and systemic engagement in the context of sexual function/dysfunction, as well as obstructions clinicians can face when providing critical feedback to clients. This book will be useful for aspiring supervisors as well as those who supervise clinicians seeking licensure or certification.

James C. Wadley, PhD, CSTS, is associate professor and chair of the Counseling and Human Services Department at Lincoln University in Pennsylvania. He is a licensed professional counselor and AASECT-certified sex therapist and supervisor. Dr. Wadley also maintains a private practice in Pennsylvania and New Jersey.

Richard Siegel, PhD, CSTS, is a licensed mental health counselor in Florida, an AASECT-certified sex therapist and supervisor, and director of the Modern Sex Therapy Institutes.

The Art of Sex Therapy Supervision

Edited by
James C. Wadley and Richard Siegel

Routledge
Taylor & Francis Group

NEW YORK AND LONDON

First published 2019
by Routledge
711 Third Avenue, New York, NY 10017

and by Routledge
2 Park Square, Milton Park, Abingdon, Oxon, OX14 4RN

Routledge is an imprint of the Taylor & Francis Group, an informa business

Library of Congress Cataloging-in-Publication Data
Names: Wadley, James C., editor. | Siegel, Richard, 1963– editor.
Title: The art of sex therapy supervision / edited by James C.
   Wadley and Richard Siegel.
Description: New York : Routledge, 2018. | Includes bibliographical
   references.
Identifiers: LCCN 2018007107 | ISBN 9781138575639 (hbk. :
   alk. paper) | ISBN 9781138575646 (pbk. : alk. paper) | ISBN
   9781351271523 (e-book)
Subjects: | MESH: Sexual Dysfunctions, Psychological—therapy |
   Sexual Dysfunction, Physiological—therapy | Psychotherapy |
   Sex Counseling | Interprofessional Relations | Mentoring
Classification: LCC RC556 | NLM WM 611 | DDC
   616.85/83—dc23
LC record available at https://lccn.loc.gov/2018007107

ISBN: 978-1-138-57563-9 (hbk)
ISBN: 978-1-138-57564-6 (pbk)
ISBN: 978-1-351-27152-3 (ebk)

Typeset in Galliard
by Apex CoVantage, LLC

I dedicate this book to my family, friends, and colleagues who offered support and encouragement in completing this tremendous task.

James

I dedicate this book to my father, my daughter, and my brother, whose support, assistance, patience, and sacrifice made this endeavor possible.

Richard

Contents

Acknowledgments

The editors would like to acknowledge the tremendous efforts of our many chapter authors. They include some true giants in the field of sex therapy, have collectively trained and supervised hundreds of sex therapists and sexuality counselors and educators, and without their wisdom and decades of experience as therapists and supervisors, this book would certainly not be possible. It is our humble wish that these contributors will continue to inform and influence the field, with the development of quality supervisors, for years to come.

We would like to thank our reviewers, Dr. Twinet Parmer, Serena Corsini-Munt, Natalie Elliott, and Larry Siegel, for their assistance in editing the manuscripts. We are in gratitude to the staff at Taylor and Francis, especially Nina Guttapalle and George Zimmar, for their patience and professionalism.

We want to acknowledge the professionalism and contributions of all of our authors and the field that has supported the evolution to produce a book of this nature. The authors of this book bring over a century's worth of experience and thousands of hours working with individuals and couples. In addition, we would like to thank the AASECT for being an organization devoted to the advancement and empowerment of professionals in the field of sexology. Without their support, this project would not have been possible.

James

I would like to thank my family including my wife, Lisa, and two children, Corbin and Cairo, for their patience and support for the amount of time and space granted to finish this project. Your collective sacrifice has not gone unnoticed and I remain grateful for the opportunity to evolve as a professional. To my parents, James and Phyllis and brother, Jared Wadley for being the "wind beneath my wings" by believing in me and my work over the years. To my professional family at Lincoln University, I am blessed to have you as my brothers and sisters who have encouraged me to play my part in advancing the excellence of our institution. To my supervisors at Council for Relationships in Philadelphia including (but not limited to) Drs. Steve Treat, Bea Hollander, Kenneth Covelman, April Westfall, Argie Allen, and Mr. William Coffey and Ms. Judith Rader, I want to thank you for being you and giving me an opportunity to learn and grow as a marriage, family, and sexuality therapist. Thank you for providing me with a blueprint for "sound clinical supervision" and the necessity of remaining mindful about the needs of supervisees and clients. A special thank you to my friend, colleague, mentor, and brother, Mr. Alphonse Pignataro, who showed me how to be a professional in the field and offer countless lessons and advice about self-care. Finally, I would like to thank those people of color in the fields of sexology, psychology, social work, counselor education, and marriage, family, and sex therapy who taught me how to try to create safe spaces for dialogue about sexuality, sexual wellness, and community engagement.

Richard

I would like to thank my dad, Bob Siegel, my oldest brother, Dr. Steve Siegel, and my exceptional and beautiful daughter, Layne Siegel. I would also like to extend gratitude to my brother, Larry Siegel, who has single-handedly served as mentor, therapist, vocational counselor, advocate and promoter, co-author, co-researcher, co-presenter, and co-conspirator—and editor—for the past 25 years. I would like to dedicate this book to the late Dr. Susan Lee, my sex therapy mentor and supervisor for 15 years, and business partner in the Florida Postgraduate Sex Therapy Training Institute and Sex Therapy Training Institute of New York. Finally, I would like to offer heartfelt thanks to my original encourager, supporter, and cheerleader: my dear, departed mom, Ruth Siegel.

Introduction

James C. Wadley and Richard Siegel

When we were first invited to put this book together, we thought about how a book of this nature has been needed in the field of sex therapy supervision for some time. There have been a few works that addressed sex therapy supervision from one vantage point or another, but there has not been a compendium of essays and readings that shed light upon the complexities and nuances of conducting sex therapy supervision. We wanted to involve as many leaders in the field as we possibly could because the field comprises psychiatrists, psychologists, social workers, professional counselors, and couples and family therapists. Thus, as you can imagine, when we put out a query for practitioners to participate in this initiative, we were overwhelmed by the response. In an informal dialogue, Dr. Richard Siegel mentioned that supervision is truly an art and that there are a myriad of perspectives and techniques to assist individuals and couples with managing sexual dysfunction. It was at that point that we decided that the book would be called *The Art of Sex Therapy Supervision* because we wanted to have as many colors (perspectives) shown through this narrative medium as possible.

The purpose of the book is to educate and bring awareness to some of the issues that sex therapists face as supervisors or supervisees. We believe that some of these critical issues may be obstructions to providing or getting necessary feedback that may ultimately impede a client's capacity to develop a healthy relationship with himself/herself and his/her partner. We hope this book will be used by counselors, therapists, social workers, medical practitioners, and especially those who supervise clinicians toward licensure or certification. In addition, the book is for those who seek to gain a robust understanding of how to skillfully manage supervisees and learn more about the sex therapy supervision process.

The chapters in this book will address individual, relational, and systemic engagement as it relates to sexual function/dysfunction. The book assumes that sex therapy supervisors may draw upon supervision techniques from their respective fields (psychology, counselor education, social work, etc.) and be able to effectively manage supervisees. Another assumption of this work is that all supervisees may not be able to offer interventions that take into account the myriad factors (sexual orientation/identity, race, ability, communication style, emotional intelligence, etc.) that shape sexual functioning/dysfunction. In the fields of sex therapy, sexuality counseling, and sex education, a book of this nature has been conspicuously lacking for a significant time.

We believe that the utilization of this book is critical for anyone who seeks to become a sex therapy supervisor, not only because of the breadth and depth of clinical knowledge and experience shared by truly renowned and recognized experts in the field, but also because it underscores the crucial role that supervision plays in the development of competent clinicians.

This textbook's proud co-editors first had the chance to co-supervise groups as pre-conference session facilitators at past annual conferences of the American Association of Sexuality Educators, Counselors and Therapists (AASECT). It was mutually agreed that the most fitting title for these sessions would be, "Sex Therapy Supervision: Where the Rubber Meets the Road," because of the shared belief that a clinician could study the fascinating subject of sexuality—"clinical sexology"—for decades, but yet still not ever change the way they "do therapy," or truly *become* sex therapists without skilled, clinical case supervision. We strongly agree that supervision prepares the clinician to put that rubber to the road, so to speak, and develop their own in-the-therapy-room style and skills. And this is not only a service to the clinician, to insure they are their most competent and confident to offer a valuable service to patients in need, but it is also an invaluable service to the profession—a vital stopgap to insure that high standards are demanded and consistently assessed and maintained, and that unqualified practitioners are not "let loose" on an unsuspecting public.

One limitation of the book warrants mention. Because of the artistic nature of the book, there is no "one size fits all" technique or method for working with individuals or couples who experience sexual dysfunctions. We believe that sex therapists must possess an intuitiveness that is agile and flexible to meet his/her clients' needs. This intuitiveness then informs what appropriate intervention(s) may be needed to address presenting issues. While some sex therapists may use broad strokes to attempt to address systemic issues, others may use more pointed and definitive gestures to help shift clients' thinking and behavior.

The editors also feel compelled to acknowledge, for posterity, that at the very point in time this text is being compiled, the incessant chatter of the 24-hour news cycle seems as much if not more obsessed with the sex scandals of celebrities and politicians than with utter government breakdown. It seems we have arrived at another historic moment, a disturbing yet also heartening turbulence from an unprecedented amount of whistle-blowing on centuries-old sexist tolerance of the sexual harassment of women by men, incriminating the most powerful power brokers in industry and the halls of Congress to the Oval Office itself. And at the same time, we face unprecedented attacks and insulting threats to decades of progress on preserving and protecting the civil rights of sexual minorities; in fact, lately it seems *all* of our civil rights are being targeted.

It is sincerely hoped that the silver lining in this period of history is that this sexual chaos, from Washington, DC, to Hollywood, will pave the way for a new sexual revolution—not one based only on busting perceived "old-fashioned" social and sexual mores, but a revolution soundly anchored in sexual health and adequately armed with education, information, and truly open communication so as to create a lasting cultural change.

Sex therapy supervisors are uniquely poised to contribute significantly to this needed change by helping to forge future generations of sex therapists—and hopefully, general psychotherapists of all backgrounds, sexuality educators, and ALL health educators, as well as the growing numbers of medical practitioners embracing sexuality as a quality of life issue for their patients.

1 The Integration of Sex Therapy and Sexual Medicine

Richard Siegel

Abstract

There continues to be a dearth of sexuality learning or training opportunities in the vast majority of medical schools, so most interested clinicians are forced to find such training on their own. The American Association of Sexuality Educators Counselors and Therapists (AASECT), as mentioned throughout this volume as the oldest and largest sexological organization and certification body, has not only been attracting increasing numbers of medical professionals but has also formalized its Certified Sexuality Counselor (CSC) criteria, thereby creating standards of competence for healthcare practitioners that had not existed before. These changes present significant opportunities for sex therapy supervisors to supervise a variety of medical clinicians toward becoming CSCs. Sex therapy supervisors who have had the opportunity to supervise medical professionals toward certification will undoubtedly attest to how mutually satisfying and enriching this type of supervision can be.

Keywords

sex therapy, sex therapy supervision, sexual medicine, sexuality counseling, sexuality counseling supervision, integration of sexual medicine

The 1990s and 2000s saw an unprecedented confluence of sex therapy and the emergent field of sexual medicine. Of course, though many would credit the FDA's approval of Viagra in 1998 as the "birth" of sexual medicine, medical professionals have been treating sexual complaints, with varying degrees of success, for many years. There most certainly has been tremendous progress since the 19th century treatment of women for *hysteria* by "induction of paroxysm" to reduce anxiety and emotional instability. Of course, this was not considered to be anything sexual and thus did not include any consideration of marriage or childhood factors (as Freud eventually did) to understand the possible psychosexual underpinnings of these women. Instead, it simply led to the invention of the vibrator (*for paroxysms—don't call them orgasms!*). Also at that time, people were introduced to the prescriptions of radical ideologue physicians, like John Kellogg and Sylvester Graham, of bland diets designed to "quell the sin" of masturbation and prevent what they referred to as subsequent ravages on the body and mind from "self-pollution" among boys and young men.

However, this new "golden era" for sexual medicine emerged while urologists were generally reassuring aging men of the inevitability of "impotence," saving such treatments as intracavernosal injections or primitive penile rods for only the most severe cases, like post-prostatectomy or advanced diabetic neuropathy. Men with cardiovascular disease, for example, were presented with a Hobson's choice of taking medication that will likely inhibit erectile ability or forgo the medication and risk a cardiac event. Meanwhile, on the "other side," this new focus on sexual medicine arrived at a time when increasing numbers of physicians, particularly gynecologists and psychiatrists, were becoming increasingly interested in female sexual dysfunction (FSD). To date, however, medical intervention for treatment of desire and arousal issues in women remains something of a holy grail in sexual medicine.

Though not widely embraced, it was known among the medical community that there were some psychotherapists that were successfully treating sexual problems like erectile dysfunction and vaginismus with cognitive-behavioral and psychodynamic therapies. Since the groundbreaking work of Masters and Johnson, who first observed and described the phases of sexual response and created protocols addressing dysfunction at each phase, sex therapy was born as a formal modality (Masters & Johnson, 1966, 1971). It seems odd that, at present, sex therapy is not recognized as a distinct therapeutic modality by the American Psychological Association. Moreover, today's sex therapy cannot claim much fidelity—or even resemblance—to what Masters and Johnson originally developed (Binik & Meana, 2009; Weiner & Avery-Clarke, 2017). Though Drs. Masters and Robert Kolodny's *Textbook of Sexual Medicine* (1979) would presage that nascent specialty, the '70s and '80s were a true heyday for sex therapy, and sex therapy training programs began to appear all over the country. Renowned pioneer sex therapists like Helen Singer Kaplan, Sandra Leiblum, Michael Perelman, Peggy Kleinplatz, Eli Coleman, Leonor Tiefer, Stan Althof, and others began to bridge the gap between therapy and medicine toward the 1990s as newer, more medically oriented groups like the International Society for the Study of Women's Sexual Health (ISS-WSH) joined established groups of sex therapists, educators, and researchers like American Association of Sexuality Educators, Counselors and Therapists (AASECT), the Society for the Scientific Study of Sexuality (SSSS), and the Society for Sex Therapy and Research (SSTAR; Perelman, 2014).

In the early 1980s, there seemed to have been little public awareness of a sex therapy heyday, likely the combined effects of a far-right, conservative movement that occupied the political leadership (lasting through 12 years of Reagan–Bush administrations) and the emergence of the AIDS pandemic. So when a not-so-effective angina medication consistently showed an unexpected side effect of erectile function in men, a new era of public discourse about sex was ushered in and Viagra, a new type of drug called a PDE-5 inhibitor, became the star of the pharmaceutical world. Where "impotence" was typically thought of as something to be lived with in quiet shame, "erectile dysfunction" (ED) and its miraculous new "cure" burst out of the shadow of shame and into public discussion. The acceptance of ED as a common medical condition reached its zenith when a 73-year-old former senator and presidential nominee appeared on a national television show, with his wife, to boast about how Viagra was "rejuvenating their marriage." Since then, several other PDE5 inhibitors have been developed and marketed (e.g., Levitra, Cialis, Staxyn, Stendra). With the success of the PDE5 inhibitors, pharmaceutical companies turned their attention to developing a comparable product for the treatment of lack or desire and arousal in women—a "Pink Viagra," so to speak. This new renaissance of sexual medicine saw the approval of flibanserin, a little-used antidepressant also discovered to have "encouraging" side effects in clinical trials and, thus, touted as the first centrally acting desire agent for women (i.e., acting directly on the brain rather than just blood-flow and "plumbing" in the pelvis). It is marketed under the name Addyi and, by all measures, has been a flop (Helfand, 2016; Rubin, 2016).

Over time, and with increased use, we began seeing increasing dissatisfaction with PDE-5 inhibitors. It is common knowledge among urologists that as many as half of all Viagra prescriptions are not refilled (Castleman, 2016). Along with the relative failure of flibanserin, this has made a strong case for integrating sex therapy and pharmacotherapy in order to make both more effective (Althof, 2010). It has also sparked more conversations than ever about sex as a quality-of-life issue among all of medical disciplines. Patients today are more emboldened to ask their healthcare providers about sexual issues, without fear of "embarrassing them" (Humphery & Nazareth, 2001; Shifren et al., 2009), and slowly but surely, healthcare providers are realizing that the subject cannot be ignored or avoided and recognizing their lack of training, in both content and counseling skills, is an impediment to adequately answer their patients' sexual questions. Unfortunately, as Maslow indicated with his "one tool" metaphor, many physicians are myopically focused on using pharmacotherapies to treat sexual dysfunctions in a manner that is less than ideal. Many physicians, for example, have begun prescribing SSRI antidepressants, such as Paxil or Luvox, for rapid ejaculators, expressly because of their notorious side effect of ejaculatory inhibition. Another example of a popular but less-than-ideal use of medication is the use of numbing agents with which to treat premature ejaculation. Numbing the penis can hardly be seen as a positive sex therapy approach and completely negates to psychological, emotional, relational, and spiritual factors that make up sexual response.

All of this has strengthened the position that sex therapy, and sexual health assessment in general, needs to be incorporated into virtually every area of medicine. PDE-5 inhibitors are not the "erection-on-demand" cures they've been touted to be, and gynecologists saw that the expected throngs of women demanding Addyi never showed up. But beyond the arguably more obvious "sexual plumbing specialists," are cardiologists addressing the fears of men wanting to resume sexual relations after a heart attack (beyond the three-flight standard)? Are oncologists discussing the possible sexual effects of their chemotherapy and radiation, not to mention surgical interventions, on sexual function? Do gastroenterologists performing "tummy tucks" and gastric bypass procedures discuss body image in the context of sexual concerns? How much is rehabilitation medicine doing to insure counseling around sex and intimacy for servicemen and women and their partners, especially in the Veterans Administration, as war veterans are returning home from Afghanistan, Iraq, and Syria with catastrophic injuries?[1] Perhaps most ironic is the avoidance of conversations around sex and sexuality among obstetricians. The very thing that makes women obstetrics patients is rarely discussed at all during pregnancy or after delivery, beyond the customary admonition, "no sex for six weeks!"[2]

Happily, more and more physicians and healthcare practitioners are beginning to "see the light." In addition to continued improvement in integrating sexual medicine with sex therapy, increasing numbers of physicians, physician assistants, advanced nurse practitioners, and physical therapists are seeking training in sexual medicine and ways to enhance their skills, both in the examination room and in the counseling offices of their practices, improving the ways in which they can ask about and discuss sexual concerns with their patients.

The bad news is that there continues to be a dearth of learning or training opportunities in the vast majority of medical schools (as continues to be the trend with most psychology and psychotherapy programs), so most interested clinicians are forced to find such training on their own. More good news is that AASECT, as mentioned throughout this volume as the oldest and largest sexological organization and certification body, has not only been attracting increasing numbers of medical professionals but has also formalized its Certified Sexuality Counselor (CSC) criteria, thereby creating standards of competence for healthcare practitioners that had not existed before. These changes are relatively recent, however, and within AASECT there are only a handful of certified CSC supervisors available to oversee this, but it also presents a significant opportunity for sex therapy supervisors to supervise a variety of medical clinicians toward becoming CSCs.

Supervision of Sexuality Counselors

Sex therapy supervisors who have ever had the opportunity to supervise medical professionals toward certification will undoubtedly attest to how mutually satisfying and enriching this type of supervision can be. These supervisory relationships are typically between established clinicians in different professions, so the relationship may not align well with the more traditional mentor–apprentice model that most of the supervision approaches espoused in this volume would imply. Instead, these dynamics may fit more closely the description of what noted cognitive-behavioral therapy (CBT) supervisor David Lane calls a "process model" of supervision (Corrie & Lane, 2015), wherein the supervisee is the expert in content (their medical specialty) and the supervisor is the expert in process (in terms of both counseling skills and supervision). Together, they can focus on how sex therapy can be integrated into existing practice, regardless of the medical specialty.

Of course, this reminds us of the importance of the unique training of sex therapists beyond their particular theoretical orientation, be it social work, marriage and family therapy, psychology, or counseling. Sex therapists arguably (bias aside) are the most "cross-trained" of all psychotherapists and mental health professionals. Sex therapists typically need to be broadly trained in cognitive therapies, behavioral therapies, psychodynamic therapies, systemic approaches, individual and couples therapy skills, practical applications, creativity principles, and medical basis, as well as having a broad-based, working understanding of complex endogenous and exogenous neuroendocrine and pharmacological principles and knowledge of a pharmacopoeia of hormones and medications.

As legendary Miami-based sexuality educator and clinical sexologist Dr. Marilyn Volker has declared for decades, the future of sex therapy and the success of sexual medicine will depend on the excited and exuberant integration of "dream teams": multidisciplinary teammates working in a biopsychosocial, body-mind-spirit way to bring about sexual health, satisfaction, and happiness. This supervisor cannot begin to express the gratitude to the obstetrician/gynecologists, nurse midwives, urologists, psychiatrists, neurologists, internists, gerontologists, and most especially, the pelvic floor physical therapists that it has been his pleasure to supervise, many of whom are now AASECT-Certified Sexuality Counselors. In fact, several of these individuals have transitioned entirely out of medicine to pursue a second career as a sexuality counselor in private practice.

Notes

1 Clinicians working with these populations would be wise to watch—and show— the profoundly moving documentary called *Love After War* (2017), co-produced by Mitchell Tepper, PhD, of The Sexual Health Network (www.drmitchelltep per.com/sexual_health_network) and Mark Schoen, PhD, of SexSmart Films (www.sexsmartfilms.com).
2 Chapter author Stephanie Buehler, PhD, has just released *Counseling Couples Before, During, and After Pregnancy: Sexuality and Intimacy Issues* (2018).

References

Althof, S. E. (2010). What's new in sex therapy. *Journal of Sexual Medicine, 7,* 5–13.

Binik, Y., & Meana, M. (2009). The future of sex therapy: Specialization or marginalization? *Archives of Sexual Behavior, 38,* 1016–1027. https://doi. org/10.1007/s10508-009-9475-9

Buehler, S. (2018). *Counseling couples before, during, and after pregnancy: Sexuality and intimacy issues.* New York: Springer.

Castleman, M. (2016). *Viagra falls: Older men aren't very into erection drugs.* Retrieved from www.psychologytoday.com/blog/all-about-sex/201603/viagra-falls-older-men-aren-t-very-erection-drugs

Corrie, S., & Lane, D. A. (2015). *CBT supervision.* Thousand Oaks, CA: Sage.

Helfand, C. (2016). *Why is Valeant's "blockbuster" libido drug Addyi a dud?* Retrieved from www.fiercepharma.com/marketing/former-sprout-investors-sue-valeant-over-shoddy-addyi-marketing

Humphery, S., & Nazareth, I. (2001). GPs' views on their management of sexual dysfunction. *Journal of Family Practice, 18*(5): 516–518.

Kolodny, R. C., Masters, W. H., & Johnson, V. E. (1979). *Textbook of sexual medicine.* Boston, MA: Little, Brown.

Masters, W. H., & Johnson, V. E. (1966). *Human sexual response.* Boston, MA: Little, Brown.

Masters, W. H., & Johnson, V. E. (1971). *Human sexual inadequacy.* Boston, MA: Little, Brown.

Perelman, M. A. (2014). The history of sexual medicine. In D. L. Tolman & L. M. Diamond (Editors-in-Chief), *APA handbook of sexuality and psychology: Volume 2. Contextual approaches.* American Psychological Association, 2013. Retrieved from http://dx.doi.org/10.1037/14194-005

Rubin, R. (2016). *Is the first anniversary of FDA's approval of Addyi a reason to celebrate?* Retrieved from www.forbes.com/sites/ritarubin/2016/08/21/first-anniversary-of-fdas-approval-of-addyi-to-boost-womens-sex-drive-a-reason-to-celebrate/2/#608637549cc2

Shifren, J. L., Johannes, C. B., Monz, B. U., Russo, P. A., Bennett, L., & Rosen, R. (2009, April). Help-seeking behavior of women with self-reported distressing sexual problems. *Journal of Women's Health, 18*(4), 461–468. https://doi.org/10.1089/jwh.2008.1133

Weiner, L., & Avery-Clarke, C. (2017). *Sensate focus in sex therapy: The illustrated manual.* London: Routledge.

2 Supervising Referral Relationships

Melanie Davis, Melissa Donahue, and Judith E. Hersh

Abstract

The physician/sex therapist/sexuality educator referral relationship has the potential to enhance client sexual health through a holistic approach. This type of business relationship thrives when the participants understand and respect each other's scope of work. The supervisor who understands the bio-psychoeducational model of sexual healthcare can help the therapist build and maintain referral relationships, address legal and ethical concerns, and maintain appropriate professional boundaries with physicians and sexuality educators.

Keywords

Sex therapy, sex therapy supervision, sexuality education, integrative practice, holistic medicine, complementary medicine, complementary practice, business practice, biopsychoeducational model, sexuality educator, sexual medicine, professional boundaries, professional qualifications, healthcare, scope of practice, referral habits

Relationships among physicians, sex therapists, and sexuality educators have the potential to enhance client sexual health through a holistic approach. The success of this approach requires the providers to understand and respect each other's scope of practice and to be willing to make referrals to each other. This type of referral network benefits patients and clients by affording them access to providers with specialized expertise; meanwhile, it provides networking partners an opportunity to build their practice with patients and clients they might not otherwise encounter. Sex therapy supervisors can support this collaboration by including professional scopes of practice in their work with therapists.

When one enters a clinical mental health supervision/professional relationship, the supervisor's role is to improve upon the professional's clinical skills, strengthen their assessment and intervention skills, and help them develop relationships with collaborating professionals. From this foundation, the specialty of sex therapy has room for growth within its scope of practice. The supervisee's professional development can be enhanced as the sex therapy supervisor helps foster—or at least encourages—relationships with highly trained peers with expertise that can expand their understanding, knowledge, and skills. The supervisor should also help foster healthy business relationships, monitor boundaries, and recommend opportunities for referrals.

The biopsychoeducational model of sexual healthcare describes relationships among three types of professionals who can address an individual's biological (medical), psychological (emotional), and sexual education (knowledge and skills) needs (Davis, 2010). The biopsychoeducational model can be initiated by sex therapists, so supervisors can appropriately propose it as a practice-building opportunity and way to ensure holistic client care. One of the chief values of the model is that it recognizes that sexual health encompasses physical, psychological, relational, and situational aspects (Levy, 2002), and because of its complexity, individuals may be unable to locate a single professional capable of providing comprehensive care. By affiliating even loosely, professionals in sexual medicine, psychotherapy, and sexuality education can offer complementary diagnosis, assessment, and treatment or counseling based on a biopsychoeducational model of sexual healthcare (Davis, 2010).

The model's efficacy rests on the willingness of professionals to correctly assess when and to whom to make referrals. The therapist must seek out knowledgeable sexual health providers and educators in their geographic area, which is not always easy, given the small number of sexuality educators in clinical or private practice and the small number of healthcare providers trained in sexual medicine. The supervisor can help the therapist identify and meet physicians trained to assess and treat sexual dysfunctions. Additional assistance may be needed to identify qualified and compatible sexuality educators, especially if the therapist is unclear on the distinction between sex therapy and sexuality education. In such situations, the supervisor can initiate discussions of the complementary but different scopes of practice of therapists and educators. For example, while therapists may have the knowledge to educate patients regarding sexual anatomy, sexual behaviors, contraceptive options, and adult pleasure products, they may better serve their clients by focusing on psychotherapy and referring clients to a sexuality educator for nonclinical aspects of care. In doing so, they can provide specialized psychological healthcare while the education and skill-building rests with educators trained to set learning objectives and to provide outcome-focused consulting and counseling. The biopsychoeducational model becomes even more useful when used with Annon's (1976) PLISSIT model (p. 72).

The PLISSIT Model

Annon's PLISSIT model should be part of any discussion of scopes of healthcare practice: P represents permission; LI represents limited information; SS represents specific suggestions; and IT represents intensive therapy. Annon developed this model to help mental health professionals understand appropriate treatment methods for sexual concerns and posited that the levels a clinician would feel competent to use would "directly depend upon the amount of interest and time he is willing to devote to expanding his knowledge, training and skill at each level" (Annon, 1976, p. 72). The model can also be used to define scopes of practice for nonclinical sexuality professionals, as illustrated by the integration of an AASECT protocol and the PLISSIT model (Kelly, 2006). The model illustrates the breadth of subject matter that can be addressed before entering into the psychotherapy domain, and it outlines the levels at which physicians may counsel patients with sexual concerns.

In the PLISSIT model, permission refers to giving reassurance to patients that "they are normal and have permission to continue doing exactly what they have been doing" (Annon, 1976, p. 75), assuming that neither they nor others are harmed by the behavior (e.g., a sexuality educator, therapist, or physician could give an individual permission to masturbate). Limited information includes "factual information directly related to a specific sexual concern" (Annon, 1976, p. 77). The provision of specific suggestions requires the provider to understand the client's concern and educate the client about behavioral changes (e.g., a client complaining of osteoarthritis pain during sexual activity could be educated on body positioning to ease pressure on painful joints). Professional boundaries begin to come into play at this level because sexuality educators are not qualified to make recommendations that require psychotherapeutic or medical assessment, diagnosis or treatment.

Kelly (2006) limits non-AASECT-certified sexuality educators to working at levels P-LI, and allows AASECT-certified counselors to work at levels P-LI-SS; AASECT-certified sex therapists work at all four levels. No mention is made of how AASECT certification might affect an educator's scope of work. Davis (2010) defined qualified sexuality educators as those with AASECT certification because physicians are accustomed to making referrals to certified professionals such as ostomy educators, diabetes educators, nurse educators, and the like. With AASECT certification included in the definition of a qualified sexuality educator, physicians and therapists need not invest the time to evaluate whether an educator is qualified.

Roles Within the Biopsychoeducational Model

Healthcare Providers

Healthcare providers play an essential role in the biopsychoeducational model by assessing, diagnosing, and treating their patients' sexual concerns from the perspective of physical medicine. They must ask questions that may vary from the script of traditional medicine by extending the patient interview in order to learn more about the patient's well-being. For example, a frequent concern among male patients is erectile dysfunction, whether partnered or alone. The primary doctor or urologist may quickly prescribe a PDE5 inhibitor (Viagra, Cialis, etc.) to use as a trial. The problem with this approach is that if the physician fails to inquire about the specific nature of the patient's erectile dysfunction (e.g., the failure to achieve erections versus maintain them, or if the symptoms are present during partnered sex but not solo), they may miss critical opportunities to provide treatment that will appropriately correct or manage the dysfunction (Goldstein, Rothstein, & Masters, 1995).

Despite the importance of their role in their patients' sexual health, many healthcare providers find the subject difficult to discuss (Leonard & Rogers, 2002); as a result, they may opt for a quick medical solution rather than refer the patient to a sex therapist or sexuality educator who can more comfortably speak to patients about sexual concerns. A similar situation may arise when a patient experiences pelvic pain during intercourse, which may be a sign of vaginismus (now referred to in the DSM as GPPPD, for Genito-Pelvic Pain/Penetration Disorder). Some gynecology patients state that when they have reported vaginal pain at previous annual visits in the past, they were told there was no medical finding, so psychological counseling was indicated. While counseling is usually important, the appropriate exam by a physician and pelvic floor therapist is more beneficial and timely regarding the presenting problem because the location of pain and its characteristics are the strongest predators of its organicity (Rosenbaum, 2007). The physician should ask when the pain occurs, what it feels like (e.g., burning, stabbing, dull, or pulling), what happens when other items are inserted (e.g., finger, tampon, or sex toy), and whether the pain has always existed or is episodic.

The sex therapist supervisor can explain to the therapist that a similar dialogue should be part of the expanding sex history taken when evaluating a patient. The supervisor may also caution the therapist against prejudging sexual pain to be the result of sexual abuse or sexual trauma, thereby teaching the therapist to view sexual pain as a pain disorder that affects sexual expression rather than assuming a link to sexual trauma (Rosenbaum, 2007). It may be part of the patient's sexual history, but it is not necessarily the cause of all pelvic pain. Psychological distress such as depression and anxiety are elevated when there is sexual pain; however, studies have failed to link vulvar pain to childhood sexual abuse or trauma (Rosenbaum, 2007). Referral to a pelvic floor therapist is also critical for the treatment of musculoskeletal abnormalities that may cause pelvic pain (Rosenbaum, 2007).

The supervisor can play an invaluable role in helping the therapist identify appropriate professional partnerships that will benefit the patient, with each professional responsible for a portion of the healing process. Another important aspect of supervision in this regard is to help the therapist recognize the value of partnership as a business and collaborative model: treatment partnerships can build the therapist's network of colleagues and open the door to referrals from physicians and pelvic floor therapists.

Physicians' difficulty addressing patients' sexual concerns relates to, but is not limited to lack of formal training, time constraints, poor reimbursements for time spent addressing sexual concerns, personal biases and assumptions, patients' reluctance to bring up concerns related to sex, and ageism, such as assuming geriatric patients are neither sexually active or interested (Krychman, 2013). An example of the limited scope of attention given to sexuality by the medical profession is the fact that the US Preventive Services Task Force provides screening recommendations ranging from aortic aneurysms and alcoholism through and including cardiovascular health, depression, diabetes, sexually transmitted infection (STI) screening, vitamin D deficiency screening, and youth violence counseling; however, screening for gender identity or sexual orientation concerns, or any other aspects of sexuality and sexual health, are mentioned nowhere except in the context of sexually transmitted infections.

Most healthcare providers are not taught even the basics of sexual health counseling, such as the PLISSIT model (Kingsburg, 2014), even though sex therapists, sexuality counselors, and sexuality educators are comfortable with it. This distinction provides an entry point for therapists and educators to take over where the medical healthcare providers' scope of practice ends.

Sex Therapists

The supervisor's role is to improve upon the professional's clinical skills, strengthen their assessment and intervention skills, and help them develop relationships with collaborating professionals. The supervisor should also help the therapist identify their sexual values, including where they were acquired and how values influence client intervention (Corey, 2017).

The therapist's role is to look beyond the presenting problem and to ask leading questions. Many concerns people bring to therapy are months and often years old, and the ability to ask questions like, "Why now?" or "How do you see this issue resolved?" can open the door to the beginning of the therapeutic relationship. Patients who wait a significant amount of time to seek help may desire to avoid feelings of shame or may hesitate to admit fault, which can lead to fragmentation in relationships. The problems people bring to therapy span every phase of human sexual response and involve relationship dynamics. The therapist's role is to hear the presenting problem and expand upon the language to go beneath the surface and uncover additional challenges that lie beneath. The therapist must meet the patient where they are and help them peel the layers back one by one.

Shulman (2016) lists the skills for helping patients as clarifying their purpose and role, reaching for client feedback, partializing client concerns, and supporting the client in taboo areas. While doing this work, the therapist focuses on the emotions attached to the issues. The work also includes processing concerns in detail and labeling feelings to understand how client's concerns manifest reactions and how those dynamics develop within and affect relationships (Shulman, 2016). While there is an education component, therapy focuses on the journey rather than the lesson. The supervisor can help the therapist maintain this focus and can encourage the therapist to refer strictly educational issues to a sexuality educator.

Sexuality Educators

While physicians and therapists address acute medical and psychological issues, educators focus on other aspects of sexual health and education according to their professional training, as described by Hedgepeth and Helmich (1996):

> all aspects of becoming and being a sexual, gendered person including biological, psychological, and social perspectives. The main objectives

of such comprehensive sexuality education are to help people feel good about themselves and their bodies, remain healthy, and build positive, equitable loving relationships—to be "sexually healthy."

(pp. 1–2)

The educator's scope of practice, according to the certification standards set by the American Association of Sexuality Educators, Counselors and Therapists (AASECT) includes, but is not limited to, the following:

> sexual health; sexual and reproductive anatomy and physiology; family planning, contraception, and pregnancy/childbirth; sexually transmitted infections; gender identity and roles; gay, lesbian, bisexual, and transgender issues; sexual function and dysfunction; sexual pleasure; sexual variation; sexuality and disability; sexuality and chronic illness; sexual development across the lifespan; sexual abuse, assault, and coercion; and sexuality across cultures.
> (AASECT, 2017, ¶ 1, AASECT Certified Sexuality Educator)

Licensure is not available to sexuality educators, so therapists must take care when making referrals. AASECT certification is one way to ensure competence, as earning the credential requires meeting academic and supervised professional experience. Planned Parenthood also offers a sexuality education certification, as does the National Commission for Health Education Credentialing. None of these certifications require individuals to gain experience consulting with individuals or couples, nor do they require familiarity with making or receiving referrals. A therapist considering making a referral should ask whether the educator has completed additional training or gained relevant professional experience. Certification does require sexuality educators to adhere to standards for ethics and best practices, so it behooves therapists to lean in the direction of certified educators for referral purposes. Relationship-building opportunities can help the therapist assess the educator's qualifications and compatibility.

Supervisors

Supervision has been an essential component in the training of clinical social workers for many years (Hensley, 2003). Therapists interested in setting up a biopsychoeducational practice model may welcome the supervisor's help to assess the qualifications of sexuality educators and providers who are geographically viable referral partners.

Supervision needs to "maximize the worker's capacity to do his job more effectively and to help the worker feel good about doing his job," while other functions of supervision are administrative, educational, and supportive (Hensley, 2003). The supervisor can foster discussions around professional scopes of practice and boundaries; provide guidance on screening clients who may need referrals for sexual medicine or sexuality education; and identify potential ethical and legal issues regarding referrals to sexuality educators, such as access to sensitive client records or history. The supervisor and therapist should inves-tigate whether and how patient referrals might affect the supervisor's profes-sional relationship with insurance carriers and state regulations.

Patient Concerns as Presented to Helping Professionals

Healthcare Providers

The most common sexual complaint women report to healthcare providers is lack of desire, which is estimated to affect 1 out of 15 women (Rosen et al., 2012). This complaint may have a physiologic component, such as elevated sex hormone binding globulin leading to low free testosterone, which may be caused by the use of combined hormonal contraception. If the complaint were strictly physiologic, medical care alone would be appropriate; however, these patients nearly always also exhibit a psychologic component (Brotto, Bitzer, Laan, Leiblum, & Luria, 2010) as well as lack of knowledge about their own or their partners' bodies. Some of these patients are also unaware that there are many models of sexual function. While the most well-known may be the Masters and Johnson four-phase model of excitement, plateau, orgasm, and resolution (Masters & Johnson, 1981), other models may suit a patient's experiences more effectively. These models include Basson's Non-linear Model of Female Sexual Response (2001), which incor-porates emotional intimacy, sexual stimuli, and relationship satisfaction; and the Circular Model of Female Sexual Response (Whipple & Brash-McGreer, 1997) based on Reed's Erotic Stimulus Pathway model of seduction, sensations, surren-der, and reflection (Stayton, 1989). The sexuality educator can use these models to help patients understand their own responses, while a therapist can delve into the patient's sexual history and feelings related to their sexual scripts.

Low sexual desire is also often related to perimenopause and menopause (Bradford & Meston, 2007), during which significant physical changes typi-cally coincide with the stressors of family life, work, and aging parents. Hor-monal fluctuations can cause irritability; sleep disturbances decrease energy; and lower estrogen and testosterone almost always negatively affect the vulvar and vaginal tissues, leading to genitourinary syndrome of menopause (GSM, formerly called atrophic vaginitis). If left untreated, low desire can progress to a sexual aversion, while GSM can lead to severe pain upon vulvar touch and penetrative sex play, which in turn tends to decrease desire.

An individual's complaint of sexual pain requires a thorough physical exam by a healthcare provider trained in sexual health. Common medical disorders which present with sexual pain include vulvodynia or vestibulodynia, pelvic floor dysfunction, endometriosis, pelvic adhesive disorder as a result of pelvic inflam-matory disease or surgery, fibroids, and interstitial cystitis. The older term, vagi-nismus, is best described as high tone pelvic floor dysfunction (HTPFD), which is simply a "charley horse" of the muscles that support the pelvic floor. The etiologies of HTPFD are varied but often include orthopedic injuries. Low tone pelvic floor dysfunction (which includes uterine and bladder prolapses) can also cause pain (Gyang, Harman, & Lamvu, 2013). These pain syndromes are best treated with a combination of medical management and pelvic floor physical therapy. If a patient has suffered for a significant amount of time, consultation with a sex therapist may become an integral part of the recovery process. Also, during medical treatment and therapy, a sexuality educator can discuss forms of sexual activity that will not aggravate a pain syndrome.

The most common male sexual complaint is erectile dysfunction (ED). The Massachusetts Male Aging Study (Johannes et al., 2000), reported up to 40% of men aged 40 are affected, and the incidence increases to nearly 70% by age 70. Many medical approaches are available to address this problem; therefore, men presenting with ED benefit from a medical consult. Low libido and pain disorders are less common in men; however, clinically low testosterone can cause depression and low desire and may be related to penile pathology such as Peyronie's disease (Moreno & Morgentaler, 2009), which can cause pain. Medical evaluation of these patients is important as well.

Sex Therapists

People visit sex therapists for many reasons, including sexual pain and changes in functionality. For females, pain is usually related to pelvic floor disorders and presents as pain with penetration related to either high tone (vaginismus) or low tone (dyspareunia; Rosenbaum, 2007). Male patients usually have concerns about erectile dysfunction and either rapid or delayed ejaculation, although some men seek help to understand their partner's different arousal templates or level of desire and seek to discuss those conflicts in their relationships. Many adults seeking therapy struggle to maintain sexual passion or navigating the frequency of sexual interaction. Of course, any of these concerns can result in a psychological struggle that can result in or exacerbate anxiety or depression.

Sexuality Educators

Anecdotal comments from sexuality educators in an online forum (personal communication, 2017) indicate that the most common complaints brought to sexuality educators are lack of or limited sexual pleasure, lack of knowledge about sexual anatomy and physiology, and pre-orgasmia. Note that the term pre-orgasmia is preferred to the outdated term anorgasmia (Black, 2001) because the former denotes the potential to experience orgasm while the latter implies an inability to do so. Other complaints include lack of dating and social skills, concerns about sexual technique, the need to broach sensitive topics such as polyamorous and open relationships, desire discrepancy, and differences in sexual values within couples (e.g., the viewing of pornography or experimentation with adult pleasure products). Creative problem solving is also in the sexuality educators' realm, such as product recommendations and discussing sexual positions and devices that work for people with physical limitations.

Sexuality education and certification processes differ greatly in whether and how they address professional scope of practice. For this reason, sexuality educators may benefit from frank conversations with sex therapists in their referral network about the types of concerns that are well suited to education and those that are within the domain of clinical practice. The supervisor can help the therapist prepare for these conversations so that both the educator and the therapist maintain a relationship as equally skilled professionals who honor each other's scope of practice.

Biopsychoeducational Case Studies

The following case studies can help supervisors appreciate the complementary nature of medical care, sex therapy, and sexuality education. The supervisor can oversee appropriate referrals and collaboration; in addition, the supervisor may help the therapist ensure that all of the referring professionals communicate effectively on the patient's/client's behalf.

One example of the biopsychoeducational model is the co-authors' practice, the New Jersey Center for Sexual Wellness (NJCSW), which has interdisciplinary offices in Bedminster and Morristown, New Jersey, as well as a sex therapy–only office in Ridgewood. The NJCSW was founded in 2008 by sex therapist Sandra Leiblum, PhD; obstetrician/gynecologist Judith Hersh, MD, FACOG; and sexuality educator Melanie Davis, PhD, CSE, CSES. Upon Leiblum's death in 2010, sex therapist Melissa Donahue, LCSW, CST, became a partner in the practice. The partners and affiliated professionals address patient/client needs related to sexual health, function, pain, knowledge, relationships, desire, pleasure, and other issues. Patients have multiple access points to the practice and are not required to start with a medical examination. The unique ability to allow multiple access points to our practice highlights our determination to take a holistic approach to sexual medicine.

Case One

MG is a 28-year-old female from a conservative religious background. She was married 3 months prior to a well woman visit to a gynecologist and has no history of prior sexual experience/exploration, partnered or unpartnered; the same is true for her husband. They have been unable to consummate their marriage. She has never used tampons. The patient states that she and her husband are happy and able to communicate. They have done some manual exploration of each other's bodies which she says "feels nice," but she does not think she has ever had an orgasm. Her exam is completely within normal limits. Her hymen is intact and the opening is of normal diameter for a woman who has not experienced vaginal penetration. She is able to tolerate a pelvic exam with a narrow Pederson speculum and guided relaxation techniques, and she can tolerate a single digit bimanual exam. After the exam, the patient is given a mirror and shown her genitalia. She expresses that she did not know what female genital anatomy looked like and thought that she "peed out of the same hole as the baby comes out of." She and her husband are highly motivated to have a satisfying sexual life and to have a family.

Discussion Case One

MG's history and physical exam indicate that both she and her husband lack basic knowledge regarding anatomy and sexual pleasuring. There is no evidence of a physical pathology. Their relationship seems stable, and their communication is good. As a first step, this patient would be referred to a sexuality educator.

SUPERVISOR'S ROLE CASE ONE

The supervisor's role is to remind the therapist that the educator is competent to teach the couple about sexual anatomy and the physiology of arousal in addition to suggesting sexual activities that might be pleasurable. By helping the therapist see the benefits of education rather than therapy in this case, the supervisor may increase the therapist's trust in the biopsychoeducational model and in the educator's skills within their scope of practice. A limitation in this referral may be the therapist's feeling of isolation from the case. The supervisor can encourage the therapist to communicate with the educator and to encourage a referral to the therapist if the couple reports any psychological issues during educational consultation.

Case Two

RG is a 58-year-old woman who has had three pregnancies and three live births. She had her last menstrual period 8 years ago and has no significant past medical history. Prior to entering menopause, she and her husband had a satisfying sex life. She reports that since menopause began, sex has become increasingly painful; therefore, the couple has avoided sexual contact for 2 years. She said the last time they had sex, "It felt like I was tearing apart, and there was blood." Upon further questioning, she admits to doing things to avoid having sex, such as going to bed early or complaining of not feeling well. She has been married for 27 years, and her husband is supportive, yet this situation is causing a strain on their relationship. She also complains of occasional loss of urine when she has to void and a bathroom is not immediately available. Prior to her exam, the patient becomes tearful in anticipation of pain. On physical exam, the patient has significant thinning of the vulvar tissues and evidence of a healed tear at 6 o'clock. The vaginal rugae are absent, and the vaginal pH is elevated. Overall, the tissues lack moisture, and she reports that the exam was painful.

Discussion Case Two

On physical exam, RG shows classic genitourinary syndrome of menopause (GSM). The lack of estrogen has caused the vulvar and vaginal tissues to become less pliable and more friable leading to tearing, especially upon attempted penetration. The lack of estrogen is also likely contributing to her urge incontinence. The higher vaginal pH is consistent with her low estrogen state. Because her symptoms have been present for such a long time, RG has developed a sexual aversion disorder, and her relationship is strained. RG will be counseled by the physician regarding medical treatment options for GSM; however, she will also need to work with a sex therapist to ensure successful treatment.

SUPERVISOR'S ROLE CASE TWO

The supervisor can encourage the therapist to explore areas where the couple might begin to re-establish intimacy and, as needed, to present interventions that rebuild intimacy and trust in the relationship. Education regarding the body's response to menopause and to medical treatment could be helpful, which may warrant a referral to the sexuality educator or to the physician for follow-up consultation.

The supervisor may help the therapist discern whether and when to work with the patient alone as well as with her partner. The goal of therapy in this case is to help the couple work toward simple physical acts that build trust, arousal, and pleasure without relying on vaginal penetration. The therapist can be encouraged to communicate with the physician about the patient's physical well-being, such as how the vaginal tissue is responding to any treatment or healing and whether a referral to a pelvic floor therapist would be beneficial.

Case Three

A female patient in her early twenties presents to the medical office because she feels she "isn't working like she should be." Upon examination, the physician finds nothing abnormal and refers the patient to the sex therapist. The patient is in a committed relationship, although her significant other is seeing other another woman. Though the patient has had multiple sexual partners prior to her current relationship, she feels sexually inadequate and expresses concern that she is not experiencing orgasms with her partner. Her partner tells her repeatedly that he can always give a woman an orgasm, so something must be wrong with her. Upon further exploration, it appears that the patient believes that the pornographic videos she has seen accurately portray what an orgasm looks like for women, including ejaculation. Further discussion indicates that this patient can be appropriately referred to the sexuality educator.

Discussion Case Three

The sexuality educator uses discussion and educational resources to explain, educate, and explore what an orgasm is and what it is not. The referral in this model illustrates that the patient's psychological distress is due to inaccurate education and information. Once the information is provided, the patient's distress decreases. She can recognize that the gentle, pleasurable spasms she experiences *are* orgasms, even though they differ from those she has seen portrayed in pornography. She can learn to appreciate her body's unique sexual responses to pleasurable stimulation. In addition to sexuality education, the patient works with the therapist to assess her relationship goals, to rebuild trust with her partner, and to gain confidence in her body. This holistic approach to the patient's needs will enable her to make informed decisions about her relationship and her sexual experiences.

SUPERVISOR'S ROLE CASE THREE

This case illustrates a biopsychoeducational collaboration, as the patient needs to work through her goals for her relationship, rebuild her trust with her partner, and gain confidence in her body. The patient would have received the appropriate intervention sooner had the reception desk staff asked appropriate screening questions upon initial contact. The therapy supervisor can advise the therapist on how to educate support staff in medical practices, who may find patient screening awkward, leading to confusion about scope of practice for therapists and educators.

Case Four

The administrators of a group home for adults with disabilities contacts the New Jersey Center for Sexual Wellness to seek assistance for a heterosexual couple seeking to consummate their marriage. Both partners are significantly impaired in terms of physical mobility and flexibility, due to contractures related to cerebral palsy. A meeting is called to bring together the sex therapist, sexuality educator, the group home administrators, and a member of the residents' care team to understand the preliminary case history and group home policies on sexual expression. The meeting is followed with a private consult for the couple, attended by both the sex therapist and the sexuality educator. During the sexual history taking, the husband states that he and his wife wanted to engage in sexual relations "like in porn" (i.e., through vaginal intercourse). The wife agrees that she would like that also, yet when they describe their physical capabilities, it becomes evident to the therapist and educator that the couple's physical limitations make penile–vaginal or penile–anal penetration impossible.

Discussion Case Four

Individuals with disabilities often benefit from having access to professionals qualified to address their specific needs. Collaboration can be the key to successful outcomes, and the supervisor can encourage the sexuality educator and sex therapist to maintain clearly defined roles. The sex therapist helps the couple address their emotions and feelings associated with learning that vaginal intercourse would never be an option for them. The therapist also addresses the stress and grief this realization caused. The educator uses 14″ artist's models to illustrate positioning options for oral and manual genital stimulation. The educator also shows the couple props and adult products that could increase their sexual options.

In a case such as this, the supervisor can highlight both the therapist's and sexuality educator's professional strengths while establishing the parameters in which they will work. This may also include parameters for employees of the group home, who may need reassurance that their role will be limited to helping the couple prepare for partnered sexual activity, as well as possible help with washing and dressing afterward. It is important to emphasize to the therapist how collaboration such as this has direct benefits to a patient's quality of life.

Counterindications to Supervision of the Biopsychoeducational Model

The success of therapy supervision within the biopsychoeducational model relies on the supervisor's appreciation of the benefits of referrals as well as familiarity with healthcare provider and sexuality educator scopes of practice. If the supervisor is not aware of the differences among physician, therapist, and educator perspectives on sexuality and sexual health, referral opportunities may be missed. Sex therapists may not find the biopsychosocial model valuable if they lack the desire to foster referral relationships. To make efficient use of supervision, the supervisor should inquire early on in the relationship whether the therapist's business goals include referral-based practice building.

Conclusion

The complex nature of sexuality may benefit from an integrative approach to sexual healthcare that is based on professional relationships among physicians, psychotherapists, and sexuality educators (Davis, 2010). This approach, best described by the biopsychoeducational model, can enhance client sexual health if referral relationships are fostered among physicians, sex therapists, and sexuality educators. Such an approach can counteract what Moser and Devereaux (2012) refer to as the isolation of various disciplines. They noted that patients deserve the benefit of a thorough evaluation of their sexual concerns through a team approach.

The sex therapy supervisor can foster the model's success by helping the therapist find qualified and willing referral partners, by discussing professional boundaries, and by overseeing the therapist's role within the model.

The biopsychoeducational model can help therapists to build their practice and increase their credibility, specifically among medical practitioners. The supervisor can assist by helping the therapist to identify potential clinical partners. One place to start is by setting up in-person meetings with the local medical center's chairpersons of obstetrics and gynecology, internal medicine, family practice, hematology, and oncology. These meetings can build relationships and educate clinicians about the relationship between sexual wellness and overall health status (e.g., oncologists tend to focus on their patients' survival rather than on their needs for emotional or physical intimacy). The therapist can explain that for many patients, sexual intimacy is an important part of being alive, even if some aspects of sexual expression may be put on hold during treatment. The therapist can say, in essence, "I am available to navigate this with you for your patient's benefit." At the same time, the therapist should emphasize that therapy will not interfere with the patient–physician relationship.

Moser and Devereux (2012) noted that an obvious obstacle to referral relationships is the distribution of expertise in a given locality. Financial and insurance constraints are additional barriers to referral follow-through for sex therapy. The supervisor and therapist can consider ways to overcome barriers, such as providing physicians with brochures on sex therapy to build patient confidence in the sex therapist. Therapy fees may be offered on a sliding scale to accommodate financially needy clients.

If the supervisor or therapist have an existing relationship with a physician, they can leverage it to gain an introduction to the head of any department with which that physician is associated. The supervisor should also consider existing relationships with hospital social workers, outreach coordinators, and nursing administrators.

A study of physician referrals for sex therapy to treat impotence (Segraves, Schoenberg, Zarins, Knopf, & Camic, 1982) indicated that male patients prefer to consider their dysfunction to be of medical rather than psychological origin; in addition, they were unwilling to discuss their erectile difficulties in their sexual partners' presence as couple therapy necessitates. As a result, the patients tended not to follow through on physician referrals for sex therapy. Additional research is needed to determine whether those research findings remain accurate today and what other trends may emerge regarding patient follow-through on referrals for sex therapy.

About the Authors

Melissa Donahue, LCSW, CST, is a partner in the New Jersey Center for Sexual Wellness. A Certified Sex Therapist through the American Association of Sexuality Educators, Counselors and Therapists, she has expertise in oncological social work and gerontology. She uses talk therapy to treat diagnoses of desire, arousal and orgasm phase difficulties, sexual dysfunctions, body image, relationship issues, pain, sexual abuse, sexuality and oncology issues, and sexuality and disability issues.

Judith E. Hersh, MD, FACOG, NCMP, IF, is a founding partner in the New Jersey Center for Sexual Wellness. She is a Fellow of the International Society for the Study of Women's Sexual Health and is certified through the North American Menopause Society. She is a partner in Women's Care Source and is a clinical assistant professor at Robert Wood Johnson Medical School. She has been a sexuality and aging lecturer for the American Medical Student Association's Sexual Health Leadership Program and is on the staff of two Central New Jersey medical centers.

Melanie Davis, Ph.D., CSE, CSES, is a founding partner in the New Jersey Center for Sexual Wellness. She is a professional development provider and speaker on sexuality, and she is on the adjunct faculty of Widener and Drexel Universities and the American Medical Student Association's Sexual Health Leadership Program. She is a Certified Sexuality Educator and Supervisor through the American Association of Sexuality Educators, Counselors and Therapists. She is the Our Whole Lives Sexuality Education Program Associate for the Unitarian Universalist Association and author of *Sexuality and Our Faith: A Companion to Our Whole Lives Sexuality Education for Grades 7–9* (2nd ed.) and *Our Whole Lives Sexuality Education for Older Adults* and was a developmental editor for *Our Whole Lives Sexuality Education for Grades 7–9* (2nd ed.). She is on the editorial advisory board of the *American Journal of Sexuality Education*.

References

American Association of Sexuality Educators, Counselors and Therapists. (2017). *AASECT Certified Sexuality Educator.* Retrieved from www.aasect.org/certification.aspwww.aasect.org/aasect-certified-sexuality-educator-0

Annon, J. S. (1976). The PLISSIT model: A proposed conceptual scheme for the behavioral treatment of sexual problems. *Journal of Sex Education and Therapy*, *2*(1), 1–15.

Basson, R. (2001). Female sexual response: the role of drugs in the management of sexual dysfunction. *Obstetrics and Gynecology*, *98*, 350–353.

Black, J. (2001). Pertinent points [Commentary]. *Journal of Sex & Marital Therapy*, *27*(2), 17–119.

Bradford, A., & Meston, C. M. (2007). Senior sexual health: The effects of aging on sexuality. In L. VandeCreek, F. L. Peterson, & J. W. Bley (Eds.), *Innovation in clinical practice: Focus on sexual health* (pp. 34–35). Sarasota, FL: Professional Resources Press.

Brotto, L. A., Bitzer, J., Laan, E., Leiblum, S., & Luria, M. (2010). Women's sexual desire and arousal disorders. *Journal of Sexual Medicine*, *7*, 586–614.

Corey, G. (2017). *Theory and practice of counseling and psychotherapy* (10th ed.). Boston, MA: Cengage Learning.

Davis, M. J. (2010). *Sexuality education as perceived by physicians and therapists: As assessment of attitudes about and interest in referring patients to sexuality educators* (Doctoral dissertation). Retrieved from Dissertations & Theses @ Widener University; ProQuest Dissertations & Theses A & I (6128043431)

Goldstein, I., Rothstein, L., & Masters, W. H. (1995). *The potent male.* Norwalk, CT: Reginesis Cycle.

Gyang, A., Hartman, M., & Lamvu, G. (2013). Musculoskeletal causes of chronic pelvic pain: What a gynecologist should know. *Obstetrics and Gynecology*, *121*(3).

Hedgepeth, E., & Helmich, J. (1996). *Teaching about sexuality and HIV.* New York: New York University Press.

Hensley, P. H. (2003). The value of supervision. *Clinical Supervisor, 21*(1), 97–110.

Johannes, C., Araujo, H., Feldman, H. A., Derby, C., Kleinman, K., & McKinlay, J. (2000). Incidence of erectile dysfunction in men 40–69 years old: Longitudinal results from the Massachusetts Male Aging Study. *Clinical Urology, 163*(2), 54–61.

Kelly, M. (2006). *Distinguishing between sex educators, sex counselors and sex therapists* [Fact sheet] (Rev. ed.). Ithaca, NY: Planned Parenthood of the Southern Finger Lakes and Ashland, VA: American Association of Sexuality Educators, Counselors and Therapists.

Kingsburg, S. (2014). *Addressing sexual desire problems of women without a prescription*. Plenary session of the North American Menopause Society Annual Meeting, Washington, DC.

Krychman, M. (2013). Counselling: A life course approach. *Gynaecology Forum, 18*(2), 13–16.

Leonard, C., & Rogers, R. (2002). Opinions and practices among providers regarding sexual function: Do we ask the questions? *Primary Care Update OB/GYNS, 9*(6), 218–221.

Levy, B. K. (2002, March). Break the silence: Discussing sexual dysfunction. *OBG Management, 14*(3), 70–85. Retrieved from www.obgmanagement.com/pdf/1403/1403OBGM_Article1.pdf

Masters, W., & Johnson, V. (1981). *Human sexual response*. New York: Bantam.

Moreno, S. A., & Morgentaler, A. (2009). Testosterone deficiency and Peyronie's disease: Pilot data suggesting a significant relationship. *Journal of Sexual Medicine, 6*(6), 1729–1735.

Moser, C., & Devereux, M. (2012). Sexual medicine, sex therapy, and sexual health care. In P. J. Kleinplatz (Ed.), *New directions in sex therapy* (2nd ed., pp. 127–139). New York: Routledge.

Rosen, R. C., Connor, M. K., Miyasato, G., Link, C., Shifren, J. L., Fisher, W. A., . . . Schobelock, M. J. (2012). Sexual desire problems in women seeking healthcare: A novel study design for ascertaining prevalence of hypoactive sexual desire disorder in clinic-based samples of U.S. women. *Journal of Women's Health, 21*(5), 505–515.

Rosenbaum, T. Y. (2007). Physical therapy management and treatment of sexual pain disorders. In *Principles and practice of sex therapy* (4th ed., pp. 157–174). New York: Guilford Press.

Segraves, R. T., Schoenberg, H. W., Zarins, C. K., Knopf, J., & Camic, P. (1982). Referral of impotent patients to a sexual dysfunction clinic. *Archives of Sexual Behavior, 11*(6).

Shulman, L. (2016). *The skills of helping individuals, families, groups, and communities* (8th ed.). Boston, MA: Cengage Learning.

Stayton, W. (1989). A theology of sexual pleasure. *American Baptist Quarterly, 8*(2), 94–108.

Whipple, B., & Brash-McGreer, K. (1997). Management of female sexual dysfunction. In M. L. Sipski & C. J. Alexander (Eds.), *Sexual function in people with disability and chronic illness. A health professional's guide* (pp. 509–534). Gaithersburg, MD: Aspen.

3 Sex Therapy Group Supervision

A Conceptual Model for Integration of Sex and Group Supervision

Douglas Braun-Harvey

Abstract

Current sex therapy and supervision literature has not conceptualized sex therapy group supervision or differentiated sex therapy supervision in a group setting from existing methods for individual sex therapy supervision. Sex Therapy Group Supervision (STGS) is a conceptual model that integrates client sexuality and group process within sex therapy supervision groups. STGS builds upon existing supervision research to propose a tripartite method emphasizing core knowledge, integrated methods, and reflective processes. A sex therapy supervision group is a space held for therapists to experientially learn through witnessing, modeling, practicing, and integrating a range of vital sexual therapy practices within a reflective group process. Specific supervision strategies for group work are outlined and explicated through case study vignettes.

Keywords

group supervision, sex therapy supervision, sex therapy training, sex therapy certification, sex therapy

It is a given among psychotherapists that supervision facilitates supervisee learning (Goodyear, 2014). Increasing attention is now being given to both clinical supervisor processes and supervisor training (Borders, 2014). Clinical supervision empirical research, credentialing, and legal and ethical guidelines have clarified and promoted supervision best practices (Borders, 2014). Emerging conceptual supervision models emphasize particular interventions set within a supervision framework that operationalizes methods of supervision correlated with basic mechanisms of change (Goodyear, 2014). The most useful emerging clinical supervision models clarify "what clinical supervision is and how it works" (Milne, Aylott, Fitzpatrick, & Ellis, 2008, p. 170). Absent from the current literature is delineation of what exactly is sex therapy group supervision and how is it differentiated from other forms of group supervision and existing methods for individual sex therapy supervision. The American Association of Sexuality Educators, Counselors and Therapists (AASECT) sex therapy certification training methods and supervision guidelines do not currently outline supervision models or group facilitation supervision methods for training supervisees (AASECT,

2017). Specialized group psychotherapy journals that review evidence based group supervision practices, training methods, group supervision outcomes, supervisee skill acquisition, and group supervision conceptual models rarely even mention the integration of sexuality within group supervision.

Today, specialists in group work write about group supervision to train group therapists but rarely discuss sex. Sex therapy supervision is done in both groups and individually, however, there are no standards or expectations for how to lead the groups. The group supervisors too often adapt individual supervision tools to a group setting. It is the lack of integrating human sexuality within existing group supervision models as well as suggested methods for group supervision in the development of sex therapists and sexologically informed psychotherapists (e.g., Goodyear, 2014; Alfonsson, Spännargård, Parling, Andersson, & Lundgren, 2017; Beidas et al., 2013; Milne et al., 2008; Borders, 2014; Bennett-Levy, 2006) that forms the basis for this chapter.

Psychotherapy training and supervision groups are no longer limited by having sufficient numbers of supervisees living in the same geographic area. Recent contributions to the literature discuss supervision methods and models adapted to web-based supervision. Technology-mediated supervision, utilizing web-based group face-to-face platforms, is an emerging group supervision practice (Rousmaniere, 2014).

Supervision ethics guide these emerging supervision models to prioritize supervision methods that protect the supervisee from harm (Ellis et al., 2014). Michael Ellis and his colleagues recently revised an existing framework for inadequate and harmful supervision. They expanded the spectrum to include minimally adequate supervision, inadequate clinical supervision, and harmful supervision. In this comprehensive review of minimal to harmful supervision practices, sexuality was only mentioned in the harmful supervision end of the spectrum. "Having a sexual relationship" or "being sexually intimate" or "sexually inappropriate" between supervisee and supervisor was the only aspect of human sexuality mentioned (Ellis et al., 2014). This is an all too frequent pattern within the teaching and supervision of psychotherapists of including sexuality when it is harmful behavior and remaining mostly silent about its inextricable link with health and well-being.

This chapter adapts a cognitive model of therapist skill development to propose a conceptual model for learning sex therapy group supervision (but it certainly can and should be generalized to all psychotherapy and counseling supervision contexts; Bennett-Levy, 2006). Sample sex therapy supervision group dialogues are meant to provide examples for moving from a conceptual framework to operationalizing a supervision intervention. The chapter includes both general psychotherapy group supervision that strives to better integrate human sexuality as well as sex therapy supervision groups whose purpose is to supervise therapists seeking to become certified sex therapists. Examples of both in-person and technology-mediated group supervision contexts are presented. Emphasis is placed on supervision models and practices that protect supervisees from inadequate and harmful supervision. The assumption for this model of group supervision is that inadequate or harmful supervision increases the risk of a therapist providing poor care or injuring their client. This chapter provides direction and motivation for clinicians, supervisors, and supervision researchers to develop and implement ethical, effective, and engaging sex therapy group supervision.

Group Supervision

Sex therapy group supervision and consultation is so much more than simply individual supervision or consultations in a room (virtual or in-person) with several people meeting at the same time. This is both good and bad news for supervisees seeking training in sex therapy. Some supervisees think that individual supervision, in which they have the exclusive focus from their supervisor, is far superior to a group supervision (Bernard, 1999), contrasted with other supervisees who intentionally seek out group supervision because they find the group process deepens their learning and broadens their apprenticeship (Bernard, 1999). Sex therapy supervisors may have similar biases. Why bother with learning all the complicated factors of managing a diverse set of people in a room? Why spend such valuable time in a group, when I can direct my full supervisory attention to one supervisee in a concentrated time? Why deal with the distractions of other sex therapists' concerns and learning especially when they may not be pertinent to everyone in the group? Given the cost of time, effort, learning, and money, why would a supervisee or supervisor give such a priority to learning how to provide sex therapy–based group supervision?

Sex therapy group supervision integrates human sexuality within all aspects of clinical case supervision while examining supervision group process in an experiential manner that provides reflection and deepening of insights into common human sexual worries, problems, and dysfunctions. The diversity that each member and supervisor brings to the meeting is the essence of group. The diversification of a supervision group is often highly valued by both supervisors and group members (Borders et al., 2012). The very formation of a sex therapy supervision group creates an entity designed to examine and throw light upon both group phenomena and group process to learn sex therapy.

Sex therapy group supervision expands supervisee sexual knowledge and clinical sex therapy skills through attending to supervision group clinical case content and "here/now" process. When supervision groups agree to focus on their own intrapersonal and interpersonal process, they enter into a vital learning resource for both exploring specific clinical issues while also being encouraged to reflect upon group meta-processes that may also be endemic to many sexual problems. "The principle strategy that takes a therapist from being average to expert is reflection" (Bennett-Levy, 2006, p. 60). How members and the supervisor process real-time group discussions through a process of applying existing knowledge and skills from other contexts to the new situation is key to the development of therapist expertise (Bennett-Levy, 2006). Training future sex therapy supervision group leaders expects the supervisor remain current with new sex research and sex therapy practices. Sex therapy group supervision capitalizes on the complexity and inherent multiple perspectives that are the hallmark of groups. It is unique and valuable learning process for therapists to acquire clinical sex therapy skills; illustrate their implementation within individual, group, and couples therapy; and understand the wide range of barriers and strengths for consolidating sex therapy principles and practices.

Sex Therapy Group Supervision Conceptual Model

Group supervision research and published models of psychotherapy supervision provide the foundation for this sex therapy group supervision conceptual model. The aim of the Sex Therapy Group Supervision (STGS) model is to provide some coherent direction for supervisors to integrate client sexuality within their consultation group content and process and to capitalize on group process for learning sex therapy within a sex therapist group supervision. Kleinberg's group psychotherapists training model defines how learning takes place in a group and identifies impediments to supervisees' learning while integrating how these same dynamics may be reflected in the supervision group (Kleinberg, 1999). James Bennett-Levy's three-part cognitive model for therapist skill acquisition and refinement is formulated around three systems of therapist training: declarative, procedural and reflective (Bennett-Levy, 2006). Bennett-Levy begins with the *declarative system*. It is here that supervision focuses upon the supervisee learning factual information. Declarative system supervisee learning is typically accomplished through lectures, observation, reading, or supervision. Learning how to and when to take action based upon the declarative system information is the system that Bennett-Levy calls the *procedural system*. It is the procedural system that builds and refines supervision rules, plans, and procedures that structure the application of supervision. Here is where supervision incrementally builds and progressively refines a therapist's repertoire of fluent and automatic basic therapy skills. The *reflective system*, Bennett-Levy's third component, analyzes past, current, or future experiences and then compares these experiences with learned information. Comparative reflection data leads to either a new plan of action, maintains the status quo, or alters stored information due to new input from the reflective analysis (Bennett-Levy, 2006). According to Bennett-Levy (2006), "Once basic skills are learned, reflection enables practitioners to discern in what context, under what conditions, and with what people, particular strategies may be useful" (p. 60).

The STGS model proposes a tripartite process for learning and practicing sex therapy group supervision. The three components of STGS are core knowledge, integrated methods, and reflective processes. Core knowledge combines fundamental domains of group supervision, sexuality, and sex therapy. Second, STGS operationalizes and integrates core knowledge into a set of STGS skills and procedures. This integrated-methods component of STGS emphasizes both technical group and interpersonal relational skills as well as attitudes and treatment methods for applying sex therapy. STGS relies upon supervisor and supervisee core knowledge and integrated methods of practice to engage sex therapy supervision groups in a reflection of both the "here/now" in the supervision group and the "there/then" of their individual, couples, or group clinical practice. This meta-process is intended to develop therapist empathy, insight, and evidence-informed, client-centered STGS. The reflective process is perhaps "one of the most important mechanisms by with humans learn from their own experience and develop life wisdom" (Bennett-Levy, 2006, p. 60).

Distinct Features of Sex Therapy Group Supervision

STGS organizes its three components into a sequential taxonomy for supervisors to facilitate their group and provide sex therapy knowledge and skills. STGS uses research-based supervision learning methods to foster core knowledge. STGS core knowledge content is individualized based upon the supervisor's level of training and experience in group therapy, sex therapy, and supervision. STGS provides a learning environment conducive to capitalizing upon group content and process for refining sex therapy principles and practices. STGS outlines specific actions that facilitate specific, desired, and observable supervision interventions while providing a space for developing interpersonal perceptual skills that deepen the identity of oneself as a sex therapist. STGS prioritizes intellectual and emotional moments in group supervision for groups to explore here/now experiences that increase everyone's—supervisors and supervisees alike—understanding and competence in providing sex therapy. STGS is a reflection practice to discern useful clinical strategies within specific contexts and conditions.

Combining group supervision with sex therapy training is inherently a reflective process. When we learn about the sexual lives of our clients and bring their sexual problems to a sex therapy–focused group consultation, the sexual attitudes, values, history, and current sexual themes of each group member spring into their consciousness. It is an explicit agreement within STGS that these individual and group thoughts and feelings are relevant for discussion in the supervision group.

Core Knowledge

Sex therapy and case consultation within a supervision group attends to each of the group members' learning. Goodyear (2014) identified four supervision learning mechanisms that have "emerged from the supervision literature as those most important in fostering supervisee learning" (p. 94). His study concluded that modeling, feedback, direct instruction, and self-directed learning were most frequently linked with psychotherapist knowledge acquisition.

Modeling

An essential element of STGS is the many opportunities for divergent feedback provided by the supervisor and group members within a here/now interaction of the supervisory group. STGS provides both novice therapists and seasoned professionals intentional or unintentional moments to observe the group leader perform both successfully or poorly at group facilitation and clinical sex therapy discussions. How are leader errors in a supervisor group an opportunity for sex therapist to learn skills for managing their own dreaded "egg-on-the-face" moments?

> Dale is a sex therapy supervisor leading a sex therapy supervision group. A new member joined an all-male group which, at that time, was comprised of cisgender gay men who all identified as white. Dale made a passing comment about the group as a "gay men's supervision group." The new member stated that he is heterosexual, not gay. Dale paused, the group became silent, waiting for what was to come next. Dale silently thought, "oops!" Embarrassment flooded his face as the awareness of his assumption sank in. He heard several group members make nonverbal "tsk-tsks" or horrified gasps. The new member was the first to speak—he smiled, pumped his fist and exclaimed, "yes!!" He had said that he was proud to "pass as a gay man," and that to him, it was a sign that he was not being perceived as harboring the types of unwanted gender and sexual orientation stereotypes commonly held by, and often projected with disfavor toward, cisgender straight men. A lively discussion ensued, and the group eventually focused their discussion on Dale.

Several members gave feedback about how gracefully and honestly Dale managed his embarrassment. The group began reflecting upon how they might have imagined their own reactions if they had been leading a group in which they said something so presumptive and prejudicial. Dale invited the group to draw parallels to their own vulnerabilities in learning sex therapy in front of the members of this group. They began to empathize with the apprehensions in learning to supervise a sex therapy supervision group as having many similarities with their own anxieties in learning to be sex therapists. The new member closed the group discussion by commenting on his relief from witnessing the group supervisor model how to be seen in a less than flattering light.

Feedback

Many group facilitation and sex therapy micro-skills are learned through supervisor and/or group member feedback. It is not sufficient to simply have experience in leading groups. Untrained group therapists can become less skilled after months of leading groups due to repeating their original mistakes without intervening corrective feedback (Yalom, 1995). The supervisor and the group provide information to another supervisee when a discrepancy is seen between the supervisee's knowledge and skills and their goals of what they want to be able to do as a therapist or supervisor (Goodyear, 2014). An important skill in the development of sex therapy group supervisors is to "behave and talk as a group therapist" (Kleinberg, 1999, p. 165). Learning to facilitate groups in effective and skillful ways combines group supervision facilitation training and mentoring while learning to lead supervision groups. Supervisor feedback in addition to group member feedback and self-observation (e.g., "I notice when your voice gets louder I feel hot, my heart races and feel an urge to bolt out of the room") enables supervisors to become more skillful at monitoring and examine how their affective cues influence their method of group facilitation and supervision.

STGS is a space for future sex therapists to hone their skills in giving and receiving feedback. Feedback within a relationship is also a common sex therapy tool. STGS leaders give feedback when supervision group members' sex talk turns into jumping to emotional conclusions or voicing rigid opinions. Sex therapists need to learn how to suspend their judgments long enough to thoroughly understand their client's sexual thoughts, feelings, behaviors, and concerns. STGS is a space to better understand this skill through listening to other group members' thoughts and feelings. The following paragraph is another example:

> Pat is a member of Garet's monthly online STGS. Pat has a recurring pattern of shifting the group's sex therapy clinical content from a specific case content to "macro-" societal contexts. In one group, Terry was presenting a case about a cisgender male and female couple. Terry was describing the couple's conflict about the male partner's combining online sexual imagery with solo sexual activity. Terry told the supervision group that, upon reflection, they noticed a distinct avoidance to ask about any details of the imagery the client found pleasurable to watch while masturbating. Terry wanted to explore with the sex therapy supervision group possible feelings that may arise when sex therapists ask clients to talk about detailed descriptions of sexual imagery. After Terry stated this goal for the clinical case discussion, Pat interjected, "Where I live, I see so many people doing what everyone in society seems to be doing these days—the minute someone is looking at porn they're called a sex addict."

Garet's challenge is to give constructive feedback to Pat while being mindful of the potential for embarrassing group members with their peers. Garet values honest here/now interpersonal feedback. Garet has come to know that the supervision group members genuinely care about their impact on each other. Garet wants to facilitate sex therapy supervision groups that help members recognize behavior patterns. STGS leader feedback needs to consider the learning goals of the supervisee, the goals for the supervision group, and the goals of the current client who is the focus of the group discussion. The supervisor feedback will ideally combine a didactic and experiential component that relies upon group process rather than continuing to focus on Pat's deflecting statement. Garet chose a more informal style of feedback by pondering aloud with the group, asking "I am curious how Pat's observation of societal rush to judgment is linked with understanding Terry's story of supervisor avoidance?" In this way, the leader has included Pat within the group process without deflecting the group content away from Terry's sex therapy supervision issue. Feedback is given through a process observation of the leader without directly stating their observation to one group member in a manner that turns the group into an audience for a dyadic "calling out" by the group leader of a group member.

Direct Instruction

Beginning sex therapists often value direct instruction. Early STGS learners are like most early learners in that they need immediate feedback with direct clear content (Goodyear, 2014), therefore it is important for STGS leaders to assess each individual group member's need for specific sex therapy skill education. Direct instruction is more frequent and necessary at the novice stage of learning sex therapy. Group supervisors direct instruction includes demonstrating a specific sex therapy interpersonal or systemic clinical intervention.

Some group supervisees may directly ask to learn a specific sex therapy skill through immediate supervisor instruction. Direct instruction is an essential supervisor tool in shaping sex therapists' openness and receptivity for transferring knowledge and skills from supervisor to therapist to client. Direct instruction is a common facilitator intervention when group members report repeating the same errors in a specific case or in response to the same clinical concern with different clients. Direct instruction eventually loses its advantage when supervisees sufficiently internalize repeated direct instruction to develop their own internal guidance (Kirschner, Sweller, & Clark, 2006). Direct instruction methods combine group supervision and sex therapy instruction while gradually scaffolding relevant procedures for facilitation of group process and clinical sex therapy practices (Aulls, 2002). Key to direct instruction is for supervision group leaders to monitor group process and sex therapy practices that are currently beyond the group's stage of learning capacity. In order to give sufficient space for STGS members to focus their attention on learning new sex therapy clinical practice that is in the general range of the group's psychotherapy and sex therapy current competence, the supervisor will choose to offer direct instruction about group process facilitation or sex therapy interventions. The following paragraph is an illustration of direct instruction:

> Dylan, a specialist in kink-informed and affirming therapy for alternative sexual interests, leads a supervision group, and is in a STGS to learn about how to better integrate group process with sex therapy. Dylan has a current supervisee, Evan, who monopolizes their group case discussions. Dylan described how Evan frequently responds to each group member's clinical case presentations by launching into an endlessly detailed description of their similar clinical supervision situations. Dylan described noticing frequent labeling and stigmatizing thoughts about Evan, like "monopolizer" or "narcissist." Dylan asked the STGS group, "What should I do?"

Direct instruction is best given by the group leader after first reviewing the supervisee's level of current knowledge. An STGS supervisor might begin by asking Dylan to talk about their group training or classroom education related to managing clients or supervisees who lack self-awareness when telling stories in great detail. Dylan talked about wanting to stop thinking such stigmatizing labels about Evan. Dylan's work with the kink community has brought to light the often condemning slurs directed to sexual outsiders. Dylan has developed a well-honed, nonjudgmental clinical style in working with sexual diversity. Dylan was struggling with finding a similar suspending judgment mental space about Evan's interpersonal pattern.

Dylan wanted to address Evan in a manner that avoided silencing a group member. To avoid a silencing trap, the STGS supervisor might invite group discussion about how sexually diverse groups have been historically silenced and draw attention to these parallels. The supervisor could represent how a majority culture discomfort with sexual diversity doesn't take into consideration the feelings of sexual minorities. In so doing, Dylan moved away from the leaders countertransference with Evan as a method to prevent a group dynamic that scapegoats Evan's interpersonal pattern. After managing the leader's countertransference, the STGS supervisor directly instructed the entire supervision group about how it is the group leader's responsibility to address Evan's interpersonal pattern. Dylan quite transparently admitted, "I somehow knew that, but needed you to tell me." The STGS leader then said,

> I so appreciate your honesty. Dylan, I believe learning to do supervision of sex therapy takes time. There is no such thing as a complete set of instructions for how to address this, but I have a few basic suggestions.

A supervisor needs to recognize that some supervisee group members may lack some social sensory system for observing the impact on others as well as perceiving the group responses (Yalom, 1995). In this circumstance, the facilitator formulates their feedback through an "I" statement. The supervisor might say to Evan, "when you [describe the specific behavior] . . . I experience [describe your experience]." When Dylan directly informs Evan of a specific behavior that leads to a specific difficulty for the leader Evan is provided self-observation information as well the supervision group witnesses a demonstration of how to engage supervisees and/or clients in similar group behavior (Corey, Corey, Callanan, & Russell, 2014).

Self-Directed Learning

Therapists learn about human sexuality and group work from books, journals, lectures, academic coursework, in-service training, traineeships, webinars, YouTube, Ted Talks, conferences, case discussions, and workshops. Supervision-specific technical knowledge for groups and sex therapy is essential for developing sound practices for STGS. How do therapists learn supervision practices that integrate their psychotherapy, sex therapy, and group work knowledge? STGS is a repetitive practice of self-directed learning to assess sex therapy circumstances and build a supervision course of action that can be held up for scrutiny and evaluation through the group, supervisor, and the therapist's own self-reflection (Goodyear, 2011). A supervisor may have a knack for keen insights about clinical sex therapy and honed their skills to individually supervise sexual problems presented by supervisees. However, the same supervisor may not have developed knowledge about essential content and process for leading a supervision group. STGS is a reflective practice to activate awareness of discrepancies between supervision performance and standards of group work and sex therapy (Goodyear, 2014). The following vignette illustrates a case about the use of technology-assisted supervision:

> Skylar is a leading researcher and sex therapist who supervises groups using technology-assisted supervision and training (TAST). TAST is an all-encompassing term for technology that supports clinical supervision or training (Rousmaniere, 2014). Skylar's motivation for providing a cloud-based, remote video-conferencing supervision group was to increase access for less costly and more flexible sex therapy supervision groups with a more diverse membership. Skylar has been a lifelong early adopter of new technologies, and is very comfortable and familiar with technologically mediated training. This is contrasted, however, with Skylar's lack of adequate training in methods for group process and group supervision process, especially when integrating a very diverse group of professionals.
>
> Kim lives in a rural Midwestern state 100 miles from the nearest large city. Kim had been a member of Skylar's online group for over a year. A forensic psychologist who evaluates men arrested for nonconsensual illegal sex crimes, Kim's goal was to become a certified sex therapist and open a sex therapy practice. There was at the time only one certified sex therapist in the state, who lived 250 miles away from Kim.
>
> In Skylar's last supervision group, Kim phoned in to the group because of a break in the online video connection. The other six members of the group were connected to both video and sound. Kim's voice was present, but on the webinar screen only the name "Kim" appeared next to the live video images of the other group members. With a clear voice connection, Kim asked the group for some time to discuss a recent forensic interview case. The wife of a man accused of sexual rape of minors contacted Kim to schedule an individual therapy session. She reported feeling depressed since learning of her husband's predatory behavior with children. Kim described some very specific details from the wife's description of her partner's predatory behavior. Skylar noticed the upset facial expressions of the other six group members on the video screen, and was aware that is was a new experience for the group to be talking about sexual predatory behavior, especially by a forensic specialist. Skylar later described "freezing," and did not discuss the group's nonverbal reaction to Kim's

account, nor did Skylar talk about the group process of silently listening yet appearing visibly distressed.

As Kim continued to discuss the case without seeing the video images of the other group members, it became clear to Skylar that this technological short-coming was an unaddressed factor in the supervision group process. Skylar realized that there was not a group agreement that members presenting a case must have properly functioning voice and video technology. The sound, without the case presenter's ability to see the group members' faces, resulted in an unequal playing field within the group. This became a liability for all involved, including the group leader. Skylar decided that the group guidelines needed to be updated to preclude any member from presenting a case when the presenter's video and sound are not working properly.

Integrated Methods

Sex therapy group supervision integrates technical supervision practices with group process relationship skills and therapist's personal attitudes. STGS train-ing emphasizes a group process that develops sex therapists use of here/now perceptions of the therapist and the client. The supervisor scaffolds supervisee learning beginning with basic sex therapy tools, gradually leading to what Bennett-Levy calls "an increasingly sophisticated range of *when-then* rules, plans, procedures and skills" (Bennett-Levy, 2006, p. 66).

The "when" is a set of conceptual, relational, and technical skills for lead-ing supervision groups. The basic assumption is that when sex therapists have specific behaviors outlined for them at the novice stage of learning followed by repetitive practice opportunities under the guidance of a group supervisor, then the supervisee will "acquire expertise by combining facilitative attitudes and skills into an increasingly sophisticated range of . . . skills, which are highly contextual: which strategy, for whom, under what circumstances?" (Bennett-Levy, 2006, p. 66). Put another way, sex therapy group supervisors invest in group facilitation practices that develop supervisees' attitudes, technical skills, treatment plans and procedures, and interpersonal relational competencies as a mechanism for moving from a psychotherapist identity to the distinct identity of a sex therapist.

Group Supervision as Experiential Learning

An empirical review synthesizing 24 studies on supervision models concluded that experiential learning is an essential component in developing competent and clinically effective supervisees (Milne et al., 2008). STGS is an experien-tial learning forum for not only observing the technical skills of sex therapist communication and treatment strategies (via taped sessions or therapist ver-bal report), but it is also particularly well suited for exploring sex therapist relational skills. The group is a forum that welcomes a supervisee's "ability to hear, see, and understand the subtleties of the client's experience and to identify markers underlying information processing difficulties that determines the quality of the therapy" (Greenberg & Goldman, 1988, p. 701). AASECT-certified sex therapy supervisors differ in their opinions about the emphasis on their groups attending in equal measure to clinical content and supervision group process. Little emphasis is currently given to developing sex therapy training in group supervision as a distinctive milieu for observing, assessing, and giving feedback about supervisees' ability to balance technical sex therapy practices with processing relational here/now therapy events. STGS supervision emphasizes exploration of the supervision group process to build supervisee spontaneity as they collaboratively create well-matched sex therapy treatment interventions. Sex therapy supervisors use the group process to increase a therapist's capacity for empathy, to "de-automate" the myriad therapist habits developed through education and training that often omit sexuality and sexual health, and to expand supervisees' minds to form complex clinical thinking and integration of sex therapy practices and principles.

Technical Skills

The first step in scaffolding supervisee sex therapy technical skills is to assess each group member's current sex therapy strengths and weaknesses. An informational individual face-to-face meeting (if STGS is an in-person group) or online in-person video conference call is suggested to review a therapist's group supervision starting point. The group leader also reviews the group supervision agreement and expectations. Some STGS can be thought of as a sexual health in psychotherapy supervision group, where the group purpose is for psychotherapists to learn and improve their methods for integrating sexual health and sex therapy within their individual, group, or couples therapy. Other STGS are groups specifically for licensed psychotherapists pursuing certification as a sex therapist. An informational meeting ensures potential members are matched well with the group purpose.

The informational meeting should also explore the supervisee's general goals and how much sex therapy and/or group facilitation training the candidate needs. It is important to clarify to each potential supervisee that STGS emphasizes a balance between sex therapy supervision group content and group process. This includes reviewing the candidate's past experiences with supervision or therapy process groups, the "nuts and bolts" of scheduling, attendance, communication with group leader and other group members, confidentiality, privacy, and finances. The leader should clarify the procedures to join the group, whether the STGS is a time-limited or ongoing group, and whether the group is for only pre-licensed professionals or a mixture of license-eligible and more seasoned practitioners. Other considerations may include whether the group will combine case consultation and supervision for those seeking to become certified sex therapists, and what types of clinical cases the supervisor most commonly supervises.

It is important to have an honest discussion of the strengths and limitations of the group supervisor. This is to protect future group members from misinformation and assumptions about the range of supervision skills and therapeutic factors most likely to be learned within this particular group. This discussion is an opportune moment for the STGS leader to observe and assess the candidate's interpersonal skills, openness to feedback, and ability to discuss the leader's and their own personal characteristics. It is unrealistic to not acknowledge the inherent subjectivity that informs these observations. This is where the experiential process of STGS begins. How does the supervisee keep track of the supervisor's and their own verbal interactions? "I wasn't clear about what you said . . ."; "I really appreciate you saying that . . ."; "Hmm, let me think about that—I may have had something else in mind for a supervision group." What personal attributes are clearly noticeable? How might these attributes be a good match for the current group and the overall goals of the STGS? Given the complexity of providing supervision in a group setting while maintaining an emphasis on sex therapy, it is incumbent upon the supervisor to practice rigorous self-honesty about their willingness and openness to work with the supervisee. Declining to accept a person as a member of a supervision group is not an easy process. The following paragraph is a scenario of the potential challenges of a supervision group:

> Chris is starting a new "mixed" sex therapy supervision group for both licensed therapists seeking sex therapy certification and professionals wanting to improve how they integrate sexual themes within their general psychotherapy practices. Evan attended a sex therapy conference panel presentation in which Chris was one of the panelists. Evan made an introduction after the panel presentation and several weeks later called Chris to schedule an informational interview to enter the new group. At that time, there was one more space in the group. On the day of their informational meeting, Evan called Chris to reschedule 30 minutes before the scheduled time due to a private practice client emergency. The day of the rescheduled appointment, Evan left a voice mail saying that "traffic was horrible." Evan apologized several times, and again asked to reschedule. Chris began to notice feeling ambivalent about scheduling a third screening appointment, and chose to discuss the situation with a mentor and close friend. Chris noticed Evan's lack of self-reflection in the phone messages. In particular, Evan expressed no curiosity about the impact of the cancellations on Chris. Was this, he wondered, a preview of future group interactions with the supervision group?

STGS combines acquiring sex therapy and group facilitation knowledge while experiencing an active group process for experientially learning. Evan demonstrated interest in the learning but did not exhibit a basic interpersonal trait of empathy or curiosity about the interpersonal experience of others. Evan did not say anything like: "Wow, I can't believe this happened again! I am trying to imagine the mess I may be creating by this delay. I would really like to talk to you in person. I don't want to interfere with your process of forming a group.

I know what's it like when I set up time and someone cancels." In both cancellations, Evan emphasized frustration at others' behavior that interfered with Evan's plans for the screening appointment. Evan seemed to want Chris to listen to these experiences in what Chris perceived as a one-sided conversation. After the mentoring discussion, Chris decided to schedule a phone conversation with Evan, but not to leave a voice mail. Chris gave Evan feedback about their process. Evan became immediately angry and defensive, and accused Chris of being unfair. Evan was not curious or interested in Chris's feedback. Chris decided not to offer to schedule another screening interview with Evan.

Relational Skills

The relational experiences in the sex therapy supervision group are as integral to the learning as the sex therapy didactic content. According to Barlow (2013), "Supervisees need to be instructed that the supervisory process focuses on both process and content of therapy and supervision" (p. 164). Sally Barlow identifies a range of group facilitation competency benchmarks for psychologists that "delineate expected levels of supervisee development in such a way as to avoid the accusation that the focus on supervision process seems too much like therapy" (Barlow, 2013, p. 161). The art of supervision is to develop competencies in giving and receiving feedback to and from group supervisees. Sex therapy supervision groups are excellent practice space for members to develop their group process relational skills.

STGS will invariably bring attention to group members' personal blind spots of self-observation or awareness. The advance agreement among STGS members states that both leader and group members will from time to time discuss here/now interpersonal or clinical supervision self-awareness for improving group facilitation and sex therapy skills. When a blind spot in a group member's personality or relational patterns is observed in a STGS, the leader has the responsibility to assist the member and the group with what to do with this awareness. Is this a "teachable moment?" Is it an observation to contain until the clinical topic is completed and there is more of a space for processing the groups interactions? Is the group willing and able to contain its collective impulses to immediately comment on the group member's behavior? Central to STGS is the supervisor guiding the incremental development of the group as a container for open group discussion about member and leader interpersonal process.

When sex therapy group supervisors invite reflection about the group's relational experiences, it deepens supervision learning within both the sex therapy clinical case content as well as the relational processes relevant to the supervision situation. Some helpful questions may be:

1. How did the you experience the group when working on this most interesting supervision situation?
2. What did the group enjoy or perhaps feel disappointed by in my (the leader's) facilitation of this supervision case?

3.   Does anyone have some feedback for someone in the group?
4.   Were there any elements of the case content that had some parallels with our group discussion?

Notice how the STGS leader's approach is to remain curious about the interpersonal process. The facilitation questions are direct and clear, and yet invite an open-ended response. The questions do not contain evaluative conclusions or labels of anyone in the group or the supervisee's clients. This is particularly important in sex therapy group supervision. Too often societal sexual health conversation patterns remain mired in glib labels, immediate judgments, humorous jokes, or opinions that create hierarchical superiority or professional smugness. It is vital to STGS that the group process not replicate normative societal sexual health conversation patterns.

Reflective Processes

Being highly educated in sexuality as a mental health professional in the United States is a chosen responsibility. Sex therapists' personal sexual selves and identity are integral to their role. Each supervisee's lifetime of sexual experiences and relationships informs how they process the relational dimensions of sex therapy and sex therapy supervision groups. Too often the group member's sexuality, sexual health, and individual array of sexual and erotic pleasures is "singularly absent from the group psychotherapy discourse, reflecting . . . a problem that goes to the heart of our models of group" (Nitsun, 2013, p. 282). In his iconic 500-page volume *The Theory and Practice of Group Psychotherapy*, Irving Yalom (1995) includes only 15 pages about sexual abuse groups, sexual fantasies, and sexual relationships. Australian narrative therapist Cyndi Darnell observed

> few practitioners discuss sex explicitly either in their personal lives or outside a context of abuse, pain or monogamous relationships. Our collective discomfort with discussing sex implies that trauma is an acceptable reason to seek therapy, but exploration and pleasure is not.
>
> (Darnell, 2017, pp. 1–2)

Individual and couples therapy are almost the exclusive domains for delivering sex therapy. Learning sex therapy principles and practices in groups is an approved method for teaching sex therapy, but is not promoted as a robust form of sex therapy or for training sex therapists.

In fact, the original proposal for this text did not include sex therapy group supervision as a topic. Wadley and Siegel are to be commended for their responsiveness to add this topic to this text on sex therapy supervision. But the omission reflects a consistent dynamic surrounding group therapy, group supervision, and specifically the teaching of sex therapy group supervision: "There is no empirical data about how frequently group psychotherapy is supervised in a group format" (Bernard, 1999, p. 153). We have no data on training sex therapy supervisors in groups. It is not difficult to presume how very rare it is for sex therapy supervision to be supervised in a group format.

In the book *Treating Out of Control Sexual Behavior: Rethinking Sex Addiction*, the authors discuss their methods for a "combined individual and group therapy principles and practices designed to facilitate corrective emotional responses and support men moving toward their personal vision of sexual health" (Braun-Harvey & Vigorito, 2016, p. xiii). The authors have only recently begun providing group supervision for training group leaders who facilitate groups treating men with out of control sexual behavior.

What might be important reflective topics and skills for STGS leaders? Watson and Soklaridis (2017) describe *reflection* as a cultivated habit of mindfulness where information is approached as a novel experience, facts are seen as conditional for this moment, situations can be seen from multiple perspectives, categorization and judgment is suspended, and a lively engagement in self questioning is prioritized. Harris and Hays (2008) surveyed marriage and family therapists and found a correlation between therapist discomfort with sexual topics and their unwillingness to formulate and implement interventions focused on their client's sexual health. In fact, the more uncomfortable a therapist was in talking about sex, the more often they avoided any discussions about sex with their clients (Harris & Hays, 2008). In a study of occupational therapy students, over 50% reported they would not feel comfortable in dealing with sexual issues (Jones, Weerakoon, & Pynor, 2005). Perceived comfort in discussing sexual topics and the related ability and willingness to talk with physicians about sexual topics is central to the communication quality between teens and their physicians (Fuzzell, Shields, Alexander, & Fortenberry, 2017). A recent study concluded that physicians need to take proactive efforts during routine medical appointments to increase sexual minority and majority patient comfort with talking about sex (Fuzzell, Fedesco, Alexander, Fortenberry, & Shields, 2016). Perez and Ussher confirmed earlier studies that found cancer treatment physicians as uncaring, incompetent, and neglectful when discussing sexuality with their patients (Gilbert, Perz, & Ussher, 2016). Comfort by the provider has a clear direct qualitative and quantitative consequence for addressing a wide range of sexual problems and disorders in healthcare settings. It is perhaps then a fair parallel recommendation to prioritize a supervisor's ability, willingness, and comfort with initiating both content and process within sex therapy–focused group supervision.

Sexual health conversations are important group leader tools for integrating sexuality within therapy groups (Braun-Harvey & Vigorito, 2015; Braun-Harvey, 2009).

> Studies suggest a troubling circumstance in psychotherapy that arises when a therapist's lack of knowledge, discomfort with talking about sex, and lack of preparation for sexual health conversation aligns with a client's defenses against talking about his sexual activities and behavior.
>
> (Braun-Harvey & Vigorito, 2016, p. 13)

Sex therapy supervision groups must move beyond the current normative privileging of therapist client case content and avoidance of group process. Sex therapy supervision groups that prioritize balancing clinical discussion with reflection practices centered on the supervision group process are poised to develop more exceptionally skilled sex therapists. Just as psychotherapy groups must overcome negative sociocultural silence about sex, supervision groups must welcome a conscious and informed conversation about the real-time supervision group process, rather than keeping it silenced.

Sex Therapy Group Supervision: Application

The core knowledge and integrated methods for sex therapy group supervision outline the supervision group leader foundational knowledge as well as the interaction qualities between group leader and supervisee. We now look at how sex therapy training in a supervision group exploits group interaction and process to teach and train sex therapy. The work of sex therapy methodologies such as behavioral, somatic, spiritual, psychoeducational, mindfulness, emotion-focused, and others is not especially different from general psychotherapy settings (Darnell, 2017). Sex therapists stand apart from most of the field of psychotherapy by holding space for the open discussion of sex, sexual problems, and sexual pleasure in a therapeutic context (Darnell, 2017).

A sex therapy supervision group is a space held for therapists to experientially learn through witnessing, modeling, practicing, and integrating a range of vital sexual therapy practices within a reflective group process. Attending to both group content and process is necessary to disrupt traditional clinical training and psychotherapy practices that reflect societal sexual silence, avoidance, illiteracy, problem focus, stigmatization, fetishizing of "normal," and reification of dominant cultural narratives. A goal for sex therapy group supervision is to undo and build new psychotherapy sexual health conversational language and interpersonal tools. The here/now relational context between group members is ideally suited to develop sex therapists. The supervision group leader balances members' comfort with discussing sexual complaints, betrayals and functioning with less familiar psychotherapy discussions about sexual pleasure, range of sexual orientations, gender spectrum, and relationship diversity while mitigating group defenses and fears associated with honest and vulnerable reflections on clinical work.

STGS balances supervision group content and process to bridge sex therapy theory with sex therapy practice. Considerable emphasis on supervision group process is "vital to the effective conduct of groups" (Nitsun, 2013, p. 266). However, the focus on the development and patterns of relationships within the supervision group can become out of balance with content-specific sex therapy methods and practices. STGS group leaders attend to three fundamental leader facilitation interventions to balance clinical case content and supervision group process: group cohesion, group interactions, and their own facilitative decisions.

Cohesion, a central action for change in psychotherapy groups, is considered an important element in sex therapy group supervision (American Group Psychotherapy Society, 2007). Supervision groups that express a greater sense of cohesion will more likely welcome individual and/or group reflections that provide vulnerable, honest, and direct feedback.

How do supervision group interactions contribute to member's perceptions of the group as an attractive, compatible, supportive, trusting space to learn and practice clinical sex therapy? How does the leader guide new groups to tolerate the tension of early conflicts when differences emerge between group members or with the leader? The universality of cultural conflict and sex is not presumed to be left at the door in a sex therapy supervision group. A sex therapy supervision group is an excellent space to work with different clinical models, professional controversies, and conflicts, as well as value differences that emerge within the minds of clients, between relationship partners, or among members of a psychotherapy group. Watson, Raju, and Soklaridis (2017) operationalize three teaching components for operationalizing cross-cultural clinical and teaching spaces through reflection, humility, and working with otherness. The sex therapy group supervisor is often attending to a member's struggle with self-criticism and anxious anticipation of group or leader judgments. STGS emphasizes group leader skills to make the implicit fears of criticism explicit within the group.

The supervision group's ability to practice self-reflection will be overly determined by the facilitator's strengths and limitations in their self-reflection capacity. Kannan and Levitt's findings about therapist training and self-criticism led them to conclude "psychotherapy training may be best approached through supervisor transparency about their own process of development, the mirroring of supervisees' experiences, and peer supervision as a medium to bolster supervision" (Kannan & Levitt, 2017, p. 11). Sex therapy supervision group supervisors are expected to go well beyond minimally adequate clinical supervision standards and requirements to facilitate the group's focus on sexual content and their ensuing process (Ellis et al., 2014). This chapter closes with a series of additional sex therapy group supervision case examples. The case discussion describes how STGS core knowledge, integrated methods, and reflective processes are organized within supervisee clinical case presentations.

Group Cohesion

David, a US sex therapist, is interested in collaborating with Alistair, a well-regarded and highly respected UK sex therapist, educator, and researcher. Three months ago, Alistair sponsored David to come to London and present a lecture to therapists on his book. Afterwards, they both found themselves interested in growing their professional relationship. David asked Alistair if he would be interested in co-leading an online sex therapy consultation group for UK-based and

EU-based therapists. Alistair liked the idea and they agreed to discuss this further via video conference.

David and Alistair began their meeting talking about the differences in addressing sexuality in psychotherapy in the UK, in particular among clients with diverse sexual orientation, gender identity, and sexual relationships. Alistair shared his experience at a recent EU sexology professional conference. "There was a high level of interest in sex but only from a pathologizing perspective. The entire conference had virtually nothing on GSRD issues." Alistair casually spoke the acronym "GSRD," as if he had been saying this term for years. David heard a familiar small voice of shame in his mind that he knew became activated at just these kinds of unexpected professional moments. He was not familiar with the acronym GSRD. A clawing question entered David's mind: "How do I address the fact that I do not know this term?" This is an all too common experience of a therapist learning about sex therapy—how to be transparent about not knowing. David had expectations of himself that he would find words that skillfully worded his cross-cultural inquiry with Alistair in an engaging, nonformulaic manner.

This common predicament of wanting to navigate cultural differences regarding sex and sex therapy was a central motivation for David and Alistair in co-leading a group. David had a vague, pre-conceived notion of how to handle his moments of ignorance, but it was unformed by real-world practice. All of this flashed in a moment through David's mind. As David remembered the priority he places on his supervisee's honesty about their not knowing, he commented, "I am not familiar with GSRD, what are these initials?" Alistair, in a matter-of-fact, kind, and precise manner replied: "GSRD is the acronym for *Gender, Sexuality and Relationship Diversities.* For some while now we've been thinking beyond LGBTIQA+ because the '+' doesn't really indicate whether cis, heterosexuals or those into BDSM get included as well as people involved in consensual non-monogamies and all the other sorts of GSRD identities." As David's mind opened, he felt a firing commotion in his brain. A novel notion had been transmitted. David began to see the cultural contrast between the American LGBTIQA+ identity-driven discourse as the privileging of an identity through language as a form of social justice. The UK transition to Gender, Sexuality and Relationship Diversities (GSRD) shifts this North American discourse from privileging diverse identities to emphasizing a broader perspective on inclusivity of all diversity. A rich discussion ensued between Alistair and David about the possibilities of merging their diverse cultural and clinical training within a consultation group focused on sex therapy work in psychotherapy.

Supervision group cohesion will more likely develop when co-leader(s) engage in pre-group reflection. The language of GSRD provided an opportunity for

David and Alistair to experience a suspended judgment zone. This was the start of their preparation, selection, and formation of their online group. David and Alistair's cross-cultural exchange would become essential in facilitating the consultation group process to build a cohesive connection among the group.

Cohesion is like a "complex chemical reaction," and the multiple complexity of the relationships between group members become the basis for this multiple systemic chemical cohesion (Burlingame, Fuhriman, & Johnson, 2002, p. 84). STGS places the supervisor's intrapersonal and intragroup interventions as central to the enhancement or attenuation of group cohesion. Supervision group cohesion is inhibited when supervisors remain in the sex expert role and approach the group by guiding individual group members rather than facilitating their group participation (Enyedy et al., 2003).

Philip is forming a new sexual-health-in-psychotherapy consultation group for local therapists. The sex therapy group provides continuing education credits for the American Association for Certified Sex Educators, Counselors and Therapists (AASECT). His pre-group formation approach began with defining basic structural components. Who joins? Will it be a closed/open group? What will be the group size? How often will it meet? What time will the group meet? How much to charge? What would preclude an interested therapist from being considered for membership? What is the purpose of the group related to sex therapy training? Philip eventually decided to form a six-member group of licensed therapists who have attended one of his previous trainings. Once the group had six members it would become a closed group. No fixed timeline for the group's ending would be established. No decision would be made about adding members should a member leave. Philip thought it would be useful to see how the relationships between the group members developed, and how they would address an empty space in the group should a departure arise. The group was to meet every month on the same date and time, with some agreed-upon months off for previous commitments.

Eventually six potential members emerged from Philip's process for establishing the group. Abby, educated with a master's degree in sexuality as well as a second master's degree in social work, is a cisgender, first-generation Chinese-American whose arranged-marriage parents immigrated to the United States from China. Abby was obtaining hours for licensure as a clinical social worker, and was eagerly anticipating to return to a professional community of sexually informed professionals; she requested that Philip waive the requirement that members be licensed. Abby, ironically, would be the most sexologically trained member of the supervision group, and yet the least trained in psychotherapy. This uncommon juxtaposition of high levels of sexuality literacy while in the early stages of psychotherapy training was the inverse of the other five group members. Some of them had been therapists for over 30 years and expressed chagrin at their novice stage of development in sexuality and psychotherapy. Three of the group members wanted to become AASECT-certified sex therapists, including

Abby. Philip wondered whether a new psychotherapist with an advanced degree in human sexuality might model a more developed ability to discuss sexual diversity, or whether it was at all likely that she would bring more experience in openly exploring her thoughts and feelings related to clinical cases involving sexual health and sexuality.

Abby demonstrated several micro-skills in giving and receiving feedback about sex therapy during the workshop. Philip noticed her well-honed ability to talk about sex with other professionals while suspending judgmental comments (which could have easily been smugly stated in a manner of "look how much I know about sex"). Yet, at the same time, Abby asked two specific direct-instruction, psychotherapy-focused questions in the workshop: "Do I call the client back if it sounded like he was getting off from talking to me about my specialization in sex therapy?" and "How do I set a boundary when it is time to end a session but a client has just revealed a crucial detail about their sexual problem with only a few minutes left in the session?" Philip began to see Abby's rare and unique individual strengths and experiences as a perfect match for the group. Each member had a strong set of skills in either sexuality or psychotherapy; no one entering the group felt an especially high degree of proficiency in both. It was thought that Abby may model what the other group members aspired to learn about sex, just as the seasoned professionals would model to Abby their well-developed psychotherapy minds.

Philip decided to invite Abby to join the group. An early reflective process within the new group was Philip's disclosure of his weighing his decision to include Abby in the group. This was a valuable early modeling of group process as a means for developing connectedness, authenticity and supervisor responsiveness. Abby shared her experience in becoming trained in sexuality and the tension between her and her parents, who viewed sexual knowledge and discussion as a source of shame and embarrassment. Abby told the group about her divided alliances in upholding her Chinese heritage and cultural norms around sexual silence and her lived American experience of pride in sexual literacy within a country that was still mostly sexually illiterate. The group had a here/now experience to learn about linking family of origin and culture with the group's determination to develop their sexual literacy as psychotherapists. Philip reinforced this group process that developed early experiences for group cohesiveness.

Group Interactions

Sex therapy group supervision is a relational experience within the didactic sexuality group consultation content. "Group supervisees have a responsibility to manage the relationships among each other" (Enyedy et al., 2003, p. 315). An important function and benefit of group supervision is the peer-to-peer observation and feedback about a member's blind spot in either relational awareness, personality, or clinical knowledge (in particular sexual knowledge and sex therapy skills). STGS is a remedy for a particularly toxic and endemic pattern among sexually illiterate or sexuality undertrained licensed psychotherapists: excessive self-criticism.

> Paul is leading a sexual-health-in-psychotherapy workshop in a large eastern metropolitan city. Among the 25 workshop attendees is a cisgendered white male psychiatrist, Bertrand, who is nearing retirement after decades of devoted work. He has stated he is proud of his ongoing curiosity and desire to learn no matter how many years he has practiced his form of medicine. About an hour into the workshop, Bertrand wells up with tears, places his head in his hand, and weeps quietly. The group conversation stops. Paul sits quietly among the waiting circle of attendees. Paul asks Bertrand if he would like to talk about his thoughts or feelings. He nods his head yes, but emotions keep him from forming the words right away. After a brief pause, he sits up and looks around the room with a reconstituted sense of self, saying, "I have just been remembering the hundreds of clients, through all my years of psychiatry, with whom I avoided talking about sex. It wasn't until this moment that I realized how many of them I could have helped so much more if I had only known how to talk with them about sex. I feel ashamed of my ignorance, and sad that I was not in a workshop like this decades ago."

Paul discussed how important it is in training therapists, and in providing sex therapy, to listen for evidence of high levels of harsh self-criticism in the supervisee or client when they learn valuable and new sexual information. Bertrand modeled how therapists may feel shame about their lack of training and skills in working with sexuality only to then feel shame about their shame, much like the wave of shame Bertrand felt and showed in his body. In groups, "the potential for shaming is exacerbated by the number of people present and possibility of sudden, unexpected exposure" (Nitsun, 2013, p. 258). Supervisor transparency about their training process while mirroring the supervision group members' experience is a useful approach for training psychotherapists (Kannan & Levitt, 2017). Paul explained how common therapist self-judgment and criticism arise when learning to integrate sexuality within psychotherapy. He invited the workshop attendees to share any judgments or self-criticism they were having about current or past clients they also may have been reflecting on as they listened to Bertrand. Several members of the workshop shared their own experiences as well as their motivation for attending the workshop. One person said "I feel better about being here today, my regret and shame about avoiding talking about sex with my clients got me here. I don't want to keep letting them down." Paul invited the group to see the pride therapists can feel in facing their patterns of avoiding sex talk and determination to change.

Leader Facilitation Concerns

The language of words is the essential medium for groups, group supervision, and sex therapy group supervision (Nitsun, 2013). STGS prioritizes the leader's use of here/now interactions to examine the interactions between language and the nonverbal physicality of communication. Sex therapy group leader interventions include the use of appropriate language, suspension of judgment, managing therapist affect stimulated by discussion of sexuality, awareness of the supervision group leader's own erotic desires, and therapist capacity for appropriate pacing of movement towards and away from sexual and erotic content, each of which will be addressed separately. Ultimately, the supervisor guides the therapist's process of the integration of sexual health information with the therapist's preferred psychological theory and style of psychotherapy.

The Language of Sex

Language is the first barrier to sexual health conversations in psychotherapy. It is the essential therapist invitation that welcomes the client's sexual life into psychotherapy. Sex therapy group supervision must often look well beyond the supervision language of psychology, psychiatry, or psychotherapy and enter the seemingly foreign territory of sexologists, sex researchers, sexuality educators, sexual health public policy makers, and sex therapists.

Group supervisors link sexual science, sex therapy, and accurate sexual language with clinical case work in their groups. Sex therapy supervision groups bridge and connect therapists to create sparks of creativity, inspiration, and passionate courage as they enter the world of sexology and sex therapy. Groups often lead to discovery of therapist strengths and potential blind spots with regard to talking about sex. For example, supervision groups or sexuality conferences can help therapists discover their unseen sex negative attitudes and sex phobic feelings. A sex therapy group supervisor may encourage their supervisees to go to sex research conferences (e.g., The Society for the Scientific Study of Sexuality) and listen to sex researchers describe their work. If so, it is always wise to suggest that supervisees pay close attention to the language used at such venues, and in particular sex research descriptions of sexual activity and behavior that are alternatives to common sex negative terminology. Sex research does not rely upon psychological theory on psychosexual disorder nomenclature that is all too often replete with value judgments, prejudices, and unfounded assumptions.

STGS focuses leaders to shift group members' language from client metaphor, pronouns, poetic imagery, and vague speech. Group supervision for sex therapy is an important practice space for therapists to move out of their habits of settling for a client generalization as sufficient dialogue to discuss their sexual worries, problems, or disorders. It is the detailed language of sex that accesses a person's feelings and insights about their sexual concerns as well as meaningful group connection. Group facilitators lead supervisees into these moments of precise and clear language to increase the likelihood of these sexual health conversation skills filtering into supervisees' clinical work. A sex therapy supervision group may also explore the balance between focusing on specific language used and the sexual functioning concern being addressed.

Tracy, a 34-year-old single cisgender African American heterosexual female clinical social worker, specializes in treating depression. Recently, a client told her "I'm frigid, I have no interest in sex." Tracy wanted to hear how other group members talk with their clients about the sexual side effects of psychotropic drugs. A STGS leader listens quietly to the supervision group's language in response to Tracy's description of the clinical question. A psychotherapy supervision group of therapists with little training in sexuality may discuss the sexual side effect question and be less curious about how Tracy addressed the clients use of the sex negative term "frigid."

The leader invites Tracy to discuss her history of talking about sexual functioning with clients. Tracy blushes a bit and says, "Oh, this is so hard, I hardly ever bring this up, that's why I joined this group." The leader asks, "What is 'this'?" Tracy looks surprised. "I'm not sure what you're asking." Another group member Lucinda says, "I know what the question is about. You said 'this' without saying what specifically you meant that was so hard to bring up about client sexual functioning." Tracy realizes she did what she sees her clients do, when sex is the topic, they become vague about what they are saying. She brushed over the details just like her clients. She was surprised how effortless this was. Tracy said, "I remember the first time I said the word masturbate in here. It was such a strange feeling in my mouth to even say the word." The leader looks around the room, takes a quick temperature of the group and waits.

The group began a lively discussion about the value of using specific sexual terms and language with their patients. The group leader encouraged the group to speak up when members review their cases using traditional terms that contain hidden value judgments, like "frigid." STGS is a space for therapists to learn how to work with the general public's often imprecise and misleading terms that can make objectively and clearly describing and discussing clients' sexual activities, functioning and pleasure extremely difficult.

Suspending Judgment

Sex therapy supervision groups emphasize treatment methods that avoid common sociocultural sex negativity. Supervisees' judgmental thoughts may surface when a group member explicitly describes the details of a client's sexual activity. Group leaders need to regulate their own internal judgments while maintaining curiosity about supervisee judgments. The effective leader listens for the familiar sequence of spoken judgments: group members will often state an opinion or make a conclusion about a sexual act or behavior, rather than describing or deconstructing their internal experience in response to the sexual content in a case presentation. Sex therapy supervision intentionally moves the group discussion away from familiar societal judgmental discourse into a dialogue of honest, informed exploration of sexual concerns or treatment dilemmas.

Pham is a single 25-year-old second-generation Vietnamese American gay cisgender male graduate student completing his internship at a lesbian and gay community center outpatient counseling center. He is a co-leader of an anxiety and phobia treatment group. Pham wanted to discuss his co-leader's response to a client reporting a severe panic attack while having anonymous sex in the home of another man. His co-leader, John, is a 53-year-old white gay cisgender male psychologist who had recently been hired as a full-time therapist and supervisor. The client told the anxiety group about his panic attack and the helpful response of his anonymous sex partner in moving past the attack. Pham noticed that John became noticeably quiet and still. Pham said the client really focused on how well he had utilized his skills for managing his panic and how much worse the attack could have been without his support from the group. Pham said: "Then John, the co-leader, asked if he thought the client's panic attack could have been activated by the client placing himself in a dangerous situation." Pham described how the group member immediately became defensive. "I didn't come here to focus on my sex life. It was not dangerous. What makes you say that?" Pham told the supervision group how he chose to remain quiet during this exchange. Pham realized he deferred to John, the experienced therapist, despite his judgmental comment. Pham reported that John went on to give his opinion about going to a complete stranger's house to have sex may not be good judgment for managing anxiety and panic. Pham said "he felt like a spectator in John's judgmental countertransference." He was visibly upset as he described his choice not to say anything in the group or in his post-group meeting with John. Pham wanted to talk with the supervision group about his guilt for not speaking up and to prepare to have a conversation with his co-leader before the next group.

The group supervision leader, hearing the familiar doubt and self-criticism of a new therapist, reinforced Pham for sharing his self-criticism about his silent response to his group leader's behavior. He invited Pham to explain to the group his motivation for bringing this case to supervision. First and foremost, Pham described his isolation and loneliness with his ambivalent feelings about talking with his co-leader. Pham found it ironic that the senior therapist of the group was being a "bad therapist" in Pham's mind. The group began to share similar stories of being disappointed with previous supervisors or more experienced therapists.

Both group leaders in this sample are cisgender gay men, however the senior therapist identifies as white, while Pham is Vietnamese American. How might the supervision group be a place for Pham to assess the alliance between the leaders, the group members and the group as a whole when viewed by the racial and cultural diversity of two leaders who share the same sexual orientation? What relevant cultural variables may be important for the group to discuss with Pham? How might adding the diversity lens contribute to understanding his guilt as well as his plans to talk with John? Might this be a valuable intern opportunity to begin skills in addressing cultural differences among therapists in their conceptualization of self-disclosure? (Chen, Thombs, & Costa, 2003).

The leader may also invite the supervision group to explore how the development of group psychotherapy and sex therapy practices by white identified professionals biased the field. Pham's situation is an opportunity for the supervision group leader to acknowledge the paucity of studies and information on multicultural practice and training in group therapy and sex therapy. Practice guidelines published by the American Group Psychotherapy Association (AGPA, 2007) are "insufficient in the articulation of specific ways in which racial-cultural minority group members' characteristics, values, preferences, and sociocultural context should be considered in promoting effective practice" (Chen, Kakkad, & Balzano, 2008, p. 1265). The supervisor may place Pham's judgment about his reaction to his co-leader in the context of no pre-group preparation to acknowledge and discuss how the co-leader relationship and facilitation process will differ. The leaders did not prepare for a situation when the leader from the racial majority responsible for most notions of psychotherapy and sex therapy conflict in their clinical approach. Pham's unique contributions from his racial-cultural beliefs, values, and expectations of therapy had not been integrated into the co-leader relationship. Had this been broached by the leaders in their own relationship development, Pham may have found his voice to move past his internal activation and directly address John's judgmental statement.

Affect Management

A supervision group that is insufficiently prepared for sexual themes and content can flood supervisees with unmanageable feelings. Unfortunately, this flooding is too often erroneously associated with the sexual content. Group members' heightened anxiety level when discussing sex may lead to errors in thinking, like "sex is too scary to talk about." Supervision groups, particularly those not specifically for AASECT certification, need proper preparation for clinical case discussion of sexual content. Without preparation, supervisees may prematurely conclude that their strong feelings or reactions to sexual themes in clinical case presentations are exclusively linked with the sexual content of the case. The sex therapy group supervisor invites supervisees' curiosity ("Hmmm, I wonder what this feeling is about") beyond merely the sexual content of the case.

Group Supervisor's Own Erotic Desires

Group supervisors must prepare to experience their own sexual stirrings when providing sex therapy supervision. Sex therapy training and supervision normalizes sexual countertransference when working with sexual themes. Group supervision is a place for supervisees to listen and learn as their colleagues move past anxieties and judgments regarding sexual countertransference and rely upon their sex therapy knowledge, psychological theory, and psychotherapy skills for help with navigating this terrain. Unfortunately, when sex therapy supervision groups do not acknowledge and discuss possible therapist sexual reactions or stirrings, the group content and process too often move towards premature clinical solutions.

Jack Morin (1995), in *The Erotic Mind*, proposes that attraction and obstacles together generate erotic feelings; attraction alone is not sufficient. Eroticism requires barriers, obstacles, and obstructions along the path of attraction. Without these barriers, the attraction remains just that: an attraction without the concomitant charge of electrical erotic energy. Sex therapy supervision group leaders can listen to group supervisees discussion of sexual countertransference through the narrative of Morin's erotic equation. What inhibitions about sexual stirrings were a sufficient enough obstruction, when combined with the supervisee's attraction, to generate erotic arousal? Sex therapy group supervision will call upon group leaders to have a basic understanding of erotic feelings as well as a method for including client "erotic maps" within clinical case work. Sexual countertransference can be welcomed into a supervision group by identifying common obstacles that are sources of erotic charge within the context of psychotherapy.

Examining the erotic themes of thousands of men and women sharing their peak erotic experiences through an online research program, Morin found four common themes that interact to focus and generate erotic feelings and sexual behavior. His "Four Cornerstones of Eroticism" were founded on the notion that the "universal challenges of early life provide the building blocks for adult arousal" (Morin, 1995, p. 74). These "existential sources of arousal enhancing obstacles" are longing and anticipation, violating prohibitions, searching for power, and overcoming ambivalence (Morin, 1995, pp. 74–75). Overlaying these concepts to John and Pham's gay men's anxiety group, it is possible to posit that John became erotically charged listening to a group member describe a forbidden or taboo sexual behavior and was thus distracted from attending to the group process by his own sudden erotic energy.

Pacing Sexual and Erotic Group Work

Sex therapy supervision group leaders need to balance the tension between supervisees' premature movement either to suppress or to move towards sexual content. Supervision groups, as mentioned before, can reflect societal limitations on sexual talk or blithely move into sexual content "ready or not." Group supervisors must pace sexual content through attuning with supervisees' affect, to familiarize sexuality discussions within supervision group process.

Sean, a sex therapist and group supervisor, trains therapists in one-day group therapy workshops. He presents content, then models the use of the workshop content by facilitating a small demonstration group of workshop participants in front of the remainder of the attendees. At a recent workshop, Sean's demonstration group of four men and four women of various ages, ethnicities, and sexual orientations were asked to discuss their reactions to the morning's didactic material on sexuality in group therapy. Sean sat quietly and let the group begin. Within the first few minutes of the group, a delightfully eager participant cued the group that he was about to disclose significant content about his current sexual life with his male partner. Sean quickly assessed the "readiness of group" to jump into the deep waters of a member's self-disclosure about their sexual life. Sean was familiar with this pattern, and at moments like this he heard the profound words of Jack Morin in his head: "To uncover what has been long hidden, be patient and gentle; allow the erotic mind to reveal itself at its own pace as it tests the waters. Practice offering yourself invitations to see more, to comprehend more, to accept more, to enjoy more. Each invitation carries with it the freedom to decline or to wait. The goal of erotic self-understanding is furthered by a willingness to ease up in the face of your own reluctance" (Morin, 1995, p. 12).

Sean did not want to risk empathic failure by letting the group move too quickly into sexual content, especially while conducting a demonstration group in front of 50 colleagues. Sean engaged with the enthusiastic learner and asked him to reflect a moment—without yet disclosing his story—on the meaning of his disclosure. He deftly asked him what his hopes were for the group that drove his desire to want to share his story. Sean asked him if there was a sense of longing held in this enthusiasm. The participant moved to a deepening affect, and his eyes welled with moisture. He identified himself to the group as a gay therapist, and began to discuss his eagerness to attend this workshop. He related how much he thought about coming to the workshop and the anxieties he felt, his isolation and hunger for training and support in the difficult work of facilitating groups of gay men who are themselves so craving for support. Sean again invited him to reflect on the content of what he wanted to discuss. The now considerably less eager group member looked around the group, realized he did not intimately know the demonstration group members, and wanted to first connect on a different level. He quickly decided it was "too soon" and chose to wait a bit longer before jumping in to such personal disclosure.

Sex Therapy Group Supervision

Delineating sex therapy group supervision from existing methods of group supervision and individual sex therapy supervision has been absent from the literature. This chapter was based on the need for integrating human sexuality within existing group supervision methods and to propose a Sex Therapy Group Supervision (STGS) model for mentoring sex therapy supervisors to capitalize on group process for teaching sex therapy in groups. The supervision literature emphasizes supervision methods that protect supervisees from harm. STGS's three-component sequential taxonomy moves from development of core knowledge, followed by integration of clinical methods which eventually leads to developing a lifelong professional reflective practice balances group content and process, to bridge sex therapy theory with the practice of sex therapy. The framework of STGS is first and foremost based on the assumption that combing the rigors of supervisory learning with the complexity of group process provides a uniquely important and essential component of learning, practicing, and excelling in providing safe, effective, and inspiring sex therapy.

About the Author

Sexual health author, trainer and psychotherapist **Douglas Braun-Harvey** bridges sexual and mental health and facilitates organizational change. In 2013 he and Al Killen-Harvey co-founded The Harvey Institute, an international education, training, consulting, and supervision service for improving healthcare through integration of sexual health. He teaches and trains nationally and internationally linking sexual health principles within drug and alcohol treatment, group psychotherapy, HIV prevention and treatment, and child maltreatment.

Since 1993 he has been developing and implementing a sexual health–based treatment approach for men with out of control sexual behavior (OCSB). His new book, *Treating Out of Control Sexual Behavior: Rethinking Sex Addiction*, written with co-author Michael Vigorito, was published in 2016. Previous publications include *Sexual Health in Recovery: Professional Counselor's Manual* (2011) and *Sexual Health in Drug and Alcohol Treatment: Group Facilitator's Manual* (2009).

He is a Licensed Marriage and Family Therapist, Certified Group Psychotherapist and Certified Sex Therapist.

References

Alfonsson, S., Spännargård, Å., Parling, T., Andersson, G., & Lundgren, T. (2017). The effects of clinical supervision on supervisees and patients in cognitive-behavioral therapy: A study protocol for a systematic review. *Systematic Reviews*, *6*(1), 94.

American Association of Sexuality Educators, Counselors and Therapists. *Supervision guidelines* [Date file]. Retrieved July 9, 2017, from www.aasect.org/guidelines-supervision

American Group Psychotherapy Society. (2007). *Practice guidelines for group psychotherapy, AGPA science to service task force, 2007*. Retrieved August 5, 2017, from www.agpa.org/home/practice-resources/practice-guidelines-for-group-psychotherapy

Aulls, M.W. (2002). The contributions of co-occurring forms of classroom discourse and academic activities to curriculum events and instruction. *Journal of Educational Psychology*, *94*(3), 520.

Barlow, S. (2013). *Specialty competencies in group psychology*. Oxford: Oxford University Press.

Beidas, R. S., Edmunds, J. M., Cannuscio, C. C., Gallagher, M., Downey, M. M., & Kendall, P. C. (2013). Therapists perspectives on the effective elements of consultation following training. *Administration and Policy in Mental Health and Mental Health Services Research*, 40(6), 507–517.

Bennett-Levy, J. (2006). Therapist skills. A cognitive model of their acquisition and refinement. *Behavioural and Cognitive Psychotherapy*, 34(1), 57–78.

Bernard, H. S. (1999). Introduction to special issue on group supervision of group psychotherapy. *International Journal of Group Psychotherapy*, 49(2), 153–157.

Borders, L. D. (2014). Best practices in clinical supervision: Another step in delineating effective supervision practice. *American Journal of Psychotherapy*, 68(2), 151–162.

Borders, L. D., Welfare, L. E., Greason, P. B., Paladino, D. A., Mobley, A. K., Villalba, J. A., & Wester, K. L. (2012). Individual and triadic and group: Supervisee and supervisor perceptions of each modality. *Counselor Education and Supervision*, 51(4), 281–295.

Braun-Harvey, D. (2009). Fundamental principles of sexual health for group psychotherapists and their groups. *Group*, 33(3), 257–271.

Braun-Harvey, D., & Vigorito, M. A. (2016). *Treating out of control sexual behavior: Rethinking sex addiction*. New York: Springer.

Burlingame, G. M., Fuhriman, A., & Johnson, J. E. (2002). Cohesion in group psychotherapy. *Psychotherapy*, 48(1), 34–42.

Chen, E. C., Kakkad, D., & Balzano, J. (2008). Multicultural competence and evidence-based practice in group therapy. *Journal of Clinical Psychology*, 64(11), 1261–1278.

Chen, E. C., Thombs, B. D., & Costa, C. I. (2003). Building connection through diversity in group counseling. In D. Pope-Davis, H. Coleman, W. Ming Liu & R. Toporek (Eds.), *Handbook of multicultural competencies in counseling and psychology* (pp. 456–477). Thousand Oaks, CA: Sage.

Corey, G., Corey, M. S., Callanan, P., & Russell, M. (2014). *Group techniques* (4th ed.). Belmont, CA: Brooks/Cole, Cengage Learning.

Darnell, C. (2017). Using narrative practices in a group sex therapy context. *Sexual and Relationship Therapy*, 1–12.

Ellis, M. V., Berger, L., Hanus, A. E., Ayala, E. E., Swords, B. A., & Siembor, M. (2014). Inadequate and harmful clinical supervision: Testing a revised framework and assessing occurrence. *Counseling Psychologist*, 42(4), 434–472.

Enyedy, K. C., Arcinue, F., Puri, N. N., Carter, J. W., Goodyear, R. K., & Getzelman, M. A. (2003). Hindering phenomena in group supervision: Implications for practice. *Professional Psychology: Research and Practice*, 34(3), 312.

Fuzzell, L., Fedesco, H. N., Alexander, S. C., Fortenberry, J. D., & Shields, C. G. (2016). "I just think that doctors need to ask more questions": Sexual minority and majority adolescents' experiences talking about sexuality with healthcare providers. *Patient Education and Counseling*, 99(9), 1467–1472.

Fuzzell, L., Shields, C. G., Alexander, S. C., & Fortenberry, J. D. (2017). Physicians talking about sex, sexuality, and protection with adolescents. *Journal of Adolescent Health*, 61(1), 6–23.

Goodyear, R. K. (2014). Supervision as pedagogy: Attending to its essential instructional and learning processes. *Clinical Supervisor*, 33(1), 82–99.

Gilbert, E., Perz, J., & Ussher, J. M. (2016). Talking about sex with health professionals: The experience of people with cancer and their partners. *European Journal of Cancer Care*, 25(2), 280–293.

Greenberg, L. S., & Goldman, R. L. (1988). Training in experiential therapy. *Journal of Consulting and Clinical Psychology, 56*(5), 696.

Harris, S. M., & Hays, K. W. (2008). Family therapist comfort with and willingness to discuss client sexuality. *Journal of Marital and Family Therapy, 34*(2), 239–250.

Jones, M. K., Weerakoon, P., & Pynor, R. A. (2005). Survey of occupational therapy students' attitudes towards sexual issues in clinical practice. *Occupational Therapy International, 12*(2), 95–106.

Kannan, D., & Levitt, H. M. (2017). Self-criticism in therapist training: A grounded theory analysis. *Psychotherapy Research, 27*(2), 201–214.

Kirschner, P. A., Sweller, J., & Clark, R. E. (2006). Why minimal guidance during instruction does not work: An analysis of the failure of constructivist, discovery, problem-based, experiential, and inquiry-based teaching. *Educational Psychologist, 41*(2), 75–86.

Kleinberg, J. (1999). The supervisory alliance and the training of psychodynamic group therapists. *International Journal of Group Psychotherapy, 49*(2).

Milne, D., Aylott, H., Fitzpatrick, H., & Ellis, M. V. (2008). How does clinical supervision work? Using a "best evidence synthesis" approach to construct a basic model of supervision. *Clinical Supervisor, 27*(2), 170–190.

Morin, J. (1995). *The erotic mind: Unlocking the inner source of sexual passion and fulfillment.* New York: HarperCollins.

Nitsun, M. (2013). *The group as an object of desire: Exploring sexuality in group therapy.* London: Routledge.

Rousmaniere, T. (2014). Using technology to enhance clinical supervision and training. In C. E. Watkins Jr. & D. L. Milne (Eds.), *The Wiley international handbook of clinical supervision* (pp. 204–237). Oxford: John Wiley and Sons.

Watson, P., Raju, P., & Soklaridis, S. (2017). Teaching not-knowing: Strategies for cultural competence in psychotherapy supervision. *Academic Psychiatry, 41*(1), 55–61.

Yalom, I. D. (1995). The theory and practice of group psychotherapy. New York: Basic Books.

4 Live Supervision of Sex Therapy

Sarah E. Wright

Abstract

Much of sex therapy supervision relies on supervisee recall. This may limit a supervisor's ability to intervene or offer feedback in areas that are outside a supervisee's awareness, or those which may be uncomfortable for the supervisee to name. Live supervision involves direct observation and real-time intervention in therapy sessions. This chapter thoroughly explores the use of live supervision to maximize in vivo *learning for supervisee development, growth, and skill acquisition, as well as enhancing clients' benefit from therapy. Various technologies and methods of live supervision are outlined, some of which allow for live supervision to happen remotely. A range of potential interventions are explored, with the developmental level of the supervisee being a critical determining factor in their selection. This chapter aims to demystify the process of live supervision and make it a viable option for sex therapy supervisors.*

Keywords

Live supervision, in vivo learning, technology, distance supervision, remote supervision

Introduction

Historically, the field of sexuality has been studied through a primarily medical lens. This has resulted in significant gains in understanding physical sexual response, the process and function of arousal and orgasm, and medical complications that can impact sexual functioning. Conversely, live supervision has been a tool mainly within the family therapy arena with the aim of seeing interpersonal dynamics in action and intervening in the here-and-now. Live supervision is an extension of this here-and-now aspect of therapy. Instead of relying on supervisee recall of events in session, supervisors watch the session as it takes place, see the interactions between therapist and client, and provide immediate feedback, guidance, and direction as it is needed instead of in hindsight when a prime opportunity for learning or challenge may have been missed. This chapter brings together the two paradigms of sex therapy and live supervision and offers suggestions for how to best use live supervision to maximize *in vivo* learning for supervisee development, growth, and skill acquisition. Various methods of live supervision will be outlined, all of which can enhance clients' benefit from therapy. This chapter aims to demystify the process of live supervision and make it a viable option for sex therapy supervisors.

Distinct Features and Challenges

Current practices of supervision of sex therapy tend to be very focused on the content being reported in session, such as symptom frequency and duration, which is another carryover of the medical roots of this field. Supervisors want to ensure that supervisees know appropriate treatment protocols, are abreast of recent research and cultural trends, and are maintaining ethical standards with vigor. Live supervision also focuses on these aspects with the additional benefit of tuning into the ever-important *process* of sex therapy. Acknowledging patterns of when a client changes the subject, where people choose to sit in the room, and the presence or absence of eye contact during certain interactions all can impact one's therapy and subsequent understanding of presenting concerns and related factors. How can we teach our supervisees to tune in to these nuances when they aren't aware of what to tune in to, or when to look for them? Live supervision takes advantage of the fact that we learn better with immediate, in-the-moment feedback, with the opportunity to change our trajectory in real time.

The American Association of Sexuality Educators, Counselors and Therapists (AASECT) has alluded to the benefit of seeing a provider engaged in clinical work. In the section on their website providing guidance on the provision of supervision for those pursuing certification as a sex therapist, it is written that "the presentation of sex-related case materials utilizing direct observation or audio/video is encouraged" ("AASECT requirements for sex therapist certification," n.d., para. 6). Even with the AASECT recommendation, there is little guidance in the field of sex therapy about how to engage in this type of supervision. Relying solely on verbal recounts and review of documentation can be challenging as there is a risk that verbal recall will be inaccurate, or that supervisees will purposefully conceal aspects of work on which they worry about being judged (Mehr, Ladany, & Caskie, 2010; Ladany, Hill, Corbett, & Nutt, 1996; Yourman & Farber, 1996). Live supervision can be an excellent tool to use when therapists or clients feel "stuck" with therapeutic progress, when novel presenting concerns are being addressed, when trying to implement a new treatment or intervention, when teaching behavioral skills, when questions exist about interpersonal dynamics within the therapy system, or when therapists are confused about a pattern of outcomes (e.g., clients terminating therapy prematurely). It can also be helpful in working with novice sex therapists to determine their comfort in addressing issues of sexuality, fluidity of using sexual terms and definitions, ability to ask personal questions relevant to presenting problems, and potential to overlook aspects of sexuality with which they do not have as much familiarity or comfort. Significant gaps in time between performance and feedback may limit the effectiveness of supervisee learning (Tracey, Wampold, Lichtenberg, & Goodyear, 2014). Further, live supervision provides a way to monitor potentially challenging ethical situations to ensure that a proactive approach is being used, instead of having to react to a potential ethical breach.

Several studies have highlighted the benefits of live supervision as described by both therapists and clients. Benefits for therapists have included receiving immediate feedback (Bartle-Haring, Silverthorn, Meyer, & Toviessi, 2009), improved conceptualization skills (Carmel, Villatte, Rosenthal, Chalker, & Comtois, 2016), increased therapist confidence (Weck et al., 2016; Miller, Miller, & Evans, 2002), rating of sessions as more effective (Rizvi, Yu, Geisser, & Finnegan, 2016), improved working alliance with supervisor (O'Dell, 2009), and finding it to be a helpful and effective learning tool (Miller et al., 2002). It has been reported that even one session of live supervision can significantly improve a therapist's perception of clinical progress (Bartle-Hering et al., 2009), and that repeated sessions have an increased positive effect (Bartle-Haring et al., 2009). Therapists have also reported feeling closer with their supervisor as a result of engaging in live supervision (Rousmaniere & Frederickson, 2013). Additionally, it has been reported that changes in the therapist as a result of live supervision generalize to other clients and across sessions (Klitzke & Lombardo, 1991). For clients, reported benefits have included increased intensity of the session (Rousmaniere & Frederickson, 2013), receiving more suggestions, hearing a greater diversity of suggestions and feeling supported (Locke & McCollum, 2001), increased effectiveness of sessions (Rizvi et al., 2016), and greater working alliance with the therapist (Weck et al., 2016; Kivlighan, Angelone, & Swafford, 1991).

Few disadvantages to live supervision have been reported, and have included coordinating schedules (Rizvi et al., 2016), potential cost of technology (Miller et al., 2002), setting up equipment, being in a room with a one-way mirror, and general worry about being watched (Locke & McCollum, 2001). As is evident, most concerns center on technology and its use, as well as general comfort on behalf of the therapist. Even with these documented concerns, Ford (2008) found that the technology used in live supervision had no negative impact on the session. Taking time to fully orient a client before the session and having a contingency plan in the case of malfunction can minimize any impediments that may occur.

Live supervision takes into consideration the various systems present in therapy. There is the therapeutic system, consisting of therapist(s) and client(s); the supervisory system, consisting of the therapist and the supervisor, and potentially others who may be involved in group supervision; and the supervisory team, which encompasses all systems involved in the care of the client (Haber, 1996). Ultimately, these systems are all working for the same goal of client betterment. Even the process of supervision is an attempt to ensure that a therapist is operating in the client's best interest, and in a manner that will prove helpful. To best facilitate this, two important areas to be considered before engaging in this type of supervision will be discussed.

Technical Considerations

The hallmark of live supervision is being able to hear and see what goes in within the therapy room while also having some means of communicating with the therapy dyad (therapist and/or client). There are a range of formats that would allow for this, and preference for setup may depend on practice setting, available funds, and the technical skills and comfort of those involved in the process. The most common methods for the viewing component of live supervision include observation via one-way mirror or remote observation of a session using a HIPAA-compliant closed-circuit video. There is more variability within the communication component, including options known as a "bug in the ear" and a "bug in the eye" (utilizing an earpiece or video screen, respectively), as well as calls via phone, the therapist stepping out of session to consult with the supervisor, or the supervisor entering into the therapy session. All communication methods will be discussed in more detail later in this chapter. The first two options require more investment in technology, while the latter require no additional equipment other than a standard telephone.

The ability status of the supervisory system is another consideration in determining which method would be most ideal. For supervisees with a visual disability, the bug in the eye technique may not be viable. Similarly, for supervisees with a hearing disability, the bug in the ear or a phone call may not work. It is imperative to ensure that whatever method chosen is the most viable for all engaged. Location can be another factor to consider, and recent research has been done on the use of remote live supervision where the supervisor is located off-site (Rousmaniere & Frederickson, 2013). This could be invaluable in the field of sex therapy, where the pursuit of certification requires supervision by a certified supervisor. Depending on one's practice location, there may not be local options available for supervision. This would make live supervision more widely available and accessible, and could greatly improve the quality of supervision around skills specific to sex therapy.

Informed Consent

As with any technique used in therapy, it is important that clients are fully informed about the rationale, potential benefits, possible risks, and process of live supervision, and have the option to either agree or refuse to participate without consequence. Supervisee confidence in the benefit of live supervision may impact the presentation of live supervision as an option, and in turn could increase client's willingness to try. Informing clients about the rationale for suggesting live supervision is an excellent place to start. Taking advantage of the expertise of a supervisor, wanting to ensure the highest quality care, feeling at an impasse in therapy, and wanting guidance on a therapeutic technique are all solid reasons to engage in live supervision.

Knowing what to expect with live supervision can help both the client and the therapist get the most from the situation. Typically, clients are educated and explicitly informed about the process of live supervision, any changes that will occur in the setting and timing of appointment, any equipment that may be present in the room, and information about anyone who may be part of the supervision team. Clients are informed that a supervisor (or supervision team) will be viewing and listening to the session from a private location, and that the confidentiality of the session will be maintained. If the session is being recorded for later review by the therapist, clients are informed of this as well, including the format of the recording, how it will be stored, who will have access to this, and how long the recording will be maintained.

Clients are made aware that the supervisor will be communicating with the therapist (or perhaps with the client, as will be discussed) via the predetermined medium. It should be made clear whether clients will be aware of this communication as it happens (as with a phone call), or if the communication will be more covert (as with a bug in the eye). If the communication will be covert, clients should know whether they will be apprised of the comments that had been offered at the conclusion of the session. Additionally, any changes to the meeting time or location should be made known well in advance of the actual live supervision session. Clients will ideally know what equipment will be present, where it is located, and how it will be used throughout the session. Finally, clients should be given the option to meet anyone who will be viewing the session, even if they are watching remotely. This can help some people feel that the process is less nebulous and more personal. Clients need to be reminded that consent can be rescinded at any time, even after the session has started. If live supervision is repeated in a future session, informed consent is to be reviewed to ensure that the client continues to desire this format. A sample informed consent form has been included for reference (see Appendix).

Skill Set of Supervisee

While live supervision is appropriate for use with trainees at all levels, the selection of specific supervisory interventions hinges on the developmental level of the therapist. Haber (1996) discusses this, and states that it is typical for beginning therapists to need more support, structure, and direction. Many novice therapists are more successful with concrete directives and guidance, while advanced therapists tend to want autonomy in the session and may fare better with less concrete interventions and more observations, questions, or challenges. Specific interventions and their developmental considerations are further discussed later in this chapter. Regarding sex therapy, it may be the case that a seasoned clinician is learning and expanding on newly acquired sex therapy skills. It is important to consider the supervisee's experience with the *skills being used* in a session, and not the development or experience of the therapist overall (Costa, 1994). Since it remains the case that most mental health graduate training programs in the United States include few, if any, courses on sexual health and sex therapy, it is likely that some providers seeking sex therapy supervision are engaging in clinical work in this field for the first time.

It is also important to consider a supervisee's ability to see this type of intervention as an asset to their learning while minimizing the evaluative components. Supervisees who work well in a collaborative, team-based atmosphere will likely benefit most from this type of supervision. Concern about potential negative evaluations can make the experience more anxiety provoking than beneficial and may lessen any potential learning that could have resulted from using this approach. Supervisees who are overly focused on evaluations, tend to strive for perfection, or struggle to name areas in need of improvement may have a harder time with this supervisory method. Reiterating this experience as one of learning and not evaluation may help supervisees maximize its effectiveness. Allowing a supervisee to observe a supervisor can also normalize the process.

Finally, consideration is ideally given to the supervisee's ability to hear and integrate feedback in the moment. Some supervisees have only had positive feedback from supervisors, and others have heard nary an encouraging word in supervision. It is important to know a supervisee's relevant history and expectation when it comes to feedback, and for all parties to have a clear idea of how feedback will be given both during and after live supervision. Having a solid supervisory working alliance is a cornerstone to successful live supervision.

Techniques

Orienting to the Session

A brief amount of time is needed before the start of the live supervision session to ensure all parties are ready to maximize its benefit. Haber (1996) recommends about 15 minutes as being ideal, and discusses this being sufficient time to engage in all necessary tasks and processing, and not so much time as to unnecessarily increase the therapist's nervousness. Costa (1994) outlines several methods to address and manage supervisee's anxiety before engaging in live supervision, including normalizing the reaction and giving permission to mess up. It has also been suggested that the opportunity to role play or to witness others engaged in live supervision can help prepare a supervisee for the experience (Rousmaniere & Frederickson, 2013; Bernard & Goodyear, 1998). Ensuring that all technical equipment is set up and functional is a primary task of this time, as is checking that visual displays, audio output, and communication media are all working and perceptible by all parties, and that all parties know how to access these tools as needed. Engaging in behavioral rehearsal with these tools before the session can increase therapist's comfort using them in session.

After all technical checks have been completed, time is spent orienting to the actual session. The therapist provides a brief conceptualization including client demographics, presenting concerns, goals for therapy, current conceptualization, and present rationale for initiating a live session. It can be helpful if the therapist has a specific goal or aspect of therapy on which to focus. As an example, a psychotherapist named Olga, in training and under supervision toward becoming certified as a sex therapist, had been working with a young male client who initially presented for therapy with concerns related to erectile functioning. After the initial assessment however, he became reluctant to engage in any discussion around this concern. Olga was feeling stuck in therapy and asked for the supervisor to help her find an opening with the client to address the issue, and to help her better attune to any dynamics in the relationship that may be impacting the client's difficulty in talking about his sexual dysfunction. This gave the supervisor a particular concern on which to focus and allowed for interventions to be tailored to the identified need.

During the orientation time, the supervisory system will solidify plans for how interventions will be offered. This may depend on the availability of technical equipment, comfort with the use of equipment, and comfort or preference of any member of the supervisory system. If multiple options are present, it should be discussed as to which are viable for the session at hand. Clients should be informed about any method of intervention that will or may be used, including the possibility that a member of the supervisory team may address the client directly. If phone calls will be used to deliver interventions, it is ideal for a land line in the office to be used. Using a supervisee's cell phone could create an unnecessary distraction as other calls, texts, or notifications may come up during the therapy session. Issues such as battery life could also become an impediment. Additionally, if calling in and speaking with the client, it would be inappropriate to contact a client on their personal phone, and it could potentially be uncomfortable for a therapist to allow a client to use their personal cell phone.

The orientation time is not intended to plan for the session. This may serve to increase the therapist's anxiety and make the therapist less present with the client. Additionally, there may be developments since the last meeting that render any pre-created plan untenable. This does not preclude a supervisor from giving the therapist an idea about possible interventions, or immediate thoughts that arise from the introductory information, such as relevant behavioral interventions or potential hypotheses for why the current dilemma exists. Finally, therapists should be reminded that the ultimate decision about whether to include a suggested intervention is theirs. It may be the case that the supervisor is offering an intervention that, unbeknownst to the supervisor, has been used in a previous session. Or perhaps the intervention offered is not in line with the therapist's orientation, skill level, or comfort. In any of these cases, the therapist must decide about which interventions are best suited to benefit the client and make the ultimate decision about their utilization. The rationale for not using an intervention offered is ideally processed with the supervision team after the session. If the issue is a lack of awareness or experience with a suggested intervention, then future supervision sessions can focus on the bolstering of necessary skills.

Live Supervision Session

Before entering the therapy space, clients should be given the option to meet the supervision team. If desired, the meeting should be brief and should include name and role in the live supervision process of all members of the supervision team.

Once in the therapy room, clients are reminded about the process of live supervision. Therapy can then begin as it typically would for that therapeutic dyad, ideally with them having 10 to 15 minutes to establish a solid working flow (Wright, 1986). There can be some initial nervousness or discomfort, especially if the session is occurring in a location other than the usual meeting room. Giving a bit of time allows for much of this nervousness to subside, and for the typical dynamic to resume. If in a supervision team, the decision is made as to whether processing about the session will happen concomitantly or if the session will be observed without discussion among the team. It has been the experience of this author that the ability to process throughout the session increases viable suggestions, aids in the enhancement of the clinical conceptualization, and increases the team's awareness of various dynamics and nuances in the session. Additionally, research has suggested that when supervisees process throughout a session while observing, they are more likely to incorporate feedback and suggestions when they have the opportunity to be observed (Moody, Kostohryz, & Vereen, 2014).

It is recommended that the maximum number of interruptions to the session be kept to five (Wright, 1986) to minimize disruption and maximize effectiveness of interventions offered. Fewer call-ins have been associated with increased client cooperation with interventions (Moorhouse & Carr, 1999). This would exclude any situation or condition that is unethical or could contribute to harm to the client. Fewer call-ins also give ample time for an offered suggestion to be considered, altered to fit the progression in the session since it was offered, and then executed. Calls being made in too rapid succession leaves insufficient time for this processing, and can negate any benefit the intervention could have had, and has also been associated with therapists giving the client less time to process in the session (Moorhouse & Carr, 1999).

Liddle and Schwartz (1983) generated a series of considerations for supervisors when engaging in live supervision and contemplating making an intervention. These include considering whether potential harm could come if an intervention is not made, the likelihood that the therapist will come to the intervention independently, how able the therapist would be to execute the suggested intervention, and whether the intervention would foster a sense of dependence on the supervisor. When the supervisor has an intervention in mind, it is helpful to hold this thought for a brief time. It may be that the therapist is having the same thought and is working to incorporate this into the session. In the meantime, if working in a team, this is an ideal time to name the awareness to the team and solicit additional input. Through this process an intervention is created. Ideally, an intervention is brief, easily understandable, and in line with the identified goals of the therapeutic system.

Methods of Intervening

- Calling in via phone and speaking to the therapist

Addressing interventions to the therapist is the most common way to deliver an intervention. The therapist is prepared and has been coached on ways to handle such interruptions. It is important to remember that calls in are just that—an interruption. Supervisors need to be mindful of the timing of a phone call, as the phone ringing is an intervention of its own. It can interrupt silence, redirect an unproductive line of dialogue, or challenge unhelpful or inaccurate comments being made by the therapist.

It has been suggested (Wright, 1986) that phone interventions start with something positive. This helps reorient the therapist temporarily back into the supervisory system. It also serves to eliminate some of the potential nervousness the therapist may feel at being watched by the supervisory team. Positive feedback offered should be genuine and should be in some way related to the intervention that will be offered. The developmental level of the therapist will determine the type of intervention used and is further discussed below.

- Calling in via phone and speaking to the client

If it is possible that the supervisor may call in and speak directly to the client, the client needs to be apprised of and consent to this before the session begins. When used, this style of intervention can help increase the client's sense of agency and can make the client feel that they are contributing to the therapeutic system. Depending on the intervention, the client may or may not be guided or encouraged to share the information with the therapist.

To highlight this, consider a case involving a heterosexual male therapist who was beginning to work with issues of sexuality and was receiving supervision around this for the first time. The therapist had just started working with a heterosexual female client who had been struggling to integrate sex into her romantic relationships in a way that was positive and empowered. In the orientation session, the therapist shared with the supervisor his difficulty asking the client directly about issues related to sexuality. He expressed concerns about how the client might perceive the appropriateness of such inquiry, and whether there would be suspicion about his motives for asking more detailed or specific questions.

Early in the session, the supervisor called in an offered a directive to the therapist to ask the client about what she saw as the function of sex in a relationship and to facilitate an exploration of her sexual values. While the therapist could execute the first part, the additional exploration did not occur and the conversation refocused on the client's emotional engagement in relationships.

For the subsequent intervention, the supervisor requested to speak with the client. The client was then asked to convey to the therapist her feelings about talking about sex in therapy. She proceeded to share that she was slightly nervous, but was looking forward to being able to talk openly in a space where she felt safe from judgment and understood by her provider. She further shared that while it was a bit more difficult to talk to a man, that she had intentionally sought out a male therapist to further challenge herself, and to have the opportunity to talk with a man about sex in a way that could provide a healthy model. It was having this overt permission from the client that finally allowed the therapist to ask the essential questions to better understand the client's concerns.

- Bug in the ear

With this form of intervention, the therapist wears an ear piece that allows the supervisor to communicate directly and continuously to the therapist. This method would preclude the option to speak directly with the client. This method also reduces the interruptions experienced with a phone call, as there is no audible indication that an intervention is being made. One aspect to consider with this intervention is whether the client will be made aware when the supervisor is speaking with the therapist. If not, this can put undue pressure on the therapist to continue to listen to the client while simultaneously attending to the message being offered by the supervisor. If the client is made aware, then there is the decision as to whether they will be informed about the message offered from the supervisor.

The bug in the ear technique also relies on much briefer interventions than what can be used via telephone. There is unlikely to be sufficient time to offer a positive comment and offer an intervention into the session. This method is more commonly used when frequent, brief feedback is needed.

- Bug in the eye

The bug in the eye technique was first described by Klitzke and Lombardo (1991), and has been found to be less distracting than other forms of live supervision (Klitzke & Lombardo, 1991; Miller et al., 2002). While it may sound unpleasant, there is nothing that actually goes in one's eye. The bug in the eye requires that a monitor be set up behind the client but in the field of vision of the supervisor. The monitor (usually a tablet or computer) is the method by which text interventions are delivered to the therapist. The monitor is intentionally placed out of the client's eyesight but within that of the therapist. In this format, text interventions are sent from the supervisor and are only left up on the screen for a short time to eliminate distraction. Messages are ideally brief with a suggested limit of seven to nine words (Scherl & Haley, 2000).

It is important with this method to ensure that there is a mutually understood way to differentiate between types of interventions (e.g., telling the therapist something to do versus making an observation). Rousmaniere and Frederickson (2013) recommend the use of symbols to denote various types of interventions. (See below for a full discussion of types of interventions.) When using this method, it is important that all members of the supervision system are aware of the text codes being used, what they mean, and which denote action on the part of the therapist. Similar to the bug in the ear, this method makes it more difficult for the supervisor to speak directly to the client. At the end of the session, it is recommended that the client be allowed to review any of the comments that had been sent throughout the session (Rousmaniere & Frederickson, 2013).

- Requesting that the therapist step out of the session for an in-person consultation

Asking a supervisee to step out of the therapy room for a consultation with the supervisory team requires the least amount of technology. A simple knock at the door could signal that it is time for the therapist to step out and consult with the supervisory system. If a phone call is considered an interruption, then this method would certainly be considered a complete disruption of the therapeutic system. It literally removes the therapist from the client, effectively breaking the bond that had been built in the session to that point. This can be a helpful intervention when the therapist seems stuck or overwhelmed, or when interventions offered via other means have not been effective.

- Supervisor going into the session

This method of intervening is ideally used as a last resort (Haber, 1996). A supervisor going into a session may send the message to the client that the supervisor does not believe that the therapist is competent enough to be helpful. Additionally, the therapist may get the implied message that the supervisor does not have confidence in their ability to serve as an effective helper to the client. However, there are times when it is appropriate for the supervisor to enter in the session. When a needed directive is too complicated to adequately describe in a brief intervention, client safety is a concern, or the therapist could benefit from *in vivo* modeling of a skill or technique, a supervisor going into the session may be the most fitting option.

When using this method, it is imperative that the supervisor be respectful of the therapeutic system, and to acknowledge its interruption. It is also helpful for the supervisor to reiterate confidence in the therapist and to be transparent about the reason for coming into the session. Once the intervention has been offered, the supervisor leaves the session and allows the therapeutic system to process the interaction and continue with the session.

One example of this was when a novice therapist was working with a client on issues of identity, depression, and inability to find a romantic partner. She brought this client for live supervision as she had thought the client might have had feelings for her, and she was unsure of how to process this with him in a way that could be therapeutically beneficial. About 15 minutes into the session, the client disclosed that he had been having thoughts of suicide secondary to loneliness and hopelessness about finding a partner. The therapist quickly jumped to reassurance and providing hope that he would one day meet someone with whom he had a connection. The supervisory system could see that an immediate safety assessment was needed, and that the current approach was likely to leave the client feeling more dejected.

The decision was made for the supervisor to enter the session and conduct a thorough safety assessment. While doing so, the supervisor took the opportunity to comment on the working relationship that had been established. The client was able to acknowledge his want to connect on a more personal level with the therapist, and worrying about being rejected. This allowed the supervisor to inform the client about the boundaries that exist in therapy and the reason for these. The client's feelings were normalized, and he was validated for feeling connected to the therapist given his ability to be vulnerable with her in a way he did not allow himself to be with others. This example gave him a framework of potential ways he could approach other relationships with the goal of increasing his sense of connection with others. The therapist continued this line of processing when the supervisor left, and offered appreciation for the client's ability to speak openly about his feelings even with her in the room. This modeling gave the therapist language to use with the client in setting boundaries in the relationship, and helped normalize his feelings without making her the focus of attention. The combination of a safety assessment in conjunction with addressing the dynamics of attraction in the therapeutic system would have been far too complex to try to convey over the phone or in a one-time consultation.

- Live remote audio

Using this approach, the therapist and supervisor are connected via phone with the therapist using a speakerphone setting. The supervisor can listen to the therapy session and share feedback at any point. It is necessary for there to be agreed methods for the supervisor to interrupt and to navigate offering interventions individually to either the therapist or client. Establishing a method for the supervisor checking in about nonverbal interactions happening in the session can also be beneficial. Getting information about body posture, seating location, or facial expressions can add to the supervisor's understanding of the clinical dynamic. Preparing a therapist that this is a likelihood will better equip them to offer this information when asked.

While this method minimizes a supervisor's access to nonverbal information, it may be ideal when there is limited access to technology or HIPAA-compliant resources, especially when involved in remote supervision. If possible, it is ideal to use a landline when engaging in this form of supervision to reduce distractions that may be more frequent from a cell phone.

Types of Interventions

Below are Haber's (1996, p. 171) suggestions for types of interventions to use, which have been supported by later research (Moody et al., 2014).

- Directive: Interventions that clearly dictate an action to be taken or comments to be made. These interventions are clear, concise, and leave little room for interpretation.

- "Ask the client about masturbation practices, and whether the presenting concerns are present during masturbation as well."

- Supportive: Interventions that offer little in the way of direction, and instead make use of validation. It can be used to highlight something effective that the therapist has done, which may increase the likelihood this will continue to happen. This can also be an effective tool when therapists are especially anxious, need frequent reassurance, or seem to be waiting for an intervention from the supervisory system.

  - "You're doing a really good job normalizing the client's discomfort with talking about sex, and then reframing your questions."

- Declarative: Statements that come directly from the supervisor to the therapeutic system. These are intended to be delivered from the therapist on behalf of the supervisor. It is a way for the supervisor to affect the entire therapeutic system simultaneously.

  - "It seems that everyone in the room is avoiding talking about the threesome that created so many problems in the relationship."

- Interrogative: Asking questions of the therapist can give them more control over how and whether to incorporate a given intervention. It can also send the message that there is no specific intervention in mind but a line of curiosity that the supervisor has. If the therapist thinks it is a viable direction, it can be pursued. If the therapist has knowledge the supervisor doesn't, or if the sense in the room indicates the curiosity may not be relevant, it can be ignored.

  - "Do you think the client's trauma history is impacting her current orgasmic function?"

- Explorative: These prompts are intended to get the therapist thinking beyond content. Whether it be exploring relevant feelings, thoughts, or reactions they are having, thinking about ways to shift to the process of the session, or incorporating experiential exercises into the session, these directives are intended to get below the surface.

  - "What feelings are you aware of having when your client talks about having an affair?"
  - "How can you use some of the imagery the client is providing to work on a metaphorical level and incorporate more emotion?"

- Reflective: These interventions rely on the supervisor's use of self as a tool. It relies on the supervisor's ability to be aware of feelings and to communicate them succinctly. It does not give direction to the therapist, yet can give some key insight about dynamics within the relationship of which the therapist might be either unaware or may have become a part.

  - "I'm exhausted watching you work this hard and only getting one-word answers."
  - "I feel sad hearing this story."

- Intensive: These interventions are usually the most vague and are intended to inject a sense of energy or urgency into the situation. Sometimes this can also be used to highlight a dynamic in the session that the therapist has become a part of without knowing.

  - "This couple is suffering and you are the only one who can help!"
  - "How will he ever be happy again if he can't get an erection?!"

Note that some of the interventions may be edited for length, complexity, or content to best fit with the technology being used. As mentioned previously, use of the bug in the eye method needs to have a predetermined method of differentiating the various types of interventions, such as the use of symbols or fonts to designate and distinguish various interventions.

Use of Reflecting Teams

When working with a supervisory team, usually in the context of group supervision, the use of reflecting teams can be a powerful adjunct to the live supervision session. In this paradigm, the end of the therapy session is not the end of the experience. The therapeutic system (both therapist and client) has the opportunity to watch the supervisory team process the session. The therapeutic system becomes the viewer while the supervisory team becomes the viewee. Depending on technology, this may require the physical relocation of the various systems (i.e., therapeutic system moving into the viewing room).

The supervision team, usually consisting of one or two supervisors and other supervisees, then processes the session. Areas of discussion may include the content of the session, other possible interventions that could be used, the relationship between therapist and client, skills evidenced in the session, growth and courage of the client, areas for future exploration, feelings that arose during the session, and differences in approach that could be viable. This part of the live supervision is typically brief and lasts for no more than 5 to 10 minutes. The conclusion of the processing signifies the end of the live supervision experience. There is not additional processing by the therapeutic system, giving both an opportunity to reflect on the feedback received until the next session.

While effort is made for this to be a genuine processing of the session, any thoughts, feelings, or suggestions that may but hurtful to the client or detrimental to the therapeutic system are reserved for the post-session processing. Such examples might include addressing a therapist's value or belief system, discussing potential diagnoses, or bringing up emotionally laden content that has not been previously processed. Because the therapeutic system will not process the feedback immediately, it is important not to offer novel observations or feedback that may be upsetting to the client.

One potential benefit to this approach is increasing the cohesiveness of the therapeutic system. It reiterates the connection between therapist and client as both are hearing feedback together about the work they are doing. Additionally, it allows the client to view the therapist as human, and not above hearing ways to further improve clinical work. It also reiterates the efforts being put into the client's care, which has been named as a benefit of live supervision, usually reported under the familiar axiom that "two heads are better than one" (Locke & McCollum, 2001). It can also create a strong sense of validation for the client. To hear a group of professionals restate one's feelings and struggles adds a sense of legitimacy for many clients. It is a powerful experience for one to genuinely feel heard.

Processing the Session

Processing this unique experience with supervisees is a crucial aspect of live supervision. Many supervisees are nervous about having their work observed firsthand. The ability to decompress and deconstruct this experience is one of the aspects that helps make it a salient learning experience. This facilitates conversations around confidence, sense of competence, the "imposter syndrome," and supervisee beliefs about their ability to be helpful to clients, especially in an area like sexuality where many therapists have received little, if any, training in sexual health and sex therapy (Reissing & DiGiulio, 2010).

After the session, many supervisees appreciate a break to use the restroom, get a drink, or generally take a breath. When processing with a supervision team, this author has found it beneficial to allow the other supervisees to share their feedback first. When a supervisor begins the processing, they tend to offer much of the feedback that the team had been thinking, which can limit the team's involvement in subsequent processing. Allowing the other supervisees to provide the initial feedback can facilitate a greater sense of cohesion and support among them. It is also good practice for developing therapists to begin to hone their supervisory skills, of which the provision of feedback is a critical element (Bernard & Goodyear, 1998). Training in the art of supervision can significantly increase one's confidence when operating in this role (McMahon & Errity, 2014).

Ideally, feedback is a blend of validation and acknowledgment of the strengths of the session with curiosity about aspects of the session that were more difficult. Instead of highlighting to a therapist that emotion is avoided in a problematic manner, approaching with curiosity about why emotion seems to be the last area of exploration will foster additional reflection and hopefully self-awareness and growth (Costa, 1994). Live supervision can leave a therapist feeling overly vulnerable, and additional delicacy can be helpful in making it feel like a learning experience instead of an exposure of all one's weaknesses.

Linking the processing back to the orientation session is a way to increase the relevance of the entire process. Responding to questions posed by the therapist, providing feedback in pre-identified areas, and hypothesizing about concerns raised all create an environment of collaboration in which the therapist feels like a pivotal part. It can also provide structure to the provision of feedback and can help ensure that the feedback is not overwhelming or out of sync with the therapist's developmental level. Offering suggestions for future focus or exploration helps the therapist know how to make best use of the feedback offered. It can display the range of options available without limiting the therapist to one prescribed course of action. It also allows other members of the supervision team to think about how different treatment approaches can vary based on the theoretical model used, demographics of the client, and other factors.

Wrapping up the processing phase is best done by providing a brief summary of the feedback offered, reminding of any future suggestions, and reinforcing the positive aspects of the session. Validating the difficulty and courage inherent in allowing one's work to be not only viewed, but interrupted and subsequently processed in detail, is no small feat! When possible, it is ideal to offer follow up feedback in writing. Providing initial verbal feedback followed up with feedback in writing has been shown to prolong the therapist's engagement with the experience and increase subsequent learning (Moody et al., 2014).

Case Example

Marisol, a female therapist working towards certification as a sex therapist, had been working with Frank, a heterosexual man in his mid-twenties, for about six months. Frank had initially presented with symptoms of depression and poor self-esteem and had made gains in this arena. In his last session, he reluctantly reported difficulty getting aroused with his current partner. He and his partner had been together for about a year and this was the first serious relationship for them both. His concerns with achieving and maintaining an erection had been ongoing for several months and were beginning to create problems in the relationship.

In orienting her supervisor to live supervision, Marisol gave a summary of the work that had been done. She stated that Frank was the younger of two boys and was raised by a single mother who had to work three jobs to make ends meet. He had not learned a lot of good coping skills and did not get a lot of positive reinforcement growing up. Therapy focused on improving his confidence and challenging cognitive distortions. Marisol reported that in the last meeting, she had trouble fully assessing issues of intimacy and sexuality. She stated that Frank would either complain about his partner's unrealistic demands or would bring up other life events that seemed unrelated. She acknowledged feeling a bit nervous about the live supervision session as she was concerned that she was asking questions that were too probing, asking them in a way that was ineffective, or doing something that she was not aware of that was hindering the process. She stated that she wanted to use live supervision to get feedback about her approach.

A one-way mirror was used for observation, and an inconspicuous microphone allowed for the session to be heard from the viewing room. It was agreed that the supervisor would call in via phone to offer interventions to either Marisol or Frank as was deemed appropriate.

At the start of the meeting, Marisol's nervousness was noted as being different from her typical presentation. Within a few moments, Marisol was calm and readily engaged with her client. Time was spent checking in about his mood, self-care activities, and general emotional well-being. It quickly became apparent that both the therapist and client were avoiding issues of sexuality, and no shift seemed to be forthcoming.

After about 15 minutes into the session, sexual issues had still not been named. The supervisor made the determination that Marisol's nervousness was a likely factor and called in with a declarative intervention. Her skill in assessing sexual health issues was reinforced, and she was directed to follow up about the arousal difficulties and to gather more information about what was happening in the relationship when they began. At the next natural pause, Marisol overtly asked about the arousal difficulties. Frank acknowledged these were ongoing, and expectedly tried to change the subject. Marisol persisted, and asked about the status of the relationship when the issues began.

Frank shared that the relationship was very positive, and that his girlfriend was everything he had wanted in a life partner. The two shared similar values, belief systems, and hopes for the future. He realized that the first time the couple had mentioned the idea of marriage was around the same time the arousal difficulties began. Frank began to talk about his fears of getting emotionally close with a woman, and fears that he would be rejected if he was not "man enough" to please her. He talked about fears of abandonment, and described feeling abandoned by his mother because of the amount of time she spent at work through most of his childhood. These fears were explored regarding his relationship and the impact they had on his sexual function.

Marisol had skillfully incorporated the first intervention and had engaged in processing of issues of sexuality and intimacy without concern or demonstrable discomfort. The determination was made to call in with another intervention that had the potential to be more challenging. The supervisor called in with an intensive intervention. When Marisol answered the phone, the supervisor commented on her apparent comfort with addressing issues of sexuality. The intensive intervention was then offered that Frank didn't think he was "man enough" to keep his partner. The pairing of reinforcement of her ability to address issues related to sexuality with the acknowledgment of the underlying dynamic in the room was intended to bring to her awareness that the fear being processed was more complex than what was being presented.

Marisol queried about what it meant to him to be "a man." He initially talked about masculine stereotypes and his attempts to reject these. She further pressed about where he learned these expectations, and he shared that he had had minimal contact with his father, making his older brother his only male role model. When this was further probed, he recalled being about seven years old and his older brother showing him pornography as a way to keep Frank occupied while his brother had friends or girlfriends over to the house.

His brother had premised the showings by telling him that it would help him "be a man." Since that time, Frank had worried that he would not be able to act in the ways the men in the movies had, and long worried that he would not be "man enough" to ever have a partner.

The therapy session ended soon after this final revelation. The therapeutic system reflected on the significant gains made and set a goal for Frank to spend some time thinking with his adult brain about what it meant to be a man.

In the processing after the session, Marisol reported feeling relieved at the outcome. She acknowledged avoiding the topic of sexuality early on, stating that she was worried about being judged by the supervisor. She stated that having the directive gave her the courage to ask the questions she had been thinking about. Further, she stated that she had been aware of the comment he made about being "man enough," but had attributed this to stereotypical gender roles. The significant processing taking place around fears of abandonment was sufficiently potent that she did not want to leave such a vital aspect unexplored.

When presenting this case for live supervision, Marisol had assumed that she was doing something wrong. By engaging in live supervision, the supervisor could see dynamics in play of which the therapist had not been aware. It is also notable that Marisol had the courage to bring a client she had been struggling with for live supervision. It is typical that challenging cases offer the greatest opportunity for therapist learning and can highlight a therapist's vulnerability as their potential shortcomings are on display. Had the supervisory relationship not been as established and trusted as it was in this case, this client may never have been considered for live supervision.

Summary

While live supervision may not have originated within the field of sex therapy, there is a range of potential benefits from its use. Most notably, allowing for the opportunity of *in vivo* learning, giving immediate feedback, and strengthening the working relationship top the list of potential benefits for therapist development. Further, clients are likely to benefit from having multiple professionals considering their concerns and experiencing an increase in the intensity of sessions. In a field wrought with taboo and cultural discomfort, it is important that sex therapists in training have the opportunity to hear feedback, be directed in the processing of potentially difficult material, and are challenged to think more in depth about issues of sexuality beyond behavioral interventions. Many therapists have rated live supervision as the most pivotal and significant aspect of their training as therapists (Bartle-Haring et al., 2009). Sex therapy needs to take advantage of this opportunity as the field continues to grow and expand in ever-changing directions. Technology availability may limit the use of this method, and hopefully the benefits will merit the relatively small investment in equipment that would facilitate the opportunity for such learning.

Appendix
Consent to Supervised Treatment

I understand that I am receiving therapy from _____, who is a licensed _____ in the state of _____. I also understand that my therapist is currently pursuing advanced certification as a Sex Therapist from the American Association of Sexuality Educators, Counselors, and Therapists (AASECT), and as such is involved in ongoing supervision with _____, **Licensed _____ and Certified Sex _____ Supervisor**, whose contact information is available upon request.

I give my permission for my sessions with _____ to be audiotaped for the sole purpose of sharing them in supervision for the betterment of my care. I understand that any identifying information will be removed, and the counseling relationship will remain confidential. I understand that these recordings will be maintained by _____ at all times and for no more than 6 months, and will be destroyed after review.

I consent to live supervision, in which _____ will be either phoned in or connected via secure video conferencing software to observe or participate in the treatment. Further details will be shared when scheduling such supervision, and I am aware that I can ask any questions about this process at any time. I will incur no additional costs or obligations as a result of this, and am aware that I can revoke this consent at any time and without having to provide rationale or advance notice.

THERAPIST(S):   *CLIENT(S):*

_____   _____

(Printed Name)   (Date)   (Printed Name)   (Date)

_____   _____

(Signature)   (Signature)

_____   _____

(Printed Name)   (Date)   (Printed Name)   (Date)

_____   _____

(Signature)   (Signature)

About the Author

Sarah E. Wright earned her Psy.D. in Clinical Psychology from the School of Professional Psychology at Wright State University in Dayton, Ohio, and is an AASECT-Certified Sex Therapist and Supervisor. She has worked clinically with issues of sexual health since 2005 in settings ranging from the Veterans Administration to various college counseling centers, and has engaged in extensive supervision training both domestically and internationally. Currently she works full time in the counseling center at the University of South Carolina (USC) in Columbia as the Coordinator of Human Sexuality Services and has over 11 years of service at USC. She also maintains a small private practice and teaches courses on the first-year experience as well as the psychology of human sexuality. She has a previously published book chapter titled "A Cultural Transformation Approach in the Group Treatment of Addiction," which appears in *Innovations in Clinical Practice: Focus on Group, Couples, and Family Therapy*, edited by Leon VandeCreek and Jeffery B. Allen.

References

AASECT requirements for sex therapist certification. (n.d.). Retrieved April 8, 2017, from www.aasect.org/aasect-requirements-sex-therapist-certification

Bartle-Haring, S., Silverthorn, B. C., Meyer, K., & Toviessi, P. (2009). Does live supervision make a difference? A multilevel analysis. *Journal of Marital and Family Therapy, 35*(4), 406–414. https://doi.org/10.1111/j.1752-0606.2009.00124.x

Bernard, J. M., & Goodyear, R. K. (1998). *Fundamentals of clinical supervision* (2nd ed.) (R. Short, Ed.). Needham Heights, MA: Allyn & Bacon.

Carmel, A., Villatte, J. L., Rosenthal, M. Z., Chalker, S., & Comtois, K. A. (2016). Applying technological approaches to clinical supervision in dialectical behavior therapy: A randomized feasibility trial of the Bug-in-the-Eye (BITE) model. *Cognitive and Behavioral Practice, 23*(2), 221–229. https://doi.org/10.1016/j.cbpra.2015.08.001

Costa, L. (1994). Reducing anxiety in live supervision. *Counselor Education and Supervision, 34*(1), 30–40. https://doi.org/10.1002/j.1556-6978.1994.tb00308.x

Ford, A. E. (2008). *The effects of two -way mirrors, video cameras, and observation teams on clients' judgments of the therapeutic relationship.* Retrieved from ProQuest Dissertations & Theses Global. Order No. 3303560.

Haber, R. (Ed.). (1996). *Dimensions of psychotherapy supervision: Maps and means.* New York: W. W. Norton.

Kivlighan, D. M., Angelone, E. O., & Swafford, K. G. (1991). Live supervision in individual psychotherapy: Effects on therapist's intention use and client's evaluation of session effect and working alliance. *Professional Psychology: Research and Practice, 22*(6), 489–495. https://doi.org/10.1037//0735-7028.22.6.489

Klitzke, M. J., & Lombardo, T. W. (1991). A "Bug-in-the-Eye" can be better than a "Bug-in-the-Ear": A teleprompter technique for on-line therapy skills training. *Behavior Modification, 15*(1), 113–117. https://doi.org/10.1177/0145445 5910151007

Ladany, N., Hill, C. E., Corbett, M. M., & Nutt, E. A. (1996). Nature, extent, and importance of what psychotherapy trainees do not disclose to their supervisors. *Journal of Counseling Psychology, 43*(1), 10–24. https://doi.org/10.1037//0022-0167.43.1.10

Liddle, H. A., & Schwartz, R. C. (1983). Live supervision/consultation. Conceptual and pragmatic guidelines for family therapy trainers. *Family Process, 22*(4), 477–490. https://doi.org/10.1111/j.1545-5300.1983.00477.x

Locke, L. D., & McCollum, E. E. (2001). Clients' views of live supervision and satisfaction with therapy. *Journal of Marital and Family Therapy, 27*(1), 129–133. https://doi.org/10.1111/j.1752-0606.2001.tb01146.x

McMahon, A., & Errity, D. (2014). From new vistas to life lines: Psychologists' satisfaction with supervision and confidence in supervising. *Clinical Psychology & Psychotherapy, 21*(3), 264–275. https://doi.org/10.1002/cpp.1835

Mehr, K. E., Ladany, N., & Caskie, G. I. (2010). Trainee nondisclosure in supervision: What are they not telling you? *Counselling and Psychotherapy Research, 10*(2), 103–113. https://doi.org/10.1080/14733141003712301

Miller, K. L., Miller, S. M., & Evans, W. J. (2002). Computer-assisted live supervision in college counseling centers. *Journal of College Counseling, 5*(2), 187–192. https://doi.org/10.1002/j.2161-1882.2002.tb00221.x

Moody, S., Kostohryz, K., & Vereen, L. (2014). Authentically engaged learning through live supervision: A phenomenological study. *Counselor Education and Supervision, 53*(1), 19–33. https://doi.org/10.1002/j.1556-6978.2014.00046.x

Moorhouse, A., & Carr, A. (1999). The correlates of phone-in frequency, duration and the number of suggestions made in live supervision. *Journal of Family Therapy, 21*(4), 407–418. https://doi.org/10.1111/1467-6427.00128

O'Dell, T. (2009). *Strength of the working alliance and subsequent development of the goal, task, and bond between supervisor and supervisee using various supervision modalities* (Doctoral dissertation). Dissertation Abstracts International Section A, 69, 3465.

Reissing, E. D., & Di Giulio, G. (2010). Practicing clinical psychologists' provision of sexual health care services. *Professional Psychology: Research and Practice, 41*(1), 57–63. https://doi.org/10.1037/a0017023

Rizvi, S. L., Yu, J., Geisser, S., & Finnegan, D. (2016). The use of "Bug-in-the-Eye" live supervision for training in dialectical behavior therapy: A case study. *Clinical Case Studies, 15*(3), 243–258. https://doi.org/10.1177/1534650116635272

Rousmaniere, T., & Frederickson, J. (2013). Internet-based one-way-mirror supervision for advanced psychotherapy training. *Clinical Supervisor, 32*(1), 40–55 https://doi.org/10.1080/07325223.2013.778683

Scherl, C. R., & Haley, J. (2000). Computer monitor supervision: A clinical note. *American Journal of Family Therapy, 28*(3), 275–282. https://doi.org/10.1080/01926180050081702

Tracey, T. J., Wampold, B. E., Lichtenberg, J. W., & Goodyear, R. K. (2014). Expertise in psychotherapy: An elusive goal? *American Psychologist, 69*(3), 218–229. https://doi.org/10.1037/a0035099

Weck, F., Jakob, M., Neng, J. M., Höfling, V., Grikscheit, F., & Bohus, M. (2016). The effects of Bug-in-the-Eye supervision on therapeutic alliance and therapist competence in cognitive-behavioural therapy: A randomized controlled trial. *Clinical Psychology & Psychotherapy, 23*(5), 386–396. https://doi.org/10.1002/cpp.1968

Wright, L. M. (1986). An analysis of live supervision "phone-ins" in family therapy. *Journal of Marital and Family Therapy, 12*(2), 187–190.

Yourman, D. B., & Farber, B. A. (1996). Nondisclosure and distortion in psychotherapy supervision. *Psychotherapy: Theory, Research, Practice, Training, 33*(4), 567–575. https://doi.org/10.1037/0033-3204.33.4.567

5 Supervision in Forensic Sexology Evaluations

Daniel N. Watter

Abstract

This chapter examines the challenges of both the practice of forensic sexology evaluations, as well as the supervision of those wishing to obtain the skill and experience required in order to ethically and effectively practice in this complex area of sexological specialization. Perhaps the greatest challenge in the area of forensic sexology is understanding the substantial difference between the mindset of a forensic sexological examiner and the mindset of the sex therapy clinician. Most mental health professionals are trained in the art of psychotherapy and psychotherapy case conceptualization. While such training makes for excellent clinicians, an entirely different set of skills is required for the forensic sexologist. Those sexologists wishing to enter the realm of forensic work must be willing to obtain substantial training and supervision. Due to the extraordinary impact a forensic sexological evaluation can have on the lives of those impacted by the legal system, the forensic sexology supervisor has a very powerful and influential role in the preparation of the forensic sexologist.

Keywords

Forensic sexology, forensic evaluation, forensic supervision, forensic sex therapy

Introduction

Recent years have seen an increased demand for and interest in the field of forensic psychology in general (Schlesinger, 1996; Shapiro, 1999), and forensic sexology in particular (Watter, 2006). When discussing forensic sexology, we are referring to the application of sexual science to issues arising from criminal, civil, and/or administrative legal matters. Examples of such cases would include situations in which someone has been arrested for a sexual crime or offense, engaged in professional sexual misconduct, committed acts of sexual harassment, and/or an accident or medical procedure that has resulted in an injury to the genitalia or sex drive. As a result, many sex therapists have been sought out to function as forensic evaluators, even though they may have little or no training in this highly specialized area of practice. This chapter will discuss some of the myriad challenges of both the practice of forensic sexology evaluations and the supervision of those wishing to obtain the skill and experience required in order to ethically and effectively practice in this complex area of sexological specialization.

Distinct Features and Challenges

One of the greatest challenges in the area of forensic sexology is understanding the substantial difference between the mindset of a forensic sexological examiner and the mindset of the sex therapy clinician. Most mental health professionals are trained in the art of psychotherapy, and psychotherapy case conceptualization. While such training makes for excellent clinicians, an entirely different set of skills is required for the forensic sexologist. Forensic examination requires an awareness and appreciation of the fact that the forensic arena is dramatically different from the arena in which most clinicians are familiar and comfortable. The field of forensic evaluation has its own rules, values, and practices, many of which will appear quite foreign to the practicing clinician. The supervisor in such settings has the primary task of assisting the practicing clinician to adapt to this changed emphasis and develop the skill set necessary to function in this specialized area of practice. The following are the most common challenges for both the clinician the supervisor to navigate. This list is by no means exhaustive, but is rather meant to provide an overview of the many dissimilarities between clinical sexology and forensic sexology practice. The supervisor faces the arduous task of helping transform the accepting and compassionate clinician into the critical and dispassionate forensic examiner.

Challenge #1: The Role of Confidentiality

Most sex therapy clinicians understand that confidentiality is the cornerstone of effective psychotherapy practice. Indeed, it is the promise of confidentiality that allows our patients to feel free to open up to us and reveal their innermost thoughts and feelings. Confidentiality provides a safety net for our patients inasmuch as the knowledge that their privacy is protected provides them the opportunity to explore, reveal, and contemplate change (Watter, 2018). However, in forensic assessment, confidentiality is not promised. It is important to begin a forensic evaluation with the caveat (i.e., informed consent) that there is no promise of confidentiality in such assessments, and anything discovered during the course of the evaluation may end up in the forensic sexologist's report of findings. As a result, examinees may have good reason to be less than forthcoming with information, which is quite different than the expectation in therapeutic consultation. Even though the clinical sexologist understands that it may take a client a while to develop the trust in the clinician required to be open and honest about their sexual function or desires, the sex therapist reasonably expects that once a caring and trusting therapeutic alliance is created, the client will express himself or herself as honestly and as openly as he/she is able. The forensic sexologist, however, works with quite a different set of assumptions and expectations. One reason for this stark difference in expectation is that in forensic evaluation, the "client" is not the person sitting in front of you. In actuality, the "client" is the referent of the case, be it an attorney, a court, an insurer, or an employer (Melton et al., 2007). The forensic examiner's primary duty is in assisting the case referent by providing information that will be of value to the referent in making a determination regarding the disposition of a legal matter. While clinical work typically has a broad focus, forensic work has a very limited and clearly defined objective that addresses a narrowly defined and specified question. As a result, the perspective of the client, which is so vital to the clinical process, is of secondary importance in forensic assessment.

Challenge #2: In Clinical Work, the Client's Perspective Is of Paramount Importance. In Forensic Work, the Client's Perspective Is Secondary

As mentioned earlier, confidentiality for the examinee in the forensic interview must be waived. As a result, clients may tend to be guarded in what information they are willing to reveal to the forensic sexological examiner. To reiterate an earlier point, while most sexuality clinicians have encountered clients who were not fully open and honest, we usually assume that much of their guardedness is the result of not yet having a solid and trusting therapeutic alliance with their therapist. Over time, as the therapeutic relationship builds and strengthens, clients tend to become more open and revealing. However, in forensic work, due to the lack of confidentiality, voluntariness, and the potential consequences the client may be facing, it may not be in the client's perceived best interests to be very revealing. Most of those we evaluate in forensic sexology are not coming to us voluntarily. Many, if not most, are mandated to evaluation and/or treatment by a court, their attorney, or some other referral source. As a result, the client may feel that they have little choice but to participate, and their narrative likely contains some significant purposeful omissions and distortions. Indeed, the forensic sexologist may find that the client is often hostile to the entire process. Should they participate, such clients are clearly invested in presenting a favorable impression in the hope they will come through the assessment process with as little punitive action being recommended as possible (Watter, 2006).

Obviously this is an extremely challenging population to work with. Yalom (2017) recalls that he observed while a resident at Johns Hopkins in the late 1950s that sex offenders were among the most difficult groups he had ever led. He recollects:

> The members spent far more energy trying to persuade me they were well adjusted than they did working on their problems. Since they had an indeterminate sentence—that is, they were incarcerated until psychiatrists declared them recovered—their reluctance to reveal a great deal was entirely understandable.

(p. 88)

In this regard, little has changed since then. Therefore, the forensic sex therapy clinician must rely more heavily on collateral information so that the examiner will be better able to ascertain the veracity of the client's version of events (Wincze, 2000). Examples of collateral sources would include information that is provided from police statements, victim statements, family members, a thorough life history, and psychological testing that includes scales to detect malingering.

Challenge #3: In Clinical Work We Expect to Work Slowly and Assessment Is Seen as a Dynamic Process. In Forensic Work We Are Expected to Work More Quickly and Have Limited Opportunities to Sit With the Client. As a Result, the Evaluation Is Seen as an Essentially Static Process

According to Melton et al. (2007), in therapeutic settings, evaluations and assessments proceed at a more leisurely pace. Diagnoses, treatment plans, and intervention strategies evolve as we become more familiar with our clients and their lives. We fully expect that it will take some time for us to know and understand our clients, and that it will take some time for them to become comfortable enough to open up with us.

However, in forensic evaluation, we rarely have more than a few hours to spend with the person we are trying to learn about and understand. Forensic assessments require that all relevant data be collected and evaluated in a matter of hours, during which there may be a records review, clinical interviews, psychometric testing, and/or collateral interviews. In that short amount of time, the examiner will be expected to render a diagnosis and treatment suggestions (Watter, 2006). What makes this especially challenging is that despite the limited contact with the client, the importance of accuracy cannot be overstated. We are preparing documents that will be used in a legal setting, and a well- done forensic sexology evaluation will become a significant factor in the final disposition of the client's case.

Challenge #4: In Clinical Work We Are Involved in a Process That Is Seen as "Sex-Positive." In Forensic Evaluation We Often Find Ourselves in a Process That Can Be Seen as "Sex-Negative"

Most sex therapy clinicians would agree that we attempt to create an environment for our clients that is sex-positive (Watter, 2006). That is, in our clinical work, our efforts go toward assisting our clients to restore, explore, and/or enjoy the expression of their sexuality. Whether we are working to improve sexual function, sexual enjoyment, and/or sexual acceptance, sexuality is seen in a positive light and as source of healthy human behavior.

Forensic sexology, however, sees sexual behavior through a decidedly different lens. While the forensic sexology examiner also would like to see sex as an expression of health and positivity, most forensic sexology is focused on controlling and limiting the expression of problematic sexual behavior. Most clients present for forensic assessment due to the fact that the expression of their sexuality has transgressed the boundaries of law. As a result, rather than focusing on helping the person sitting in front of us in embracing their sexual desires and predilections, we find ourselves attending to the restraint or cessation of a sexuality that they may feel most comfortable with or desire most. Philosophically this may be at odds with the view of sexuality that many sexology clinicians find themselves aligned with. That is, some may find the mindset of a forensic sexologist to be too judgmental and condemnatory of one's sexual expression. While this is certainly a valid argument, it also represents one of the most important differences between the clinical sexologist and the forensic sexologist. The forensic sexologist works within the legal arena, and this world is quite different from the clinical world. This distinction cannot be made strongly enough. If one is unable to accept the parameters of legal decision making, then forensic sexology may not be the best fit for the sexologist.

Challenge #5: In Clinical Sexology We Are Typically Dealing With Clients Who Are Experiencing Personal Distress. In Forensic Sexology We Are Often Dealing With Clients Who May Cause Society Distress, But May Not Be Experiencing Distress Themselves

Much of the work in clinical settings is directed toward relieving the client's distress. Indeed, it is often such distress that motivates the client to seek sex therapy services and to do the work that is necessary in order for change to result. Whether it is the result of sexual dysfunction, difficulty accepting one's own sexual desires and interests, or sexual differences that have negatively impacted the quality of a relationship, the client seeking out sex therapy services is experiencing emotional distress and is looking for a positive resolution.

In contrast, many if not most forensic cases involve a client who may experience little to no personal distress regarding their sexual behavior. Their principal distress may be that they have been arrested for the expression of their sexual behavior and are now facing the possibility of incarceration or some other substantial punishment. In other cases the examinee's behavior may not be illegal but may be causing concern or distress to a partner. This issue is often present in complicated and antagonistic high-conflict divorce cases. It is not unusual for an aggrieved spouse or partner to try to use one's sexual interests and behaviors as a means of limiting or restricting child custody and/or visitation. The forensic examinee may wish to be able to continue practicing their illegal or preferred sexual behavior so long as they would not experience negative consequences. This is a particularly complicated situation for the forensic sexologist, as the forensic sexologist needs be wary of those situations in which a wounded or aggrieved spouse or partner wants to use the legal system to punish a spouse or partner by means of suggesting that their sexual behavior is somehow pathological and/or harmful. This, most assuredly, is not the role of the forensic sexologist. Our role is not to pass judgment on the "correctness" of one's sexuality. Rather, we use our science and our knowledge to inform the referent in order to assist them in their decisions regarding the disposition of the case. Once again, the forensic sexologist must be aware of the conflicting agenda between the referent and the client. While the clinical sexologist seeks to develop a common treatment agenda with the client, the agenda of the forensic clinician and the forensic examinee are likely to appear dramatically different.

Skill Set of the Supervisee

Most supervisors of clinicians would likely agree that in order to be an effective sex therapist, the clinician needs to be skilled in developing relationships that are characterized by empathic understanding, caring, and trust (Melton et al., 2007). These skills are required in order to build a strong therapeutic alliance with the client. Fernandez and Serran (2011) add skills such as warmth, genuineness, respect, attentive listening, directiveness, flexibility, self-disclosure, and supportive challenging as essential elements in the skill set of the effective clinician.

In forensic sexology, however, such a skill set needs to take a subordinate role inasmuch as the forensic examinee is unlikely to engage in such a relationship. Nor would such a relationship be productive, given the role of the forensic sexological examiner. As mentioned earlier, the forensic examinee often approaches the forensic sexological assessment with wariness, skepticism, and a reluctance to be too open or revealing. As a result, the forensic sexologist is looking to create a relationship that is characterized by an emotional distance between examiner and client.

It is critically important to recognize the distinction between a forensic sexologist and a clinical sexologist working with a forensic population. As mentioned earlier, the forensic sexologist is typically working on behalf of a court, an attorney, or another third party. The clinical sexologist working with a forensic population, such as sex offenders (those who have been arrested for a sex crime), may be working with a difficult population, but the skill set of the psychotherapist in nonforensic settings is also the required skill set for the effective treatment when working with sex offenders. As Yalom (2017) mentioned, the sex offender population may also be reluctant to be too revealing, inasmuch as they desire to be freed from treatment. As a result, they are often evasive, wary of the motives of the clinician, and are likely to overemphasize "good" behavior. Nevertheless, while the ability to form a strong therapeutic alliance may be particularly challenging, it is the establishment of a warm, caring, genuine, trusting, and supportive therapeutic relationship that will make the difference if the client is desirous of change. Sexological clinicians working with a forensic population need to be prepared to work extremely hard and be encouraging and energetic, especially within a group therapy setting (Fernandez & Serran, 2011).

The skill set of the forensic sexologist begins with the ability to accurately determine what is being asked of us, and what our role in the adjudication process should be. In clinical work, our objective is clear; we are being asked to assist a client or clients in changing behavior and/or relieving emotional distress. In forensic work, we are asked to assist the court in answering a legal question through the application of sexological/psychological science and methods. Often we are being asked to assist in making determinations of guilt, amenability for treatment, potential for harm, and/or level of dangerousness. The forensic sexologist must, however, be careful to not cross the boundaries between the responsible application of our science and mere speculation. While one can be quite helpful in assisting the court, the forensic sexologist is not the arbiter of guilt or innocence, truth or fiction. The forensic sexologist needs to remain mindful that we are severely limited in our ability to discern fact from fabrication. Even with a great deal of collateral information, we are never fully able to ascertain the veracity of what our examinee is telling us. Indeed, as forensic examiners there is little in our training that makes us any better equipped than the average person to be able to tell fact from fiction (Szasz, 2001). Similarly, when asked to assess dangerousness, we are really being asked to assess the risk of someone committing an additional offense in the future. Here too, we tread on precarious ground. While our ability to assess risk has greatly improved over the years, largely due to actuarial assessment tools, we have little data that suggests that our ability to predict future offenses is consistently reliable (Zimring, 2004).

The forensic sexology supervisor must be certain that his/her training in forensic examination is extensive and that he/she is clear on the different skill sets required of the clinical sexologist and the forensic sexologist. Assisting the forensic sexology supervisee to develop the skill set necessary to do forensic work requires a supervisor who is astute in identifying the many pitfalls that could easily befall the sex therapy clinician as he/she looks to move into the realm of forensic sexology. Earlier we looked at the importance of creating a relationship that is characterized by an emotional distance and detachment. This is a critically important skill, given that the forensic sexologist must remain objective and emotionally uninvolved in the outcome of the evaluation. If the forensic sexologist has an emotional investment or bias in a case, the credibility of the examiner, and the usefulness of the evaluation, will be irreparably damaged. It is for this reason that most forensic experts caution against a professional assuming multiple roles (AFCC, 2010). Multiple roles can often create a conflict of interest that will seriously compromise the results of the examination. For example, the forensic sexology examiner should never be the person who has in the past, or is currently, functioning as the examinee's sex therapist. The roles of the forensic sexologist and the clinical sexologist cannot be combined without significantly compromising the evaluation process. A clinician who has served as a person's therapist cannot be objective, as they have already assessed someone through a therapeutic lens, and have already established a supportive and emotionally involved relationship with the examinee. Not only would such prior emotional investment compromise the evaluation, but it would also very likely jeopardize the therapy relationship as well. For example, when a sex therapy clinician is working with a client, it is reasonable to expect that the therapist will serve as the client's support, advocate, and confidant. Should the sex therapist then become the forensic examiner and confidentiality is no longer applicable, the examiner must view the situation through an impartial and objective lens, and the client may no longer believe that he/she can trust the clinician to act on his/her behalf. The therapist naively believing that they can successfully navigate the two conflicting roles has derailed too many otherwise successful therapies.

The forensic sexologist must also keep current on the research and laws regarding the expression of sexuality. This would include being conversant regarding issues such as childhood sexual development, paraphilias, sexual dysfunctions, relationship issues such as separation and divorce, domestic violence, relationship conflict, medical issues that affect sexual functioning and behavior, and the impact of culture on the determination of acceptable versus unacceptable sexual expression. In addition, the forensic sexologist must be familiar with the current research on the impact of personal biases, personal beliefs and attitudes, and personal values that could impair the forensic sexologist's objectivity. It is also imperative that the forensic sexologist be familiar with the ethical codes of conduct that governs his/her primary discipline. Because this area can be so challenging, and because the outcomes can so dramatically impact the lives of those we examine, ongoing supervision and case discussion is a necessity. Those clinicians who do not believe they will be able to adjust to this different mindset are well advised to not enter the forensic area. Obviously, it is one of the most important tasks of the forensic sexological supervisor to help their supervisee(s) recognize whether or not they are suited for this type of work.

One final skill that is necessary in order to be regarded as a competent forensic sexologist is a facility with report writing. Since much of what the forensic sexologist does is educate the court or other referents, the forensic sexologist must be able to communicate clearly, in writing, their thoughts, processes, rationales, and opinions in a manner that is professional yet free of confusing professional jargon. Written reports need to be sufficiently detailed and well organized to be of value to those making the determination of how best to dispose of the legal matter. Those who do not feel comfortable with their writing skills may consider either taking seminars or workshops in legal writing for mental health professionals or not accepting the role of a forensic sexologist. Obviously, a significant aspect of the forensic sexology supervisor's role is to advise the supervisee of any deficiencies in their report writing skills.

Techniques

Many of the techniques used by clinicians in a general sexological interview will be also useful for the forensic sexologist. The forensic assessment may be more structured than a general clinical interview, but the skills and techniques involved in getting clients to respond to inquiries are similar. Open-ended questions, the judicious uses of silence, being able to discuss sexuality in non-euphemistic language, and so forth are techniques that most all sexuality clinicians are already well acquainted with.

For the forensic sexologist, many of the essential techniques have already been delineated above. The challenges of becoming comfortable with the mindset of the forensic examiner, and its myriad differences from the mindset of the clinical sexologist, are often the greatest obstacles. The forensic sexology supervisor has the task of assisting the practicing clinician with this transformation.

The process of informed consent must be especially detailed and clear when doing forensic work. A proper forensic informed consent makes a precise statement about the limits of confidentiality, including specifically who will be receiving information from the assessment. Those clients who have had prior psychotherapy experiences may assume that whatever is said within the walls of the examiner's office is protected by confidentiality. At the outset of the assessment, it must be made clear that such confidentiality does not apply in the arena of forensic evaluation. In addition, since the forensic sexological examiner will be utilizing and relying on several collateral sources for information, the informed consent must list the names of the individuals and/or agencies that the forensic sexologist will be communicating with. The language in the informed consent must be easily understandable to the nonsexology professional and essentially jargon-free. According to the Association of Family and Conciliation Courts (2010), the informed consent form should also include information about the nature and course of the evaluation, risks and benefits of such evaluation, professional fees charged, and how payment will be expected and collected.

Because forensic sexology works within the legal arena, proper and extensive documentation of the evaluation and assessment procedures is required. Precise documentation and record keeping is essential when explaining to the court or other referent the process, theoretical rationale, and assessment tools the forensic sexology examiner has relied upon in formulating the diagnosis and/or recommendations that may be proffered in determining how best to dispose of the legal matter. Documentation should be reasonably contemporaneously written, and reports should be written soon after the evaluation is complete. In addition, sufficiently detailed documentation will be required should the forensic sexologist be asked to testify in a court of law. When giving expert testimony, the forensic sexologist may be asked intricate questions about his/her interview procedures, testing protocols, and the scientific literature that has guided the examiner's case conceptualization, conclusions, and recommendations. Such testimony can be exacting and grueling, but this, too, is another area in which the forensic sexologist must recognize the difference between this work and the clinical. Forensic testimony often feels like a battle between the examiner and an attorney representing the opposing side that seeks to discredit or impugn your conclusions and recommendations. It is important to be skilled in the techniques of legal testimony and to be prepared for aggressive challenges to your work product. One common strategy of an opposing attorney may be to maneuver the forensic sexologist into testifying and making statements beyond the scope and limits of his/her knowledge, expertise, and/or role. The forensic sexologist should respectfully decline to provide any information or opinion that exceeds such scope and limits. Indeed, there is little that will diminish the findings of the forensic sexological examiner more than the suggestion of a lack of credibility and integrity. Therefore, it is imperative that the forensic sexologist beware of attempts to lead him/her beyond the bounds of what the evaluation can support. Of course, these attacks and challenges are not personal. Indeed, such vigorous and powerful confrontations are de rigueur in legal settings. Nevertheless, the stakes are high and the forensic sexologist must remain mindful, alert, and vigilant throughout the potential clashes with attorneys. Again, one must have the temperament for this type of forensic work, as well as the education and training to understand the workings of the legal arena and the techniques required to adequately and appropriately respond to the expected challenges.

Some Cautionary Thoughts on Diagnosis in a Forensic Setting

The forensic sexologist must recognize that his/her thoughts, judgments, reports, interventions, opinions, and testimony will likely have a great impact on the lives of those we evaluate. Therefore, we cannot be cavalier about any diagnostic labels we may choose to use. Unfortunately, sexual diagnoses have frequently been used in unhelpful, indeed often harmful ways. Moser (2001) and Szasz (2001) remind us that the DSM diagnostic process and diagnostic labels have been manipulated to create bias and prejudice toward the sexual behaviors and interests of men and women for decades. This is especially true regarding paraphilic or "nonmainstream" sexual behavior. Paraphilia diagnoses have been misused in criminal, civil, and administrative proceedings as indicators suggestive of the inability to parent, inability to control one's sexual behavior, being unfit for employment, and/or as grounds for divorce due to mental illness and other psychiatric maladies (Moser, 2009). Of course, we have also seen unfortunate uses of nonsexual DSM diagnoses. Experienced clinicians will easily relate tales of clients and patients diagnosed with mood disorders who were then denied life insurance, disability insurance, and long-term care insurance. The assigning of DSM diagnoses, while a necessary evil in order to obtain insurance reimbursement for clients (at least in the United States), carries immense weight and should be used thoughtfully and cautiously, with an awareness of the long-term implications of such labeling.

For the clinical sexologist, diagnosis is seen as a dynamic process that is likely to change or be refined over time. Yalom (2002) asserts that it is typically easier to assign a DSM diagnosis at session 1 than it is at session 10. As we learn more and more about our client, their clinical picture or narrative becomes increasingly complex and their suffering multidetermined. In essence, a static diagnosis is often an impediment to clinical work because the astute clinician recognizes the need for flexibility in case conceptualization, as well as the individuality and uniqueness of each client. As a result, he/she doesn't feel the urgency to hastily decide on a diagnostic label.

The forensic sexologist, however, does not have the luxury of time in determining a DSM diagnostic formulation. Evaluations must be completed in a matter of hours, and with information obtained from an often less than cooperative source. Collateral sources are vital to the evaluation process, but they too may be reluctant to provide information, may have their own agendas, and/or may be unable to provide meaningful insight into the mind of the examinee. As a result, the forensic examiner must be thoughtful, prudent, and cautious when assigning a DSM diagnosis. The determination we make with such limited time and information will carry great weight in a court of law. Our words will be accorded substantial authority in answering the psycho-legal questions before the court. Perhaps for this reason above all else, the responsibility of the forensic sexologist and the forensic sexology supervisor is immense. Clinical work resides in the realm of vagary, but forensic work expects precision. The forensic sexologist must be vigilant of not stepping beyond the bounds of what the evaluation and our science and professional knowledge can support when making diagnostic pronouncements.

One particularly complicated and current dilemma in the sexological community surrounds the phenomenon of hypersexuality, or sex addiction. The assessment and treatment of hypersexuality or sex addiction is a controversial and fervently debated topic in present-day sex therapy (Watter, 2017). Indeed, its very existence has been questioned (Moser, 2011; Ley, Prause, & Finn, 2014; Ley, Brovko, & Reid, 2015). Despite the frequent references to sex addiction in the press, popular literature, much of the professional literature, and complaints patients bring into therapy, hypersexuality and sex addiction were not seen as having adequate empirical support for inclusion of the latest edition of the DSM (DSM-5; APA, 2013).

Nevertheless, Ley et al. (2015) assert that sex addiction is playing an increasingly significant role in many types of forensic matters. They remark that claims involving sex addiction are appearing in criminal, civil, and administrative matters despite the fact that the DSM has not recognized the legitimacy of the diagnosis. While courts have been inconsistent in their acceptance of sex addiction as either a defense (mental illness) or as an exculpatory factor, the claim of sex addiction as a legal strategy has seen a substantial upsurge in recent years. Parker (2014) has reported that 48% of the nonsubstance addictions reported by state bar associations to the American Bar Association involved claims of sex addiction. The forensic sexologist will likely see attempts to assert sex addiction in cases related to child pornography, divorce and/or custody and parenting time, and professional licensing board complaints. It is, therefore, imperative that regardless of the forensic sexologist's opinion or the forensic sexology supervisor's opinion related to the legitimacy of the diagnosis of sex addiction, in a legal setting such a diagnosis is considered ambiguous at best, and the diagnosis has no official status. As a result, Ley et al. (2015) recommend courts should be encouraged to understand that at the present time, sex addiction is not a disorder or mental illness that is recognized by the DSM. Therefore, it should not receive the same recognition or privileges as those disorders that are recognized by the DSM. It may very well fall to the forensic sexologist to provide such education to the courts when sex addiction is referenced in a pending legal matter. Both the forensic sexologist and the forensic sexology supervisor need to remain current on the status of sex addiction as a diagnostic entity.

Case Study

Pat

The following represents a composite of several different cases. Aside from the name of the supervisor, all other names are fictitious, and not meant to describe any particular sexologist or client.

Pat was a 38-year-old clinical social worker and AASECT Certified Sex Therapist. Pat had been practicing sex therapy in the community for approximately 10 years. As one of the few sex therapists in the area, Pat was called upon by a local attorney to assist in preparing a defense for Dr. Jones, a local family practitioner who had been accused of professional sexual misconduct. As a result, Dr. Jones was facing criminal prosecution and the loss or suspension of his medical license. Specifically, it was alleged that Dr. Jones inappropriately touched an adult female patient during the course of an examination. It had been claimed that Dr. Jones fondled a woman's breasts for the purpose of his own sexual arousal and gratification. Dr. Jones's attorney was looking for a forensic sexological expert who would do a forensic sexological examination in order to find either an explanation for Dr. Jones's behavior that would be exculpatory, or to ascertain whether or not Dr. Jones was even guilty of such behavior in the first place.

Pat, who was an experienced clinical sexologist, had never been asked to function in such a role and didn't know anyone else in the community who possessed the expertise in sexual behavior that the case could be referred to. As a result, Pat wisely decided to seek supervision on the matter from Dr. Daniel N. Watter. Dr. Watter was a psychologist and AASECT Certified Sex Therapist, as well as an AASECT Certified Sex Therapy Supervisor. In addition, Dr. Watter had extensive experience in both clinical sexology and forensic sexology.

Pat had already had an initial consultation with Dr. Jones before contacting Dr. Watter, and felt uneasy following the interview. Dr. Jones had denied any wrongdoing whatsoever, and Pat was unsure how to proceed with the case. Dr. Watter asked if Pat had received any information from the referent prior to the interview with Dr. Jones. Pat had not received any information prior to the meeting, and as a result had only Dr. Jones's words to go by. Dr. Watter informed Pat that in order to do a competent assessment, Pat would need to request all pertinent discovery materials from Dr. Jones's attorney. In a matter such as this, there would likely be a police investigation report, a victim statement, a consent order or investigatory documents from the medical board, a report from a database identifying any of Dr. Jones's past infractions or appearances in front of the medical board, and so forth. Without these materials, Pat would have no chance of preparing a credible or useful report of findings. Pat had assumed that if there were more data available, Dr. Jones's attorney would have provided it automatically. While many attorneys would do just that, some will wait until the forensic examiner specifically requests the background information. This is especially likely to be the case in those cases in which the background material is potentially damaging to their client and the attorney may hope that a naïve examiner will overlook this information and develop a novel explanation that the defense can use to their benefit. Dr. Watter explained to Pat that this is precisely why the agreement between forensic sexology examiner and the referent needs to be clearly delineated, and that the forensic sexologist has all of the information that is pertinent to the case. Dr. Watter also educated Pat about the need for appropriate psychometric testing and collateral interviews, if available.

Pat contacted Dr. Jones's attorney to request all of the discovery materials. They were quickly dispatched and Pat was able to see that this was not Dr. Jones's first complaint of this nature. She was then able to reinterview Dr. Jones and question him about the details of prior allegations, as well as the current one. Dr. Jones, realizing that he could no longer deny, began to discuss the details with Pat. Dr. Jones explained that he was not honest during the first interview because he suffers from a diagnosed sex addiction. This was extremely embarrassing to him, and he said he has a difficult time admitting his affliction to anyone. He has been in sex therapy treatment since the lodging of the first complaint, and believes he is doing very well in overcoming his mental illness. Dr. Watter advised Pat to obtain permission and a release to talk with Dr. Jones's therapist. Dr. Jones was reluctant to consent, but Pat advised that while it is Dr. Jones's right to refuse consent, such refusal would be incorporated into the report of findings. Dr. Jones's then agreed to allow Pat access to his therapist. Dr. Jones's therapist told a markedly different story from that of Dr. Jones. The therapist related that Dr. Jones had been inconsistent in attendance at sessions, and when he was present, he resisted engagement in the therapy process. In essence, Dr. Jones's therapist was of the opinion that Dr. Jones had made little to no therapeutic progress.

Dr. Watter and Pat discussed the implications of the information they had received thus far, as well as the vagaries and inconsistencies related to the diagnosis of sex addiction. After looking carefully at the discovery material, the results of psychometric testing, and the collateral conversation with Dr. Jones's therapist, Pat was able to see a dramatically different picture of Dr. Jones than was seen at the initial consultation. Pat and Dr. Watter worked on crafting a written report of findings indicating Dr. Jones's lack of progress in therapy, lack of remorse for and acknowledgment of his actions, as well as testing suggestive of a narcissistic personality disorder, and submitted this to the referent. Clearly the referent was hoping for a different assessment outcome, but was hopeful that the court would recommend further treatment for Dr. Jones, and not permanent loss of license, heavy fines, and/or incarceration.

This case clearly illustrates some of the major differences between clinical sexology and the forensic sexological examination. The supervisee and the supervisor must embrace the differing mindset of the clinician versus the forensic examiner. Pat initially approached this case as a clinical sexologist, meeting Dr. Jones without reviewing discovery information prior to the initial meeting with the client. As a result, Pat was at a disadvantage in performing the forensic sexological examination. It was the supervisor's role to educate and guide Pat through the assessment process, and to keep Pat on track regarding the conceptualization of the case from the vantage point of a forensic sexologist as opposed to a clinical sexologist. Ideally, Pat would receive further training in forensic sexology and forensic examination before getting to the point of case supervision. As can be seen from this case example, there is much to learn about forensic work and the intersection between the legal and the sexological domains. It would also be helpful if the forensic sexological supervisor was to recommend that the forensic sexological supervisee become involved with one of the professional organizations, such as ATSA (Association for the Treatment of Sexual Abusers, www.atsa.com), in order to become more proficient in the process of forensic sexological evaluation, and to become engaged in a community of other professionals doing a similar type of work.

Conclusions

This chapter attempted to elucidate the myriad differences between the work of the clinical sexologist and the forensic sexology examiner. The forensic sexological supervisor has the formidable task of guiding the trained practicing clinical sexologist through navigating the bumpy terrain of the psycho-legal arena. The forensic sexology supervisor has the responsibility for ascertaining whether or not the forensic sexology supervisee possesses the requisite training, skill, temperament, and maturity to be able to function effectively in this most complicated area of practice. Many clinicians who have ventured into forensic work have quickly been dissuaded from continuing due to the complexity and demanding nature of the charge. Those sexologists wishing to enter the realm of forensic work must be willing to obtain substantial training and supervision inasmuch as the rules and expectations of the legal arena are quite different from the rules and expectations of the clinical. Forensic sexologists are there to assist the court or other governing body in making determinations regarding the appropriate course of action to take with a client whose behavior has transgressed the boundaries of law and/or society. Many will find themselves not well suited to this work and are best advised to confine their involvement to the clinical work they may find more palatable. The forensic sexology supervisor has a very powerful and influential role in the preparation of the forensic sexologist. Both parties are advised to be mindful of the extraordinary impact a forensic sexological evaluation can have on the lives of those impacted by the legal system.

About the Author

Daniel N. Watter specializes in the treatment of individuals and couples experiencing sexual and/or relationship problems. He received his doctoral degree from New York University in 1985 and earned a post-graduate certificate in Medical Humanities (with a concentration in Medical Ethics) from Drew University. He is licensed by the State of New Jersey as both a psychologist and a marital and family therapist. In addition, he is Board Certified in Sex Therapy by both the American Association of Sexuality Educators, Counselors, and Therapists (AASECT), and the American Board of Sexology (ACS), of which is also holds Fellowship status.

He has recently completed two terms on the New Jersey Psychological Association's Ethics Committee where he spent two years as the Committee's chairperson. He is the former chair of the Diplomate Certification Committee for the American Association for Sexuality Educators, Counselors, and Therapists (AASECT). He is also past president of the Society for Sex Therapy and Research (SSTAR).

References

American Psychiatric Association. (2013). *The diagnostic and statistical manual of mental disorders* (5th ed.). Washington, DC: Author.
Association of Family and Conciliation Courts. (2010). *Guidelines for court-involved therapy*. Retrieved from www.afccnet.org

Fernandez, Y.M., & Serran, G.A. (2011). Characteristics of an effective sex offender therapist. In B. K. Schwartz (Ed.), *Handbook of sex offender treatment* (pp. 69.1–69.21). Kingston, NJ: Civic Research Institute.

Ley, D., Brovko, J.M., & Reid, R. C. (2015). Forensic applications of "sex addiction" in US legal proceedings. *Current Sexual Health Reports, 7*(2), 108–116. https://doi.org/10.1007/s11930-015-0049-7

Ley, D., Prause, N., & Finn, P. (2014). The emperor has no clothes: A review of the pornography addiction model. *Current Sexual Health Reports, 6*(2), 94–105.

Melton, G.B., Petrila, J., Poythress, N.G., Slobogin, C., Lyons, P.M., & Otto, R.K. (2007). *Psychological evaluations for the courts: A handbook for mental health professionals and lawyers* (3rd ed.). New York: Guilford Press.

Moser, C. (2001). Paraphilia: Another confused sexological concept. In P.J. Kleinplatz (Ed.), *New directions in sex therapy: Innovations and alternative* (pp. 91–108). Philadelphia, PA: Brunner-Routledge.

Moser, C. (2009). When is an unusual sexual interest a mental disorder? *Archives of Sexual Behavior, 38*(3), 323–325. https://doi.org/10.1007/s10508-008-9436-8

Moser, C. (2011). Hypersexual disorder: Just more muddled thinking. *Archives of Sexual Behavior, 40*(2), 227–229. https://doi.org/10.1007s10508-010-9690-4

Parker, M. (2014). Addicted to lying, or lying about addiction? Distinguishing genuine addiction from gaming the system in assessing mitigated sanctions for process additions. *Georgetown Journal of Legal Ethics, 27*(3), 805–827.

Schlesinger, L.B. (1996). *Explorations in criminal psychopathology: Clinical syndromes with forensic implications.* Springfield, IL: Charles C. Thomas.

Shapiro, D.L. (1999). *Criminal responsibility evaluations: A manual for practice.* Sarasota, FL: Professional Resource Press.

Szasz, T. (2001). *Pharmacracy: Medicine and politics in America.* Westport, CT: Praeger.

Watter, D.N. (2006). Forensic sexology versus clinical sexology: Some cautionary comments. *Sexual and Relationship Therapy, 21*(2), 143–148.

Watter, D.N. (2017). Existential issues in sexual medicine: The relation between death-anxiety and hypersexuality. *Sexual Medicine Reviews, 6*(1), 3–10.

Watter, D.N. (2018). Protecting my patients' story: Beneficent or paternalistic? *Patient Education and Counseling, 104*(4), 758–759.

Wincze, J.P. (2000). Assessment and treatment of atypical sexual behavior. In S.R. Leiblum & R.C. Rosen (Eds.), *Principles and practice of sex therapy* (3rd ed., pp. 449–470). New York: Guilford Press.

Yalom, I.D. (2002). *The gift of therapy: An open letter to a new generation of therapists and their patients.* New York: HarperCollins.

Yalom, I.D. (2017). *Becoming myself: A psychiatrist's memoir.* New York: Basic Books.

Zimring, F.E. (2004). *An American travesty: Legal responses to adolescent sexual offending.* Chicago, IL: University of Chicago Press.

6 Sex Therapy Supervision With Couples

Stephanie Buehler

Abstract

Just as sex therapy is often marginalized in graduate school or post-graduate programs, supervision of couples sex therapy is a topic rarely addressed. Supervision of couples sex therapy requires knowledge of common and uncommon sexual difficulties, as well as underlying couples' dynamics that may be the cause or result of such problems. A sexological ecosystemic approach can be used by both the supervisor and supervisee for case conceptualization. Couples' sexual difficulties due to mental health problems, genito-pelvic pain/penetration disorder, and sexuality before, during and after pregnancy are provided as examples. The chapter also covers the ethics of couples sex therapy.

Keywords

Supervision, couples therapy, sex therapy, couples sex therapy, sexological ecosystem

Couples have likely had sexual problems since humans were first aware that sex could happen outside of its procreative purpose. Fortunately, today we have couples' sex therapy to help people find contentment in their intimate relationships. The field of marital and relationship therapy has grown exponentially, with the supervision of couples' therapy well defined by the American Association of Marriage and Family Therapists (2007). Members of other professions, including psychology, social work, and professional counselors, may also treat couples and need proficient supervision of their work. Meanwhile, the field of sex therapy has seemingly lagged behind. This is not the case, however, at the American Association of Sexuality Educators, Counselors and Therapists (AASECT), which has been certifying sex therapists and educators since 1978 (Valentine, personal communication, 2017).

In clinical practice, some sex therapists have a practice that includes a mix of individuals and couples. As a rule, if an individual has a partner, then they are expected to come to therapy as well because, as in any systemic therapy, if one partner has a sexual issue, then both partners have a sexual issue (Weeks, 2013). Sexual issues generally do not occur solely because one's genitals are not in good working order; they can be a symptom of problems in the relationship. However, addressing relationship difficulties is not a guarantee that the sexual issues will be resolved—a stance which, unfortunately, many couples therapists not trained in sex therapy seem to believe. To treat both sex and relationship problems, an integrated approach to couples' and sex therapy is usually required (Hertlein, Weeks, & Gambescia, 2015).

Challenges of Couples' Sex Therapy Supervision

Supervising couples' sex therapy requires the ability to work with supervisees who may or may not already have experience working with clients with problems of a sexual nature, let alone with couples. This is challenging, given that doing each type of therapy requires a sophisticated skill set and the flexibility to move among and between theoretical models, as presenting problems may require a variety of interventions to reach a satisfactory resolution. But historically sex therapy has been at the margins of psychotherapy.

This marginalization of sex therapy was graphically presented in a diagram of systems theory (Jordan & Fisher, 2016). At the top of the genogram, medicine branched to psychiatry, the field within which Freud practiced. Freud's psychosexual model of development then branched off to Masters and Johnson (a medical doctor and researcher, respectively) and Kaplan (a psychiatrist) to develop sex therapy. Another line of theoretical development also starts with medicine, which then branched off to gynecology and obstetrics (conspicuously neglecting urology). Gynecology and obstetrics first branch to sexology (a science completely absent from most university programs), and then to Kinsey, a researcher and educator. All sexuality-related branches come to an end in the 1960s. Meanwhile, the diagram displays the remaining branches of the "family tree" of systems theories blossoming into structural and strategic therapy, narrative therapy, brief therapy, and so on.

Fortunately, there has been recent cross-pollination among couples therapists and sex therapists. Hertlein et al. (2015) have contributed an edited textbook regarding systemic sex therapy. Metz and McCarthy (2012) exemplify the use of cognitive-behavioral systems theory for working with sexual problems such as erectile dysfunction and premature ejaculation. The sexological ecosystem (Buehler, 2016) is another approach to understanding not only how one's sexuality developed within one's family of origin, but as a result of interactions between and among subsystems, for example, sex education in one's school versus what is learned about sex from one's culture.

The supervisor needs to put supervisees through their paces, not only in terms of understanding their client's sexuality but also the couple's dynamic, both in and out of the bedroom. If the supervisee is knowledgeable in couples' therapy, some guidance at the beginning of supervision in applying tenets of couples' therapy to sexual difficulties is useful. If the supervisee has not had training or experience in couples' therapy, then the supervisee will need more education, both from the supervisor and from their own study of one or more theoretical approaches. Bowen's theory (1993), for example, can be applied to understand how anxiety and projection occur when a partner has erectile dysfunction or anorgasmia. Or, when a couple has mismatched desire, the supervisee can help each partner become more differentiated, which is helpful in diminishing anger and blame before the couple can work together on the presenting sexual problem.

Providing Competent Couples' Sex Therapy

The Supervisee's Understanding of Sexuality

A large percentage of mental health professionals (MHPs) have never had a single course in sex therapy, or have minimal exposure to the subject. For example, the State of California requires just eight hours of education in human sexuality before graduates in doctoral programs can sit for the licensing exam. Mental health professionals who want to practice couples' sex therapy are often highly enthusiastic and motivated enough to seek additional training required to treat couples with sexual complaints, even seeking certification through organizations such as the American Association of Sexuality Educators, Counselors, and Therapists (AASECT). However, whether or not a couples' therapist seeks specialized training, a variety of circumstances may bring couples' sexual issues to the forefront. In many cases, couples who seek help for getting their relationship back on track after an incident of infidelity or treatment for cancer need assistance with sexual issues, and they expect couples therapists to be able to talk about sex.

In order to practice competently from the start, the supervisee needs to be made aware of their own ideas about sexuality. Each of us holds a *sexological worldview*, defined as "the result of the socialization process that is comprised of values, beliefs, opinions, attitudes, and concepts specific to sexuality, including any and all sexual behavior and identities" (Sitron & Dyson, 2012). One's sexological worldview needs conscious examination for biases that may cause harm in the therapeutic alliance. One can hold to the view that sex means intercourse in the missionary position between a married man and woman, but that will not get them very far with LGBTQ couples, couples in committed relationships who are not legally married, couples in open or polyamorous relationships, and couples that enjoy sexual experimentation with less "vanilla" forms of sexual expression.

Socialization and sexual development take place within each individual's unique *sexological ecosystem* (Buehler, 2016). The sexological ecosystem contains five subsystems that can help the supervisee assess where problems might occur, as follows.

Microsystem

This subsystem contains the elements closest to the individual, including their biological and psychological makeup, family of origin, and extended family members. This is the area that is assessed for overall health, sexual and mental health, messages about sex from parents, and messages sent verbally or by example from extended family members.

Mesosystem

The mesosystem is an abstract subsystem in which the interactions between and among systems take place. This is where interactions between partners occur, as well as between the dyad and other systems, for example, the healthcare system. To illustrate, consider one case in which a male partner was diagnosed with prostate cancer and received excellent information and support regarding sexual late effects, while in another case the male partner received virtually no information or support. The interaction between couples and healthcare providers will be very different in each case. Another illustrative case might be that of a young woman whose parents did not permit to have the Gardasil vaccine for human papilloma virus (HPV) before sexual debut, and who now faces cervical cancer, which impacts her sexual relationship with her partner.

Macrosystem

The macrosystem includes institutions that exert direct effect on one's sexual development and identity, such as school, church or temple, healthcare providers, the legal system (e.g., avoiding sexual activities that could lead to arrest), and the workplace (e.g., the impact of work/life balance on one's relationship).

Exosystem

The exosystem includes social influences that affect the individual indirectly. This could be myths and cultural messages about sexuality, media images of sexual behavior, and even Supreme Court rulings on civil rights or public policy decisions.

Once the supervisee understands their own sexological ecosystem, they can develop a broader view of each partner's sexual development. The process of gathering information can also help the couple understand one another's sexuality, and introduce themes they may have never considered without guidance, such as more or less restrictive views of premarital sex, or how one's sexuality might change after the birth of a child (Buehler, in press). The sexological ecosystemic assessment becomes an ongoing process, both for the supervisee and the clients who can think about having a lens that allows them to focus in tightly, perhaps on hormonal changes, or broadly, such as the portrayal of multiorgasmic women in pornography as a comparison to oneself.

Sitting in Nonjudgment

Because everyone carries sexual shame and guilt, the supervisee's empathic and nonjudgmental stance is critical to effective treatment in couples sex therapy.

Shame and guilt regarding sexuality make it difficult for couples to reach out for help, let alone talk about it openly in the therapy room. Couples come in with a wide variety of sexual complaints. Some will be common: mismatched sexual desire, or difficulty reaching orgasm. Others will be less common, from a desire to experiment with BDSM (bondage, dominance, sadism, masochism) or with open relationships, to coping with a partner coming out as bisexual or gay. Some couples will speak pragmatically about sex, while others will be so frank it might make a new couples' sex therapy professional blush. Through it all, the supervisee needs to remain relaxed, present, and attentive to listen to the complaint with openness and curiosity, just as they would with any client.

If couples sense that the therapist is uncomfortable with sex-related topics or an alternative form of sexual behavior, they may stop treatment prematurely, and then sometimes will go from therapist to therapist seeking someone who will give them appropriate help. Many couples report that coming in for help with sexual issues marks the first time they have had an adult-to-adult conversation about sex; those couples who are more open about sexuality also appreciate having a therapist who they feel really understands them, especially if they have been to therapists who have judged their behavior. In general, if supervisees hold to the value that humans as a whole need healing from sexual wounds, both small and large, then they can meet the couple where they are and take them from being distraught over their sexual relationship to contentment.

Sexual Health in the Couples' Relationship

To practice effectively, the supervisee ideally has had some experience working with couples in a variety of settings, as the couples' sex therapists must be astute not only at diagnosing sexual problems, but relationship difficulties as well. Few MHPs, however, learn what constitutes a healthy sexual relationship. One such framework for understanding and treating couples is the Good-Enough Sex Model (Metz & McCarthy, 2012). In this model, a healthy sexual relationship is described as including regular, varied, and enjoyable sexual activity; good overall physical and emotional health; and realistic expectations for sexual encounters. The purpose of sex might also be varied, from release of tension to a spiritual experience. The couple sees themselves as an "intimate team" in co-creating a sex life that is based on pleasure rather than performance.

Supervisees need to recognize that treating sexual issues refers to more than "body parts and friction," as Masters and Johnson famously said. Couples present with sexual difficulties resulting from childhood sexual abuse and other trauma, erotic revival after infidelity, and coping with discovery of a partner's secret sexual behavior. Sometimes one partner can no longer suppress questions regarding their sexual orientation or gender, which tests the relationship to see if it can survive or necessarily come to an end. Differences in religion or culture sometimes interfere with sexual enjoyment, so the couples' sex therapist needs to be savvy enough to explore these related issues as well.

Couples, Sex, and Mental Illness

As mental health professionals, supervisees must be aware of the intersection of mental illness and sexuality (Buehler, 2011). Most training programs do not provide education regarding the effects of sexual difficulties on mental health, which can include depression and anxiety, and of course the impacts that depression and anxiety can have on sexual problems. However, diagnoses including, but not limited to, attention deficit hyperactivity disorder (ADHD; American Psychiatric Association [APA], 2013), substance abuse, eating disorders, autism spectrum disorder, and even learning disabilities can all impact sexual function. For example, couples in which one (or in some cases, both) partners have ADHD may struggle not only due to lack of organization in the affected partner, but with sexual problems that range from delayed ejaculation for men and anorgasmia in women to impulsive sexual acting out that perils the relationship altogether. In the case of sexual function, there are novel interventions that can help, such as the use of a variety of sex toys (vibrators, dildos, massagers, etc.) to inject novelty and increase stimulation for the ADHD partner. Certain relationship dynamics, such as the non-ADHD partner acting in a "parentified" role or the ADHD partner masking an avoidant personality by "forgetting" important occasions, can drive a wedge in the couples' intimate relationship.

Other mental disturbances may also mask sexual difficulties. A person might use alcohol to boost sexual confidence or slow down the process of ejaculation; couples sometimes incorporate recreational drugs or alcohol in order to be more disinhibited during sex. It is not unusual for one partner to be anxious or sad if the other partner gives up alcohol and spoils some of the fun. If one or both partners become sober, it can change the couple's sexual routine; sometimes couples even need to grieve the loss of their old sex life.

High-functioning autism is another area where supervisees might need more than usual assistance in helping couples resolve sexual issues. Common complaints when a partner has autism include a lack of spontaneity, "robotic" or mechanical sex, and sexual dysfunction that may include erectile dysfunction or delayed ejaculation. In all cases, the supervisee must facilitate communication, empathy, and exploration of new sexual behaviors that both can enjoy.

A more severe instance where couples may struggle with sexual problems and mental illness is when there has been a history of sexual abuse. However, any type of trauma may create sexual problems, including physical abuse, neglect, or military service due to emotional numbing, difficulty relating to a partner, or low libido or drive. The supervisee must take extra care in working with such couples to remain neutral and not push an agenda of sexual activity. The supervisee needs to facilitate an agreement to "take a vacation" from sexual activity while both partners take time out to understand one another's sexual expectations and struggles, the sexual activities that "trigger" the survivor, and introducing sensual activities at a pace that allows the survivor to have "healthy control."

When a couple in which one partner has depression, anxiety, ADHD, or another problem presents for treatment of sexual issues, the supervisee has a decision to make. Will the supervisee be able to treat the couple's sexual complaint *and* the emotional problem simultaneously? Or will the supervisee need to refer the partner for individual treatment and/or a psychiatric evaluation? In cases where there is mild to moderate anxiety, for example, both partners can often benefit from certain aspects of anxiety management, including relaxation, mindfulness, and addressing negative cognitions. Couples can also explore the role of the symptom in their relationship: Is one partner's anxiety a red flag that they are not asking for, or receiving, appropriate support? How is anxiety interfering with the couple's sexual relationship? Is it a turn-off? Does it cause friction, or even fatigue?

When one partner's problem is more severe, especially if the treatment does not lend itself to having partner involvement, then the couple may need to make a decision about whether to continue couples sex therapy or to wait until the identified problem is better managed. There is no one right answer, but sometimes the identified partner may feel overwhelmed by demands. On the other hand, they may also be relieved that they now have an answer for why their sexual relationship has been difficult. Often, they will want to remain in couples' sex therapy so that they can learn more about, say, symptoms of ADHD and how to manage them in the bedroom.

Treating Sexual Pain Disorders

Another often neglected area in regard to training couples' sex therapists is the diagnosis and treatment of genito-pelvic pain/penetration disorder (GPPPD). GPPPD is diagnosed when a woman fears that penis–vagina intercourse will be painful and therefore avoids all sexual activity, or she in fact experiences painful intercourse either due to vaginismus (hypertonic pelvic floor muscles that prevent vaginal penetration) or dyspareunia (penetration is possible, but intercourse is painful; APA, 2013). GPPPD can be diagnosed at any point in life, but often its symptoms are reported in young women who may have been unable to consummate a marriage, women after having given birth by any mode, or women who lack education about coping with vaginal changes due to menopause (e.g., dryness and atrophy). Note that lesbian women who desire vaginal penetration (e.g., with a sex toy or finger) may also complain about GPPPD.

Couples affected by GPPPD often delay treatment for months and even years, creating strain on their relationship. As is often the case, couples may not have received good sex education, or any education at all, which requires the couples' sex therapist supervisee to learn how to explain basic human anatomy, the human sexual response and the role of arousal in comfortable intercourse, and the importance of open communication about sex. Couples often benefit from sensate focus exercises (slow, sensual touching), in which partners are directed to explore one another's bodies without the aim of attempting intercourse. At the same time, the supervisee can educate the couple about how they can enjoy other sexual activities while working on resolving GPPPD symptoms. In this regard, the couples' sex therapist supervisee will need to develop their educational approach, including the location or development of handout material and a library of books to recommend to clients.

The supervisee can explore the couple's motivation for having intercourse. Some couples come to treatment expressing a wish to conceive. The supervisee should not take such a wish at face value. Sometimes there is pressure from extended family to produce children before the couple is psychologically or otherwise equipped, or even truly onboard with the idea of parenthood. Occasionally, a woman develops GPPPD because she fears the pain of labor and delivery. While working through their concerns, big and small, about becoming parents, they may need to set boundaries with family members, lest they feel that their sexual activity (or lack thereof) is being monitored, possibly by an entire extended family, creating even greater pressure to perform.

The supervisee treating GPPPD needs to gain competence with a collaborative approach, as these problems generally require working with the client's gynecologist or uro-gynecologist and a specialized pelvic floor physical therapist. It is recommended that the supervisee explain the release of information in full to the couple, and to ascertain any information that the couple does not want disclosed to the medical provider. The supervisee may need to facilitate ethical referrals and communication between and among members of the treatment team, which includes assistance from the partner, for example, learning how to treat vaginismus with internal vaginal massage between physical therapy sessions.

There are other physical issues that similarly affect a couple's sexual relationship. Any cancer of the reproductive system (e.g., breast, uterine, or prostate cancer) has the most direct effect on one's sexuality, but other illnesses including diabetes, arthritis, and even psoriasis can affect overall feeling of well-being, body image, and sexual function. Wanting to be sensitive to one another, couples sometimes stop engaging in sexual activity to avoid drawing attention to the effect of the illness on their relationship. In such cases, supervisees can combine medical family therapy (Tyndall, Hodgson, Lamson, White, & Knight, 2012) with sex therapy. For example, medical illnesses can impact a couple's usual roles, making it a challenge to relate to one another and to organize daily life. Sometimes one partner must be in the caregiver's role, changing dressings or drains and administering medications. Such changes not only "medicalize" the couple's relationship but also desexualize it. Supervisees need to recognize that they may need to help the couple through a grieving process over how their sex life used to be, and to embrace a "new normal."

Common Issues in Couples' Sex Therapy

There are a variety of common situations that couples frequently present in sex therapy. For example, supervisees conducting couples' sex therapy often will find that there is a need to dispel "sexual myths," such as the male partner in a heterosexual relationship always has more drive than his female partner, or that all gay men like to engage in anal sex. Power struggles that are sometimes played out covertly in daily life become overt when the couple engages sexually, where both partners may try to attain sexual dominance, or a partner who claims to enjoy being the passive partner is, in actuality, directing the other partner. Couples may have different "sexual styles" (McCarthy & McCarthy, 2011), with one partner being more experimental and the other appreciating routine; they may seek help negotiating a way to get both needs met.

Although attachment theory is predominantly focused on emotional interactions between partners, supervisees can apply emotionally focused therapy (Johnson, 2017) to sexual interactions. It is often easier to start by examining each partner's attachment style outside of the bedroom. Securely attached partners are the most likely to report that they get along well and spend quality time together, but their sex life needs help. Someone with an anxious attachment style may overwhelm the other with their need for sexual attention and validation; someone with an avoidant style may frustrate their partner as they fail to notice their partner's sexual needs, or even their own needs, for that matter.

These anxious or avoidant styles often morph into the "pursuer-distancer" pattern of interaction (Betchen, 2013), which is very common when it comes to complaints regarding low sexual desire or, in many cases, a sexless marriage if both partners are "distancers." In general, the supervisee must listen for, or track, the couple's description of the way in which each partner initiates or declines having sex, and their reasons for doing so. The proof is often in the pudding if the couple ignores the supervisee's simple suggestions, such as taking turns initiating, or putting sex on the schedule. More exploration will often reveal who is usually the pursuer, who is the distancer, and what might cause them to eventually switch roles. Making couples aware of this pattern is often enough of an intervention to create change.

Couples frequently complain that "the thrill is gone," and that sexual passion has grown cold. Couples also may compare themselves unfavorably to friends who like to brag about sexual exploits (e.g., "One couple we know has sex every day!"; "We have sex in a variety of positions that is very satisfying!"). Supervisees need to normalize that some couples experience the same diminishment in excitement over the years they are together. Supervisees will need to help the couple explore what they want or need *now* from their sexual relationship, and to intentionally create it. Supervisees can also educate the couple about so-called *responsive desire* (Basson, 2000). Unlike Masters and Johnson's (1986) *linear model*, in which an individual feels desire, seeks out a partner, has an orgasm, and returns back to their former, pre-desirous state, in the responsive model an individual may not feel spontaneous desire ("horniness"), but if all is well, then when the partner initiates sex, they may be willing to engage, become aroused, and then feel desire for sexual activity.

Supervisees in couples' sex therapy must also be aware of the issue of consent. Sometimes a couple comes to therapy because one partner wants the therapist to tell the other partner that "anything goes" in the bedroom, and that refraining from a particular behavior is prudish, stubborn, or immature. The supervisee can start with the premise that all sexual activity should be consensual, and that if someone does not want to do something, they should never be told they *must* do it. However, that does not mean that the discussion of acceptable and unacceptable sexual activity comes to a close. If one partner wants to engage in a variety of sexual behaviors, then the supervisee can facilitate an exploration of what activities the partners are willing to do, might agree to try, or are off the table altogether.

Couples' Sex Therapy Before, During, and After Pregnancy

Perhaps one of the most neglected areas that supervisees need to know about is the treatment of couples' sexuality in regard to reproduction (Buehler, in press). Many couples report that their sex life "went off the rails" after the birth of their first, or subsequent, child. Often, that is where the discussion ends, probably because of the persistent myth that lower sexual frequency happens to every couple who become parents. The fact is, however, that most couples resume sexual activity after the delivery of a child (Hipp, Kane Low, & van Anders, 2012). The question becomes, then, why did this particular couple stop having sex at this time and not really resume being intimate?

One of the reasons that therapists may avoid talking about sexuality and reproduction is that mixing motherhood with sexuality has traditionally been taboo. Once again, the supervisee needs to examine their sexological worldview if they are to compile a complete sexual history for the couple. The supervisee might begin with an exploration of whether there were any difficulties becoming pregnant and, if so, whether they sought infertility treatment. Having a diagnosis of infertility, in and of itself, can create distress in each partner, and in the couple's relationship, as hopes are dashed that they will be able to have a baby in the "normal way." The treatment of infertility can be difficult as well as costly, creating sexual difficulties including low drive, anorgasmia, and erectile dysfunction. Conversely, sexual problems such as vaginismus and delayed ejaculation can create infertility. Infertility clinics do not always inquire into a couples' sex life, making it possible for a couple to become pregnant through artificial reproductive technology, then to deliver a baby without resolving their sexual concerns.

Some couples engage in sexual activity during pregnancy, with less in the first trimester because a woman may not feel well. During the third trimester, couples may sexually engage with one another less because sex becomes awkward. However, there are changes that can cause sex to be uncomfortable for the female partner at any time, including the tone of pelvic floor muscles and hormones. In addition, while some women may feel sexy and positive about themselves and their bodies during pregnancy, others may feel awful and dislike the physical changes. Men, too, have different responses to the pregnant female form. "I'm afraid of hurting the baby," may be true, or it may be a polite way for a man to excuse himself from being sexual during the pregnancy. The supervisee might explore if the couple was sexually active during the pregnancy or, if they refrained from sex, whether one or both partners were alright with this decision.

In the postpartum period, couples may face the stereotypical stress that comes with having a newborn (e.g., lack of sleep and less time than needed to manage all of the tasks associated with caregiving an infant). Since some couples figure out a way to resume their sex life, the supervisee needs to discover what obstacles the couple in treatment may have faced. Sometimes there was unrecognized postpartum depression or birth trauma that was seen as a reaction that would naturally pass. There could have been an episiotomy or changes to the pelvic floor that caused fear and avoidance of intercourse. Sometimes one or both partners gained weight during the pregnancy and became overly conscious of their body image. The supervisee needs to ensure, however, that there is no blame on one partner over the other. Whatever occurred, it can be seen as a symptom that was not recognized or understood by the couple because they were, perhaps, distracted. Now that they understand the root cause, the couple can join together to overcome the problem and get their sex life back on track.

A final area that couples' sex therapy supervisees need to be prepared to explore is that of family planning. Couples sometimes avoid having intercourse because of inadequate contraception, using the withdrawal method, or one partner or the other refusing to use condoms. There may be a need to discuss experimenting with a variety of condom types and lubricants to find one that both partners can accept, or even to explore the couple's feelings about vasectomy. Finally, couples that do not have adequate birth control often need a referral so that they can discuss options with a medical provider, usually a gynecologist.

Treating LGBTQ Couples

The topic of treating clients who identify as LGBTQ is covered in depth in Chapter 11 and it is here touched on briefly because of the supervisee's role in couples' sex therapy with this population. Namely, supervisees should not simply extrapolate what they know about working with heterosexual couples. Even though Americans have become more accepting of sexual minorities and gay marriage is the law of the land, LGBTQ couples still experience *minority stress* (LeBlanc, Frost, & Wight, 2015). Being, or feeling, outside of the American mainstream means that there can be an internal struggle to maintain self-esteem, as well as outer struggles to make a good life for oneself. Minority stress compounds naturally occurring relationship stress and can also affect sexual function. Again, supervisees must be aware of their sexological worldview in order not to make assumptions about LGBTQ couples.

Open Relationships and Nonmonogamy

Open relationships are becoming more common (Moors, 2017), with heterosexual couples increasingly engaging in polyamory and other nonexclusive arrangements. In addition, LGBTQ couples—who could not marry until recently—who have adopted such arrangements may feel validated and speak freely about their lifestyle. Supervisees and supervisors need to examine their own views regarding alternative lifestyles, lest they cause harm by judging the couple's lifestyle choice. The supervisee can use their systems training to help couples to define roles and rules, communicate about feelings, and set boundaries as needed. When couples are in polyamorous relationships, when possible it is advisable for the core constellation of participants to come into the office, where the supervisee can explore roles, rules, boundaries, enmeshment, and so on among members.

Acceptance, however, does not mean that the supervisee cannot explore why the couple decided to open their relationship, or in what ways an open relationship may have lent complexity to their lives. The exploration of such issues should take place not out of curiosity, but to understand the relationship history and discover longstanding patterns of interaction. The supervisee must also take care to understand the couple's goal. Is the goal to better a clearer agreement regarding rules, or to set boundaries regarding what is off-limits, like one partner asks the other about sexual activities outside of their relationship?

The couples' sex therapist supervisee can also help couples that want to explore whether or not such an arrangement is right for them. There are many avenues of inquiry in such cases. Do both partners want to open the relationship? If not, the supervisee can facilitate an open dialogue about each partner's feelings. The supervisee can also help the couple find compromise; for example, some couples conclude that a "hall pass" arrangement ("what happens in Vegas stays in Vegas") may work for them; that they will each have only one other partner who is known to the other partner; or that one partner (who often has come out as bisexual or gay) may have opportunities for sexual encounters on a frequency that both partners agree upon. Couples can be reminded that their agreement can be revisited at any time, perhaps with ongoing assistance from the therapist.

Ethics in Couples' Sex Therapy

Any time a mental health professional works with couples, there are particular ethical considerations, especially in regard to confidentiality if a clinician sees the partners separately. From the outset, the supervisee needs to make clear their stance regarding who they consider to be the client—is it two individuals coming for treatment together, or is it the unit, together as a whole, that is being seen? Legitimate arguments can be made either way, however, the therapeutic alliance with one or both partners can be ruined if a supervisee's policy is not made early on. If, for example, the supervisee does not explain their "secrets policy," and meets with one partner, that partner might tell them something that undermines the therapy if it cannot be shared.

Sometimes sex therapists want a sexual history from each partner. Since one or both partners may not want to disclose such private and personal information in front of the other, the supervisee may decide to see partners individually, explaining that no information from history-taking sessions will be shared. The "no secrets" policy can then be put into place thereafter, if the supervisee wishes to do so. It is not advisable to have an open discussion about the "no secrets" policy, in case one partner wants everything to be open, and the other partner has expressed a wish that the supervisee hold secrets, which might make proceeding in couples' therapy awkward: "What is my partner hiding?"

A related situation may arise if one person wants to be seen in sex therapy prior to coming in with their partner, usually because of embarrassment, but sometimes because they want to disclose something about their sexual behavior to the therapist, for example, that they have a private fetish or that they visit sex workers. Before starting treatment, the supervisee may inform the individual that in some cases a referral to a couples' therapist may need to be made, for example, if the supervisee feels that information disclosed may impact the alliance if and when the other partner joins therapy.

Other sex therapists will not keep secrets under any circumstances, and they would not switch modalities from individual to couples' sex therapy. They may go so far as to tell partners that even if contacted separately, they will tell the partner in the next session about the contact and the nature of its content. Still others have a compromise solution, something akin to what therapists do when they are seeing teens, which is to tell the couple that information from separate sessions will be kept confidential unless there is something harmful that the therapist deems needs to be shared, for example, having unsafe sex or being diagnosed with an STI. In that case, the supervisee would facilitate disclosure, usually in a conjoint session.

Record keeping often comes up in regard to couples therapy. It is acceptable to keep a single record for a couple's therapy session. However, if there is concern regarding third-party reporting, such as to an insurance provider, then the supervisee might be advised to keep a separate record for each partner. The supervisee also may need to be reminded or told that if a single record is kept, should there be a request to release the record from one partner, then all information about the other partner must be redacted. Because mental health professionals do not have dual relationships with their clients, it is also acceptable to have in the informed consent a notification that since couples therapy is not being conducted for forensic purposes, no records will be released for legal purposes unless ordered by a judge. This can be important because there are cases where one partner has used information about the other partner's sexual activity (e.g., BDSM) to exert leverage in questions regarding child custody.

Relationship Dissolution

Couples sex therapy supervisees need to be able to recognize when a couple's relationship might be coming to its end. Signs that this may be the case include when one partner breaks an agreement that the couple created together in treatment, or if partners return to each and every appointment without having accomplished an assignment. The couple may also clearly be incompatible not just along one dimension, but along nearly every dimension of an intimate relationship; neither partner will be able to—nor necessarily should be expected to—change enough to satisfy the other. The couple may also display intense conflict in every session as well. If this happens, the supervisee may need to ask the couple if they want to work on sexual issues or on resolving conflict in a healthy way. At times, the supervisee may want to make a referral to a couples' therapist who specializes in high-conflict couples, with the proviso that the couple can return to sex therapy when they are ready.

Sometimes a supervisee may sense that a couple is headed for separation or divorce. The supervisee can be encouraged to ask if either partner has considered ending the relationship. Couples also may ask if the supervisee thinks they should divorce at some point in treatment. The wise supervisee never answers this question or gives recommendations that the couple should split. The supervisee can explore with the couple what their life might look like if they choose to separate or divorce. Sometimes this type of reality testing can help a couple decide to stick with treatment and continue to work on their relationship. Though it may be nerve-wracking, the supervisee needs to weather the couples' storm as they grapple with their ambiguous feelings.

Case Example

A supervisee (Jean; pronouns she/her) began working with a couple originally from India who reported that though they had been married for 3 years, they were unable to become pregnant. Jean reported that the couple was highly distressed about their predicament, but Jean was mostly curious about the couple's arranged marriage. She could hardly believe that such marriages still occurred, and expressed that it was "no wonder" the couple had not gotten pregnant. Jean was encouraged to explore her own sexological worldview regarding her assumptions about how people develop attraction to one another. Jean identified that she adhered to the American ideal that individuals must be given the freedom to find their own romantic partner, without any say from parents or extended family.

This lead to testing Jean's assumption: could there be any merit to having input from parents regarding one's choice of mate? Could two people learn to love one another over time, especially if they had the full blessing and support from everyone around them? Could chemistry grow between two people as they got to know one another, or did chemistry need to be something instant? The supervisor then asked Jean if she knew that couples in arranged marriages often reported high levels of relationship satisfaction and lower divorce rates than in American marriages. Jean did not, but after learning more about arranged marriages, she understood how this might be.

The supervisor also inquired as to why Jean had not asked them about their sex life in the first appointment. Here Jean admitted that she had assumed the couple would be highly uncomfortable talking about sex, given their cultural background. The supervisor referred Jean to the idea that she had covert permission to talk about sex, given that the couple was trying to become pregnant but had not succeeded. The supervisor and Jean then explored Jean's own embarrassment in talking about sex. Jean admitted that talking to the conservative couple from India felt like talking to her own conservative parents about sex—something she could not imagine doing. Jean was encouraged to be gentle with herself as she overcame the ideas about sex her parents had instilled in her. This gave Jean an entrée into the microsystem—a place to begin talking about sex with the couple by asking if their own parents had ever spoken to them about sex.

After the second session, Jean reported that she had learned a lot about the couple. While the wife had never had any sexual partners, the husband, who had studied in England, had a few prior girlfriends with whom he had sexual relationships. He reported that he knew right away that there was a sexual problem on their wedding night, as he had been unable to have penetrative vaginal intercourse. Jean was able to ask more questions to ascertain whether the wife perhaps had vaginismus. The wife thought so, but had been too upset and embarrassed to see a physician to get an accurate diagnosis. Jean noticed that the husband looked disgruntled and asked him about his feelings. The husband reported that he had made more than a few appointments for his wife to see a gynecologist, but she was too embarrassed to expose her "private parts" to the doctor.

Jean asked the supervisor how to help the wife overcome her negative body image regarding her genitals. The supervisor and Jean first discussed how to explore how the wife came to view her body with shame, and then to normalize that this is common in conservative societies. The supervisor also asked Jean various ways she could acquaint the wife with her own reproductive system, which Jean thought might include looking at diagrams and perhaps, when the wife felt ready, to use a mirror to identify the parts of her own external genitals.

The supervisor then asked Jean to talk more about the couple's dynamic. Did they seem to be joined together as a team to treat the problem? Were they locked in a pursuer–distancer pattern in which the more the husband tried to persuade the wife to seek treatment, the less inclined she was to do so? What was the final impetus for coming to see a therapist? Had the couple talked about separation? Furthermore, had the wife had any negative experiences with doctors? Or had she heard friends mention negative experiences about doctors, particularly gynecological examinations? Jean was encouraged to flexibly use the sexological ecosystem to explore various themes of interaction in the mesosystem. Jean could also help the couple develop empathy for one another's upbringing regarding sex and to amplify places where the couple might join together, such as the husband's willingness to attend medical appointments with his wife.

The supervisor and Jean met again after Jean had seen the couple for four additional sessions. Jean realized that she began to see merit in all different types of relationships, and all different ways of finding a suitable partner. She began to read source material on her own about Indian culture, and learned that the *Kama Sutra*, or book of sexual positions, was just one part of an ancient text on sexuality that had been suppressed when other more conservative cultures conquered the original people of the Indian subcontinent. She thought about bringing these ideas up in a session, when appropriate, to help both partners understand the influence of culture on sexuality, and how it could change depending on the times.

Jean also reported that the couple had gone together to see a gynecologist that she had recommended, and that the wife had both vaginismus and vulvodynia, or pain around the *introitus*, or entrance, to the vagina. When the gynecologist had lightly touched a cotton swab at points all around the introitus, the husband reported he watched in genuine amazement and compassion as his wife yelped in pain at the slightest touch. The gynecologist had prescribed an estrogen cream to be applied around the introitus, and once the skin in this area had healed, the wife would be referred to a pelvic pain physical therapist (PT). The husband stated that he would also go to the initial appointment with the PT to help his wife ease into treatment.

Jean then reported that the husband's response to the wife's experience of pain made her curious. She had gently asked the husband why he was so surprised. The husband admitted that he thought his wife was withholding affection from him, that she did not really find him attractive at all, and that the arranged marriage had been a farce. The wife reassured her husband that she truly loved him and was looking forward to resolving her condition.

The supervisor and Jean agreed that the initial steps of the treatment plan had been met, and that new steps could now be devised. Jean now saw her role as supporting the work of the PT, and decided to get a release of information so that the couple could feel even more confident of a positive outcome because they had a team working for them. She also decided to help prepare the couple to have eventual intercourse by providing sensate focus activities so that the partners could explore one another's bodies without feeling pressured.

Jean then expressed concern to the supervisor that the couple might have sex in order to conceive a child and then, having fulfilled their obligation, the wife might regress back to avoiding any sexual contact. Once again Jean examined her cultural beliefs that marriage is primarily about love and romance, and considered that the Indian couple might feel that marriage is about providing offspring to make their families happy. She also realized that the couple might have different views of the purpose of sex between married partners, and that exploring this difference with them might prevent some future heartache.

Jean did not mention the couple again until they were able to have pain-free intercourse. Husband and wife had, in fact, different views of sex within marriage. The wife was not fond of intercourse, but had experienced orgasms while her husband had explored her body. She thought that she could get used to the idea of having regular sex even after they became pregnant. The husband professed to be happy that he had it all—a wife with whom he could have sex and a life partner with whom he could raise a family. And a year later came proof of effective treatment—a photo of a beautiful newborn. Jean admitted that she thought she would be helping couples have better sex, not encouraging them to have any sort of sex at all, and she certainly did not expect to help a couple to conceive, which turned out to be a happy surprise that she and the supervisor could celebrate.

About the Author

Stephanie Buehler is a licensed psychologist and AASECT-certified sex therapist affiliated with Hoag Hospital in Newport Beach, California. She is the author of a bestselling textbook, *What Every Mental Health Professional Needs to Know About Sex*, and a new book for 2018, *Counseling Couples Before, During, and After Pregnancy: Intimacy and Sexuality Issues*. As Director of the Buehler Institute, she provides continuing education and sex therapy training in the United States and internationally. Her articles have been published in the *Journal of Sexual Medicine, Sexual Health Review*, and the *Journal of Sex and Marital Therapy*.

References

American Association of Marriage and Family Therapists. (2007). *AAMFT approved supervisor designation standards and responsibilities handbook*. Retrieved from https://dx5br1z4f6n0k.cloudfront.net/imis15/Documents/Approved_Supervisor_handbook.pdf

American Psychiatric Association. (2013). *Diagnostic and statistical manual of mental disorders (DSM-5®)*. Washington, DC: Author.

Basson, R. (2000). The female sexual response: A different model. *Journal of Sex &Marital Therapy, 26*(1), 51–65.

Betchen, S.J. (2013). *Intrusive partners-elusive mates: The pursuer-distancer dynamic in couples*. New York: Routledge.

Bowen, M. (1993). *Family therapy in clinical practice*. New York: Jason Aronson.

Buehler, S.J. (2011). *Sex, love, and mental illness: A couple's guide to staying connected*. Santa Barbara, CA: ABC-CLIO.

Buehler, S.J. (2016). *What every mental health professional needs to know about sex* (2nd ed.). New York: Springer.

Buehler, S.J. (in press). *Counseling couples before, during, and after pregnancy: Intimacy and sexuality issues*. New York: Springer.

Hertlein, K.M., Weeks, G.R., & Gambescia, N. (2015). *Systemic sex therapy* (2nd ed.). New York: Routledge.

Hipp, L.E., Kane Low, L., & van Anders, S.M. (2012). Exploring women's postpartum sexuality: Social, psychological, relational, and birth-related contextual factors. *Journal of Sexual Medicine, 9*(9), 2330–2341.

Johnson, S. (2017). An emotionally focused approach to sex therapy. In Z.D. Petersen (Ed.), *The Wiley handbook of sex therapy*. Hoboken, NJ: John Wiley & Sons.

Jordan, K., & Fisher, U. (2016). History and future trends. In K. Jordan (Ed.), *Couples, marriage, and family therapy supervision*. New York: Springer.

LeBlanc, A. J., Frost, D. M., & Wight, R. G. (2015). Minority stress and stress proliferation among same-sex and other marginalized couples. *Journal of Marriage and Family, 77*(1), 40–59.

Masters, W. H., & Johnson, V. E. (1986). *Human sexual response*. New York: Bantam.

McCarthy, B. W., & McCarthy, E. (2011). *Discovering your couple sexual style: Sharing desire, pleasure, and satisfaction*. London: Routledge.

Metz, M., & McCarthy, B. (2012). The good enough sex (GES) model: Perspectives and clinical applications. *New Directions in Sex Therapy: Innovations and Alternatives, 2*, 213–230.

Moors, A. C. (2017). Has the American public's interest in information related to relationships beyond "the couple" increased over time? *Journal of Sex Research, 54*(6), 677–684.

Sitron, J. A., & Dyson, D. A. (2012). Validation of sexological worldview: A construct for use in the training of sexologists in sexual diversity. *SAGE Open, 2*(1). https://doi.org/10.1177/2158244012439072

Tyndall, L. E., Hodgson, J. L., Lamson, A. L., White, M., & Knight, S. M. (2012). Medical family therapy: A theoretical and empirical review. *Contemporary Family Therapy, 34*(2), 156–170.

Weeks, G. R. (2013). *Integrating sex and marital therapy: A clinical guide*. New York: Routledge.

7 Supervision Issues With Couples in Nonconsensual Affairs and Infidelity

Tammy Nelson

Abstract

Therapists working with couples and individuals with infidelity issues may need supervision from a clinician with experience and proven interventions. Infidelity presents unique challenges in therapy. The therapist must know how to treat the issue and have a clear plan for each of the three identifiable stages of infidelity recovery. Therapists must also be aware of potential countertransference issues and how to utilize that self-knowledge to enhance the therapeutic relationships as opposed to harming them. Finally, supervisors must work through their own countertransference issues in order to effectively guide their supervisees. The author uses a case study of a couple who has experienced infidelity to illustrate the approach and the supervision of the treating therapist. The supervision is critical to the success of the treatment plan of the therapist. The methodology includes a step-by-step rationale and suggestions for specific questions that should be asked at each level of the intervention: of the client(s), of the therapist/supervisee, and of the supervisor themselves. The result of this particular approach, based on the author's seminal work on the topic, covered in her book The New Monogamy, *is that the therapist and the clients both come to appreciate monogamy on a spectrum. The clients and establish a consciously crafted monogamy agreement to create a new relationship, stronger than prior to the infidelity.*

Keywords

infidelity, affairs, supervision, sex therapy, monogamy, new monogamy, monogamy agreement

Introduction

Infidelity issues are challenging for both supervisors and supervisees. Therapists and clinicians find that countertransference issues are personally difficult and there is a lack of research about how to respond to affairs (Vaughan (2002, 2010). In order to help supervisees help their clients, there needs to be a clear treatment plan with identifiable stages for a path to healing (Solomon, 2006).

There is a spectrum of responses that therapists experience when their clients present with affairs, including pathologizing the infidelity, aligning with the victim, defending the perpetrator, overempathizing the sex positivity in order to help the couple justify the affair, overrelating with the victim because of personal experience, and maintaining a neutral position which creates distancing and clinical withdrawal and/or a superiority in the session (Solomon (2006).

This chapter will include a case example of supervision with supervisees where a couple experience betrayal, and where the supervisee will learn to help the couple either end (I prefer the term "complete") their marriage, end their affair with integrity, or create new monogamy agreements. We will discuss creating new monogamy agreements later in this article.

This chapter will also make intervention suggestions for clinicians to move into erotic recovery and long-term healing where empathy creates passionate monogamous and/or transparently open partnerships. Many new or more traditionally trained practitioners struggle with these new paradigms of looking at affairs not from a victim/perpetrator/rescuer model but as a therapeutic opportunity for growth. Until now there have been few clear models of recovery for couples with direction for measurable outcomes (Fife, Weeks & Gambesica, 2008).

Using the following method, couples can save and restart their marriages through three phases of treatment and a recovery process that avoids shame and retaliation. There are three phases of recovery in affair recovery work: the crisis phase, the insight phase, and the vision phase. Each phase of recovery has its own goals in therapy. The goal of the work in the crisis phase in therapy is to shift from goals focused on away from trauma and intrusive thoughts and a desire for forgiveness and a search for blame to self-care and stabilization. In the insight phase, the goals of therapy are to move from lack of trust to increased insight and awareness, away from power struggles in the relationship to responsibility for one's own actions and empathy toward the partner. In the vision phase of affair recovery, the goal is to focus on erotic recovery and the possibilities for a new relationship with the current partner or an intentional separation.

Being aware of and knowing how to recognize and work through all of these phases consciously is the goal of the supervision.

There Are Three Phases of Recovery After an Affair:

The crisis phase
The insight phase
The vision phase.

The *crisis phase* occurs when there has been disclosure or discovery of an affair and when the couple is in acute distress. Things are chaotic at this point, and therapy should focus on safety and addressing painful feelings. The person who has been cheated on can experience repetitive fantasies of the affair, intrusive thoughts and blame, and anger, and may have self-loathing, low self-esteem, body shame, and guilt. The person who had the affair may have a desire for forgiveness, guilt, shame, or anger; they may blame their partner; they may feel relief that the secret has been exposed; and they may be anxious to either discuss the affair or avoid the conflict.

An affair can be a "wake up" or "break up" time. In the crisis phase, a couple may begin to look at their relationship in a new way, but may not be ready to confront their history or what brought them to this place where the infidelity could occur.

Affairs are defined by three things (Nelson, 2013): the outside relationship, the sexual relationship, and the dishonesty. For each couple, the wounding or the disappointment or the betrayal is dependent on which part of the affair is the most hurtful.

The outside relationship might be an emotional relationship (Glass, 2003), a long-term parallel marriage (Brown, 2013), or an online relationship (Vaughan, 2017). The sexual relationship might be sexual contact with a paid sex worker or an ongoing physically intimate connection. The dishonesty can be lying to the partner directly when confronted, or hiding infidelity under the guise of protecting them from the truth (Spring, 2013).

The *insight phase* begins when the couple stops defining the affair as "her" affair or "his" affair, and uses language in the session that refers to the affair as "our" affair. They begin to report that the infidelity happened to "us." This is the phase of therapy where they can explore the story of *why* the affair happened.

Becoming observers of the affair, the couple is encouraged to begin to tell the story of the history of the relationship. Repeating endless details of sexual indiscretions won't help, but taking a deeper look at what each partner longed for and may not have been getting in the partnership may help them find empathy for one another and begin a deeper level of healing.

The *vision phase* is the final healing stage of affair recovery, where the couple can decide if they want to make the relationship work. In the vision phase, erotic connection can be revived. The meaning of monogamy changes in this phase from a moralistic overall prohibition on sex outside the marriage to a search for deeper intimacy *inside* the marriage. The marriage will have to end in its current version. The couple needs to know that their vision of what they had initially created, their original monogamy agreement, is no longer viable. They have an option now to create a new relationship, a new monogamy, one that works for each of them, if they choose to do so.

If they decide to stay together, the therapist can help create new monogamy agreements, fashioning a broader, more well-defined vision for a new marriage or partnership. A vision of the new relationship can include negotiating a commitment to the future.

Couples' Therapy

After infidelity, couples usually present for therapy in the crisis phase of affair recovery. Their relationship may be unstable, and couples' therapy can be volatile. Inexperienced therapists can feel hopeless and lost without a clear path to recovery. Supervision can help guide them through the phases of recovery which can be complex, giving the supervisee the tools to follow through each stage of recovery.

If clients presenting with infidelity are coming in as a couple, it can be a set up for the therapist to experience what is known as a trauma triangle (L'Abate, 2009). Because there are three people in the room for relationship therapy after an affair, there is potential for the therapist to (consciously or unconsciously) align with the victim, defending their position because they are the ones who have been cheated on. Instead, the goal is for both partners to be heard, to be validated and empathized with. One way to move the focus from the therapist as rescuer is to use the active Imago dialogue process (Hendrix, 1998), as listed below.

If the therapist has experienced their own betrayal, countertransference can be confusing. They may overempathize with the hurt partner. They may feel triggered with hurt and pain or anger. They may see the "perpetrator" or the cheater as being distant or withdrawn or acting superior or entitled. These are all valuable feelings to explore in supervision. They give important information to both the clinician and the supervisor and can help explore important issues in the sessions.

The therapist may also overidentify with the perpetrator, feeling sympathy and an alliance that can create a blind spot in the treatment, removing the therapeutic distance necessary for couples treatment (Garfield, 2004).

One thing supervisees need to know is that all triangulation (Scheinkman, 2005). is temporary. The "perpetrator" will eventually express their own feelings of hurt, neglect, and betrayal. At that time, the therapist may switch alliances, and this can throw off the balance of the setup of the relationship dynamic. If the cheating partner wants to protect the feelings of the hurt partner, they may see the therapist as damaging to the system. And so the triangle of victim/perpetrator/rescuer spins around. Roles may shift during the session and the supervisee must be aware of the role that he/she plays in facilitating dialogue between the couple.

Couples therapy after an affair is also a parallel process to an affair. A parallel process is when therapy becomes a process of reconstructing a similar pattern that is happening in the patient's personal life. Therapy then can deconstruct the pattern and create a new pattern or story by working on a preferred narrative (Zimmerman and Dickerson, 1993). For instance, therapy can recreate the dynamics of an affair with one outside partner and the roles, patterns, and communication styles may repeat unconsciously within the treatment room. This is an important point to discuss in supervision. *What are the roles of each person in the room? The supervisee/therapist? Each partner in the couple?*

There is a professional and a couple in the room. The opportunity is present to work through the issues that created the infidelity and/or continue the patterns of betrayal. Deeply entrenched in each of the client's backgrounds are their emotional needs and their personal psyches, so it makes sense that the therapy can feel like it is a setup for the therapist from the moment the couple walks in the door. Often they are coming in to therapy after they have decided that the relationship has ended and are merely using therapy as means of concluding that they have tried everything to salvage the partnership.

Sometimes supervision includes parameters around whether the affair should end before the treatment can begin. It can be difficult for the therapist to determine if the affair is really over or if it is continuing. A treatment plan should avoid these types of ultimatums. If the therapist threatens the couple by telling them he or she will not continue treatment until any outside affair has ended, the therapist is putting themselves into the relationship in a way that violates the couple's boundaries.

Such a request assumes that the therapist has the power to make that decision for the couple. It also assumes that the person cheating will tell the therapist the truth about ending the affair. This assumption, that the therapist has control over the couple's infidelity, shows inexperience in the therapist, and many new clinicians may fall into this trap.

If a spouse is lying or hiding an affair from their partner, it is likely he/she will hide and lie about it to the therapist as well. If the therapist insists that the partner end the affair, for *them*, they are only perpetuating the dysfunction in the relationship and the "threesome" is now continued in the therapy. What does a client gain from lying in therapy? What can the therapist do to increase the likelihood that clients don't lie?

The therapist can have a conversation with the clients about disclosure and assure them that therapy is a safe place to talk honestly. By its nature, one assumes that the client understands the nature of the therapeutic relationship and that disclosure is in their best interest in order to do the most work in the sessions, but this should not be taken for granted. Some clients will need many sessions before they feel they can trust the therapist to disclose the truth.

Also, if the client is lying to their partner, it is unlikely that a simple assurance that they can now open up in the session to a therapist will not create enough of a safe place for them to disclose ongoing lies.

This can create the continuation of crisis, acted out in the treatment room. Many couples will quit therapy after only a session or two, after failing to establish a safe relationship with the clinician. In supervision, there is a method to discuss cases that can help.

The Four Question Method to Discuss Cases

In supervision, discussing cases is critical in order to avoid the pitfalls of triangulation, and of overidentifying with the clients after infidelity. This is a simple formula that can be used in each phase of infidelity recovery. In the crisis phase of recovery after infidelity, this Four Question Method to Discuss Cases (Nelson, 2008) is helpful in supervision, to focus on the client's needs, and to be objective about the couple and their experience in treatment. It can also provide valuable experiential information that can be used to assess and treat the couple by being aware of countertransference reactions and simplifying the supervisor's role.

There are four questions that supervisees can use to describe a case, and this can be used to process their questions.

Four Question Method to Discuss Cases in Supervision:

One: What problem does the couple present with?
Two: What are they actually there for, in your estimation?
Three: What does it feel like to sit with them in your office?
Four: What is your actual question about this couple?

In Question One, What problem does the couple present with?, the supervisee is asked to make a succinct summary of what the issue is that brought the couple in for therapy. It is not necessary to give a background or history at this time. The client's childhood or familial interactions are secondary to what is happening in the sessions. Because the therapist is seeing them as a couple, all of the interactions are live and present. The session is a mini-version (re-enactment) of the couple's life at home, and all of the drama that happens in an hour or two is representative of what has happened over the course of the relationship.

In the first session, the couple will arrive with a complaint, in this case, a trauma to their relationship: infidelity. The therapist will be fundamentally invested in a positive treatment outcome. This, for many clinicians, may mean saving the relationship or marriage at all costs, or repairing the relationship rift.

This goal could mean the therapist is missing an opportunity to meet clients where they are, in other words, to find empathy for both partners, and avoid the "trauma triangle" of the session.

The victim, perpetrator, and rescuer are common roles in the initial stages of treatment with couples. The therapist may offer a way out of the pain of the crisis for the couple (rescuer), the couple will see him/her as the solution to the pain and confusion of their current relationship issues. The couple will present with the defining problem as a betrayal by one guilty partner (perpetrator) and a resulting emotional betrayal by the other (victim).

If the couple comes in with high-intensity emotion, they may say that their goal is simply to stop the pain. Or they may want to know "why" the affair happened or "why" they or their partner did it. They may want to learn more details about the sexual behavior of their partner.

This may not be the real reason they are in treatment, but a symptom of the crisis phase.

Why Do People Cheat?

An affair can sometimes be a way of expressing a desire for an entirely different self, sometimes separate from a marriage. An affair can be a way to achieve an identity that is not developmentally complete in one's own maturity as an adult.

Some affairs are what I call "a can opener" affair, for partners who are unable to articulate for themselves or unable to remove themselves from the relationship on their own.

Sometimes, an affair is a way to end a relationship. A partner may use an affair to create a crisis in their marriage, to empower themselves to leave, or begin an honest conversation with their spouse about what they feel is lacking in the marriage.

An affair can be a way to "wake up" or "break up."

Sometimes clients in the office will say, "I didn't even know what I wanted until the affair was over and I realized that what I really wanted to do was to end my marriage," or "I had no idea that I used the affair as a way to wake up our relationship."

Cheating can bring up guilt, shame, and fear for both partners and for the therapist (and for the supervisor). [Just a note here: It can be confusing here to add a fourth person to the treatment—a supervisor. But in fact, this is one way to end the triangulation of the three-person couple's therapy. It is important to recognize that any of the countertransference reactions that the therapist being supervised is experiencing the supervisor could and will experience at some point as well. This can be valuable information for the supervision process. If the supervisor has experienced strained or difficult relationships, they may have judgments about the supervisee's handling of a case, or their alignment or values. They may also be less than objective and should discuss this with their peer supervision group and be transparent about it with the supervisee. For example, the lying, hiding and dishonesty that is inherent in an affair can create discomfort or stress in any relationship, include a therapeutic one. Over time this can lead to a stressful life, strained personal and work relationships, insecurity and low self-esteem. This can affect how a therapist works with clients, how they collect fees, how they work with a supervisor and how they are in a supervision group.]

For supervisees who have experienced relationship trauma in their own lives, an affair in the treatment room may trigger judgment and premature evaluation of the client's causal factors.

Fear of Judgment

It can be frightening for the supervisee to wonder how the supervisor will react if they are honest about their own personal life. If they tell the supervisor that they have had or are having an affair, the supervision can quickly devolve into a therapy session. If they do not disclose it, this can be seen as withholding important information and may even be a parallel process to what is happening in the session.

Questions for the Supervisee to Ask Themselves:

Can an affair be a way to keep a marriage together?
Can partners cheat even when their relationship is strong?

How does the supervisee define cheating and how might that belief system play itself out in therapy?

In Question Two, in your estimation, what is presenting issue of the client and why are they coming in to see you at this moment in their relationship?, the supervisee should discuss what they believe the couple is in therapy trying to resolve. Sometimes, for example, an affair can be a "can opener" (see *The New Monogamy* by Tammy Nelson) as stated above, and the couple may have reported that they were in therapy to repair or save their marriage, when in fact, in the therapy it feels like staying married is not a choice.

Perhaps the affair is continuing, or a partner is using the infidelity as a reason to end the relationship. In this case, the real goal in therapy may be to have the clinician facilitate a separation or divorce. Sometimes the therapist is hired to help one or both partners find the language or even the awareness that they want to end their marriage.

The supervisee, in supervision, can explore some ideas about why they believe the couple is in therapy. If they report initially that their positive, measurable treatment outcome is to "save the marriage," but they seem to be moving toward "completing" their marriage, then the therapist is at odds with the goals of treatment and will not be successful, or helpful. In order to discuss it with them directly, the supervisee and supervisor can explore what are the goals they are seeking to accomplish in therapy.

The therapist may be working against the goals of the clients. If the couple wants to end the marriage, but the therapist believes that couples should stay together no matter what, then the treatment may not be therapeutic. Many times one partner wants to work on the relationship while the other partner is ready to end the marriage. This can create confusion in the treatment for the therapist and for the clients.

Committing to a limited number of sessions can help. Asking the clients to commit to a finite number of weeks, anywhere from 3 to 12 weeks, suggesting you all re-evaluate at the end of that time period, gives a container to the therapeutic process (Liberman, 1970).

Some Questions for the Supervisee to Ask Themselves:

Do you think it is possible for a marriage to be more intimate and connected after an affair?
What do you think is a relationship deal breaker?
What can happen in a relationship that can be too damaging to repair?

Probably the most important Question in the Four Question Method is Question Three: What does it feel like to sit with them in your office?

Sitting with people is bound to bring up feelings, emotions, and physical reactions in the body. These can help the therapist to identify countertransference, and thereby insight into the couple's narrative. Using the clinician's countertransference (and avoiding diagnosing), the therapist's self-awareness can be an important tool to assess mood swings, boredom, and hopelessness in a couple.

In supervision, the supervisee can describe what they feel when they are with the couple in several ways:

What I feel in my body. . . .
What I feel in my emotions. . . .
What I am experiencing with them. . . .

The completion of these sentences "stems" gives the supervisor access to information that they would otherwise not be aware. For instance, if a therapist finds themselves nodding off, feeling sleepy, this can be a direct indicator that the couple is not in their feelings. Yes, it may be about the therapist, but it is worth checking out with the couple; are they intellectualizing, are they exploring their emotions or avoiding?

Another example of countertransference: if the therapist feels anxious before a session with a couple, this may not be the clinician's anxiety; it may the couple's anxiety. Therapists can pick up emotions, feelings, attitudes, and are sensitive to experiences which can help with the therapy and the supervision.

In Question Four, What is your actual question about this couple?, the supervisee is asked to come up with one succinct question to focus on in the supervision. It can be helpful to first identify what process the therapist will use to work with the couple. The therapist's question may be determined by one or more of these three constructs:

1. Their experience as a child growing up and personal history
2. Their capacity to determine and distinguish their issues from their clients (countertransference)
3. Their educational and theoretical history regarding couples in dyadic clinical treatment.

Which stage of recovery is this couple currently experiencing? To narrow down the treatment focus, the supervisee can try to identify what phase of recovery the couple is currently experiencing:

The Three Phases of Recovery After An Affair:

The crisis phase
The insight phase
The vision phase.

Crisis: If a couple is in the crisis phase, the supervisee's question may be about safety, medication assessment, housing, children and temporary custody, or whether or not the couple should separate or stay together. These are all decisions that the therapist may have to participate in during the course of treatment, particularly in this first crisis phase.

If the partners are experiencing crisis levels of affect, the therapist should refer out for medication. If the partners are unable to control their rage or are physical with one another, a temporary separation may be necessary and talking about housing should be the priority.

It is a good idea to ask the couple to put divorce or permanent separation on hold for now. No long-term decisions should be made during the crisis phase.

This is not the time to do deep work on attachment issues or trauma bonds. The partner needs to stabilize their emotions, take care of their children, and find a safe place to sleep for the moment.

Insight: Moving out of the crisis phase, the therapist may be discussing more advanced topics with the couple, including erotic recovery. Sex and healing can be more challenging for the therapist in the sessions, since every movement forward in this area can trigger a backslide to the crisis phase.

It is important for the therapist to remind the couple that these backslides into crisis are part of the healing process. Many times having sex can bring them back to the original wounds of the betrayal.

During the insight phase, the most intense psychotherapy work is done, as well as the sex therapy interventions. Discussions about what led to the affair and the stories each partner makes up about what created the environment for the affair to flourish need to be discussed. The couple will need a container, or a dialogue system in order to create a safe space to be heard and to share. Using the dialogues in *Getting the Sex You Want* or *The New Monogamy*, couples can talk in a structured way about creating a new sexual connection, each being heard, validated, and empathized with.

Love Maps

Couples set each other up to create scenarios that match the stories of how they feel about *themselves*. In other words, the stories that they tell themselves are deeply embedded in their psyches. The wounds they experience as adults come from the way they were reared.

It is important during this stage of recovery to begin to guide the couple into discussion around what their family and relational history may have been and how it has contributed to the dysfunction in the marriage that they are currently experiencing.

As the therapist, confronting the couple on what they longed for in their childhood is the goal to go deeper, below what they blame their partner for not giving them. This insight can help the couple move out of blame and into empathy.

For the Therapist to Ask Clients:

In what ways have you been abandoned or neglected throughout your formative years?
What did you long for as a child but not receive?

The answer to these difficult questions can give information about what has helped to form the couple's individual personalities, or "love map" (Money, 1993). The love map is the cathexis that is formed which determines attraction as an adult. Throughout an adult's life, they will move toward pattern recognition that mimics their childhood, both positive and negative. Men and women, gay or straight, will look for certain behaviors in a mate that will heal them from childhood wounds. The partner they choose will also seemingly repeat behaviors they have experienced from caretakers in their childhood (see *Love Maps* and *Getting the Love You Want*). This is the story of their relationship in adulthood, and why it will echo that of childhood.

What Is the Story of the Affair?

The story the couple tells in the insight phase of recovery will be the lens through which they see and judge their partner. They will understand the story of the affair and may revise the meaning and even the history of the whole relationship or marriage in order to fit the beliefs they have, not just about their partners, but about *themselves.*

Discussing the meaning of the story in the session is more important than taking a long sexual history or plotting their childhood background.

Questions to Ask Clients:

What is the story you make up about why the affair happened?
What is the story you make up about what the affair means about you?
About your partner?
About your marriage or relationship?

This then, forms the basis of Question Four, What is the supervisee's real question about this couple?

It does not serve the supervision to ask a vague "Why did one or both partners cheat?" or "How can I help them heal?" but rather to help the supervisee dig deeper, to look at all of these issues: What are the stories that the couple makes up based on their love maps, their personal history, and their childhood wounds? What is the question that will help the supervise to narrow in on a sex therapy intervention or a relationship exercise or a dialogue that can most help the couple?

If the supervisee identifies that the couple is in the **vision** stage of the relationship, there are some specific exercises that can help explore the desires and longings the couple may have and create a new, more connected and passionate relationship going forward.

It will be important that the therapist is comfortable facilitating frank discussions about sex at this stage, and discovering what both partners desire from the relationship. It is possible that one or both of may be curious about having a relationship that is more sexually fluid than a traditionally monogamous relationship, or they may agree that sex only between the two of them will work for both at this point in their marriage. Either way, it is the discussion of this new monogamy agreement that is the most crucial element of the discussion.

In order to have the couple explore all of their options, the supervisee will need to understand what those options are and how they can help the couple to discuss them.

All monogamy is on a continuum, from totally closed to totally open. During the vision phase of recovery, the therapy should move into an explicit discussion exploring where the new relationship will be on the monogamy continuum, at least initially.

Because an affair needs to be repaired in the erotic area, the relationship will need to continue to grow in this area as well. A new monogamy agreement should include a discussion of the couple's expectations around sexuality and what that will look like in the immediate future.

The Couple Will Need to Discuss Their Sexual Relationship

How often will we have sex and what kind of sex and how will we discuss it? What type of discussions will we have around monogamy?

If the therapist is uncomfortable discussing these questions in session, they can give the couple assignments to take home (see References). But in supervision, this reluctance should be explored and the reasons discussed to determine if this is situationally based or an issue that may come up with all clients. The supervisee may want to grow more comfortable talking with the couple about sex, or refer out.

A relationship that has suffered from an affair has had unspoken implicit assumptions, and will benefit from having each partner's expectations about the future of the relationship brought into the open. One way to facilitate more discussion in this phase, and to focus on deeper questions, is to create exercises for the clients.

One simple exercise that can be done in the session is the visioning exercise. And this can be done by the supervisee as well.

The Supervisee Can Answer the Following:

What is my vision for this couple? _____
My fears:
My worries:
My desires:

The Partners Can Do This Exercise in the Session, Or As a Take-Home Dialogue

What is my vision for us as a couple? _____
My fears:
My worries:
My desires:

Case Study

Lydia and Frank

Lydia and her husband, Frank, had been married for 15 years. Frank discovered that Lydia had been having an affair. They came into therapy and he reported that he felt hurt, and hopeless about their marriage.

In the first session with Dr. Sarah, a mature therapist who had a specialization in sex therapy, Lydia reported that she wanted to focus on their sex life and a vision of a better future together. Dr. Sarah had been trained in some affair recovery, but research in this area was somewhat dated, and she knew that she would need to use supervision to stay on top of this complex case.

Dr. Sarah found out in the session that Frank had been reading Lydia's emails between Lydia and her outside boyfriend and he had read that not only was Lydia sleeping with Frank, she had been having group sex with him, and they had been to sex clubs together. He was devastated.

In therapy, Dr. Sarah determined that they were in the crisis phase. She asked if they needed to decide where to live, they said they would stay together but needed to negotiate if they were sleeping in the same bed.

Dr. Sarah had her first supervision session with Dr. Smith. Dr. Smith suggested that she remind the couple not to make any decisions about divorce or long-term commitment at this time.

In the next few therapy sessions, Lydia and Frank wanted to know how to create new boundaries around their relationship and determine the differences between privacy and secrecy for their relationship.

Dr. Sarah came back to supervision for several more sessions when she found herself struggling with the couple's insight phase of recovery. They had explained in detail in the couple's session that they had always enjoyed sex together throughout their marriage. There was nothing they could not discuss. There were, in fact, still having sex three to four times a week. However, reading the details of Lydia's affair online had devastated Frank because he felt that there was nothing missing or wrong in his marriage to Lydia until he found out she had fantasies of kinky sex, group sex, and sex clubs. Now the stories he made up were that he had wrongly believed in the past that their sex life was perfect. He thought that they loved each other. But now he wasn't sure.

Dr. Smith asked Dr. Sarah in supervision to discuss her history, training, and beliefs about affairs, what she thought about marriage and infidelity and what she thought the couple was presenting for (Question One in the Four Question Method).

Dr. Sarah said that she had been taught in her training as a graduate student that marriages were only at risk of affairs if there was a fundamental crack in the foundation of the relationship, or if the marriage was sexless, or one partner had little or no desire for the other.

Dr. Smith and Dr. Sarah talked about how this might affect her treatment strategy. If the couple could sense that Dr. Sarah believed the marriage was fundamentally flawed, it was possible that they could rewrite the whole history of their marriage to align with Dr. Sarah's beliefs.

Dr. Smith told her to look out for statements from them that sounded like,

> "We never should have married," or "We have never been happy," or "She always . . ." or "He always . . ."

When couples used "always" or "never" in a session, they were many times projecting, Dr. Smith said. In the supervision, Dr. Sarah said she thought the couple wanted to stay together, no matter what. Dr. Smith asked her if she felt that was the real reason they were in treatment, to stay together.

Dr. Sarah said she could sense that Lydia was still deciding whether she should give up the affair. When asked how her sex life with Frank was, Dr. Sarah had said "It is lovely." Dr. Nelson asked her to have Sarah explore this story, to see if "lovely" was satisfactory for her and for her partner.

Dr. Smith asked Dr. Sarah what she felt in her body when she sat with the couple. Dr. Sarah reported she felt anxious, restless, and "like she wanted to get up and run out the door" during the session. Dr. Smith asked Dr. Sarah if she thought that was because of the couple, or her own countertransference, or something more personal. Dr. Sarah said,

> "I think that is how Lydia is feeling. She always has one foot pointed toward the door, she sits on the edge of the couch. She makes me nervous."

Dr. Smith suggested Dr. Sarah use this information in the session. When Dr. Sarah met again with the couple, she asked Lydia about her posture. Lydia said,

> "Yes, I feel like I want to escape. This is very difficult."

Dr. Sarah asked Lydia if she was willing to go deeper and explore this in the therapy. Lydia agreed she would explore her childhood story. Dr. Sarah asked her what she had wanted to escape in her childhood. Lydia cried and said,

> "I couldn't wait to get out of my house. It was awful, my father was drunk and bossy and I was always running out at night to escape. I would literally run down the road to hide from him."

In the next supervision session, Dr. Smith asked Dr. Sarah to refine her questions to one question she had, or something she was struggling with regarding the couple. Dr. Sarah reported that the couple loved each other and felt there was too much to lose to get divorced and to end it now.

Dr. Sarah admitted that she had her own personal history with infidelity, and she actually doubted that Lydia could really love Frank if she had cheated on him. Dr. Smith asked Dr. Sarah what she meant. Dr. Sarah said,

> "Perhaps Lydia is just using therapy a safe space to *confess*."

Dr. Smith pointed out that Lydia had just used supervision as a place to confess her own infidelity. Perhaps there was a parallel process happening in therapy and in supervision, or she was projecting her needs onto the client.

Dr. Smith asked Dr. Sarah what stage the couple was in, currently. Dr. Sarah said definitely they were still in stage two. They had begun to tell the story of the affair and what had led to it. Dr. Nelson asked Dr. Sarah what she felt in her body when she was with the couple. Dr. Sarah said,

> "I feel tense. I feel like there are hidden things we are not discussing. I feel drawn to Frank, and resistant to Lydia."

Dr. Smith asked her what the feelings in her body told her.

Dr. Sarah said she felt a tightness in her chest, like her heart was hurting. She said that indicated to her that there was hurt. She said,

> "Lydia did not confess before she was caught." She wondered, "What was the point of keeping the secret? Maybe it is the dishonesty that is the thing that has damaged the relationship, not the sex."

Dr. Smith asked Dr. Sarah what was getting triggered for her about this idea of "confession."

She said, "When you do something wrong, you should confess. Forgiveness comes with confession."

Dr. Smith asked, "Any chance that feeling comes from a religious background of your own?"

Dr. Sarah said she had been brought up Catholic as a child but had long ago given up church or confession for herself.

Dr. Smith said it made sense that Dr. Sarah would feel that sex and affairs should be handled with integrity. Dr. Smith told her that people cheat for a variety of reasons. Dr. Smith asked Dr. Sarah to examine the stories she was telling herself around why this couple had cheated.

She asked her to think about the following:

What is the story you make up about why they cheated?
What is the work this couple needs to do on their relationship?
Can this marriage be saved, and should it?

After several more supervision sessions, Dr. Sarah said she was able to discuss the vision of what they both wanted sexually in their future. Dr. Sarah could honor both of their voices, and taught them to mirror (the process of accurately reflecting a message sent by the partner; see Imago dialogue process below), empathize, and validate (reflecting or imagining the feelings of the receiver; see Imago dialogue process below). Dr. Sarah said that she could see the affair from both sides now, and that she was helping the couple to do the same.

Getting to know the couple during these sessions, Dr. Sarah could see that the affair may have been a way for this couple to "wake up" their marriage. They had been having sex but not talking about fantasies or changing the way they had sex for over 15 years. Resentment had built up over the years. There was no guilt or pressure in the sessions, and that allowed Dr. Sarah to continue without pressuring the couple or creating guilt or shame for them around their sexuality.

Dr. Smith and Dr. Sarah reviewed the three phases of affair recovery. It seemed the couple was ready to review a new monogamy agreement, and Dr. Sarah referred them to the books, *The New Monogamy*, *State of Affairs*, and *After the Affair*. They continued to explore their sexual agreements, and Dr. Sarah continued to explore her own story around her projections.

Confronting Values

Every therapist needs to confront their own hidden countertransference and prejudices, their sexism and stereotypes, before they work with individuals and couples.

Some of the **things that supervisees should consider** during affair recovery supervision:

> *What does it mean to be a therapist—how do your background, beliefs and prejudices affect your ability to work with couples and individuals recovering from infidelity?*

Some Questions for the Supervisor to Ask Themselves:

Why did you choose to become a therapist?
How did your family value monogamy?
What do you feel about your own marriage or relationship?

Questions for the Supervisee To Ask Themselves:

Do you push clients, give them advice, or collude with them?
How much should you reveal about yourself?
Do you share about your own affair, infidelity, relational betrayal, or secrets?

Even though our ideas about sex and sexuality have greatly advanced over the last half century, our culture still holds a pathological idea about infidelity. An affair can be a way of expressing a desire for an entirely different self—either separate or remain in the marriage or relationship.

Many infidelity treatment approaches today are based on the idea that the unfaithful spouse is a perpetrator—someone who wronged the other. While the pain caused by infidelity cannot and should not be denied, what is generally not understood is that many people cheat because they struggle with their individual identity in their own lives and lack of empowerment in their relationship.

An affair makes up to some extent for a lack of adult development. For some, understanding that an affair as an unconscious bid for attention, a desire for self-worth, search for intimacy, or a response to feeling stuck is important in understanding how to have a more mature, connected relationship and a fuller, more mature adulthood.

Supervision can help therapists move toward a greater understanding and healing for all involved.

Addendum

One way to create a safe dialogue process after an affair is to use the Imago dialogue process.

The dialogue process uses mirroring, validation, and empathy.

Mirroring: The process of accurately reflecting a message sent by the partner (Sender). It requires the listener (Receiver) to be fully present. It indicates to the partner that you are willing to hold your own reactivity for the moment and attempt to understand the dialogue from their point of view.

Validation: A communication to the Receiver that the information being received and mirrored "makes sense." It indicates that your partner's point of view has validity—it is true for the Receiver. It is a way to let your partner know that their subjective experience is not crazy, it has its own logic and is a valid way of looking at things. It may include an understanding of your partner's childhood wounds.

Empathy: The process of reflecting or imagining the feelings of the receiver. Being able to understand the feelings that the other is experiencing about the event or situation. This deep connection helps both partners to experience the other's emotions. Empathy allows both partners to meet on common ground.

Adapted from Harville Hendrix, *Getting the Love You Want*, and Hedy Schleifer.
Dialogue Sentence Stems:

- What I need from you when I tell you my feelings:
  - Mirror
- What scares me most:
  - Mirror
- What I really want to know:
  - Mirror
- What I cannot stop thinking about:
  - Mirror
- What I want you to know about me right now:
  - Mirror
- What I need each day going forward:
  - Mirror

About the Author

Tammy Nelson, Ph.D., is a licensed psychotherapist in private practice, a relationship expert and international speaker, an author, a faculty member and teacher with a Doctorate in Philosophy in Clinical Sexology. She is a Board Certified Sexologist, a Diplomate of the American Board of Sexologists, a Licensed Professional Counselor, an AASECT Certified Sex Therapist, a Registered Art Therapist, a Licensed Alcohol and Drug Counselor, a Certified Imago Relationship Therapist, and an Advanced Imago Clinician.

References

Brown, E. (2013). *Patterns of infidelity and their treatment.* London: Routledge.

Fife, S. T., Weeks, G. R., & Gambescia, N. (2008). Treating infidelity: An integrative approach *Family Journal, 16*(4), 316–323.

Garfield, R. (2004). The therapeutic alliance in couples therapy: Clinical considerations. *Family Process, 43,* 457–465. https://doi.org/10.1111/j.1545-5300.2004.00034.x

Glass, S. (2003). *Not just friends.* New York: Free Press.

Hendrix, H. (1998). *Getting the love you want.* New York: Henry Holt.

L'Abate, L. (2009). The drama triangle: An attempt to resurrect a neglected pathogenic model in family therapy theory and practice. *American Journal of Family Therapy, 37*(1), 1–11.

Liberman, R. (1970). Behavioral approaches to family and couple therapy. *American Journal of Orthopsychiatry, 40*(1), 106–118.

Money, J. (1993). *Lovemaps: Clinical concepts of sexual/erotic health & pathology, paraphilia, & gender transposition in childhood, adolescence and maturity.* New York: Prometheus.

Nelson, T. (2008). *Getting the sex you want; shed your inhibitions and reach new heights of passion together.* Beverly, MA: Fair Winds Press.

Nelson, T. (2013). *The new monogamy; redefining your relationship after infidelity.* Oakland, CA: New Harbinger.

Scheinkman, M. (2005). Beyond the trauma of betrayal: Reconsidering affairs in couples therapy. *Family Process, 44,* 227–244. https://doi.org/10.1111/j.1545-5300.2005.00056.x

Solomon, S., & Teagno, L. (2006). *Intimacy after infidelity: How to rebuild and affair-proof your marriage.* Oakland, CA: New Harbinger Press.

Spring, J. (2013). *After the affair, updated second edition: Healing the pain and rebuilding trust when a partner has been unfaithful.* New York: HarperCollins.

Vaughan, P. (2002/2010). *Help for therapists (and their clients) in dealing with affairs.* San Diego, CA: Dialog Press.

Vaughan, P. (2017). Retrieved from www.dearpeggy.com/2-affairs/com010.html

Zimmerman, J. L., & Dickerson, V. C. (1993). Separating couples from restraining patterns and the relationship discourse that supports them. *Journal of Marital and Family Therapy, 19,* 403–413. https://doi.org/10.1111/j.1752-0606.1993.tb01002.x

8 A Sex Therapist Is a Person Too

Attending to Countertransference in Sex Therapy Supervision

Katherine Ellin

Abstract

Countertransference is ubiquitous in psychotherapy, and clinical supervision is the field's primary tool for teaching clinicians to effectively deal with it. In sex therapy, countertransference can be especially challenging, both to deal with and to discuss. This chapter examines the role of clinical supervision in helping therapists deal optimally with countertransference in sex therapy with individuals and couples. Different kinds of countertransference that are likely to arise in sex therapy are explored, and examples of working in supervision to address a range of countertransference experiences are presented.

Keywords

countertransference, supervision, sex therapy, erotic transference

Introduction

Countertransference is ubiquitous. Every therapist experiences it. Yet it is hard to define and even harder to effectively deal with. Talking about sex inevitably takes therapy to the tender places quickly. In sex therapy, we often speak with our clients about what may have felt unspeakable or unaskable. We enter a private sphere with an individual or couple. And in that private, vulnerable, intimate space, intense feelings that are messy and complex inevitably emerge for everyone in the office, including the therapist. Managing those subjective experiences is key to a positive therapeutic outcome. Clinical supervision is an essential vehicle for learning how to effectively use countertransference to enhance the therapy rather than to interfere with and impede it (Agass, 2010; Aponte, 1994, 2009; Bean, 2014; Falender & Shafranske, 2004; Gehlert, 2014; Guiffriday, 2015). This chapter focuses on the crucial role of clinical supervision in helping sex therapists learn several strategies to address countertransference. In addition, it offers practical guidance for supervisors to effectively address countertransference with sex therapy supervisees.

Definition

Definitions of countertransference vary considerably. Different theoretical orientations understand and explain the concept of countertransference in a variety of ways. Countertransference was initially identified by Freud (1957) as a phenomenon that occurred when the therapist's own unexamined and unresolved conflicts contributed to problematic reactions in the therapy. Since then, perspectives on countertransference have expanded. Heimann (1950) suggested that countertransference refers to all the feelings the therapist has towards the client, and that it can be used to increase understanding in order to improve the therapy. Recently, in therapeutic models that emphasize the intersubjective nature of interaction, there is the recognition that counter-transference and transference are mutually constructed phenomena that client and therapist create together, and therefore countertransference is an essential tool for the therapist that, when used well, is likely to have a profound effect on the success of the therapy (Beebe & Lachman, 2002; Beebe, Knoblauch, Rustin, & Sorter, 2005; Ehrenberg, 1992; Gelso & Hayes, 2007; Langs, 1982; Searles, 1986; Stern, 1985; Stolorow & Atwood, 1992).

For the purpose of discussing countertransference in sex therapy supervision, this chapter is grounded in the broadest, most comprehensive understanding of this phenomenon: the therapist's experience of being in the therapy room with the client. In this perspective, countertransference encompasses the therapist's entire subjective experience that emerges as a result of interaction with the client, including feelings, thoughts, and somatic reactions. It can be conscious or unconscious. It can be a deeply felt experience or a small sense of something. Sometimes, as Freud (1957) suggested, it is a result of an unresolved or unexamined conflict. It may also be related to the respective cultural backgrounds of the therapist and the client, to identity issues, to family background, or to personal circumstances in the moment. In other words, countertransference is just who a therapist is as a person in interaction with who a client is as a person.

Importance of Addressing Countertransference in Sex Therapy Supervision

In and of itself, countertransference is neither bad nor good. It is simply a fact. All therapists experience it and all contend with it. It is what we do with it that matters. Countertransference that remains out of awareness, or that is poorly managed, is likely to interfere in the therapy and can even cause damage to the client or the therapeutic process. At its worst, it can lead to ethical boundary crossing and violations, including sexual activity with clients (Pope, Sonne, & Greene, 2006). Used well, however, countertransference can provide us with important and useful information about our clients, information that can be leveraged as a powerful and enormously effective therapeutic force (Baum, 1969–70; Ehrenberg, 1992; Tauber, 1979; Gelso & Hayes, 2007; Grossman, 1965; Heimann, 1950). Often, the client's most salient issues are discovered through countertransference. The therapist's unconscious experience reflects something about the client's experience that may not have been made explicit (Heimann, 1950). For this important information to reflect something meaningful about the client, we must be sure that it is not distorted by the therapist's personal issues. While this is true in all forms of therapy, therapy that focuses on sex can be uniquely difficult. Speaking about sexuality can accelerate and complicate transference and countertransference reactions. It can elicit primal issues that the sex therapist may not have noticed, understood, or fully resolved within him/herself (Celenza, 2010; Pope, 2000). This means that sex therapists need to be even more exquisitely attuned to their own somatic, cognitive, and emotional experience in interactions with clients, in order to do good, effective sex therapy. They also need to develop skills for articulating their thoughts, feelings, and behaviors.

Clinical supervision is an important component of a sex therapist's training. It is our field's primary method of teaching how to actually practice therapy. The sex therapist learns about sexuality, effective therapeutic approaches, strategies, and techniques through specific readings and courses. But it is in clinical supervision that the conscious and deliberate use of self is delineated and refined. Supervision is the context in which the intersection of personal and professional dwells, which means it is the space in which the sex therapist can engage fully in learning to use who they are as a person in their role as a therapist. Supervision can be specifically targeted to focus on countertransference. Supervision can be intentionally designed to improve and enhance the therapist's capacity to notice, examine, and effectively use countertransference (Aponte, 2016). While seasoned therapists may be more tuned into their own internal reactions and patterns, reflecting on possible countertransferential issues remains a crucial aspect of providing good and effective sex therapy. Early career sex therapists may require more help from the supervisor in identifying and noticing possible countertransference reactions. They may need additional guidance to learn how to reflect on and understand their inner experience. Then, most importantly, they need to develop approaches to use what is learned from the countertransference in ways that are beneficial for the therapy. Being a good, effective sex therapist requires a disciplined openness to perceiving all that the client brings to the therapeutic encounter. This requires allowing for uncertainty, inviting complexity, and being clear and spacious enough of mind and body to notice what exists in the moment. It requires putting aside the personal, and holding space for all that the client is as a person and all that they carry with them. Maintaining this level of self-awareness and spaciousness of self is hard to do in an ongoing and consistent way. Clinical supervision is where sex therapists can take the time and space to explore and generate purposeful and effective ways to use their countertransference reactions to benefit the client. Attending to countertransference in clinical supervision is integral to developing the disciplined and rigorous use of self, and the constructive use of countertransference that is so important to advancing sound therapeutic work.

Discerning what aspects of the subjective experience belong to the therapist and what is actually about the client is essential, and clinical supervision is where this process can be learned and practiced. This is not an easy task, so it is important for sex therapy supervisors to directly address countertransference with supervisees (Aponte, 2016). Since sex is potentially a highly charged issue, it is crucial for sex therapists to be able to speak openly in supervision in an effort to cultivate an acute awareness of their own countertransferential experience in sessions. Cultivating the capacity to bring to awareness what is going on internally during a therapy session and learning what to do with that personal experience is key to becoming a good, effective sex therapist. It is not easy to be fully aware of one's feelings, especially when those feelings seem wrong to feel. It is incredibly difficult to speak about feelings that are deeply personal, raw, or are not in line with what seems appropriate. Yet, this is exactly what a sex therapist must do.

We know that much of what happens in human interaction is nonverbal and occurs out of awareness. It is no different in psychotherapy. Therefore, the therapist's nonverbal communication is of extreme significance (Bernstein, 1979, 1984; Chace, 1975; Lichtenberg, 1983; van der Kolk, 2014). When therapy is focused on sex, the communication of bodies in the therapy room can be uniquely potent. Since much of who and how people are sexually and relationally developed in the context of nonverbal early relationships, and, for the most part, occurs outside of awareness, creating change in the here and now through implicit communication can be a powerful therapeutic tool (Beebe & Lachmann, 2002; Karen, 1994; Stern, 1985; Slade, 2002, 2003; Slade & Holmes, 2013; Tobias, 1995). Using facial expression, gaze, gesture, tone of voice, posture, movement, and other nonverbal communication in disciplined, purposeful ways in sex therapy can create change on an implicit level (Beebe & Lachmann, 2002, 2005; Chace, 1975; Ogden, 2008; Robbins, 1986; Siegel, 1984; van der Kolk, 2014). For therapists to cultivate this capacity to interact on a body level, along with the ongoing verbal communication, they must be keenly sensitive to their own internal experience. Countertransference must be carefully monitored in order to use nonverbal communication as a change agent in sex therapy.

While the full subjective experience of the sex therapist is important to consider in sex therapy supervision, it is often the highly charged reactions that are difficult to deal with that need special attention. The most emotionally activating and potentially damaging countertransferential reactions can be related to traditionally taboo topics, including sex (Celenza, 2010; Pope et al., 2006). Bringing these countertransference reactions into awareness and then discussing them openly in supervision can be deeply distressing. It can elicit a flood of unacceptable thoughts and feelings in a therapist. The astonishing, wonderful, and surprisingly fabulous thing about this is that, often, it is in the therapist's genuine struggle in response to a client that the deepest understanding and the most profound opportunity for positive change can be discovered.

Supervisory Issues in Addressing Countertransference

In supervision that successfully addresses countertransference, the supervisor does the following: (a) establishes safety and clarifies shared expectations; (b) serves as a nonreactive presence in the face of the supervisee's anxiety and dis-comfort; (c) normalizes countertransference; (d) emphasizes the importance of countertransference; (e) helps the sex therapy supervisee notice signs of countertransference; (f) promotes, guides, and supports self-exploration; and ultimately (g) helps the sex therapist find ways to manage the countertransfer-ence so that it advances rather than interferes with the therapy.

Safety

Effective clinical supervision for all types of therapy relies on a foundation of basic safety and trust (Agass, 2010: Aponte, 1994; Bean, 2014; Falender & Shafranske, 2004; Gehlert, 2014). Generating and maintaining a safe, accepting atmosphere is key to promoting honest self-reflection. For sex therapy supervi-sees to make the most use of supervision, the supervisor needs to create condi-tions that promote genuine self-exploration. Supervisors need to cultivate the sense that supervision is a judgment-free zone, which often means focusing on shame reduction for the supervisee. It is the supervisor's responsibility to create the context in which the therapist can speak about all their feelings, including those that feel threatening to think about. This is not always easy to do, espe-cially when supervisees have concerns about being evaluated. There are many ways to cultivate an accepting and safe supervisory space, and supervisors do this in a variety of ways. Notably, this is an instance in which the supervisor's use of self is conspicuous. Supervisors need to be worthy of trust, which includes being knowledgeable, predictable, reliable, benevolent, humble, compassionate, sensi-tive, consistent, honest, effective, warm, collaborative, and clear.

Recognizing the inherent difficulty of speaking candidly about counter-transference is a key element for creating the necessary safety to successfully address these issues in supervision. It can be difficult for a supervisee to speak openly about many countertransference reactions. Some of the most diffi-cult topics that supervisees struggle with include feelings related to perceived flaws, competence and incompetence, and therapeutic mistakes. A therapist may have enormous difficulty speaking about issues that threaten their sense of self. When the feelings go against the clinician's idealized image of a therapist or when feelings emerge that are not in line with how they view themselves, saying it out loud to another person can be harrowing. It can be painful for a therapist to admit, even to themselves, let alone a supervisor, that they despise or even hate a client, have unwanted biases related to race and ethnicity, dis-ability, religion, and other controversial reactions (e.g., being attracted to a client). Even more so, supervisees are understandably reticent to speak about feelings that violate societal taboos. It may be hardest to talk about emotions when it feels wrong to feel what they feel. It can be frightening partly because of some confusion between thoughts and actions (Pope et al., 2006). Indeed, differentiating between thought and action, such as feeling sexually attracted to a client and actually having sex with a client, is a crucial distinction. It can be reassuring for the supervisee to remember that thoughts and feelings *are actually* facts, no matter how irrational or unwanted they may be, and that it is through speaking about these irrational facts that they can be digested and dealt with in positive and productive ways.

Supervisors may also create safety through normalizing and serving as a nonreactive presence. It can be reassuring and freeing to remind the supervisee of the basic humanity of us all, therapists included, and to convey to the supervisee that it is human to have a wide range of feelings, not all of them nice and pretty. It is "normal" to experience a complicated mess of emotions as a therapist (Aponte, 2016). Another approach is to emphasize to the supervisee that therapy is a practice, a work in progress. And we practice and practice, with the knowledge that we are imperfect and that our emotional wounds and idiosyncratic ways of seeing the world can insert themselves into our work. Fortunately, we have the gift of clinical supervision, a time and place to make sense of it all so we can help our client as much as possible. That is the practice of doing therapy. Another valuable means to create safety is to encourage the supervisee to allow for uncertainty, and to view mistakes as cherished learning opportunities. Supervision must be a confidential space, in which it is okay for the supervisee to dare to "not know," so mistakes can be discussed openly, with the goal of effectively recovering from them with the client and learning from them for future clinical work. In order to create this safe container for a supervisee, supervisors work to meet the supervisee where they are in their professional development, and maintain a nonjudgmental and positive frame for the supervisee. Using self-disclosure in a thoughtful way also can be an extremely useful technique for reducing shame and creating safety. Making the power differential explicit and discussing the facts about it are important. As in therapy, being a nonreactive presence using both words and body language, in the face of anxiety contributes to cultivating a safe space for discussing whatever thoughts and feelings the supervisee is experiencing.

Expectations

In addition to creating a safe container as soon as possible in supervision, it is useful to explain early the importance of talking about countertransference. Setting expectations that this will be a crucial component of the supervision creates clarity and allows the supervisee to bring up issues more easily. When the supervisee understands the reasons for speaking openly about personal feelings, it increases motivation to do so. Understanding that the therapist's self is the primary tool of therapy, and that countertransference provides information that allows the therapist to better understand and help the client, creates context for having countertransference-focused explorations in supervision. Supervisees need to understand that for therapists to be effective, they must have access to the full range of countertransference responses, including and perhaps especially, for sex therapists, countertransference responses related to erotic and sexual feelings and gender issues. It is also worth emphasizing early on the dramatic difference between thought and behavior. Having a thought or feeling about hurting someone is not the same as hurting them, and having a thought or feeling about kissing someone is not the same as kissing them. Not speaking about the feelings that are hardest to talk about can lead to the behaviors that actually do cross a boundary. In contrast, talking about the messy feelings can prevent thoughts from becoming action (Pope et al., 2006). This is unquestionably tremendously important.

Creating safety and shared expectations is an ongoing process in sex therapy supervision, and as new issues arise, doing what is necessary to help the supervisee trust and feel emotionally safe is essential in exploring emergent countertransference issues. The supervisor continues to hold space and to make space for the supervisee's countertransference.

Notice and Name

Noticing, naming, and understanding countertransferential emotions, thoughts, attitudes, and behaviors in supervision form the core process for effectively handling countertransference. In the context of an emotionally safe supervisory container, the supervisor helps the sex therapist identify, explore, and productively use the countertransference material.

Noticing the countertransference is the first and, frequently, the most difficult task. Finding ways to invite the experience into the room is often the supervisor's main challenge. The therapist may communicate countertransference issues directly or indirectly to the supervisor. Supervisors learn about the presence of countertransference through the supervisee's self-report, their description of the therapy, their behavior in supervision, and parallel process.

Some therapists are sensitively attuned to their own internal reactions and patterns and can reflect on possible countertransferential issues. When the supervisee is aware of their feelings with clients, they may speak about dreading a session, or feeling distracted or bored with a particular client, or having voyeuristic urges. For example, in speaking about a case in which she felt stuck, a therapist noted that she felt bored in sessions, and during supervision she became aware that she was not remembering much about this particular client, which was unusual for her. Once she recognized this, she remembered that the client had a trauma history that had not been part of the therapy, and she wondered if she was experiencing the client's defensive "forgetting" about this experience, and the emotional shutdown that can make a person feel emotionally dull and "stuck." This sex therapist used supervision to notice, name, and explore her countertransference in an open, fluid way, without help from the supervisor. She discussed with the supervisor ways to use this new insight about the client and the therapy, and developed some ideas that could potentially deepen and enliven the therapeutic process.

At other times, the therapist is not consciously aware of the reaction they are having, but will demonstrate it in the supervision. Just as in therapy, supervising requires careful attention to the spoken and unspoken. When a therapist does not explicitly raise countertransference issues, supervisors must be attuned to clues, which can communicate useful information to the supervisor and supervisee about countertransference issues. There are some common reactions indicating the presence of countertransference in supervision. A supervisee might talk about a client with a different tone of voice or a peculiar vagueness or unusual intensity in the telling. In this case, the supervisor observes and shares observation with the supervisee. For example, "I notice that when you talk about this couple, you seem bored with them. It's not usual for you. What's it like to be with them?" Another valuable clue is the therapist's nonverbal behavior. A therapist might use unique body language when they speak about a particular client. For example, in one of the case examples that follows, a supervisee exhibited obvious flirting nonverbal behaviors while speaking about a client. This allowed for the beginning of an important exploration of her attraction to her client. Another indication that countertransference is at play is when a therapist describes to the supervisor behaviors that are outside their usual therapeutic frame. This might include unusual amounts or kinds of self-disclosure, or extending sessions. One supervisee found himself sharing significantly more personal information with a client with a history of childhood sexual trauma. He believed he was doing it so that the client would feel she knew her therapist well enough as a person to trust him. Paying close attention to what and when he disclosed, the therapist realized that, while this was true, he also was achingly aware of the client's professional accomplishments, the financial and business success that the therapist's family had always wanted for him, a path he rejected by becoming a therapist. This realization allowed the therapist to differentiate between self-disclosure that allowed the client to feel she knew the therapist as a person well enough to trust him, and self-disclosure that was for the therapist to feel admired by this client for his own benefit.

Another indicator of countertransference might be consistent themes with several clients. In this situation, the descriptions of different clients sound surprisingly similar to one another, which might reflect a particular lens through which the therapist tends to see their clients. One supervisee consistently described the male partner in heterosexual couples as "clueless and useless." The repetitive and persistent descriptions of heterosexual couples as "she's great, but he's useless" alerted the supervisor that this could be countertransference. This eventually emerged as a personal theme from the supervisee's own early life with an incompetent, weak father and a competent, overfunctioning mother. Understanding that she was likely to see couples in this way helped her begin to clear this aside in order to have a less obstructed view of the couples she worked with. It is extremely important for the therapist to become aware of the lens through which they see a couple or an individual. Our lives have shaped us, and inevitably the therapist, who is also a person, perceives the world through a particular lens. This perception is further colored by the unique interpretation or way of understanding what is seen. Recognizing and attending to this is crucial to one's work as a therapist.

Of course, supervision itself is a relational experience prone to countertransference and transference reactions. Therefore, another indicator of possible countertransference is the supervisor's subjective experience of the therapist and in the parallel process that can occur in supervision.

Explore and Do Good

Once the therapist and supervisor together notice and name a particular subjective experience, the supervisor supports and guides the therapist in an exploration of this countertransference. In the exploration process, the supervisor continues to create and maintain emotional safety for the supervisee. Remembering that it can be extremely anxiety provoking for a therapist to speak openly and candidly about countertransference, the supervisor works to find a balance of support and curiosity that allows the therapist to self-reflect on potentially sensitive countertransference experiences. The supervisor continues to remind the supervisee that there is no such thing as an unbiased therapist, and that the important thing is to be aware of one's own judgments and the impact they have on therapy. While continuing to emphasize the fact that everyone has unresolved personal issues, the supervisor initiates conversations that spark genuine curiosity in the supervisee about what might color their perception and approach as a therapist with this client.

As part of the effort to optimally deal with countertransference, it is important for the supervisor to assess the supervisee's capacity for self-awareness and for speaking about these issues in supervision. The supervisor must develop an understanding of the ways in which the therapist manages intense feelings, including anxiety about having the feelings, as well as the therapist's capacity to step back from their own subjective experience in order to think clearly enough about the client to generate a reasonable formulation about the individual or couple in their office. The supervisor provides support in developing these capacities so that exploring countertransference becomes easier and more automatic for the therapist.

Once the countertransference has been noticed and described, supervision provides the time, space and structure for the supervisee to reflect: What am I feeing? What contributes to this feeling? What part of this is the client? What part of this is me—my personal history, my current life situation, my biases? And, most importantly, how can I use this information to benefit the therapy? What can I do with this subjective experience of mine to benefit the therapy and do no harm? In addition, the supervisor can encourage the sex therapist to examine what this countertransferential experience reveals about who they are as a therapist, and how they can best use their natural tendencies in clinical work.

How to Ask?

Examining and working to understand countertransference can feel threatening. To counteract this threat, the supervisor asks questions that invite curiosity and exploration in a safe, nonjudgmental atmosphere. Questions are powerful and can shape the answer. Therefore, supervisors, like therapists, must ask questions carefully and thoughtfully. A supervisor can ask about specific interventions: How did you choose that intervention at that moment?

What went into your decision to say that at that time? A supervisor can ask about the overall experience: What is it like to be with the client? What is it like for you to talk with me about the client? Do you have a sense of the client's thoughts and feelings about you? A supervisor can help the therapist tune into their somatic experience, which often reflects the not yet explicit experience: What do you notice in your body when you are with the client? What are you noticing in your body when you tell me about the client? A supervisor can ask about feelings of wanting to be more connected or more distant from client. A supervisor can ask about feelings, including impatience, frustration, anger, disgust, envy, love, attraction, or excitement. The goal of the questions is to spark curiosity and interest in the supervisee so that the exploration becomes increasingly led by the supervisee.

In sex therapy, it is enormously important to have competence around the vast diversity of sexual expression (Nichols, 2006). Especially for new sex therapists who may have intense responses to the range of sexual interests and activities they are hearing about, it is vital to closely monitor and discuss whatever emerges for them. Helping them to notice their visceral, automatic, not fully conscious reactions is critical. When hearing about sexual activities or interests that are new to them, a therapist might experience discomfort, arousal, shock, fear, disgust, interest, curiosity, envy, and more. As with any countertransferential experience, intense internal responses might lead them to behave in detrimental ways in the therapy. Typical reactions include over- or underfocus on certain issues, withdrawal or overinvolvement, and especially unconscious nonverbal communications.

Our bodies do not lie, and we have less awareness and less control over our bodies than our words. The verbal component of therapist behavior is easier to manage, but in situations that evoke intense visceral reactions, therapists often display subtle physical, nonverbal alterations in their bodies. Slight shifts in therapist nonverbal behavior can hurt or heal. A very slight expression of disgust can reaffirm all the shame that a client has ever felt, while an open, relaxed body expression can offer relief and make space for whatever the client wants to focus on, without the need to deal with a therapist's personal reaction to them. Providing information and developing cultural competency around the diversity of ways people are sexual is a significant aspect of a sex therapist's professional development (Nichols, 2006). It is imperative that supervisors help the sex therapist develop strategies to notice, understand, and use their countertransference reactions to sexual topics. As with all countertransference, it is likely that countertransference to sexual themes can reveal important information that can be used to benefit the client. For instance, it may reflect how others often react to the client and what the client experiences in the world of people. This might inform the therapist's approach in sessions, motivating them to carefully and deliberately interact with the client in ways that repair this experience of feeling marginalized or having aspects of the self rejected, or feeling "not normal." When a therapist has any kind of strong countertransference, it can make a therapist want to withdraw and create distance from the client, or feel compelled to get too close. The supervisor can help the therapist maintain the right balance of connection to the client, staying present while maintaining clear boundaries.

One supervisee at the beginning of her training came to realize in supervision that she felt repulsion when hearing a client's detailed description of his interest in a specific sexual activity that he was deeply ashamed of and had never actually spoken about it with anyone before. This brand new clinician believed that all sexual expression, including what he described, was totally acceptable. She stated that she believed that all sexuality should be embraced. But, as she spoke about this client in supervision, her mouth made tiny movements, as if she had just tasted something bad that communicated disgust. In spite of her best efforts to embrace all kinds of sexuality, her body betrayed her most basic feelings of disgust. Although she felt ashamed of her automatic, visceral response, she was able to use this awareness to bring a deeper understanding of the intensity and pervasiveness of social response that her client was likely to be surrounded by. She realized that whether people voiced it or not, their bodies communicated disgust towards his sexual interests. She understood on a deeper level that for most of his life he was surrounded by these implicit communications. This helped her to better understand the pervasive self-hate he felt, which became an important theme in the therapy.

In the exploration of countertransference issues, respect for the therapist's privacy must be honored. The boundary between supervision and therapy is an important one, although the distinction may at times be fuzzy. One way to prevent intrusion into the therapist's personal, private life is to help the therapist identify a countertransference reaction as one that occurs due to personal issues, and then set that aside, shifting the focus to how this information can increase understanding of the particular client, and how it can be used to move the therapy forward. It is useful for the supervisor to help the supervisee identify and name the personal issue just enough so that it can be separated out from their clinical work, but not to linger too long on it. Then, the therapist can choose to work on their personal issue either in psychotherapy or some other way. The level of personal disclosure in supervision varies from person to person and supervision to supervision and is based on a variety of factors. Keeping the focus on the clinical work, on the client and the therapy, is important.

This intersection of personal and professional self that is explored in supervision reflects who and what a therapist brings to their clinical work. It can be uncomfortable, and both the supervisor and supervisee might be reluctant to delve into the countertransference experience. But we know that when we as therapists put words to whatever is going on internally, all of the messy, complicated experience, including fears, worries, and all that feels "wrong" for a therapist to feel, it changes our experience. Sharing our thoughts and emotions and how they impact the therapeutic process may enhance our capacity to remain self-aware and centered within our sessions. Voice it and it takes less energy and mental space. It becomes easier to hold and to maintain awareness. It is possible that new ways of seeing the client may emerge when we explore the unnamed reality that is our own personal experience with a client.

Kinds of Countertransference and Two Cases

Common countertransference reactions that sex therapists experience include sexual attraction or aversion to the client, the response to the client's sexual attraction or aversion to the therapist, feelings of sexual inadequacy or envy, the wish to be perceived as desirable, rescue fantasies, pity for a client, feeling overly responsible for outcome, feeling incompetent or powerless, focusing on what to do or not do rather than being absorbed in the therapy experience (therapy "spectatoring"), self-doubt, need for approval from clients, performance anxiety, aligning with one partner over another, the sense that the therapist would be a better partner for the client than the partner they have, imposing the therapist's own values on the client, repulsion to sexual practices the client describes in therapy, anger about infidelity, the role of money related to sex, and boredom, among others (Dalenberg, 2000; Fine, 1965; Grossman, 1965; Kiesler, 2001; Pearlman & Saakvitne, 1995; Pope, 1993; Schaverien, 1995; Schover, 1981; Searles, 1959; Tobin & McCurdy, 2006). The possibilities are truly endless. Each therapist brings their unique being into the therapeutic endeavor and meets another unique being, and together a particular and distinctive interaction occurs.

Case 1

"Julie," an experienced therapist who was relatively new to sex therapy, entered supervision one day and said "Now I know I'm losing it! I really need to deal with this directly. Yesterday I wore a push up bra because I knew I was meeting with Kurt." Julie was self-aware and able to notice her behavior and to bring it to supervision. She felt safe enough with the supervisor to express it openly. She spoke about how hard it has been for her to be recently divorced, feeling lonely, longing for physical closeness and sex. She recognized that in some ways, Kurt would be the kind of man she would like to date if he were not her client. Once she described her feelings, she felt enormously relieved. She immediately recognized that it was understandable that she would feel these things. After more discussion, Julie noted that Kurt has never been in a relationship without having affairs, that when his wife is away he goes to a bar to pick up a woman to have sex. Indeed, his stated goal for therapy was to be completely monogamous and to stop having sex with other women when his wife went away. As Julie thought back to her experience in the therapy room with him, she recognized that he sustains eye contact with her in ways that can be uncomfortable, that he asks about her in ways that assume their common life situations. As she examined this interaction more carefully, she could ask herself, "is his behavior seductive?" and "is this something he is aware of?"

In supervision, Julie was able to (a) notice the countertransferential feelings, (b) name the feelings, and (c) explore the feelings and what was contributing to her experience, including her loneliness, her current life circumstances, his age and intelligence. At some point in her exploration, she also began to notice something he might be doing to contribute to her experience. She then asked herself the final and most important questions: How can I use this information to benefit the therapy? What can I do to not harm the therapy? On a personal level, this experience and conversation helped Julie to consider the possibility that she might be ready to begin to date. As Kurt's therapist, she realized that she would need to begin to notice moments when he displayed seductive behavior, and to gently give voice to them, so that he could begin to identify what he was doing and what it meant for him.

Over the course of the next five or six months, Julie discussed the case in supervision to make sure she was staying on track. She noted that Kurt is now able to notice when he was engaging in what they had come to call "his flirty things," and over the course of the therapy she had been able to identify that he did it when he felt uncertain, vulnerable, or scared. This was one way into his being able to understand that his picking up women for sex when his wife was away was about feeling abandoned, rejected, uncertain, and scared. He came to realize that he sought comfort in sex with women. Knowing this allowed him to express what he really needed: nurture and connection when his wife was away, and it helped him to stop the behavior that was disturbing to him.

Julie's use of her countertransference in this case opened up what turned out to be a core issue for Kurt, and helped move the therapy in a positive direction.

Case 2

Another supervisee, "Sally," was far less aware of her inner experience, so working through her countertransference was challenging, and far less successful, leading to less than optimal therapy practice and outcomes. "Sally" was also recently divorced. Blonde, blue-eyed, and physically fit, Sally could have been in an L.L. Bean catalogue, except everything was tight and necklines were low. In supervision, Sally spoke about a male client in his mid-forties. A physician with a good reputation, he was married for 15 years and had two children, ages 12 and 9. According to Sally he was athletic and nice-looking. He came to therapy because he wanted to stop having sex with women who were not his wife and to reduce his use of porn. He had been unfaithful to his wife for the past five or six years because, he said, she was not interested in sex and was busy with the children and her work as the director of a small nonprofit focused on helping homeless women and children.

Sally said she liked him, and that she felt his wife did not understand him and that she was "uptight" because she did not like that he watched porn as much as he did. She said that she, herself, had no problem with porn, and could totally understand why he was tired and fed up with his wife and she could see why he would have affairs. She expressed frustration with the wife: "Why can't she be less uptight?"

In supervision, her nonverbal behavior while speaking about this client was different from her usual body language. She sat up straighter, stuck out her chest, and twirled her hair. She exhibited seductive behavior. Her supervisor wondered aloud if she thought she would be a better wife for him." "Absolutely!" she replied. When her supervisor identified this as countertransference, it was difficult for Sally to accept it. She believed that it was "just a fact." Given her difficulty acknowledging the countertransferential nature of some of her experience and reactions to this client, the supervisor focused on preventing the countertransference from doing harm to the therapy, while working towards increased self-reflection on Sally's part. Speaking about what she wore on days she met with him turned out to be useful. Initially, she said she did not dress differently when she saw him. After further exploration, she acknowledged that "maybe" she *did* think more about what she wore on the days he was in her schedule. "But, he's a wealthy man and I have to look put together for him to respect me as a therapist," she reasoned. Over time, the supervisor continued to point out Sally's behaviors and comments that suggested countertransference. She continued to disagree with this, and insisted that she was "completely objective" about him.

The supervisor became increasingly concerned that her unacknowledged countertransference was not only getting in the way of doing good therapy but was actually causing harm, especially in the man's relationship with his wife. The supervisor's super-countertransference kicked in and she felt annoyed with Sally for being unable to recognize what seemed so obvious to her in her supervisory role. In addition, the supervisor thought that the wife sounded lovely and imagined her to be someone she herself would like. At this point, the supervisor sought consultation with another supervisor to explore approaches. She decided to reinforce the supervisee's sense of safety in the supervision and to emphasize how common countertransference was and how it could be really useful. The supervisor assured Sally that it is common for sex therapists to experience these feelings, and that it would be especially understandable, given that she recently divorced and wanted to meet a man to date. "Plus, it can be hard to be alone and not get validation as a woman." This last phrase—"not get validation as a woman"—resonated for Sally. She disclosed that her husband had affairs and left her for another woman, which left her feeling inadequate. She began to see that she was seeking "validation as a woman" in all kinds of places, including with this client. Once she was able to see some of what was happening in this case, her experience of the client shifted. She became increasingly receptive to much more of the information that she had been dismissing and minimizing, and she was able to have a more complete formulation of the case and a better therapeutic approach. While the countertransference in this case took longer to acknowledge and to deal with in an effective way, ultimately Sally was able to stop being defensive and to start thinking about how her own relational history was impacting her professional stance with her client. As a supervisor, finding the way to allow the supervisee to really see their countertransference can be difficult and frustrating. At these moments, going back to the initial steps of the process can be helpful. Unlike the linear, smooth process with Julie, the process with Sally in supervision was more back-and-forth: create safety, normalize, notice and name, create safety, normalize, notice and name, create safety, and normalize. Normalizing became especially important for Sally to feel able to recognize the countertransference. Eventually she was able to get to self-reflection that, though somewhat superficial, was enough to prevent harm. During this supervision, Sally was unable to actually use the information to enhance the therapeutic process in the way Julie did. Sally used supervision to manage the countertransference so it would not contribute to or worsen the problem the client was working on.

Super-Countertransference

The supervisor's job is to find ways to help the supervisee use the supervision well. But what happens when a supervisor's subjective experience of a supervisee gets in the way of supervision? Supervisors pay attention to the interpersonal process with the supervisee, particularly when something appears to be getting in the way of effective supervision, or when something arises in the supervisory dynamic that may reflect therapy issues. With Sally, the supervisor felt frustrated and impatient. She found herself feeling powerless as Sally rejected every effort the supervisor made to deal with what was obvious countertransference. In consultation with another colleague, it became apparent that the supervisor's irritation and impatience prevented her from being the nonanxious presence Sally needed. Once, the supervisor was able to effectively deal with her own feeling of powerlessness, her sense that she would be a better therapist to this client (note the parallel process), and her own frustration and impatience, she was better able to calm down and slow down. This allowed her to do more of the safety building work that was necessary for Sally to allow herself to notice what she actually felt with her client. The supervisor had to recognize more fully just how raw and deeply painful Sally's experience of "not feeling validated as a woman" was, in order to provide adequate support for her to recognize and effectively manage her countertransference with this client.

Just as the therapist must be sensitive to personal reactions to the client, the supervisor must be mindful of how their own personal issues and reactions to the supervisee show up in the supervision. Maintaining self-awareness and making time and space for ongoing self-reflection about their work with supervisees is vitally important for supervisors. It can be tempting to ignore the supervisory process and relationship, but as in therapy, that can be where the rich and valuable material lies. Common issues that affect supervisors include an investment in being valued, admired, liked and respected; wanting to protect; issues related to culture, ethnicity, and identity; disappointment due to unrealistic expectations; feeling that they could do a better job with the client than the supervisee; feeling that the supervisee is actually a better therapist than they are; anxiety about perception that supervisee is not doing a good job; and a wish to impart wisdom, among an infinite number of other countertransferential issues towards the supervisee.

The process for effectively managing super-countertransference in supervision is similar to that of managing countertransference in therapy. It requires noticing, naming, exploring, and determining the best approach to using the internal countertransference reaction. Often supervisors are more relaxed with supervisees than with clients and boundaries can be more flexible. This somewhat more flexible frame allows for more collegial connection, which is important. But at times this can make it harder to notice super-countertransference. The clues that are worth paying attention to include supervision that feels too much like a conversation with a friend, supervision in which cases are not discussed, supervision that becomes repetitive or overly focused on theory, supervision that is boring or painful. It is useful to notice feelings towards the supervisee that differ from the usual, including fantasies, dreams, avoidance, and protectiveness. Identifying super-countertransference and using it well in supervision can deepen the supervisory relationship and serve as a model for the supervisee on ways to use countertransference to benefit therapy. As therapists and supervisors, we bring our imperfect, value-laden selves to our work as therapists and as supervisors. The best we can do is recognize our issues, our values, our biases, and who we are overall, and pay close attention to how we communicate verbally and nonverbally.

Conclusion

As sex therapists, we hold space for another human being (or two or more) so they can explore and heal and flourish. That means listening deeply, fully, and generously. To listen and hold space for another requires full presence. It requires being fully in one's body and mind. It requires self-awareness that includes our flaws, hurts, and vulnerabilities as well as our capacity for joy, vitality, and openness to life. When we enter the "land of therapy" (the extremely personal space in which people speak about sexuality, deep passion and joy, and heartbreak and despair), we have subjective and personal responses to the interaction. It is crucial that we manage our own subjective experience so that it enhances, rather than diminishes, the client's progress in therapy. Clinical supervision provides the opportunity to learn how to use countertransference in the service of the client.

Often stories about sexuality and intimacy meander. People speak about the messy complexity of their sex lives. They speak about deep unspoken memories. They speak about tender moments and about harrowing experiences. They speak about joy and pleasure. They speak about what they crave and are starved for. They speak about boredom and about vitality and passion. As sex therapists, our job is to listen. As sex therapy supervisors, we listen. We listen to stories and stories of stories. As our own personal story interacts with the story we listen to, it becomes another story. Sorting through these intertwined stories and teasing apart what is about whom is essential to successful therapy. It is not an easy task.

Clinical supervision is how sex therapists truly learn to practice good therapy. It is in supervision that the most important practical details in the relationship between the therapist and clients can be discussed in an authentic manner. Who a therapist is as a person is inextricably linked to who they are as a therapist, and it is in supervision that who the sex therapist is as a person in the context of doing therapy can be better understood. The skillful use of the person of the therapist interwoven with therapeutic skill is what makes a good sex therapist. Countertransference plays an enormous part in this. What the sex therapist feels and thinks in the context of a therapeutic encounter matters. Clinical supervision helps sex therapists deal effectively with countertransference in order to cultivate the capacity to hold space for another, so that the client might explore, understand, and heal, allowing their sexuality to flourish. Helping sex therapists listen wisely, generously, and open-heartedly is what sex therapy supervision is all about.

About the Author

Katherine Ellin, Ph.D., MSW, DTR, is a clinical psychologist, AASECT Certified Sex Therapist and Supervisor. Her 30-plus years of clinical experience also includes trauma-focused therapy, leadership and staff positions in community mental health centers, residential programs, and psychiatric hospitals and at the Institute for Sexuality and Intimacy. Her clinical work integrates psychodynamic thinking, attachment theory and research, cognitive-behavioral techniques, solution-focused therapy, family system approaches, and an awareness of the mind–body connection, reflecting her dance therapy training and lifelong yoga practice. She founded and directed the Time Trade Circle (http://timetradecircle.org) and serves on the board of Our Spirit (http://ourspirit now.org).

References

Agass, D. (2010). Countertransference, supervision and the reflection process. *Journal of Social Work Practice, 16*(2), 125–133. Retrieved from https://doi.org/10.1080/0265053022000033694

Aponte, H. J. (1994). How personal can training get? *Journal of Marital and Family Therapy, 20*, 3–15.

Aponte, H. J. (2009). Training the person of the therapist in an academic setting. *Journal of Marital and Family Therapy, 35*, 381–394.

Aponte, H. J. (2016). *The person of the therapist training model: Mastering the use of self.* New York: Routledge.

Baum, O. E. (1969–1970). Countertransference. *Psychoanalytic Review, 56*, 621–637.

Bean, R. D. (2014). *Clinical supervision: Cultivating self-awareness and competence.* Hoboken, NJ: John Wiley & Sons.

Beebe, B. K., Knoblauch, S., Rustin, J., & Sorter, D. (2005). *Forms of intersubjectivity in infant research and adult treatment.* New York: Other Press.

Beebe, B. K., & Lachmann, F. M. (2002). *Infant research and adult treatment: Co-constructing interactions.* Hillsdale, NJ: Analytic Press.

Bernstein, P. L. (1979/1984). *Theoretical approaches in dance-movement therapy* (Vol. 1). Dubuque, IA: Kendall/Hunt.

Celenza, A. (2010). The guilty pleasure of erotic countertransference: Searching for radial true. *Studies in Gender and Sexuality, 11*(4), 175–183.

Chace, M. (1975). *Marian Chace: Her papers* (H. Chaiklin, Ed.). New York: American Dance Therapy Association.

Dalenberg, C. (2000). *Countertransference and the treatment of trauma.* Washington, DC: American Psychological Association.

Ehrenberg, D. B. (1992). *The intimate edge: Extending the reach of psychoanalytic interaction.* New York: W. W. Norton.

Falender, C., & Shafranske, E. P. (2004). *Clinical supervision: A competency-based approach.* Washington, DC: American Psychological Association.

Fine, R. (1965). Erotic feelings in the psychotherapeutic relationship. *Psychoanalytic Review, 52,* 30–37.

Freud, S. (1957). The future prospects of psychoanalytic therapy. In J. Strachey (Ed. & Trans.), *The standard edition of the complete psychological works of Sigmund Freud* (Vol. 11, pp. 139–152). London: Hogarth Press.

Gehlert, K. M. (2014). A trainee's guide to conceptualizing countertransference in marriage and family therapy supervision. *Family Journal: Counseling and Therapy for Couples and Families, 22,* 7–16.

Gelso, C., &. Hayes, J. (2007). *Countertransference and the therapist's inner experience: Perils and possibilities.* Mahwah, NJ: Lawrence Erlbaum.

Grossman, C. M. (1965). Transference, countertransference, and being in love. *Psychoanalytic Quarterly, 34,* 249–256.

Guiffriday, D. (2015). *Constructive clinical supervision in counseling and psychotheray.* New York: Routledge.

Heimann, P. (1950). On countertransference. *International Jounal of Psychoanalysis, 31,* 81–84.

Karen, R. (1994). *Becoming attached: Unfolding the mystery of the infant-mother bond and its impact on later life.* New York: Warner Books.

Kiesler, D. J. (2001). Therapist countertransference: In search of common themes and empirical referents. *Journal of Clinical Psychology, 57,* 1053–1063.

Langs, R. J. (1982). Countertransference and the process of cure. In S. Slipp (Ed.), *Curative factors in dynamic psychotherapy* (pp. 127–152). New York: McGraw-Hill.

Lichtenberg, J. D. (1983). *Psychoanalysis and infant research.* Hillsdale, NJ: Analytic Press.

Nichols, M. (2006). Psychotherapeutic issues with "kinky" clients. *Journal of Homosexuality, 50*(2–3), 281–300.

Ogden, G. (2008). *The return of desire: A guide to rediscovering your sexual passion.* Boston, MA: Trumpeter.

Pearlman, L. A. & Saakvitne, K. W. (1995). *Trauma and the therapist: Countertransference and vicarious traumatization in psychotherapy with incest survivors.* New York: W. W. Norton.

Pope, K. S. (1993). Therapists' anger, hate, fear, and sexual feelings: National survey of therapists' responses, client characteristics, critical events, formal complaints, and training. *Professional Psychology: Research and Practice, 24,* 142–152.

Pope, K. S. (2000). Therapists' sexual feelings and behaviors: Research, trends, and quandries. In L. S. (Ed.), *Psychological perspective on human sexuality* (pp. 603–658). Hoboken, NJ: John Wiley & Sons.

Pope, K. S., Sonne, J. L., & Greene, B. (2006). *What therapists don't talk about and why: Taboos that hurt us and our clients.* Washington, DC: American Psychological Association.

Robbins, A. (1986). *Expressive therapy: A creative arts approach to depth-oriented treatment.* New York: Human Sciences Press.

Schaverien, J. (1995). *Desire and female therapist: Engendered gazes in psychotherapy and art therapy.* New York: Routledge.

Schover, L. R. (1981). Male and female therapists' responses to male and female sexual material: An analogue sudy. *Archives of Sexual Behavior, 10,* 477–492.

Searles, H. R. (1959). Oedipal love in the countertransference. *International Journal of Psychoanalysis, 40,* 180–190.

Searles, H. R. (1986). Countertransference: A path to understanding and helping the patient. In H. R. Searles (Ed.), *My work with borderline patients* (pp. 189–200). Northvale, NJ: Jason Aronson.

Siegel, E. (1984). *Dance-movement therapy: Mirrors of our selves.* New York: Human Sciences Press.

Slade, A. (2002). Moments of regulation and the development of self-narratives. *Journal of Infant, Child, and Adult Psychotherapy, 2,* 1–10.

Slade, A. (2003). Intersubjectivity and maternal reflective functioning. *Psychoanalytic Inquiry, 23,* 521–529.

Slade, A., & Holmes, J. (2013). *Attachment theory* (Vols. I–VI). London: Sage.

Stern, D. (1985). *The interpersonal world of the infant: A view from psychoanalysis and developmental psychology.* New York: Basic Books.

Stolorow, R. D., & Atwood, G. E. (1992). *Contexts of being: The intersubjective foundations of psychological life.* Hillsdale, NJ: Analytic Press.

Tauber, E. S. (1979). Countertransference reexamined. In L. E. Feiner (Ed.), *Countertransference* (pp. 59–70). New York: Aronson.

Tobias, K. E. (1995). *The relation between maternal attachment and patterns of mother-infant interaction at four months* (Unpublished doctoral dissertation). City University of New York, New York.

Tobin, D., &. McCurdy, K. G. (2006). Adlerian-focused supervision for countertransference work with counselors-in-training. *Journal of Individual Psychology, 62,* 154–167.

Van der Kolk, B. (2014). *The body keeps the score: Brain, mind, and body in the healing of trauma.* New York: Penguin.

9 Sex Therapy Supervision Through a Systemic Lens

Neil Cannon and Amanda Sasek

Abstract

Supervision is a critical component of a therapist's development and growth. When engaged in sex therapy supervision, it is to the benefit to the supervisee and their clients that the supervisor is engaging with them through a systemic lens. When the client is viewed in the context of the entire system, the therapist has more context and the client will have more awareness and insight. When looking at the system of an individual client, for instance, the system will include entities such as individual mental and physical health concerns, current and past romantic relationships, family of origin, church and faith communities, cultural context, and supervisory alliance between supervisor and supervisee. The history of systems theory, systemic sex therapy, and systemic supervision will be reviewed in this chapter. Case studies will be utilized to illustrate systemic sex therapy supervision in practice.

Keywords

supervision, systemic supervision, sex therapy, sex therapy supervision, systems theory, self of therapist, supervisory alliance

Systemic Sex Therapy Supervision

Little to no research or literature exists for systemic sex therapy supervision, which is why the authors reviewed the three domains in which literature does exist (systems theory, systemic sex therapy and systemic supervision). This chapter will be based upon the three named research areas, as well as authors' knowledge/experience in systemic sex therapy supervision.

A systemic supervisor in sex therapy knows:

1. Each client is a part of many macro- and microsystems. When these systems are discussed and explored, change and growth happens. These systems are myriad. Things included in one client's system include family of origin, the family they live with, work, friends, societal, cultural, religious, and more.
2. Supervisees will do best when they treat their clients holistically and collaborate with the entire treatment team.

3. The relationship between supervisor and supervisee matters and plays out in the supervisee's clinical work. This concept is conceptualized by the authors as "supervisory alliance."
4. If the supervisee is treating an individual client who is in an intimate relationship, the supervisee is ethically and legally bound to treat the individual client. Clinically, however, we want supervisees to expand their thinking to include the client's system while focusing therapy on that which is in the client's control.

History of Systemic Thinking: Basic Ideas and Theory of Change

There are many influences on what we know today as systemic thinking and family therapy. Following is a summary of some of the major contributors and ideas, but this summary is not intended to be a comprehensive list. Nathan Ackerman was among the first to classify the family system as the client, as opposed to only one individual within the family system (Volini, 2015). He also required all family members to be present in every session. Ludwig von Bertalanffy was an Australian biologist and the founder of general systems theory. In 1968, Bertalanffy identified guiding principles in systems theory that could move scientific inquiry forward (Smith-Acuña, 2011). Bertalanffy introduced us to the idea that a system as a whole is greater than the sum of its parts (Nichols & Schwartz, 2001). This idea from Bertalanffy sets up supervisors and supervisees alike to examine the interdependent nature of the various parts of a system. By doing this, one understands the entire system better (Volini, 2015).

> Systems theory can be defined as a set of unifying principles about the organization and of functioning of systems. Systems are defined as meaningful wholes that are maintained by the interaction of their parts.
>
> (Smith-Acuña, 2011, p. 6)

Another major influence on systemic thinking is the field of cybernetics. Cybernetics is a transdisciplinary concept that was developed from the study of machines in during World War II. One of the concepts that evolved from cybernetics is the feedback loop. The feedback loop is the idea that a system gets the information necessary to maintain the status quo or a preplanned goal.

Feedback loops can be negative (maintains the status quo/reduces change) or positive (causes the system to change/deviate from the status quo). This influenced systemic thinking and family therapy in that it invited professionals to consider how families function to enforce or challenge homeostasis (Nichols & Schwartz, 2001). Homeostasis is defined by the tendency of a family to resist change in order to maintain status quo (Volini, 2015).

Gregory Bateson (1972) brought cybernetics to family therapy by introducing a new way of thinking that involved looking at psychopathology not solely as result of past events such as a medical disease, but instead as something that is a part of an ongoing, circular feedback loops. This is called circular thinking.

Circular Causality Versus Linear Thinking

Systemic therapists do not focus solely on the causes of the problems that an individual or couple brings to therapy (linear thinking), but rather the patterns of interaction that form sequences (circular thinking, Lee & Nelson, 2014).

Linear thinking assumes that A causes B (Nichols & Schwartz, 2001). If we utilize this way of thinking in therapy, it does our clients a disservice, as it assumes only simple cause and effect, rather than the intricate patterns that are often intertwined into our relationships.

Circular thinking instead looks at the patterns between client and the system. Therapists' hypotheses change based on various responses to questions asked of their clients. New information leads to new questions and results in change (Nichols & Schwartz, 2001).

For example, suppose a supervisee is in a therapy session with a couple discussing a recent affair. The injured partner is stuck in anger about the betrayal. The clients do not benefit from the therapist staying stuck in a linear causality, but instead would benefit from more circular thinking. For instance, a systemically focused clinician might help the clients understand what made their relationship vulnerable to the affair (Snyder, Baucom, & Coop Gordon, 2007). A linear-focused way of looking at an affair would assume easy causation between a partner who is "unhappy in the marriage" and the subsequent infidelity. This is not to say that linear causation is never the answer. However, it is to the benefit of the client to look at the affair not just in a linear way but also in a circular way. Systemic therapists slow down and look at the entire system. Because the angry partner often has much perceived power following the discovery of infidelity, it is easy for therapists to stay with the anger of the injured partner rather than explore deeper issues. Systems theory, however would have us explore an expanded system and its patterns once the system starts to stabilize. Author and couples therapist Esther Perel discusses the complicated topic of infidelity in her book *The State of Affairs: Rethinking Infidelity*. The way Perel looks at and explores affairs exemplifies taking a systemic look at affairs. Perel (2017) notes that "sometimes, when we seek the gaze of another, it isn't our partner we are turning away from, but the person we have become" (p. 151). She goes on to say, "So often, the most intoxicating other that people discover in the affair is not a new partner, it's a new self" (Perel, 2017, p. 151). Systemic sex therapists utilize knowledge of the system as a whole, and do not stop at linear explorations.

Major Family Therapy Theorist Influences and Family Therapy Models

Systemic thinking and family therapy was influenced by myriad theorists who had their own unique way of looking at systems and families. The following is a review of some of the theories and models helpful when considering your work as a systemic sex therapy supervisor.

Strategic, Systemic, and Structural Family Therapy

Strategic therapy was born from Gregory Bateson and his team in Palo Alto, California. He was joined by several others on both coasts that all had different ideas about what strategic therapy meant. Strategic therapy looks at power and hierarchy in the family, as well as how what they are doing maintains the problem. The strategic therapist believes they are responsible for helping the family change with specific interventions that directly impact the presenting problem (Piercy, Sprenkle, & Wetchler, 1996). One specific strategic intervention is calling "prescribing the symptom." This is a behavioral prescription aimed to change the meaning of the symptoms or behaviors clients are presenting with (Smith-Acuña, 2011). A systemic sex therapy supervisor may help their supervisee explore benefits of utilizing this theory by helping them to encourage a client with an erection difficulty to practice "losing" his erection and coping effectively with it. Previously, the meaning behind losing the erection may have been shame, anger, or confusion. By purposely losing his erection for the purposes of therapy homework, the client may be able to create more functional meaning behind it. This may reduce anxiety and shame related to the erectile difficulty.

Salvador Minuchin provided a way of understanding and reorganizing families with structural therapy. Structural therapy's theory of change involves looking at the network individuals are a part of and how the structure of these networks maintains the "problem." Structural therapy believes that a change in structure of the family system will reinforce positive change (Piercy et al., 1996).

Virginia Satir brought a humanistic and more emotional way of thinking to family therapy with a focus on the humanity and self-esteem of individuals within the family (Nichols & Schwartz, 2001). Satir helped families understand that family dysfunction was often born of one or more family members lacking healthy self-esteem. She encouraged open communication about this to create change (Volini, 2015). Satir and Carl Whitaker are known as the leaders of experiential family therapy.

Systemic therapy was also influenced by the work of Gregory Bateson, and also like strategic therapy, had several theorists with different ways of carrying out the main ideas. Systemic therapists also utilized circularity as a concept as well as neutrality and curiosity in their work to stay open to client's behaviors as having multiple origins (Piercy et al., 1996).

Murray Bowen developed Bowen Family Systems Theory and coined the term "differentiation of self" as it relates to therapy. This concept refers to an individual's ability to balance thinking with feeling, thus balance individuality with togetherness. Individuals who are highly differentiated are able to act rationally while experiencing anxiety, depression, or anger (Volini, 2015). This concept is helpful to family therapists as it helps them look at how much a person's emotions are impacting their relationships. "The more autonomous one's intellect is from automatic emotional forces, the more differentiated one is" (Piercy et al., 1996, p. 34).

When working with couples, it is important that the supervisor help the supervisee assess the level of differentiation in each couple. A therapist may assess the couple's levels of differentiation by observing or asking questions about how they hold on to their boundaries and values with their partner. Someone who is differentiated is able to effectively balance their own boundaries and values while being mindful of how this impacts their partner (Schnarch, 2009).

This concept is critically important to remember when working with couples due to the importance of balancing levels of differentiation in a healthy relationship. For example, if the partner of someone who experienced sexual assault is struggling to maintain their own anxiety related to their partner's post-traumatic stress, that anxiety may in fact cause the post-traumatic symptoms to worsen. The partner with the anxiety must learn to reach out emotionally to their partner about their anxiety without overburdening them with it.

Bowen discovered that the more differentiated key family members were, the more differentiated the entire family was (Nichols & Schwartz, 2001). Bowen also gave us the genogram, which helps couple and family therapists draw out a client's family system and detect patterns within it. Bowen was very interested in a client's family of origin and the patterns within the system. Bowen believed that unresolved emotions within the family structure are doomed to repeat themselves (Nichols & Schwartz, 2001). Below is an illustration of a genogram and how family therapists use the genogram to both to gain insight into a system and utilize the process of making a genogram with a client as a catalyst for change.

One favored method of supervision is to draw upon Bowen Family Systems Theory and invite supervisees to present their cases in a way that allows the supervisor/supervisee to draw a genogram for each case being supervised. To do this, a supervisor may ask their supervisees to start the case presentation by describing the client's therapeutic goal, their gender(s), and ages. The system will then take shape as the case presentation unfolds. The supervisor may instruct supervisee to create the genogram in supervision with supervisor present, or to create it in session collaboratively with their clients. Below is an illustration of a genogram and how family therapists may use this approach to gain insight into a system to positively help therapeutic outcomes. In this case, the supervisee constructed the genogram collaboratively with clients, with her supervisor supporting her with ideas for exploration in between her sessions with the couple. As the supervisor takes notes on the case, drawing a genogram of the case supports the wide-angle lens of systemic thinking.

Case Study

Molly and Jeff

Molly and Jeff presented to the supervisee for their first session of sex therapy and couples counseling. Molly's therapeutic goals were to be better connected with her partner and have less conflict. Jeff's therapeutic goals were surrounded in frequency of sex and communication problems.

The supervisee explained to the supervisor that the couple had been together for 12 years and married for 10 years. The supervisee explained that the couple spent much of their first session bickering about past events and resentments. The supervisee found Molly to have some anxiety and Jeff to have some attention concerns. After several sessions, the supervisee reported she learned more about the conflict patterns of the couple. She stated that when the couple fights, Molly pursues Jeff relentlessly to the point that he puts his hands over his ears and leaves the room, or sometimes even the house. The supervisee learned that the catalyst to setting up a therapy appointment was one of these fights that escalated to Molly breaking down the bathroom door when Jeff was inside. Both reported no trauma or abuse histories, and neither was particularly religious. The supervisee was unable to answer many of the supervisor's questions about their family of origin. The supervisor encouraged the supervisee to learn more about Molly's and Jeff's families of origin during the next session.

The supervisee came to the next supervision session and reported that she expanded the system and deeply explored the family of origin. The supervisee explained that Molly revealed that her mother was 16 years old when she had her, and described her as extremely narcissistic, unpredictable, and sometimes punitive. The supervisee also reported that Molly recalled tearfully that when she angered her mother, her mother would punish her by retreating to her large master bedroom for hours at a time. Molly would be kept on the outside of the locked bedroom door, often times begging and crying for her mother to come out. She stated her Mother would not come out until Molly wrote 100 punishment lines saying, "I am sorry for being a bad child," then have to slide the punishment lines under the door. Molly's father was an accountant and rarely came home from work until late, and they never ate dinner together as a family except on weekends. Molly described him as a good provider but also often absent from the family.

Figure 9.1 The genogram from session one. This is a simple genogram of the couple in therapy.

As for Jeff, he recalled that throughout his childhood his mother raged at his father at least once per week, generally about something that she perceived him to have done wrong. Whenever this happened, Jeff's father would simply go to the local golf club and drink the night away, which enraged his mother even more. When Jeff was 12 years old, his father had been caught having an affair with his secretary and his parents divorced. The divorce was devastating to Jeff and he had committed to himself that he would not get a divorce under any circumstances.

The supervisor asked about the children and what their household was like. The supervisee didn't have much information on that; however, she agreed to expand the system and explore what Molly and Jeff's household looked like today.

During the next supervision session, the supervisee reported that the children were 4, 6, and 8 years old. Molly and Jeff described the children as unruly and that the household often felt chaotic. Molly and Jeff often had conflicts about parenting issues, especially how to stop the children from fighting. Both Jeff and Molly were tired by the time they got home from work, which made parenting effectively particularly difficult for Molly. Molly described herself as the primary caretaker for the children and that she was becoming resentful for Jeff's lack of help and his focus on video games. The children were a stressor on the relationship and another thing that impacted Molly's lack of interest in sex with Jeff.

By looking at the expanded system, it became clearer to the supervisee and the supervisor that Molly and Jeff were simply replaying in their marriage many of the things that had been modeled to them as children. As Molly and Jeff did that, they had also created a chaotic household of their own in which sex was the last thing of interest to Molly. Although they had initially reported no trauma history, they

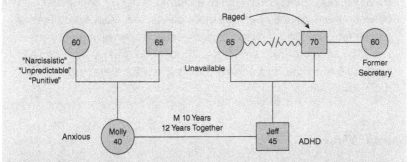

Figure 9.2 The genogram from session three. This genogram expands the system and includes the family of origin.

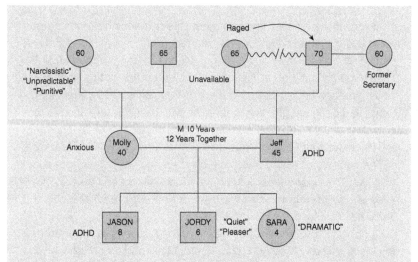

Figure 9.3 This genogram expands the system further to also include the children.

each did experience deep childhood wounds that impacted their adult intimate relationships. With this increased awareness and insight, the supervisee could begin helping them change their relationship patterns and provide them with new skills to better manage conflict. Jeff and Molly had fewer fights and learned to resolve conflict in productive ways, which included reflective and empathetic listening. They were able to remain better connected, be more regulated, and build on their strengths. The supervisee also helped Molly and Jeff learn for themselves and then express to the other what they needed to feel loved and connected based on their histories. As Jeff and Molly settled into a healthy groove with each other, the children fought less and the entire house became less chaotic. Jeff and Molly worked hard between sessions to have positive, predictable, and safe interactions with each other, which led to a shared feeling of connectedness between them. As they became more connected, Molly found herself much more open to increased sexual frequency and ultimately wanted sex with Jeff more frequently. After 6 months of weekly systemic sex therapy, the couple had achieved their goals for therapy and terminated counseling.

Systemic Thinking

As in this the case with Jeff and Molly, systems theory and family therapy tells us that there will inevitably be many different ideas of what the problem is, and we do not have to pick one culprit. Smith-Acuña (2011) suggests:

In systems theory, this shift in perspective allows us to examine the difference between "either/or" and "both/and" kinds of thinking. When we engage in "both/and" thinking, the questions we ask begin to change. Instead of which perspective is current, we can ask, "How do these things relate to each other?"

(p. 6)

Systemic Sex Therapy

Systemic sex therapy is an approach to psychotherapy and supervision, which utilizes the Intersystem Approach, developed by Weeks and later applied to numerous clinical settings (Weeks & Gambescia, 2015). It is a framework of clinical treatment for sexual concerns grounded in systems theory that takes into account the individual, couple, intergenerational, and external factors in both assessment and treatment of the presenting problem (Hertlein, Weeks, & Gambescia, 2015). The approach challenges the notion that traditional sex therapy is nonsystemic, and that couple and sex therapy can be treated in isolation of each other (Hertlein et al., 2015). We will apply this approach when appropriate as we discuss systemic sex therapy in this chapter.

When assessing/treating a sexual issue, we must look at it from many different vantage points and realize that the client is connected to many systems and subsystems that are not always obvious in the therapy room.

The Intersystem Approach considers all domains of individual or relational client systems. Specifically, it addresses the interplay between relational and sexual dynamics, recognizing that these issues become embedded within each other; thus, it is impossible to treat them in isolation (Weeks, Gambescia, & Hertlein, 2016). By its very nature, a relational problem, such as the lack of trust, may manifest as a sexual presentation such as low desire or avoidance of intimacy. It is impossible to treat the sexual problem without considering the relational factors that maintain the sexual symptom.

The Intersystem Approach allows the clinician to assess and treat sexual dysfunctions and concerns via four main domains:

1. Individual (biological and psychological)
2. Relational/couple factors
3. Intergenerational (family of origin) influences
4. Contextual considerations.

These domains occur simultaneously and influence the behaviors, thoughts, and feelings of all members of a client system. For example, the individual domain follows the assumption that therapy is contextualized by exploring the biological/medical and psychological issues within each partner. Examples of this would include assessing for medical conditions/medications that may affect sexual functioning as well as any comorbid diagnoses, which often include mood disorders and other sexual dysfunctions (Gambescia & Weeks, 2015). The couple domain examines emotional and behavioral patterns of the couple. Each person brings their individual perspective to the couple relationship, and the intersection of these two ideologies is especially important to examine when the presenting issue is a sexual concern. The intergenerational domain explores the influences upon the individual partners from their respective families of origin. Utilizing this domain, the clinician may inquire about family beliefs about sex and sexuality, how discussions of sexuality emerged, how internalized sexual beliefs manifested throughout the client's life, and how the client learned the family "rules" related to sex and sexuality. Finally, systemic sex therapists must be aware of environmental and contextual factors which often exacerbate a sexual/relational problem. These external factors include society, culture, religion, and history (Weeks et al., 2016). It is important that clinicians look holistically at the situation, presenting problem, and therapeutic goals. In addition, consideration should be given to the various systems, and subsystems present in their life and recognize the influence of relationships, work, friendships, religious beliefs, family of origin, and so forth.

For example, if a client presents with a "low libido," we do not assume the cause is solely biological, solely physical, or solely relational. Furthermore, we do not assume that because one partner's desire is higher than the other that one partner gets labeled with "low desire" and/or the other partner gets labeled as a "hypersexual," a nymphomaniac, or a "sex addict." Treating the system from a systemic and strength-based lens (Coulter, 2014), clinicians should remain careful not to use labels that can potentially be harmful to the clients. Words do indeed matter, and the supervisor in systemic sex therapy works relentlessly to reinforce this concept with their supervisees.

Supervisors work with their supervisees to be curious and explore the various subsystems, and to understand that each partner is likely to have a different perspective on the problem. For instance, the higher desire partner may be absolutely convinced that their partner "doesn't find them attractive," and the lower desire partner may see the problem as having no relation to attraction, but instead a variety of other factors. After we have done a thorough assessment of the system, we often find several layers of complexities that can include negative messages about sex from childhood, unresolved trauma histories, medications that are inhibiting libido, and a long list of other factors that could affect the system.

Systemic Supervision

What does systemic supervision look like? Marriage and family therapy supervisors are tasked with bringing systemic interventions into supervision by ensuring that within the relationship, systemic interventions can be isomorphically experienced (Yingling, 2000). Systemic supervisors are aware of the processes within the process. They recognize that they themselves are a part of the system, and use insight gained from this to impact the system in positive ways (Lee & Nelson, 2014).

Systemic supervisors encourage their supervisees to reflect upon their own system and family history and how this may impact their clinical work (Lee & Nelson, 2014). In sex therapy, many issues and concerns may come up that trigger the clinician's own relationship or family dynamic. This does not always mean that the clinician cannot do effective therapy with an issue that is "close to home," however, but this is when it becomes important for the therapist to reflect and gain awareness around how this particular client may trigger their own feelings. This is often explored in supervision and is important for the wellness of the system.

Likewise, systemic supervisors must also reflect on their own system, particularly as it relates to sexuality. Certified Sex Therapists through the American Association of Sex Educators, Counselors and Therapists (AASECT) are required to engage with their own feelings related to various aspects of sexuality through a training called "Sexual Attitude Restructuring" (SAR), AASECT defines the SAR as a minimum of 10 clock hours of structured group experience consisting of a process-oriented exploration of the applicant's own feelings, attitudes, values, and beliefs regarding sexuality. This type of growth is helpful and necessary, but should not stop there. Sexual attitudes and values are ever changing and ever growing. For example, something such as the life stage and relationship status of the supervisor impacts their view on sexuality. This is not good or bad to the supervisory relationship, but rather something very important to reflect on related to its impact on larger training system. As such, sex therapy supervisors want to think systemically about how to be aware of how our values enter the supervisory relationship. Reflecting in this way is often referred to as "self of therapist work." In order to intervene with clients effectively therapists must know themselves, their biases, values, and beliefs and how these things enter into the therapy room (Piercy et al., 1996).

Content Versus Context

Another important systemic concept is looking at the context in a therapy session versus the content. To illustrate this, we will look at a supervisee discussing with his supervisor a case of heterosexual couple presenting with early ejaculation. The supervisee states that the client's wife gets angry every time her husband reaches orgasm too quickly (early ejaculation). The angrier she gets, the more the more the husband experiences early ejaculation. The male client reports how emotionally difficult it is for him when he ejaculates sooner than he would like, and it turns into a fight between himself and his wife, and the husband is currently refusing to have sex with his partner. The supervisee reports that every session with them is high conflict in nature and he is struggling to defuse the couple's anger in session. The systemic supervisor then engages with their supervisee in a conversation about content versus context. The supervisor does this by asking the supervisee to flesh out what is going on in session, and what is content and what is context. The content of the sessions includes high-conflict interactions, not listening, criticism, defensiveness, and anger. The systemic sex therapy supervisor then encouraged her supervisee to explore how he might help direct the couple into a direction of focusing on context instead of content. The supervisor does this by helping their supervisee be aware of the larger systemic context and process.

Some questions the supervisor may ask to help the supervisee with this concept are:

1. Might there be an underlying erectile issue?

   It is important to rule out other sexual dysfunctions that could be impacting the presenting issue. Sometimes men with early ejaculation are rushing through sex to avoid an erection issue.

2. What might be below the wife's anger?

   The anger could be a manifestation of deeper sadness, fear, or shame. For instance, the wife might be feeling shame for treating her husband badly, and/or feeling like the problem has something to do with her.

3. What is below the husband's anger and avoidance?

   Much like the wife, the husband is likely experiencing shame and/or fear of failure.

4. What other issues are they having in their marriage besides the ejaculation issue?
5. Under what circumstances does she yell at him and blame him outside of the bedroom, and how does that impact their sex life?
6. What might the husband have to gain from maintaining sexual distance from his wife?
7. How does emotional safety for each of the partners play into this?
8. What family of origin issues might be playing out in their bedroom and in their arguments?

Common Factors in Supervision

Common factors research suggests that the therapist is a direct precursor to change in the client (Blow, Sprenkle, & Davis, 2007). Similarly, we believe the person of the supervisor and the relationship between supervisor and supervisee is related to positive outcomes in supervision and with the supervisee's clients. The authors call this concept *supervisory alliance*. In reviewing the common factors research, much of it seems to be geared towards newer clinicians. Sex therapy supervision often happens with more advanced clinicians, many of whom have years of experience as licensed mental health professionals. Due to the nature of the topic (i.e., sex), and lack of graduate course work offered in this area, sex therapy supervisees are in many ways "green," and it should not be assumed that they are advanced enough not to need basic supervision. Morgan and Sprenkle (2007) suggest that there are also common factors in supervision that we believe should be taken into account with sex therapy supervision.

Central to this schema is the emphasis in two domains in supervision on (1) clinical competence versus professional competence and (2) specific clinical issues versus certain topics. The authors believe these two important learning objectives are on two ends of a continuum, with the supervisor placing emphasis on each deemed helpful. Clinical competence focuses on the application of specific models and interventions, and professional competence focuses on helping the supervisee become a competent professional through teaching ethical and legal standards of the profession, or by examining self of therapist concerns. Taking into account these two dimensions, Morgan and Sprenkle (2007) developed four roles of supervision. These roles are *coach* (help supervisees accurately execute certain skills), *teacher* (help supervisees learn more general clinical knowledge, *mentor* (focus on the personal development of the supervisee as a professional), and finally the supervisor as an *administrator* (help with the professional, legal, and ethical standards of the profession). The literature asserts that good supervision involves the supervisor working from multiple roles, and that sometimes the roles overlap (Morgan & Sprenkle, 2007). A systemic sex therapy supervisor is aware of the relationship between themselves and their supervisee (supervisory alliance) and attuned to implementing different roles at different stages of the relationship.

By applying common factors of clinical supervision to sex therapy supervision, we will note how these roles developed by Morgan and Sprenkle may be played out in this arena specifically. One role that sex therapy supervisors may serve as are coaches, who help their supervisees execute a specific skill set related to sex therapy. This is done by helping supervisees follow the sex therapy certification requirements. The supervisor ensures that they not only have learned these skills in an educational setting, but can utilize them with their clients. Sex therapy supervisors may coach their supervisees through various ways: commenting on live data from the practice of the supervisee, helping them through a case conceptualization, and encouraging them throughout the process of their learning. Systemic sex therapy supervisors are also teachers, in that they teach specific techniques or ideas that might be helpful to their supervisee's clients. An example of using the teaching role with systemically focused sex therapy supervision is helping ensure supervisees have learned a systemic approach and are applying systemic thinking to sex therapy. Sex therapy supervisors are also mentors, helping with the professional development of a supervisee. This is done by guiding supervisees to explore the use of self as it related to sex therapy. Finally, sex therapy supervisors are administrators, ensuring that their supervisees have the proper training in sex therapy and have met all of the requirements.

Isomorphism

Systemic therapists recognize that the relationship between the supervisor and supervisee, and how cases are discussed and conceptualized, will manifest itself in the supervisee's clinical work. This concept is referred to as isomorphism in supervision (Lee & Nelson, 2014). Applying this concept to systemic sex therapy supervision, we postulate that the sexual values and how the supervisor discusses sex and sexuality will show up in their supervision, and subsequently in the supervisee's work. For example, if a supervisor is not well versed or comfortable with specific communities (e.g., LGBT communities, BDSM communities, polyamorous communities), this will show up in supervision when discussing those in the aforementioned communities. This may then filter down to the supervisee's clinical work with these populations.

Furthermore, the supervisor's knowledge of systems therapy is paramount to the supervisee utilizing a systems approach in their clinical work. If the supervisor is not asking systemic questions and providing systemic coaching in the context of supervision, the supervisee is more likely to also not use that lens, particularly if they were not trained within a systems framework. Isomorphism essentially shows up in many different aspects of the supervisor–supervisee relationship.

Attachment

Attachment refers to the emotional bond between people. Emotionally focused therapy (EFT) is an empirically based model of therapy that highlights attachment needs among couples as imperative to healthy and lasting relationships. EFT looks systemically at the problem in terms of the structure of the relationship, and the patterns the couple has adapted (Johnson, 2004). Johnson notes that attachment needs are not just important in developmental years, but also across the lifespan. Exploring the attachment style of each partner and how each one enacts their attachment dance can help partners create more secure bonds, and in turn resolve conflict.

Similarly, it can be helpful to explore the attachment styles of the supervisee and the supervisor. The relationship between the supervisor and supervisee is an important and, at times, delicate one. Just as a child depends on their caregivers(s) to be there for them when needed, supervisees depend on supervisors similarly. Children need caregivers to be "there" for them emotionally and take care of their basic needs. A supervisee depends on their supervisor to be "there" for them and help them as they develop their professional competence as a therapist.

Systemically, the attachment style of the supervisee or supervisor can show up in the supervisee's therapy. Let's say, for example, you have noticed your supervisee to generally have an anxious attachment style. Later on, you begin to notice that anxious attachment is showing up in supervision as they discuss a case. The supervisee is having a hard time with a couple presenting where one member of the couple reports out of control sexual behaviors. The supervisee reports her client appears to be avoiding having deeper conversations about some of the familial and emotional substrates that may subsume some of the sexual acting-out behaviors. The supervisee reports this person often withdraws and is shut down from the conversation. The supervisee reports she continues to try to challenge him to engage in exploration without any progress. The male's husband seems to be following the therapist's lead on this and continues to pursue as well. This pursuer–distancer style of the couple is being enforced by the therapist's anxious attachment style. A systemic supervisor in this case may be curious with their supervisee about how they feel when the avoidant partner is withdrawing. Examples of questions the supervisor could ask are: *When clients withdraw, what feelings are brought up for you? Does the withdrawing remind them of anyone in their family?*

Furthermore, it would be helpful for the supervisee to be aware that this avoidance may be related to the clients' own discomfort with emotional closeness or their tendency to use sex to soothe other anxieties within the relationship. Crocker (2013) found that avoidant attachment style may be a particular manifestation of out of control sexual behavior (Braun-Harvey & Vigorito, 2016).

The supervisor in this case may want to encourage the supervisee to explore in supervision how her attachment style may be showing up in her treatment and how her client's resistance to her challenging him may be a reflection of both the supervisee's and the client's attachment style.

Attachment is a systemic issue. If an individual has an attachment injury, it is likely to be rooted in childhood. In therapy, it often becomes necessary to help our clients repair old attachment injuries before addressing current issues. Likewise, a therapist may find themselves needing to explore their own attachment and how it impacts their work and their clients. Due to the relationship between sexuality and attachment, systemic sex therapy supervisors remain keenly aware of this with their supervisees.

Supervisors work with their supervisees to be curious and explore the various subsystems, and to understand that each partner is likely to have a different perspective on the problem. For instance, the higher desire partner may be absolutely convinced that their partner "doesn't find them attractive," and the lower desire partner may see the problem as having no relation to attraction, but instead a variety of other factors. After we have done a thorough assessment of the system, we often find several layers of complexities that can include negative messages about sex from childhood, unresolved trauma histories, medications that are inhibiting libido, and a long list of other factors that could affect the system.

Collaborating With Other Providers

In systemic sex therapy, there will often be many levels of care for each client, with all providers working in collaboration. These providers can include primary care physicians, obstetrician/gynecologists, urologists, psychiatrists, psychologists, social workers, physical therapists/pelvic floor specialists, body workers, and/or sexual surrogates. It is also important that we encourage a medical evaluation early in treatment to rule out or determine any biological causes. Sometimes other providers may need some education and explanation of the work we do and how we can help them, and how they can help us. As the sex therapist on the care team, it is helpful to encourage supervisees to "quarterback the team" by taking a leadership position to ensure that the client care is truly a collaborative effort.

Case Studies

Active learning is a tangible way of being able to use the ideas explored in this chapter in one's practice. As such, what follows are case studies exemplifying the concepts outlined in this chapter. Each case study example will demonstrate the effectiveness of systems work in sex therapy; each will include a conclusion for items the supervisor should consider about in the scenario.

Case Study

Jasmine

Jasmine is a 15-year-old, African American, male-to-female transgender youth brought to therapy by her biological mother seeking a letter from the therapist for hormone therapy (HT). During supervision, the supervisor queried about how the rest of the family system was supporting Jasmine's transition. The stepfather was angry about it and the maternal grandmother (age 64), who lives with Jasmine's family, had not been told. From a systemic lens, understanding the family of origin helped to identify potential land mines as well as opportunities. The supervisor asked the supervisee how she would feel about asking Jasmine and her mother if they would be interested in the therapist's support to include the stepfather and grandmother in family therapy. The therapist thought it was a good idea, as did Jasmine and her mother, who had not realized family therapy was an option for them. Like the supervisee, they viewed their therapeutic issue from a microscopic lens focused solely on needing a letter for HT. In this case, once in family therapy it turns out the angry stepfather wasn't angry after all. He was afraid of what his friends would think, and that fear was being expressed as anger. In the safety of the therapist's office, and with the therapist's coaching, Jasmine shared with her stepfather for the first time just how miserable her lived experience had been for the past 3 years. Through sobbing tears, she told her stepfather that having a penis had been so unbearable since going through puberty that one night she sat locked in her room for almost three hours with their large kitchen knife, seriously contemplating cutting her penis off right then and there. When the stepfather learned just how much pain that Jasmine was in, he was able to better support her. As for the maternal grandmother who lives in the same family home but did not know about Jasmine's gender complexities, family therapy gave Jasmine the option to come out to her grandmother in the safe space of her therapist's office, with the support of her therapist. The grandmother responded with nothing but warmth and love.

In this case, expanding the system in therapy helped the entire system create better connection and understanding.

Considerations for the Supervisor/Supervisee

Many mental health disciplines do not look at the client's many systems and how they may be impacting the presenting issue. In this case, the family greatly benefited from the supervisor looking outside the individual/biological system of the client to the intergenerational system. A sex therapy supervisor who considers the entire system helps the supervisee to expand their conceptualization of each case.

By encouraging their supervisees to look at all systems present, they are able to see how they may have a chance to impact them in a positive and long-lasting way. Furthermore, a systemic sex therapy supervisor knows that there may be treatment considerations beyond what the client is presenting with. In this case, it was important to know that support (or lack thereof) from family members makes a big impact on someone in the processing of transitioning.

Case Study

Benny

Benny is a 24-year-old, Caucasian, cisgender, heterosexual male who presented for individual therapy to understand what he described as a diaper fetish and to explore what options were available to him for treatment. Benny reports he has a partner that he has been with for 2 years. When Benny first started therapy, he reported that he came from a loving home, had a sister 2 years his junior who he was very close with, and he was also very close to his parents. After 4 months of therapy, Benny had a dream in which he saw himself being anally raped by his now diseased uncle. Benny immediately attributed causation of his diaper fetish to the rape and blamed his parents for not protecting him. Benny was furious and confused. Benny's reaction to the dream and subsequent interactions with his parents had made the tension so intense within the family that Benny and his parents had become estranged. They had not spoken in 2 months. His sister wanted to stay close to Benny, however Benny told her that if she remained in relationship with their parents, then she couldn't be in relationship with him. He forced her to choose, and she begrudgingly selected her parents. The supervisee reported to the supervisor that she was utilizing Eye Movement Desensitization and Reprocessing (EMDR) to help Benny with the trauma of recalling the rape. She also had created a safe space for Benny to start talking about his diaper fetish for the first time in his life. The supervisor asked the supervisee about whether she had conversations with Benny about repairing the family system. The supervisee said she had not and that she was focused on treating Benny.

After the most recent supervision session, the supervisee started her session with Benny by asking if he missed his sister. She asked how it felt to think about not being with his family for the upcoming holidays. Benny expressed deep sadness. The therapist asked if

Benny would like to start talking about this part of his life. It was a very emotional session with Benny being quite tearful. Benny said he was exhausted at the end of the session, however he was glad they were talking about it and wanted to start working on the possibility of ending the estrangement and on what terms. He said his mom called him last week, left him a voice mail, and he had been feeling sad and very guilty for not returning her call.

The supervisor helped her see that she had several options that would all support a systemic approach. One option would be that the therapist could continue individual therapy with Benny alone, using an intergenerational lens, focusing on the things within Benny's control. Another option is the possibility of family therapy with his parents and sister. This could be done with the current therapist or by referring out to another systemically trained family therapist. There are many complexities in deciding what is in the best interest of the client in this scenario, which is why consultation about the various options is important. After discussing the pros and cons, the supervisee decided she wanted to offer family therapy to Benny and his family if they were all interested.

Several months later, the supervisee reported in supervision that Benny and his family had been very committed to the process and were participating in family therapy nearly every week. Each member of the system had their own unique hopes, fears, and concerns that they were able to process as a family.

At the supervisee's next supervision session, a few weeks had passed and the therapist gave an update on Benny's situation. Benny was able to express how conflicted he felt about reuniting with his family. On one hand, Benny very much wanted to reunite with his family. On the other hand, Benny was angry that his parents had not protected him and they were taking the side of the now diseased uncle, saying he would have never done such a thing.

Considerations for the Supervisor/Supervisee

While the supervisee was doing great work treating this client at an individual level, she had not been aware of how she might have been able to help at the intergenerational level. Once Benny was feeling more comfortable and stable related to his fetish and trauma, the supervisee could begin conversations about repair work in the family.

Furthermore, it would also be important to expand the system but helping Benny discuss how these recent revelations have impacted his relationship with his partner of 2 years. The therapist may also want to help Benny discuss any insight gained in therapy about these concerns with his partner.

Case Study

Hank

Hank is a 45-year-old, married, Caucasian, cisgender, heterosexual male who presented for individual therapy to overcome what he reported was a sex addiction. The supervisee reported that Hank had previously seen a sex addiction therapist who said that his masturbation, foot fetish, and desire to be sexually dominated by his wife were all part of his sex addiction. The sex addiction therapist helped him set the goals for therapy to stop masturbating and stop fantasizing about his foot fetish and desires to be dominated. The sex addiction therapist had a change in his schedule so it was no longer convenient for Hank to see him. As such, Hank sought out a new therapist, which is how he came to find the supervisee.

In supervision, the supervisee reported that Hank and his wife had been married for 12 years and have two children. Hank felt like he had made very little progress in the 10 weeks he was being treated for sex addiction. The lack of progress and continued transgressions of masturbation were making his wife angry, resentful, and distant. Hank often promised her that he would stop masturbating and looking at pornography, however he had difficulty stopping and she caught him several times, which made her not trust him. The wife refused to participate in Hank's fetishes or desires to be sexually dominated. As of their last therapy session, the couple had not been sexual in any way in nearly six months.

The supervisee said she was working with Hank on making behavioral changes so he could stop looking at porn and stop masturbating, however the supervisee struggled with supporting her client and his wife's desire to stop these behaviors, knowing this may not be the best route of treatment. The supervisee reported that she and Hank both believed the wife to be stubborn and unreasonable. Hank's wife had come to one session with the previous therapist which he stated did not go well. As such, Hank was not very interested in couples counseling and his wife had previously refused.

The supervisor helped the supervisee with her countertransference related to her reaction to the wife's demands for sexual sobriety. Countertransference is defined by a therapist attributing qualities that reflect unresolved issues from a previous relationship onto a client (Volini, 2015). The supervisor pointed out that yes, Hank is the client, however we can still treat the system. Part of treating the system is honoring the beliefs of those who are not directly in therapy with us. Rather than just treat the sexual behaviors, the supervisor suggested that the supervisee work with Hank on that which is within his control, and see if he would like help making the marriage better as well, even if his wife never participates in one therapy session.

One month later the supervisee said she had been working on her countertransference related to this case with a peer, as well as in her own individual therapy. She said that had helped her have more compassion for the wife. The supervisee also reported that Hank very much wanted help improving his marriage even if his wife did not come in for counseling. The supervisee said that when she asked Hank what his wife would say about the strengths and problems in their relationship, Hank didn't have a lot of awareness. He continued to mostly blame his wife for their marital problems, and the supervisee felt stuck with how to help him move forward.

The supervisor said she was very impressed how the supervisee took such a positive approach to look at her countertransference. The supervisor suggested that next time she meets with Hank, she could try these two things:

1. Ask Hank to take a pad and paper and finish this sentence with has many things as he could come up with. My role in our disconnected marriage is _____.
2. Ask Hank how he would feel about asking his wife to write a letter to him that he had permission to share with the supervisee. If he agrees, have the wife write a letter explaining how he has hurt her over the years, what she is resentful about, what she longs for from Hank, and what changes she would like to request in order for your marriage to thrive. Ask the wife to complete this sentence in a similar letter. I will be ready for sex with Hank when _____ _____.

One month later in supervision, the supervisee was beaming with pride. The letter revealed that his wife believed Hank to be contemptuous and highly critical, and that Hank displayed angry outbursts at times that frightened her. The wife explained that she was attracted to what she described as the nice part of Hank, but she hated the mean part. She reported that if Hank was kinder and more caring with her, she would be ready for sex with Hank. The wife also said she wished that Hank would go to marriage counseling with her and did not understand why he had refused her requests for so long. Once the supervisee looked at the system, everything slowly started to change for Hank and his wife.

The supervisee referred Hank to an excellent couples counselor while the supervisee continued to work with Hank on the things within his control. Once the system was expanded, it turns out there were many things for Hank to work on, and he did.

Considerations for the Supervisor/Supervisee

Once this supervisee was able to look outside the individual system and into the couple system, she immediately had more information that would help her to help her client. If one part of the couple system will not participate in couples therapy, helping the client explore what they have control over is often a helpful intervention. Furthermore, exploring the intergenerational and cultural system may also be an important part of this case. The supervisor will want the supervisee to explore Hank's family of origin and see where he learned to be critical and learn about the origins of his contempt and anger. The supervisee could also explore Hank's sexual preferences from a cultural/societal lens to learn about what these desires mean to him in a larger sense.

Case Study

Sharon

Sharon is a 55-year-old, cisgender female. Sharon presents for sex therapy after reaching a point in her marriage where she has come to believe that her parents had some ideas about sex that were damaging to her. Sharon reported to the supervisee feelings of shame and guilt related to sex. She also reported a goal of wanting to rid herself of feeling dirty during sexual activity. The supervisee immediately identifies with the woman, being from a similar generation and having similar experiences in her own family of origin. The supervisee worked for many months of sessions to help the client let go of her family and their belief systems. The supervisee reports to the supervisor that the client has fallen into depression and the supervisor is confused as to why. The supervisor suggests that the supervisee engage in some self-of-therapist work related to countertransference. During the supervisee's reflections, she gained insight that she had allowed her own experience of estranging from her own family to impact the therapy she was providing to Sharon. The supervisor invited the supervisee to consider taking another approach in her next session with the client. The supervisor suggested that the supervisee start by helping her client explore the family's strengths, and ask her client under what circumstances she might want to re-engage with her family and explore boundaries. The supervisor also suggested family therapy.

Considerations for the Supervisor/Supervisee

This supervisee was likely experiencing countertransference with her client due to her poor attachment and her own emotional cutoff from her family. In this case the supervisee was able to gain insight quickly. If, however, she needed more exploration, it would have been appropriate for her supervisor to help her work through her own genogram, identifying related family patterns and emotional cutoff. This could be done in supervision with the supervisor or in the supervisee's own personal therapy. Helping supervisees identify their own self of therapist entering in the therapy room is a crucial part of systemic sex therapy supervision.

Conclusion and Areas for More Research

Systems therapy is a critical component in treating a sex therapy client. Utilizing a systemic lens in sex therapy supervision helps identify relationships with various systems present in a client's life. It also helps the supervisor be aware of possible systemic concerns within the supervisor–supervisee relationship. For sex therapists who do not have sufficient training in systems, supervisees and supervisors alike are encouraged to build this strength. This can be done through live training, books/articles, or observing skilled therapists who are educated and trained in couples counseling and systems theory.

Supervisors hold great responsibility for our supervisees' therapy. By the nature of supervision, supervisors only get to see a certain amount of cases from supervisees. However, when supervisors teach principles like those explained in this chapter, those principles will spill over into the entire body of work that supervisees will do over the course of their career. Teaching supervisees to conceptualize cases with a systemic lens can positively impact an entire community of people and the larger system.

More empirically validated research is needed on the topic of systemic sex therapy supervision due to the multitude of therapists practicing sex therapy with a systemic lens.

About the Authors

Neil Cannon is a sex therapist and couples counselor in Denver, Colorado. He has a master's degree in Public Health and a doctorate degree in Human

Sexuality. In addition to having post-graduate certification in Marriage and Family Therapy, he also has post-graduate certification in LGBT Family Systems. He is an instructor at the University of Michigan Sexual Health Certificate Program and a Professor of Marriage and Family Therapy at Denver Family Institute.

Amanda Sasek, MS, LMFT, is a Licensed Marriage and Family Therapist and an Approved Supervisor with the American Association of Marriage and Family Therapy (AAMFT). She is an owner and therapist at Sexual Wellness Institute in Plymouth, Minnesota. She is a faculty affiliate and adjunct faculty at the University of Wisconsin–Stout Graduate Certificate in Sex Therapy Program. She is passionate about her work with sexuality as well as her work with new therapists.

References

Bateson, G. (1972). *Steps to an ecology of mind*. New York: Dutton.

Blow, A. J., Sprenkle, D. H., & Davis, S. D. (2007). Is who delivers the therapy more important than the treatment itself? The role of the therapist in common factors. *Journal of Marital and Family Therapy, 33*(3), 298–317.

Braun-Harvey, D., & Vigorito, M. A. (2016). *Treating out of control sexual behavior: Rethinking sex addiction*. New York: Springer.

Coulter, S. (2014). The applicability of two strengths-based systemic psychotherapy models for young people following type 1 trauma. *Child Care in Practice, 20*(1), 48–63.

Crocker, M. (2013). *Looking for attachment solutions in all the wrong places: Out of control sexual behavior as a symptom of insecure attachment in men (Doctoral dissertation)*. University of Pennsylvania, School of Social Policy and Practice; Philadelphia, PA.

Gambescia, N., & Weeks, G. (2015). Systemic treatment of erectile dysfunction. In K. Hertlein, G. Weeks, & N. Gambescia (Eds.), *Systemic sex therapy* (2nd ed.). New York: Routledge.

Hertlein, K. M., Weeks, G. R., & Gambescia, N. (2015). *Systemic sex therapy* (2nd ed.). New York: Routledge.

Johnson, S. M. (2004). *The practice of emotionally focused couples therapy: Creating connection* (2nd ed.). New York: Brunner-Routledge.

Lee, R. E., & Nelson, T. S. (2014). *The contemporary relational supervisor*. New York: Routledge.

Morgan, M. M., & Sprenkle, D. H. (2007). Common factors in supervision. *Journal of Marital and Family Therapy, 33*(1), 1–17.

Nichols, M. P., & Schwartz, R. C. (2001). *Family therapy concepts and models* (5th ed.). Needham Heights, MA: Allyn & Bacon.

Perel, E. (2017). *The state of affairs: Rethinking infidelity*. New York: HarperCollins.

Piercy, F. P., Sprenkle, D. H., & Wetchler, J. L. (1996). *Family therapy sourcebook* (2nd ed.). New York: Guilford Press.

Schnarch, D., & Schnarch, D. M. (2009). *Intimacy & desire: Awaken the passion in your relationship*. Melbourne: Scribe.

Smith-Acuña, S. (2011). *Systems theory in action*. Hoboken, NJ: John Wiley & Sons.

Synder, D. K., Baucom, D. H., & Coop Gordon, K. (2007). *Getting past the affair.* New York: Guilford Press.

Volini, L. (2015). *The national licensing exam for marriage and family therapy: An independent study guide.* Waconia, MN: MFT Licensing Exam LLC.

Weeks, G., & Gambescia, N. (2015). Couple therapy and sexual problems. In A. S. Gurman, J. L. Lebow, & D. K. Snyder (Eds.), *Clinical handbook of couple therapy* (5th ed.). New York: Guilford Press.

Weeks, G., Gambescia, N., & Hertlein, K. (2016). *A clinician's guide to systemic sex therapy* (2nd ed.). New York: Routledge: Taylor & Francis Group.

Yingling, L. C. (2000). What is a systemic orientation—really? In AAMFT (Ed.), *Readings in family therapy supervision: Selected articles from the AAMFT Supervision Bulletin* (pp. 36–38). Alexandria, VA: AAMFT.

10 Sex Therapy Supervision Through a Psychology Lens

Rachel Needle

Abstract

Psychotherapy supervision is a fundamental educational component in training competent therapists. Within the context of therapy, presenting complaints relating to sex and sexuality with either an individual or a couple comprise a complex combination of interrelated biological, psychological, and contextual variables. When engaging in supervision for sex therapy cases, looking at the client or couple through a psychological lens involves conceptualizing cases using any one of a number of psychological theories. Supporting the supervisee in understanding the importance of conceptualization and the manner in which questions are presented is crucial. Sex therapy supervision utilizing a psychological lens views the client as a whole person, not just as a sexual dysfunction or presenting issue. Supervisors can support supervisees in understanding their client by looking at biological/hormonal, contextual, interpersonal, intrapersonal, ideological, and historical factors contributing to the client's presenting concern. Supervisors help supervisees recognize when their own history, views of sexuality, and biases might be getting in the way. Development is facilitated by the relationship between the supervisor and supervisee, through self-reflection, focus on clinical skill development, discussion, and conceptualization.

Keywords

sex therapy, supervision, conceptualization, psychology, psychologist

Psychotherapy supervision is a fundamental educational component in training competent therapists. Within the context of therapy, presenting complaints relating to sex and sexuality with either an individual or a couple comprise a complex combination of interrelated biological, psychological, and contextual variables. More often than not, these factors interact and result in distress and interruptions of "normal functioning." In some instances, psychological factors may precipitate a sexual dysfunction or further worsen and complicate an existing sexual issue (Althof & Needle, 2011). When engaging in supervision for sex therapy cases, looking at the client or couple through a psychological lens involves conceptualizing cases using any one of a number of psychological theories. Supporting the supervisee in understanding the importance of conceptualization and the manner in which questions are presented is crucial.

Sex therapy supervision through a psychological lens uses a framework that approaches the client holistically, not just as a sexual dysfunction or a presenting issue. Supervisees are encouraged to look at all the pieces of the puzzle. It is important to also consider the context of the supervisee–supervisor relationship and the impact the supervisor can have on the supervisee. Several models of supervision currently exist, but limited information has been gathered on the niche of sex therapy. Through certification and training programs, individuals are encouraged to examine the influence of their own culture and views of sexuality on their work with clients. The supervisor plays many roles including that of an educator, consultant, facilitator of growth, and counselor.

Sex Therapy Supervision Through a Psychology Lens

Psychotherapy supervision is a fundamental educational component in training competent therapists. The dynamic of professional supervision is complex and intricate. The many different theoretical perspectives, coupled with differences in personality types, relationships, values, and skill, creates a unique experience. Within the context of therapy, presenting complaints relating to sex and sexuality with either an individual or a couple comprise a complex combination of interrelated biological, psychological, and contextual variables. More often than not, these factors interact and result in distress and interruptions of "normal functioning." In some instances, psychological factors may precipitate a sexual dysfunction or further worsen and complicate an existing sexual issue. When engaging in supervision for sex therapy cases, looking at the client or couple through a psychological lens involves conceptualizing cases using any one of a number of psychological theories. Supporting the supervisee in understanding the importance of conceptualization and the manner in which questions are presented is crucial.

Sex therapy supervision through a psychological lens uses a framework that approaches the client–therapist relationship holistically. Supervisees are encouraged to look at all the pieces of the puzzle. It is important to also consider the context of the supervisee–supervisor relationship and the impact the supervisor can have on their supervisee. Several models of supervision currently exist but limited information is gathered on the niche of sex therapy. Through certification and training programs, individuals are encouraged to examine the influence of their own culture and views of sexuality on their work with clients. The supervisor plays many roles including that of an educator, consultant, facilitator of growth, and counselor.

Biopsychosocial Model

The biopsychosocial model was designed as an alternative to the biomedical model, which posits that mental disorders including sexual dysfunctions have a physical cause. Thus, effective treatment occurs by treating the biological (including neurological) causes. On the other hand, a biopsychosocial model examines how biological, psychological, and social causes impact an individual, their behavior, and their mental health. The biopsychosocial model is a systems approach to looking at the presenting issue. A supervisor implementing this approach will take care to challenge the supervisee to examine all the facets that combine to create the individual and their identity, and to avoid the myopic tendency to focus only on the presenting issue at hand. The facets in question may include a comprehensive sexual history, culture and the development of dialogue with self, sexual preferences, gender, lifestyle, their worldview and how they see themselves in it, and the influence of their partner(s) and stereotypes.

The three main components of this comprehensive model are biological, psychological, and social systems. To add to it, a careful and comprehensive assessment helps supervisees to delineate all the factors—medical/biological, psychological, interpersonal, intrapersonal, developmental, and contextual— that contribute to the onset and maintenance of the sexual dysfunction. For example, a client may disclose in their introductory session that they have been experiencing erectile dysfunction (ED). The biomedical model will look to treat the ED utilizing a solely pharmaceutical intervention. However, when utilizing the biopsychosocial model, the supervisee would be encouraged to gather more information about the ED, such as when the problem first presented, what the client's sexual history reveals, if there have been any changes in the individual's environment (e.g., job loss, death, change in relationship, change in health, trauma), and what the client's social landscape looks like (Althof & Needle, 2011). This information will prove valuable, as supervisees are encouraged to create a picture of a client and all of the factors that have contributed to the client's development including the presenting issue. The cause of the erectile dysfunction may have nothing or everything to do with biological factors, but without generating a holistic view of the client and their full story or picture, a sex therapist may lack information that is vital to understanding the client and their current presenting issue(s). In utilizing a wide psychological lens, a supervisor supports their supervisee in seeing the client's full picture rather than solely focusing on the sexual complaint through a narrow lens. This understanding contributes to a thorough conceptualization aiding in treatment planning.

The supervisor will work with their supervisee to understand all aspects of the client's history and to complete a thorough psychosexual assessment to include looking at a couple's sexual history, current sexual practices, relationship quality and history, emotional health, and contextual factors (young children, chronic illness, financial concerns, cultural beliefs, etc.) currently influencing their lives. The client's developmental history is examined for influences upon current functioning (e.g., sexual or physical abuse) or the impact of a serious medical illness. Assessment of all the relevant medical and biological factors is necessary to understand the genesis and maintenance of the current difficulty. Supervisors often explore and encourage supervisees to look for and understand treatment avoidance and resistance.

The benefits of using a comprehensive model of assessment goes beyond helping the supervisee to better understand and treat the client or couple. Doing so also allows for effectively managing countertransference. An individual's sexual purviews are created from years of life experiences, education, family, culture, and social influences. It is crucial for a supervisee to fully understand their own sexuality, including views and biases. The supervisor is responsible for supporting the supervisee in identifying how their personal beliefs or views might be impacting the therapeutic relationship and treatment. Additionally, providing the supervisee with resources, including readings and information, can support them in becoming well-rounded in the vernacular that may arise in sessions with individuals and couples who are of differing backgrounds. Understanding the impact of their messages, spoken or otherwise, will assist the supervisee in preventing the perpetuation of stereotyping and marginalization as a result.

Other Models of Supervision

Multiple models of supervision currently exist for psychotherapy, though little is designed to target sex therapy specifically. Supervisors can assist their supervisees by approaching the session with empathy and understanding. As part of this goal, it is recommended that supervisors get to know their supervisee, including their learning style, theoretical orientation, and therapy style, in order to implement a model that will complement the clinician, whether they are novice or experienced. Just as the biopsychosocial model applies a systems approach to understanding and addressing the client and their chief complaint, supervisors should approach their supervisees in much the same way. As such, there is no one model of supervision that provides a "one size fits all" type of standard. Instead, supervisors benefit by creating an integrative approach incorporating components from multiple models of supervision. The appropriateness of the models should be examined in a case-by-case basis for each supervisee and may want to be explored with the supervisee(s).

Developmental models of supervision focus on the growth of the supervisee and consider the stage of the clinician being supervised, much like the concept of applying the transtheoretical model of change. For supervisors, accurately defining the stage of their supervisee's development will not only help them provide appropriate feedback for that stage, but it will also support their supervisee in progressing as a clinician. Building off the concepts of Vygotsky's theory of scaffolding, new skill development of the supervisee will utilize existing knowledge with the guidance of the supervisor facilitating learning and progression.

Some supervisors use the theoretical approaches they use in therapy to help supervisees will skill development. "Theoretical orientation informs the observation and selection of clinical data for discussion in supervision as well as the meanings and relevance of those data" (Falender & Shafranske, 2008, p. 9). Thus, a psychoanalytic approach to supervision would include using clinical data such as defense mechanisms, transference, and countertransference. Cognitive-behavioral supervision utilizes observable cognitions and behaviors, and some of the techniques used in supervision "include setting an agenda for supervision sessions, bridging from previous sessions, assigning homework to the supervisee, and capsule summaries by the supervisor" (Liese & Beck, 1997). Person-centered supervision, like person-centered therapy developed by Carl Rogers, centers around the idea that the supervisee has the resources they need to develop as a therapist and that the supervisor acts as a collaborator with the supervisee as opposed to an expert. In this model of supervision, the relationship between supervisor and supervisee plays a key role in facilitating effective to facilitate valuable learning and growth in supervision (Smith, 2009).

The transtheoretical model of clinical supervision (TMCS) is based on Prochaska and DiClemente's and Prochaska and Norcross's stages and processes of change (Aten, Strain, & Gillespie, 2008). The application of the transtheoretical model on supervision allows for integration of individual approaches and values of the supervisee-supervisor relationship.

> First, no one supervision model can account for or capture the complexities of the supervisory process (Gilbert & Evans, 2001). Therefore, a clinical supervision model of this nature may provide a template for supervisors that informs their understanding of the needs of their supervisees and aids in the selection and integration of supervision modalities to help meet those needs. Second, supervisors should expect supervisees to enter into and move through clinical supervision with varying degrees of apprehension and motivation and fears of performing incompetently. Third, the TMCS can be used to facilitate supervisees' holistic professional growth and development or be used to target and address deficient or problematic behaviors. Fourth, supervisees' openness and ability to grow and change will vary across skill sets and behaviors. It is possible for supervisees to be operating at more than one stage of change simultaneously. Fifth, supervisors will be the most efficacious when they are able to accurately assess supervisees' needs across the stages of change and then aptly employ corresponding processes of change. Sixth, using the TMCS, supervisors and supervisees will operate with increasing intricacy as each gains experience in their respective roles and the supervisory alliance is strengthened. Seventh, the TMCS differs from other psychotherapy-based models of supervision because it promotes the inclusion of other supervision constructs, modalities, and interventions. Eighth, supervisors using the TMCS may be uniquely suited to address diversity issues because they have the tools to assess the need for and the flexibility to integrate multicultural (Constantine, 2001; Falender & Shafranske, 2004), feminist (Prouty, 2001), gay and lesbian affirmative (Halpert & Pfaller, 2001), and religious and spiritual (Aten & Hernandez, 2004) approaches to supervision. Finally, the utility of this model may be limited by supervisors' level of experience and abilities. More experienced supervisors will

likely be able to develop more complex, integrative, and personalized approaches to supervision, whereas novice supervisors may struggle to successfully use the model offered as a means of conceptualizing clinical supervision.

(Aten et al., 2008, p. 2)

The TMCS exemplifies some of the challenges that may arise within the context of supervision. It postulates that supervisees go through five stages of change—pre-contemplation, contemplation, preparation, action, and termination—while growing as clinicians. The benefit of utilizing the TMCS is the implication that more is going on with the supervisee than knowledge-based practice, and that these changes might not always occur in a linear fashion. The supervisee will experience personal growth as well as professional development. In becoming more competent sex therapists, supervisees will explore their biases as they pertain to preferences, culture, gender, and practice.

Considerations for Supervisors

Supervision for mental health providers currently lacks structure and definition of what a competent supervisor should possess, and even less is published about the supervision dynamic with sex therapists. Nevertheless, the approach to the supervisor–supervisee relationship should be one that promotes empathy, understanding, and communication. It is important for the supervisor to be aware of how their method of providing information might impact their supervisee. Style and delivery of feedback and information can play a role in how the supervisee takes in and processes the information. Each supervisee will be different, so it is important for the supervisor to be conscious of the skill level, potential anxiety, and current ability to process and respond to feedback. Periodically checking in with supervisees to assess their understanding of and response to supervision is encouraged. The most effective supervision is a collaboration between two individuals. While the supervisor is expected to be more expert and competent in the area of presentation, supervision also helps supervisees to be cognizant of additional factors both within themselves and the client that they might not have previously seen or understood.

Supervisors are expected to demonstrate competence and understanding of various models, methods, and interventions, ethics and professional concerns, especially as it relates to the psychological welfare of the client/therapist relationship, conducting assessment and evaluation, exhibiting an understanding of differences and diversity, and creating an environment that nurtures an openness to, and utilization of, self-reflection and assessment.

Conclusion

Clinical supervision is often considered to be a process of observing, guiding, and providing feedback. It is so much more. While supervision is different than psychotherapy, models of supervision are informed by specific styles and orientations utilized by both supervisor and supervisee. Sex therapy supervision utilizing a psychological lens views the client as a whole person, not just a sexual dysfunction or presenting issue. Conceptualization is key to understanding the client and all of the potential factors contributing to and maintaining their presenting issue. Supervisors can support supervisees in understanding their client by looking at biological/hormonal, contextual, interpersonal, intrapersonal, ideological, and historical factors contributing to the client's presenting concern. Supervisors help supervisees recognize when their own history, views of sexuality, and biases might be getting in the way. Development is facilitated by the relationship between the supervisor and supervisee through self-reflection, focus on clinical skill development, discussion, and conceptualization.

About the Author

Rachel Needle is a Licensed Psychologist and Certified Sex Therapist in private practice at the Center for Marital and Sexual Health of South Florida (www.cmshsf.com). She is also the founder and executive director of the Whole Health Psychological Center (www.wholehealthpsych.com), a comprehensive psychological practice with therapists in a broad range of specialty areas. She is the founder of the Advanced Mental Health Training Institute, which provides continuing education and certification trainings, and Co-director of Modern Sex Therapy Institutes, which provides continuing education and trains sex therapists around the world. She has an ongoing blog and personal website (www.drrachel.com).

References

Althof, S., & Needle, R. (2011, May). Psychological factors associated with male sexual dysfunction: Screening and treatment for the urologist. *Urologic Clinics of North America*, 38(2), 141–146.
Aten, J.D., Strain, J.D., & Gillespie, R.E. (2008). A transtheoretical model of clinical supervision. *Training and Education in Professional Psychology*, 2(1), 1–9.
Falender, C.A., & Shafranske, E.P. (2008). *Clinical supervision: A competency-based approach*. Washington, DC: American Psychological Association.
Liese, B.S., & Beck, J.S. (1997). Cognitive therapy supervision. In C.E. Watkins, Jr. (Ed.), *Handbook of psychotherapy supervision* (pp. 114–133). Hoboken, NJ: John Wiley & Sons.
Smith, K.L. (2009, September). *A brief summary of supervision models*. Retrieved January 12, 2018, from www.marquette.edu/education/grad/documents/Brief-Summary-of-Supervision-Models.pdf

11 Clinical Supervision, Sexuality, and LGBTQ Issues

Daniel J. Alonzo

Abstract

The intersection of clinical supervision, sexuality concerns of clients, and LGBTQ issues is a new and largely unexplored terrain. This chapter examines the unique challenges involved in supervising a therapist whose LGBTQ clients are seeking support or direction in their sexual lives. Supervisors must consider appropriate theoretical frameworks that honor the lived experience of LGBTQ clients, the adoption of a multicultural and diversity-focused lens, the assessment of a supervisee's knowledge base of LGBTQ populations, and the assessment of a supervisee's competence in intervention and treatment planning. In addition, the supervisor must pay considerable attention to the actual process of supervision in the consultation room. Several case studies will highlight the process of contextually sensitive, theoretically sound, and LGBTQ-affirmative supervision.

Keywords
Supervision, LGBTQ, sexuality, sex therapy, theory, multiculturalism, competency-based

Introduction

Supervision of sex therapists and other mental health professionals who work with clients around sexuality issues is a largely undocumented area. Even more unexplored is the intersection of clinical supervision, sexuality concerns of clients, and LGBTQ issues. There are unique challenges when supervising a therapist whose LGBTQ clients are seeking support or direction in their sexual lives. This is an endeavor that requires supervisors to be both knowledgeable about sexual minority issues and sensitive to personal factors in the supervision room that have the potential to skew the process. A vignette may help illustrate the density of this endeavor.

Mark, a 40-year-old gay white male and a licensed marriage and family therapist, sought supervision when he started to see a female couple for relationship and sex therapy. Mark had considerable experience with gay male couples but not female couples. "It's pretty remarkable," he explained to his supervisor in his assessment of his couple. "They are so enmeshed. They keep interrupting each other and taking offense at what the other one says. They don't seem to have any insight into how their separation-individuation issues are keeping them stuck. Laura—she's the older of the two—seems driven to take care of Joanne. She complains that Joanne never wants to have sex, but even in session she smothers Joanne with a lot of caretaking. No wonder Joanne doesn't feel attracted to her anymore. But Joanne doesn't help the situation. She gets all rebellious like a teenager. She either talks back, or she says she's bored. Clearly she's acting out her attachment issues. And each of them has a lot of internalized homophobia."

"Whoa, let's slow this down a bit," his male supervisor cautioned. The supervisor wanted Mark to feel confident in his assessment abilities, but the supervisor also did not want Mark to miss factors that could be impacting this female couple and the therapy that Mark was providing. "Yeah, it sounds like they can become very reactive in the room with each other. Tell me more about them. You mentioned their ages. What else? For example, tell me about their ethnicities."

"Well," Mark began, "Joanne's Caucasian, and Laura's Hispanic. But she's pretty acculturated. I don't think that's having much an effect here."

"It might be something to explore," the supervisor said. "I'm wondering what narratives and stories Laura absorbed in earlier parts of her life. How many generations is she away from the first family members who immigrated here? What did she learn about a woman's place in a relationship? How is love demonstrated in her culture?"

Mark grew slightly anxious. "I'm not sure. Are you saying that their internal object relations are not playing any part in their relationship dynamics?"

"No, honest, I'm not dismissing that," his supervisor responded. "I think you're on to something, the way they react so quickly and angrily to each other. I just want us to look at look at all the pieces of the puzzle here. Maybe it is 'enmeshment.' But you know, a lot of lesbian couples get labeled with that, when, really, closeness and nurturance may be one of their strengths. Maybe Joanne is reacting to something else, that's all I'm saying. We just don't want to make assumptions. We want to learn from them."

"I understand," Mark said. "I know I can be too analytical sometimes."

"Well, welcome to the club," the supervisor responded sincerely. "We were all trained to analyze via the medical model. So let's take a look at other pieces. How do they feel about having you as a therapist?"

Mark's discomfort grew. "I haven't explored that yet. Are you saying they should be with a lesbian therapist? I'm trying to get more sex therapy experience with couples. I'd hate to refer them to someone else."

"No, I'm not saying that. I'm just wondering what it's like for two women in a mixed-ethnicity couple, in an intimate relationship, to be talking about sex with a white gay man in a therapy room. What is their experience of that?" Mark seemed stymied by the question. He said he realized he had no answer to that.

Actually, Mark had a good reputation of being a solid relationship therapist in the local LGBTQ community. He had a warm and encouraging presence in the room with clients. He had a healthy private practice and he never wanted for referrals. He had a strong interest in sexuality, and his intention was to pursue an advanced professional designation as a certified sex therapist. The goal of supervision here was to help him transition from being a good therapist to being a contextually sensitive therapist, open to new possibilities and frameworks when working with sexual matters.

This view, in a nutshell, is the essence of supervision of therapists who address LGBTQ issues around sexuality. Supervision in these circumstances includes the following distinct components: choosing a framework that ulti mately validates the client's dignity and individuality; assessing the supervisee's knowledge base, skill level, and personal development; and being mindful of the delicate process of supervision in the room with the supervisee. These components are further illustrated in the sections below.

Distinct Features and Challenges

Essential Theoretical Frameworks

In sexuality supervision, it is necessary that supervisors help supervisees adopt theoretical frameworks that honor the lived experiences of clients. One of the most important considerations is to hold a systemic point of view. A system is an intricate organization of parts that is distinct from other such organizations and entities (Jackson, 1957, 1965). A system is a naturally occurring phenomenon, the whole greater than the sum of its parts, and all parts interacting with each other. Systems theory is interested in what happens as these whole entities, each with their own set of rules and roles and structure, must incorporate change and solve problems (Bateson, 1972). Family systems theory investigates the organization of families and the impact that such an organization has on its individual family members. Every family is a whole unto itself, but every family is also embedded in larger systems, such as the extended family, the larger community, and powerful social and cultural forces (e.g., religion, ethnicity, gender narratives, political events; Stanton & Welsh, 2012). It is an important—but challenging—paradigm shift away from the sole focus on the intrapsychic. It is a contextual point of view, taking into account the larger forces that rock and shape our clients' lives (Bronfenbrenner & Morris, 2006; Stanton & Welsh, 2012). Furthermore, family systems theory can be applied to any client, whether an individual, couple, or family (Haley, 1987; Kerr & Bowen, 1988). Sex therapists and other mental health professionals who wear blinders and only work to solve one complaint (such as premature ejaculation) or change just one pattern in a relationship (such as instructing a couple how to touch each other) are asking for frustration and failure. Supervisors must help supervisees take into account the larger picture, the greater context, so that supervisees can see all the factors that are affecting a client's progress. Examples of this could include helping supervisees wonder about family-of-origin messages about sexuality, helping supervisees understand the rhythms and give-and-take of a couple's usual communication style, and helping supervisees understand social mores and dictums may that have limited their clients' growth.

One of the social forces that has shaped the lives of LGBTQ people is the culture's dominant viewpoint of same-sex attraction and gender identification. For centuries, individuals who have not fit into binary systems of sexuality and gender have been marginalized, harassed, or persecuted. Early psychotherapeutic approaches pathologized same-sex attraction and variant gender identity, and those same approaches influenced the supervision that was provided to trainees (Pett, 2000). Although it may seem obvious and self-evident, it is important to state that the supervisor of sexuality professionals must start from an active LGBTQ-affirmative stance. The use of an affirmative model is essential so that the dignity of LGBTQ clients is ultimately affirmed and championed. Supervisors must start from an affirmative stance where all sexual orientations and gender variations are equally valid (Halpert, Reinhardt, & Toohey, 2007). Such supervision includes the process of cultivating an awareness in supervisees of the impact of homophobia, heterosexism, and oppression on the everyday lives of clients (Pett, 2000).

With an affirmative stance as the foundation, other theoretical viewpoints can add strength to the supervisory structure. A feminist therapeutic lens reminds us that therapy must commit to social change, empower clients, and value goals of interdependence and self-nurturance (Brown, 2010; Enns, 2004; Worell & Remer, 2003). Feminist-informed therapy helps supervisors and supervisees move out of the constrictions of a binary view of gender. Another theoretical viewpoint that can facilitate supervisee growth is social constructionism. Social constructionism tells us that our knowledge of reality is based on language and constructed through interactions with others (Gergen, 1999). As a result, therapists adopt a collaborative approach to working with clients, as therapists cannot be the experts of their clients' lives. Therapists and other mental health professionals must work to explore clients' perceptions and worldviews, and in getting to know their clients' experiences, they can intervene in sensitive and affirming ways (De Jong & Berg, 2008). Coming out of the social constructionist revolution, the postmodern approaches to therapy (most frequently, solution-focused and narrative therapies) contribute an important pillar to the therapeutic structure, adding important components of optimism, a focus on the future, and a trust that clients are competent and resourceful and able to craft solutions to the problems in their lives (Bertolino & O'Hanlon, 2002; Freedman & Combs, 1996; White & Epston, 1990).

Hand in hand with social constructionism and postmodernism is the adoption of a multicultural and diversity-focused lens. Diversity encompasses race, ethnicity, culture, gender, sexual orientation, gender identity, religion, social class, age or position in the lifespan, immigration status, and level of ability/ disability, just to name a few (Sue & Sue, 2016). These aspects of diversity are core parts of the self. They help us understand who we are, they connect us to others, and they provide a scaffolding on which we can fill in the specifics of identity and personal experience. What is important for supervisees to understand is that diversity affects sexuality. People experience their sexualities differently depending on how they view themselves and how others view them. As a result, there is a unique texture to the interweaving of LGBTQ issues and diversity considerations. Supervisors must help supervisees understand the unique challenges of intersectionality, or the convergence of various aspects of diversity (Cole, 2009). For example, how does being LGBTQ intersect with other aspects of identity, such as race and ethnicity? How can an African American gay male handle the stereotypes that all black men are supposed to be sexually dominant, always ready for sex, and frequently "on the down low"? (Calabrese, Rosenberger, Schick, & Novak, 2015). How can an Asian American lesbian handle the expectations that she is supposed to be quiet, passive, and inscrutable? (Reid & Bing, 2000). Supervisors must help supervisees understand the stress of such overlapping aspects of diversity. As Lewis and Grzanka (2016) point out, the stress is both additive and multiplicative. Without this understanding, supervisees may contribute to the marginalization, stereotyping, and invisibility of their LGBTQ clients.

The importance of larger contextual and systemic variables is illustrated in the opening vignette. Mark wonders about enmeshment of his lesbian clients, but it is important to factor in cultural variables. Laura's Hispanic culture is one that values *la familia*, community, and connection. What may look like a violation of boundaries in US culture is actually loving and nurturing in the Hispanic culture. Is Mark completely wrong? No, not necessarily. Laura may be caretaking too much. But the supervisor had to consider other cultural worldviews or else Mark might have come to false conclusions. The supervisor invited Mark to consider what it must be like having an intersection of multiple identities of being Latina, being a woman, and being a lesbian. Perhaps there was not much space for Laura's exploration of her sexuality in a Hispanic culture that prizes the larger good over the individual's need. On the other side of the fence, Laura's partner Joanne may have been acting like a sulking teenager, but maybe it was a challenge for her to fully own her personal power in the face of societal prejudice toward lesbians. These are the questions that supervisors must ask as they employ systemic viewpoints and culturally sensitive frameworks.

A Solid Knowledge Base of the LGBT Experience

Supervisors must ensure that their supervisees have an in-depth knowledge of LGBTQ populations and their experiences in the world (Bieschke, Blasko, & Woodhouse, 2014). If supervisees have gaps in their knowledge of LGBTQ populations, or if they lack an overall understanding of the LGBTQ experience as a minority in the United States, then it is the supervisor's responsibility to find ways for the supervisee to fill those gaps and cultivate an expanded perspective.

One of the primary areas of necessary knowledge is that of LGBTQ psychosocial development. Supervisees need to grasp what it is like to grow up "different" in a culture that prizes conformity, popularity, and adherence to majority group values. Whereas other minority children may feel isolated and different from their peers and classmates in school and on the playgrounds and other settings, they can usually return home at the end of the day to parents who look and sound like them. A Muslim immigrant child from Syria certainly might feel different from the majority of her peers in a US classroom, but when she returns home at night, she will see family members with the same complexion, hear the cadences of her native language reflected in theirs, join in a family dinner with familiar aromas, and perhaps end the day with a religious ritual that all family members practice. On the other hand, a child or young adolescent growing up LGBTQ will most likely not see or hear his or her reality reflected in her parents' or siblings' lives. Unless this child is growing up in a same-sex parental household, she will feel isolated from those to whom she should feel closest, scared to disclose or talk about her growing awareness that she is different from her family in a very significant way. The stress of having to hide one's true identity until one is strong enough and independent enough to come out of the closet is huge. Supervisees must understand that this stress is an interruption to an LGBTQ person's natural trajectory, and it can have a profound effect on trust, intimacy, and sexuality in adult life.

Another developmental consideration is the frequent internalization of negative messages about same-sex attraction from the larger culture. The term used to describe a queer person's absorption of society's negative messages about same-sex attraction is "internalized homonegativity" (Szymanski, Kashubeck-West, & Meyer, 2008a). This internalization happens during one's formative years, as LGBTQ youth are flooded with messages in the media that privilege heterosexual relationships and marriages. Heteronormative frameworks pervade most cultural institutions—and, at least by implication, cast doubt on the health of same-sex attraction (Szymanski et al., 2008a). In a school climate that tolerates widely accepted, typically ignored, blatantly homophobic comments like "that's so gay," these doubts are reinforced, over and over again, and eventually these doubts become a part of the internal psychic structure of the LGBTQ person. Internalization of these doubts leads to fear and questioning of one's identity. This is a process that leads to low self-esteem, poor self-concept, and lack of comfort in intimate relationships (Mohr & Daly, 2008; Szymanski, Kashubeck-West, & Meyer, 2008b). Freedom and enjoyment in adult sexual relationships is bound to be compromised or limited in someone who has not yet learned how to divest himself or herself of these socially constructed, toxic messages. Supervisors must make sure that their supervisees have knowledge about internalized homonegativity so that the supervisee is not viewing this phenomenon as further evidence of individual psychopathology in the client.

Another crucial area of knowledge is that of minority stress. If developmental considerations are important because they spell out the early journey of the development of the person's self, then the understanding of minority stress is important to understand present-day challenges. There is currently a tendency to minimize the stress that LGBTQ people experience on a daily basis. After all, many observers point out, this is not 1967, the year of the Stonewall riots and generally marked as the beginning of the gay rights movement: that was over 50 years ago! Many people ask, "Haven't gay people achieved what they wanted? Haven't they permeated popular culture? Anybody can marry anybody now, right? Is anyone really still shocked to find out that someone is gay?" These questions, although they remind us of tremendous progress, still expose a big measure of naiveté. Large population centers in the United States appear to be safe havens for LGBTQ persons, but—to point out the obvious—not all queer people in the United States live in large metropolitan areas. LGBTQ people continue to experience marginalization, subtle prejudice, and microaggressions, or subtle and brief everyday messages that put down targeted people (Sue, 2010). Sometimes these microaggressions are not so "micro," as they achieve a cumulative, dispiriting, and hurtful effect (Sue, 2010; Shelton & Delgado-Romero, 2013). Furthermore, hate crimes against queer people continue to happen at alarming rates (FBI, 2015). Due to perceived threats, both large and small, many queer adults prefer to stay out of harm's way by living quiet lives, out of the glare of the larger community, and away from the gay political scene. All of this is part of the minority stress that LGBTQ persons experience on a daily basis, and supervisees must grapple with this fact.

One of the sources of minority stress for LGBTQ couples is relational ambiguity (Green & Mitchell, 2015). Part of the internalized homonegativity that LGBTQ individuals experience when they are growing up is the discounting and pathologizing of their relationships. Although same-sex couples can now marry, due to the 2015 *Obergefell* ruling by the US Supreme Court, LGBTQ individuals still spend many years worrying about not being able to find love and having doubts about the viability of long-term relationships (Mohr & Daly, 2008). When an individual finally finds a person with whom she thinks she can build a future, the doubts about the sturdiness and form of that relationship begin to surface. In therapy, same-sex couples report obsessional thinking about the strength and sustainability of their relationships: Are we a couple, or are we just friends? Will we last? Do I really love this person, or am I just desperate, because a part of me is afraid that people like me are never really able to find true love? Should we model our relationship after heterosexual models, or should we forge our own path? Do we want goals that heterosexual couples seem to desire—commitment, marriage, children, house in the suburbs, a middle-class lifestyle—or can we elect to push against traditional structures? Do we want monogamy or not? Is our relationship truly over, or are we shutting it down too soon?

Furthermore, when LGBTQ individuals wait years to come out of the closet and participate in the rituals of meeting, dating, courting, having sex with and committing to others, they often come to relationships with huge expectations. Individuals can demand constant mirroring, insisting that their partners be completely understanding of all their needs, share the same interests, have the same viewpoints, have the same level of sex drive, and be turned on by the exact same expressions of sexuality. Kohut (1971) identified these demands as unmet "twinship" or "alter ego" self-object needs, and they can be too much for any relationship to withstand. When relationships frequently buckle under these pressures, LGBTQ individuals resort to reified and practiced thoughts that maybe society at large was right after all, and maybe they were not meant to have relationships. Supervisees must be aware of these internal challenges to same-sex relationships.

Finally, supervisees must also understand the frequent lack of social support for LGBTQ persons. Although some people are fortunate enough to come out in loving families, live in tolerant metropolitan areas, and find a large queer community to welcome them, many people are not so lucky. They may be coming out in smaller cities, rural communities, or in deeply conservative parts of the country. Also, the ethnicity of their immediate circles of family and friends may be one in which same-sex attraction is not valued or even recognized as valid, or worse, so vilified or forbidden as to make some fear for their safety. Support systems are crucial to the health, satisfaction, longevity, and management of stress in same-sex relationships (Kertzner, Meyer, Frost, & Stirratt, 2009; Syzmanski, 2009). LGBTQ persons who cannot find meaningful support systems are more likely to isolate, remain closeted, and look for other closeted with whom to explore their sexualities (Kertzner et al., 2009). This is a recipe for frustration and heartbreak. Therapy for sexual concerns with LGBTQ individuals and couples requires that the supervisor have a deep and broad knowledge of all these variables in order to be truly effective.

Skill Set of Supervisee

Supervisees/clinicians must show competence in skillful intervention and treatment planning (Falender, Shafranske, & Ofek, 2014). This skill must be demonstrated in the initial contact with clients, whether that be over the phone or in an initial intake session. It is especially crucial that the supervisees demonstrate strength in sensitive communication with clients. For example, because the term "homosexual" has been associated so frequently in the past with deviance and mental illness, it is important that supervisees avoid this term with clients, either as a noun or adjective, instead using terms such as gay male, lesbian, bisexual person, same-sex attraction, male–male sexuality, and so forth. Supervisees should avoid language that equates sexual orientation with specific sexual behaviors, as queer people enjoy the same spectrum of sexual activities as heterosexual people. Supervisors must listen carefully for any sweeping generalizations that their supervisees might make about same-sex sexuality (Halpert et al., 2007; Pett, 2000).

Skillful assessment and treatment planning must follow similar guidelines. In assessing the nature of a presenting problem of a client, supervisees must be careful not to make assumptions about onset and duration of sexual problems. Not all sexual problems can be traced to shame or internalized homonegativity on the part of the client. Sometimes, problems develop due to all sorts of precipitating factors (job stress, a new relationship, a recent loss, etc.) that have nothing to do with one's sexuality or gender identification. The same applies to treatment planning. Assuming that LGBTQ clients will respond better to longer, exploratory psychodynamic interventions rather than efficient and focused interventions from cognitive-behavioral therapy or solution-focused therapy is a biased trap. Such an assumption assumes that LGBTQ people are fragile, easily traumatized, and need years of depth work to heal from rejecting families, early gay-bashing, and institutionalized oppression. Although it is true that early experience can have a profound impact on the development of one's identity and sexuality, it is also true that queer people are strong, remarkably resilient, and capable of bringing change into their lives.

One of the most important skills for supervisees to develop is that of creating warm and collaborative therapeutic relationships. Research continues to show that relationship factors account for much of the success of the therapeutic venture (e.g., Norcross & Lambert, 2011; Norcross & Wampold, 2011). LGBTQ clients must sense that their clinicians genuinely like them and want to help them. It is easy for supervisors to overlook the relationship-building skills of their supervisees because supervisors can become lost in the details of specific sex therapy interventions. Supervisors must shape a supervisee's personal presence in the room as much as a supervisor might shape a specific technique. Brilliant interventions will do no good if the therapist has not earned the trust and respect of the client by adopting a strong, unwavering LGBTQ-affirmative stance. When possible, supervisors should monitor a supervisee's performance through live supervision, video recording, or at the very least, audio recording. Merely relying on a supervisee's oral report of what transpired in session may miss some of emergent challenges (countertransference, bias, professionalism, etc.) of what makes sex therapy work or not.

Concurrent Personal Development

If supervisees, as part of their skill set, are expected to create warm and encouraging relationships with their clients, then it is imperative that supervisees continue to grow as people themselves. The supervisor's function here is to assess the supervisee's willingness to engage in an ongoing exploration of one's thoughts and feelings around issues of sexuality and gender. The supervisor needs to assess the following questions: How comfortable is my supervisee with his or her sexual orientation and gender identity? If my supervisee is an LGBTQ person, does she or he have a solid identity and know who she or he is? Is my supervisee able to reflect on his or her sexual history, understanding how it has affected his or her entrance into this field? This is important, because LGBTQ clients will examine their therapists very closely for signs of disapproval, pity, or squeamishness. Supervisors must assess if a supervisee is uncomfortable talking about either the larger picture or the details of same-sex sexuality by commenting on the supervisee's reactions. Supervisors especially need to assess whether their supervisees have the ability to be a nonreactive, nonanxious presence in the face of client frustration, exhaustion, distress, and hopelessness—four feeling states that frequently appear as LGBTQ clients grapple with issues around sexuality and sexual health. Furthermore, it is imperative that any such reactivity be addressed by having the supervisee attend appropriate training, such as a Sexual Attitude Reassessment (SAR).

A special note should be mentioned at this point: for supervisors to assess and monitor their supervisees' personal development, supervisors must also be willing to do ongoing self-assessment of their own personal development (Pett, 2000). Especially after working in the sex therapy field for a significant period of time, it is easy for supervisors to become jaded and closed to their own personal blind spots, basking in their expertise but unaware of how personal events, relationship history, political events, and even the aging process can affect one's point of view. Being a self-aware, thoughtful supervisor requires constant, personal vigilance.

A brief case study highlights a number of issues in enlarging a supervisee's skill set. Janelle, a 38-year-old heterosexual African American marriage and family therapist intern, was starting to see Rebecca and Ellie, both white and both in their early thirties, for sex therapy. They had been together 1 year, and although they reported being in love with each other, they said they frequently had trouble "getting in sync" with each other's sexual style. Ellie, who identified as bisexual, said she enjoyed more penetrative sex, especially using sex toys, whereas Rebecca, the older of the two who identified as lesbian, said she felt uncomfortable with penetration, either in the active or receptive role.

The supervisor's first job was to assess Janelle's knowledge base. Was she able to take a careful sex history of each woman's experiences? Janelle felt reasonably comfortable with taking such a history, although she confessed she felt a tiny bit nervous because she had never done so with two women before. In gathering the history, Janelle discovered that Rebecca actually struggled with a significant amount of internalized homonegativity. Rebecca had been sexually abused by her stepfather when she was 10, and she said that she used to worry that her attraction to women was due to the abuse. "I know that's not true," she told Janelle, but she wondered if that is why she felt uncomfortable with penetration. The supervisor talked with Janelle about how sexual abuse can muddy and confuse identity development in the mind of the survivor. The supervisor directed her to published literature to learn more about this. The supervisor also asked Janelle to use all her counseling skills in developing a collaborative and therapeutic relationship with the couple so that they could safely explore what penetration, sex toys, and sexual roles meant to each woman. The supervisor discovered that Janelle was very skillful in the creation of a warm and accepting therapy environment. When the time came later in the therapy, she was also skillful in suggesting shared sexual exercises for the couple to practice, including exercises that expanded the idea of intimacy to include nongenitally focused behaviors.

The supervisor also assessed Janelle's knowledge about challenges common to same-sex relationships. Janelle recognized that Ellie actually seemed to need a fair amount of mirroring and validation from Rebecca, perhaps because Ellie grew up in a home where she received little mirroring and attention from her parents. The supervisor talked with Janelle about the frequent occurrence of relational ambiguity, and Janelle said it fit with Ellie's confusion about relationship parameters: Ellie confessed that she often remained sexual with previous partners for months after a relationship ended because "I never knew how to call it off"—perhaps out of fears of hurting others, or perhaps out of a fear of being alone.

Finally, the supervisor assessed Janelle's personal development and how it might be affecting her work with the couple. The supervisor guided Janelle through an exploration of her countertransference. Janelle said she felt very comfortable with her own sexuality and gender identification, and she was able to identify similarities between her own sexual and relational journey and that of the couple. However, she acknowledged that it was challenging for her to remain objective and nonanxious. Janelle said with a laugh, "A part of me wants to get in there and solve the problem. I've been a fixer as long as I can remember, and I have to pull myself back and let my clients do the work." The supervisor felt assured that the couple was in good hands, because Janelle seemed to have a keen self-awareness and a strong ability to control well-meaning impulses.

Techniques of Supervision

In addition to using contextually sensitive theoretical frameworks and assessing the developmental needs of supervisees, supervisors must use techniques that pay attention to the actual process of supervision in the consultation room (Falender et al., 2014). That is, the supervisor must not merely structure the *content*, or the *what* of supervision (the supervisee's oral report of what she said and did with her clients, and the specific directions the supervisor provides), but must also address the *process*, or the *how*, of supervision, the roles and stances that each person takes, the feeling tone between supervisor and supervisee, and the implicit messages of the communication (Falender et al., 2014). The supervision endeavor will be limited if the environment is one where the supervisor acts as expert and comments on every error and misstep, an environment where the supervisor dictates exactly what interventions should be used with a client. Supervision will be more effective if the supervisor is a collaborator with the supervisee, trusting that the supervisee will learn by engaging in reflexive conversations and thoughtful analysis of personal reactions.

The most important consideration in terms of use of effective techniques is the supervisor's creation of an environment of safety. This creation is based on the idea that there is an isomorphic process at play here—that is, a parallel process of sorts, so that what goes on in the supervision room will be a reflection of what is happening in the therapy room between therapist and client—and vice versa! If supervisors want their supervisee's clients to feel safe and welcome, then the supervisor must create an environment of safety for the supervisee. Although many supervisees will already be individuals with a significant amount of professional experience or may already be licensed in their disciplines, they will still need the room to experiment and make errors as they develop their own effective, ethical style of sexuality consultation and sex therapy intervention with clients.

It is important to note that even though a sex therapy supervisor and a sex therapy supervisee may both be licensed and may have other similar life experiences, supervision—by its very nature—involves a power differential. The supervisor is in the role of monitoring and evaluating supervisee performance. In other words, the supervisor has more power in this relationship than the supervisee. Power is not something that is easily talked about in a field where therapists value equality and social justice. Supervisors need to initiate discussions about the reality of the hierarchical nature of supervision, and they need to invite an honest discussion of how that power will be used, how decisions will be made, and how supervisees can participate in the co-construction of a fair means of evaluation (Bieschke et al., 2014). Even experienced supervisees—professionals themselves who may be supervisors of other clinicians in other settings—will bring anxieties and apprehension into the supervision room because they know they are being evaluated. The transparency and fairness that a supervisor can bring to the supervision room will invite the supervisee to create transparency and fairness in the therapy room with the client.

In terms of LGBTQ issues in supervision, supervisors must gently guide supervisees away from several common errors that supervisees make with their clients. One error is the idealization of LGBTQ clients at the expense of providing appropriate support—including supportive confrontation—for clients struggling with self-destructive behaviors (Ritter & Terndrup, 2002). Supervisees may glamorize queer clients who have stood up for their rights or have been in committed relationships for many years. Such clients are certainly worthy of our admiration, but supervisors need to caution supervisees not to overlook serious problems that can affect any group of people—such as partner/spousal abuse, chemical dependency, out of control sexual behavior, and hurtful relationship dynamics. Supervisees are sometimes reluctant to confront their LGBTQ clients on self-destructive patterns of behavior because those same clients have to deal with so many other struggles in their daily lives as sexual minorities. Some heterosexual supervisees say, "Well, I'm not gay, so I don't really know what it is like to live with all that stress and oppression. Who am I to tell them what to do?" Supervisors need to remind supervisees that clients come to mental health professionals precisely because they need help and because they value the professional's expertise. It does no client any good if the professional ignores problems out of some misguided attempt to be politically correct.

In a similar vein, not all client challenges can be tied to a minority sexual orientation or gender identity. Some supervisees may assume that clients are only experiencing difficulties because they have been subjected to societal prejudice, homophobia, and discrimination. Although it is essential that client challenges be considered through a larger, contextual point of view, supervisors must also help supervisees see that some sexual problems, after an initial assessment, need a more focused and specific level of intervention (such as addressing pain during sexual play, or finding a sexual position that provides pleasure for both partners) that would be missed by a more macro point of view.

A related error is when supervisees assume that all LGBTQ clients have a shared value system, a similar worldview, and a matching way of life.

Supervisors must remind supervisees that LGBTQ clients are as diverse as any other group: some may be politically liberal, and others may be radically conservative; some may be part of a highly active social scene, and others may be much more content staying at home with a small group of accepting friends; some may push sexual boundaries and be breathtakingly adventurous, and others may be as "vanilla" as vanilla can be! In a similar vein, supervisees may assume that their LGBTQ clients share *their* value system (that is, supervisees think that their clients see the world exactly as supervisees do). This is wishful thinking. Supervisees often assume their clients are as open and accepting of difference and variety as we sexuality professionals strive to be. In fact, many clients encounter sexual difficulties because they have very rigid ideas about sexual pleasure, sexual frequency, sexual activities, relational commitment, and sexual/gender identity. Assuming a shared sexual worldview with clients is a recipe for frustration and ineffective intervention. Some supervisees may assume a similarity between themselves and their clients because it can seem to make empathy easier and the pathway to treatment clearer. Supervisees may assume a congruence between themselves and clients as a way of calming their own anxiety, or they may be doing this as a way of liking their clients more. Supervisors must help supervisees explore the reasons why they may be working too hard to assume a congruence between themselves and their clients.

A final note about the process of supervision concerns the match between supervisor identity and supervisee identity. Will sex therapy supervision be more effective if there is a match between supervisor and supervisee along variables of sexual orientation and gender identification? Or to ask this a different way, will an LGBTQ client be more likely to experience success in sex therapy if both the therapist and her supervisor also identify as LGBTQ? Most recent research (e.g., Bieschke, Blasko, & Woodhouse, 2014; Gatmon et al., 2001; Halpert et al., 2007; Harbin, Leach, & Eells, 2008) indicates that supervision is not negatively affected if the supervisor and supervisee differ in respect to these variables—as long as two conditions are fulfilled. First, the supervision must be grounded in LGBTQ affirmative models. Both supervisor and supervisee must be committed absolutely to an approach with clients that affirms their basic dignity, worth, health, and resilience. Second, the supervisor must initiate conservations about the similarities and differences in the supervision room. Supervisees report a stronger alliance with the supervisor and a greater satisfaction with supervision when supervisors initiate conversations about cultural variables (Gatmon et al., 2001). It is not so much about an identical match between supervisor and supervisee that leads to satisfaction with the process— and by extension, to better outcomes with clients. What is more important is that the supervisee feels heard, feels safe, and feels free to be oneself in the room. Transparency, honesty, genuineness, and straightforwardness on the part of the supervisor will contribute significantly to the success of supervision.

A final case study exemplifies several of the challenges discussed above.

Case Study

David is a 45-year-old white, married heterosexual male and a licensed marriage and family therapist. He has been licensed for 12 years and he is now pursuing his certification as a sex therapist. David has many strengths: he has a warm, personal presence; his clinical skills are readily apparent; and his diagnostic abilities are well honed after specializing for many years in trauma and chemical dependency. Some of his finest work is situated in helping couples reconnect after one of the partners has returned from a tour of duty in the wars in Iraq and Afghanistan. David is wanting to pursue his sex therapy certification because he sees how intricately sex is tied into satisfaction in relationships.

In the pursuit of this certification, David has been open to expanding his learning and working with clients who are outside his experience and comfort zone. In this vein, he was referred a same-sex couple—Brian and Christopher, who have been together 10 years. Brian is a 43-year-old white gay male and a successful clothing designer. Christopher is a 34-year-old African American gay male who is pursuing acting as a career. Christopher seroconverted to being HIV-positive 3 years ago shortly after he and Brian had opened up their relationship. This was a big shock to the relationship, but the men reaffirmed their commitment to each other. Both men curtailed their extradyadic sexual contact with others, although the option for having occasional safer sex with others remained on the table, and Brian began prophylactic antiviral medication to avoid being infected with HIV himself. However, both men reported that they have not able to get their sexual intimacy back to a satisfying and erotic place. Brian reported having difficulty maintaining his erections, and Christopher reported not being interested in sex.

David's supervisor is a gay man who is slightly older than David. The supervisor's first responsibility was to assess David's competence in working with same-sex couples. David seemed fully onboard in terms of adopting a gay-affirmative theoretical stance, and he seemed knowledgeable about systemic dynamics in relationships. He seemed quite comfortable in his own identity as a married heterosexual male, and he seemed equally comfortable with gay men and variations in sexual orientation. His skills in communication helped him develop supportive therapeutic relationships with clients who struggled with a history of trauma. However, he admitted that he was having some countertransference with the couple's initial decision to open the relationship—and their subsequent desire to keep it open.

"I know I'm being judgmental here, and I feel bad about it," David admitted. "I really don't have anything against open relationships. But I keep thinking, that's what got them in this fix to begin with. It's almost as if they are not learning from their mistakes."

"I'm glad you're examining your sexual attitudes," the supervisor told David. "But I'm hearing a contradiction, and I'm wondering if you are aware of it. On the one hand, you say you don't have anything against various relational arrangements. But then it sounds as if you see their arrangement as a mistake."

"But isn't Christopher's seroconversion a consequence of their open arrangement?" David asked.

"Christopher's seroconversion is a consequence of making a poor choice and not practicing safer sex with one of his other partners. It's not a consequence of the openness of their relationship," the supervisor gently explained. This was an opportunity to further assess David's competence in the domain of knowledge. The supervisor reminded David about the pervasive, heterosexist messages in the larger culture that LGBTQ people must endure on a constant basis. The supervisor talked with him about the stress that same-sex couples live with every day. The supervisor talked about the marginalization that this couple must feel, especially with the intersection of race and sexual orientation. He also talked with him about the relational ambiguity with which gay male couples struggle: because gay male couples have been exposed to so many stereotypes about gay men (e.g., gay men cannot sustain lengthy and committed relationships, or that gay men are incapable of being monogamous)—and because it is probable that these men have internalized some of these stereotypes—this gay male couple may have experienced some confusion about exactly what a relationship should look like and what the parameters should be.

"Ah, okay, I see all that," David said thoughtfully. "Wow. I feel stupid. Maybe I have some unconscious bias I didn't realize."

"Well, don't be too hard on yourself. It's just important that you take a look at it," the supervisor told him. The supervisor knew it was important to create an atmosphere of safety where David could talk about his reactions to sexual material. The supervisor understood the isomorphic process of supervision: if the supervisor creates an atmosphere of safety in the room with David, then David is more likely to create an atmosphere of acceptance and safety for his couple. Furthermore, even though David had 12 solid years of experience, he was aware that his supervisor has the responsibility in this supervisory relationship to evaluate David's progress. Therefore, the supervisor proceeded sensitively so that David would continue to open up. "So let's say for the moment that you do have a bias. What might that bias be about?"

"I honestly don't think I have any prejudices toward gay people. My younger brother is gay. I'm close to him. He's in a relationship right now, and I wouldn't want anything bad to happen to him. I'm always telling him to be careful."

"Sounds like you feel protective of your brother. Do you think you might be feeling some protectiveness toward this couple?" It occurred to the supervisor that David may be overromanticizing same-sex relationships: David's logic might proceed along the lines that being in a relationship is better than being single because it protects one against bad things. In an attempt to make the supervision more collaborative, the supervisor thought aloud about ways to have both of them explore the dynamics of this couple. The supervisor continued, "I wonder if your reactions mirror some processes in their relationship. Maybe we can investigate together what's going on with Brian and Christopher. I wonder if either member of the couple is feeling protective of the other."

"I think Brian feels protective of Christopher," David said. "I wonder what it was like for him to hear about Christopher's seroconversion. He was probably shocked, afraid, angry, and wanting to protect him, all at the same time. And Christopher—wow, he must have felt guilty, ashamed, and afraid of losing Brian's love."

"Yes, those are all possibilities, but we don't want to jump to conclusions. We just want to explore these themes with them. I don't know what will be revealed, but just making room for a process where the two of them can have a discussion about all of this will be helpful. Along these lines, it would also be helpful to explore the fact that Brian is older than Christopher, and he earns a heck of a lot more, because Chris is a struggling actor. What does all this mean to them? How do they talk about it? How does power get shared? And if Brian does have more power because of his age and income, how does the racial difference play out between them? Has Christopher had to struggle for recognition and dignity as a gay black man in our culture? And how does he ensure his dignity in this relationship? So now he's come to couple therapy, but you, the therapist, you're also white, and I wonder what it is like for Christopher to be the only black man in the room. On so many fronts, he may feel that he is losing more power in this relationship. Maybe that's connected to his lack of desire for sex?"

David was now fully appreciating this inquiry. "And maybe Brian, feeling protective, is now having trouble seeing Chris as a sex object? Or maybe he's still angry at Chris. Any of these reactions could contribute to his erectile dysfunction. Could that be?"

"Yes, maybe, and that's why we have to get them talking about all this. And, you know, maybe Brian's challenges with arousal are nothing more than medical side effects from recently starting prophylactic mediation. Unlikely, but possible. But we always have to be conscious of medical issues. So do you see how productive it would be to explore all this in session?" The supervisor continued, "I don't know what Brian and Christopher's truths are, but more will be revealed, and just the process of opening up these discussions can shift the reality for these men. So, David, let me ask you about *our* process. What is it like having this conversation with me today? I'm gay, and you're straight, and you've told me about a gay couple you are seeing. What's that like?"

"I have to admit I worry a little that you'll think I'm incompetent. I don't want to sound like an expert in sex between men when I've never had sex with a guy. It's complicated, and it's got all these layers, and I feel stupid sometimes, but that's what I want. I want to be challenged. I feel like I'm learning something in here."

David's statement is a good summary representing the best qualities of sex therapy supervision around LGBTQ issues: it's got layers, it's complicated, and it's a place where learning can take place. The following questions invite further consideration:

> How does a systemic view of clients' sexualities help supervisees develop an empathy for their clients?
> What are the risks in avoiding considerations of intersectionality when dealing with sexual orientation, gender identification, and other cultural variables?
> How can supervisors help supervisees expand their knowledge of minority stress so that they can have more compassion for their LGBTQ clients?
> How can supervisors increase their own comfort in directly dealing with process-related challenges in the room, including relational

tension with supervisees and anxieties about dissimilarities between supervisor and supervisee?

Consideration of these questions will lead to more effective supervision of supervisees who address LGBTQ issues.

About the Author

Daniel J. Alonzo, Psy.D., is a Licensed Psychologist, a Licensed Marriage and Family Therapist, and a Certified Sex Therapist and Certified Supervisor through the American Association of Sexuality Educators, Counselors and Therapists (AASECT). He specializes in sex therapy, couple therapy, and LGBTQ mental health in Los Angeles, California. He is a frequent presenter at national conferences for AASECT, the Society for the Scientific Study of Sexuality (SSSS), the American Psychologist Association (APA), and the American Association of Marriage and Family Therapists (AAMFT). He is a Staff Psychologist in University Counseling Services at California State University, Northridge, and he is also a member of the Adjunct Faculty at Pepperdine University. His professional writings have included contributions of chapters to professional volumes such as *Couple Therapy* (edited by Michele Harway), *Counseling Fathers* (edited by Chen Oren), and *Quickies: The Handbook of Brief Sex Therapy* (edited by Shelly Green and Douglas Flemons).

References

Bateson, G. (1972). *Steps to an ecology of mind*. New York: Dutton.

Bertolino, B., & O'Hanlon, B. (2002). *Collaborative, competence-based counseling and therapy*. Boston, MA: Allyn & Bacon.

Bieschke, K. J., Blasko, K. A., & Woodhouse, S. S. (2014). A comprehensive approach to competently addressing sexual minority issues in clinical supervision. In C. A. Falender, E. P. Shafranske, & C. J. Falicov (Eds.), *Multiculturalism and diversity in clinical supervision: A competency-based approach* (pp. 209–230). Washington, DC: American Psychological Association.

Bronfenbrenner, U., & Morris, P. A. (2006). The bioecological model of human development. In R. M. Leerner & W. Damon (Eds.), *Handbook of child psychology: Volume 1, Theoretical models of human development* (6th ed., pp. 793–828). Hoboken, NJ: John Wiley & Sons.

Brown, L. S. (2010). *Feminist therapy*. Washington, DC: American Psychological Association.

Calabrese, S. K., Rosenberger, J. G., Schick, V. R., & Novak, D. S. (2015). Pleasure, affection, and love among Black men who have sex with men (MSM) versus MSM of other races: Countering dehumanizing stereotypes via cross-race comparisons of reported sexual experience at last sexual event. *Archives of Sexual Behavior, 44*(7), 2001–2014.

Cole, E. R. (2009). Intersectionality and research in psychology. *American Psychologist, 64,* 170–180.

De Jong, P., & Berg, I. K. (2008). *Interviewing for solutions* (3rd ed.). Belmont, CA: Brooks/Cole, Cengage Learning.

Enns, C. Z. (2004). *Feminist theories and feminist psychotherapies: Origins, themes, and diversity* (2nd ed.). New York: Haworth.

Falender, C. A., Shafranske, E. P., & Ofek, A. (2014). Competent clinical supervision: Emerging effective practices. *Counseling Psychology Quarterly, 27*(4), 393–408.

Federal Bureau of Investigation (FBI). (2015). *Latest hate crime statistics released.* Retrieved from www.fbi.gov/news/stories/2015-hate-crime-statistics-released

Freedman, J., & Combs, G. (1996). *Narrative therapy: The social construction of preferred realities.* New York: Norton.

Gatmon, D., Jackson, D., Koshkarian, L., Martos-Perry, N., Molina, A., Patel, N., & Rodolfa, E. (2001). Exploring ethnic, gender, and sexual orientation variables in supervision: Do they really matter? *Journal of Multicultural Counseling & Development, 29*(2), 102–116.

Gergen, K. (1999). *An invitation to social construction.* Thousand Oaks, CA: Sage.

Green, R-J., & Mitchell, V. (2015). Gay, lesbian, and bisexual issues in couple therapy. In A. S. Gurman, J. L. Lebow, & D. K. Snyder (Eds.), *Clinical handbook of couple therapy* (5th ed., pp. 489–511). New York: Guilford Press.

Haley, J. (1987). *Problem-solving therapy* (2nd ed.). San Francisco, CA: Jossey-Bass.

Halpert, S. C., Reinhardt, B., & Toohey, M. J. (2007). Affirmative clinical supervision. In K. J. Bieschke, R. M. Perez, & K. A. DeBord (Eds.), *Handbook of counseling and psychotherapy with lesbian, gay, bisexual, and transgender clients* (2nd ed., pp. 341–358). Washington, DC: American Psychological Association.

Harbin, J. J., Leach, M. M., & Eells, G. T. (2008). Homonegativism and sexual orientation matching in counseling supervision. *Counseling Psychology Quarterly, 21*(1), 61–73.

Jackson, D. D. (1957). The question of family homeostasis. *Psychiatric Quarterly Supplement, 31,* 79–90.

Jackson, D. D. (1965). The study of the family. *Family Process, 4*(1), 1–20.

Kerr, M., & Bowen, M. (1988). *Family evaluation.* New York: Norton.

Kertzner, R., Meyer, I., Frost, D., & Stirratt, M. (2009). Social and psychological well-being in lesbians, gay men, and bisexuals: The effects of race, gender, age, and sexual identity. *American Journal of Orthopsychiatry, 79,* 500–510.

Kohut, H. (1971). *The analysis of the self.* New York: International Universities Press.

Lewis, J. A., & Grzanka, P. R. (2016). Applying intersectionality theory to research on perceived racism. In A. N. Alvarez, C. T. H. Liang, & H. A. Neville (Eds.), *The cost of racism for people of color: Contextualizing experiences of discrimination* (pp. 31–54). Washington, DC: American Psychological Association.

Mohr, J. J., & Daly, C. A. (2008). Sexual minority stress and changes in relationship quality in same-sex couples. *Journal of Social and Personal Relationships, 25,* 989–1007.

Norcross, J. C., & Lambert, M. J. (2011). Evidence-based therapy relationships. In J. C. Norcross (Ed.), *Psychotherapy relationships that work: Evidence-based responsiveness* (2nd ed., pp. 3–21). New York: Oxford University Press.

Norcross, J.C., & Wampold, B.E. (2011). Evidence-based therapy relationships: Research conclusions and clinical practices. In J.C. Norcross (Ed.), *Psychotherapy relationships that work: Evidence-based responsiveness* (2nd ed., pp. 3–21). New York: Oxford University Press.

Pett, J. (2000). Gay, lesbian, and bisexual therapy and its supervision. In D. Davies & C. Neal (Eds.), *Therapeutic perspectives on working with lesbian, gay and bisexual clients* (pp. 54–72). Philadelphia, PA: Open University Press.

Reid, P.T., & Bing, V.M. (2000). Sexual roles of girls and women: An ethnocultural lifespan perspective. In C.B. Travis & J.W. White (Eds.), *Sexuality, society, and feminism* (pp. 141–166). Washington, DC: American Psychological Association.

Ritter, K.Y., & Terndrup, A.I. (2002). *Handbook of affirmative psychotherapy with lesbians and gay men.* New York: Guilford Press.

Shelton, K., & Delgado-Romero, E.A. (2013). Sexual orientation microaggressions: The experience of lesbian, gay, bisexual, and queer clients in psychotherapy. *Psychology of Sexual Orientation and Gender Diversity, 1,* 59–70.

Stanton, M., & Welsh, R. (2012). Systemic thinking in couple and family psychology research and practice. *Couple and Family Psychology: Research and Practice, 1,* 14–30.

Sue, D.W. (2010). Microaggressions, marginality, and oppression: An introduction. In D.W. Sue (Ed.), *Microaggressions and marginality: Manifestation, dynamics, and impact* (pp. 3–22). Hoboken, NJ: John Wiley & Sons.

Sue, D.W., & Sue, D. (2016). *Counseling the culturally diverse: Theory and practice* (7th ed.). Hoboken, NJ: John Wiley & Sons.

Syzmanski, D.M. (2009). Examining potential moderators of the link between heterosexist events and bisexual men's psychological distress. *Journal of Counseling Psychology, 1,* 142–151.

Szymanski, D.M., Kashubeck-West, S., & Meyer, J. (2008a). Internalized heterosexism: A historical and theoretical overview. *Counseling Psychologist, 36,* 510–524.

Szymanski, D.M., Kashubeck-West, S., & Meyer, J. (2008b). Internalized heterosexism: Measurement, psychosocial correlates, and research directions. *Counseling Psychologist, 36,* 525–574.

White, M., & Epston, D. (1990). *Narrative means to therapeutic ends.* New York: Norton.

Worell, J., & Remer, P. (2003). *Feminist perspectives in therapy: Empowering diverse women* (2nd ed.). Hoboken, NJ: John Wiley & Sons.

12 Supervision of Therapists Working With Transgender Clients

Margaret Nichols

Abstract

The supervision of therapists working with transgender and gender nonconforming clients presents special challenges. First, both the supervisor and therapist must have medical, legal, and sociopolitical knowledge as well as clinical expertise. The paradigm for understanding the transgender phenomenon has changed so recently that many counselors will have to "unlearn" the old, pathologizing model before understanding the new. Working with this population forces both therapists and their supervisors to confront ingrained attitudes about gender binaries, roles, and expression. Interventions such as the use of puberty blockers and early social transition are so new as to be untested and uncertain. Supervisors have a responsibility to keep close watch on the research literature as new findings about medical treatments and outcome can appear overnight. Finally, supervisors have to manage their own countertransferential feelings as well as guide their supervisees in self-analysis: in few other areas of mental health do decisions facilitated by clinicians have such permanent, life-altering consequences.

Keywords

transgender, trans, gender queer, nonbinary, gender binary, FtM, MtF, TGNC, gender nonconforming

Introduction

Supervision of therapists working with the transgender and gender nonconforming community is very different from almost any other kind of supervision, because the clinical work with such clients is so specialized. Perhaps no area of clinical sexology practice has changed as much since the beginning of the 21st century as that of transgender healthcare. This is because the paradigm through which we understand gender variant people has been totally upended and changed. Psychiatry and sexology used to regard gender variance as deviant and disturbed, a "mental illness." This was the view held throughout the 20th century and the beginning of the 21st century. In 2011, the World Professional Association for Transgender Health (WPATH) declared gender diverse identities and expressions part of the normal range of the human experience (Coleman et al., 2011). This position was in direct contrast to the view prevailing since Kraft Ebbing's formulation in the 1800s of transvestism and inversion as psychiatric disorders (Coleman et al., 2011). In 2013, psychiatrists agreed by defining the renamed "gender dysphoria" an impairment only if gender variance caused great distress (APA, 2013). Moreover, the Revision of ICD-11 (*International Classification of Diseases*), anticipated at this writing to be released in 2018, is removing gender variance entirely from the chapter on psychiatric disorders and placing it in a new chapter on sexual conditions (ICD-11 Beta Site, n.d.). Generations of therapists—and many sex therapists—had to throw most of what they had learned out the window and start from scratch. The situation is remarkably parallel to that confronting sex therapists after the removal of homosexuality from the DSM (*Diagnostic and Statistical Manual*) in 1973 (Nichols, 2014; Lev, 2005). When the Institute for Personal Growth, the New Jersey psychotherapy organization I founded, began working with gay and lesbian clients in 1983, most practicing therapists still regarded homosexuality as an illness caused by disturbed early parent–child interaction. Today, only therapists doing so-called reparative or conversion therapy believe such antiquated and disproved ideas. Similarly, at the moment many sexologists and therapists still believe that transgender people suffer from a mental illness caused in early childhood. Just as the removal of homosexuality from the DSM of psychiatrists laid the groundwork for the development of "gay affirmative therapy" (Bayer, 1981), this paradigm shift has led to the birth of "gender affirmative therapy" (Hidalgo et al., 2013; Ehrensaft, 2011b Lev & Alie, 2012; Menvielle, 2012). Gender affirmative therapy takes as its founding premise that gender diversity is a normal human variation and that gender variant people need support and validation, not pathologizing.

Admirably, many mental health professional groups, including some in sex therapy, have met the challenge of helping members reject what they learned in graduate school. WPATH itself now offers trainings towards certification as a gender specialist, and the standards to become a sex therapist, set by AASECT (American Association of Sexuality Educators, Counselors and Therapists), now include the requirement that candidates take course work on transgender issues. This education includes information on the nonbinary gender spectrum, typical issues faced by transgender and gender nonconforming people at different stages of life, and gender affirmative therapy techniques. Other professional groups for social workers and psychologists are endeavoring to provide the same trainings. While the effective treatment of sexual dysfunction requires a sex therapy background, work with transgender clients does not. Sex therapists arguably see more of these clients than nonsex therapists, but working with trans clients is like working with lesbian, gay, and/or bisexual (LGB) clients, in that sex therapy certification is not necessary to do sound clinical work. Therefore, the information in this chapter is relevant to the supervision of all clinicians who may be treating this population.

The changes in the mental health paradigm, including diagnosis and standards of care, have followed huge changes in the culture at large. Before the

1990s, transgender people were largely isolated from each other (Stryker, 2008). With the advent of the internet, transgender communities arose and along with them, political and advocacy groups. Just as gay activists made the DSM diagnosis of homosexuality an early target of reform efforts, trans activists by the end of the 1990s aimed to change not just the psychiatric diagnosis of gender identity disorder but also the gatekeeper status of psychiatrists, psychologists, and social workers (Wilchins, 2014). They have had substantial success; the changes in the DSM are significant. The name change of WPATH—it was formerly called the Harry Benjamin International Gender Dysphoria Association—symbolized a change in leadership that included two transgender presidents since 2006 and a radical change in perspective. Not only did the WPATH SOC 7 (Standards of Care, version 7) normalize gender variance, but it also declared the gender binary to be an illusion. Moreover, it greatly reduced the power of mental health professionals: transgender people desiring medical intervention no longer have to spend any time in psychotherapy, and adults can obtain hormones through an informed consent procedure without needing a letter from a therapist. The removal of homosexuality from the DSM in 1973 is widely considered to be the foundation of gains made since then (Bayer, 1981); the parallel changes in the mental health conceptualization of gender variant people may help further civil rights for the entire transgender community.

Trans activism has also meant trans visibility. Transgender people are "coming out" in increasing numbers, and at increasingly younger ages. Two studies from the Williams Institute (Flores, Herman, Gates, & Brown, 2016; Herman, Flores, Brown, Wilson, & Conron, 2017) reported that the number of trans adults in the United States was 1.4 million—double what had previously been believed—and that 0.7% of young people aged 13–25 now identify as transgender. To illustrate what that means, a high school class with 300 students will have an average of two transgender students. As visibility increases as a result of media attention and more people coming out, more and more people know someone who is transgender, and large numbers of people have some information about gender variance.

Definitions

Because the paradigm shift has been so recent, clinicians who are not yet working with transgender clients will not be familiar with common terms, and may not be familiar with some of the terms and concepts discussed in this chapter. Here are some of the terms that will be used here, and that are important for all supervisors to know:

> *Transgender.* An umbrella term that encompasses a spectrum of gender identities and presentations, ranging from those who want complete medical transition to another gender (the people who used to be called "transsexuals") to those who identify as gender queer or nonbinary (see below).

Cisgender: People who do not identify as transgender.

Gender binary: The common misconception that there are only two genders, male and female. In fact, even on a biological level there are many variations on XX and XY.

Gender spectrum: The concept that gender varies on a continuum.

Nonbinary: people who place themselves somewhere other than the end points of the gender spectrum; those who feel they are neither male or female, or both, or something in between. Other terms for the same phenomenon are "gender queer" or "gender fluid."

Assigned gender: The gender assigned at birth, usually determined by genitalia.

Affirmed gender: The gender with which one may identify.

Gender identity: An individual's internal sense of gender.

Gender expression: The way you manifest your gender identity in appearance and actions; your gender presentation. Individuals can be gender nonconforming in their gender expression while retaining a cisgender identity (e.g., boys who want to wear dresses but still consider themselves male).

Social transition: To live full time as your affirmed gender, with or without medical intervention.

Medical transition: Body modification to achieve the physical appearance of your affirmed gender, including cross gender hormone treatment and various surgeries.

Puberty blockers: Medication used to help children who are transgender; given in the early stages of puberty, they suppress the development of secondary sex characteristics of the child's assigned gender. When followed by cross gender hormones, the individual develops most of the physical characteristics, including height, body shape, and voice of their affirmed gender.

TGNC: transgender and gender nonconforming, an umbrella term that includes transgender people and those with an unconventional gender expression.

What Makes Supervision of Therapists Working With Trans Clients Unique?

The recent dramatic changes in the way we view gender variance, and the intersection of medical and mental healthcare inherent in the treatment of transgender clients, make supervision of therapists working with these clients particularly challenging. To begin with, supervisors need to be extremely well versed in the new paradigm, which means acquiring a lot of new knowledge. Unless the supervisor is very young, it also means they must challenge their own inherent biases, attitudes that were validated by their profession starting with grad school. Such supervisors will have to "unlearn" what was taught as part of their original professional training. In addition, clinicians and supervisors working with this population need to frequently examine their countertransference. Historically, mental health practitioners have actually added to the oppression of trans people through excessive "gatekeeping" (i.e., limiting access to medical care; Beemyn, 2014). In the past, transgender people wanting hormones or surgery have been denied this care by clinicians for superficial and judgmental reasons (e.g., the therapist doesn't believe the person will "pass" well in their affirmed gender). So it is critical to examine interventions in this light, especially interventions that involving making a client wait for a letter recommending medical procedures. This is made more complicated by the fact that while the WPATH SOC 7 decries gatekeeping, it still requires mental health letters before surgical procedures. Clinicians and supervisors walk a fine line between unfairly imposing their own biases on their transgender clients and simply being a rubber stamp for anyone who wants surgery or hormones.

In addition to understanding the new paradigm and being proficient in the principles of gender affirmative therapy, supervisors of therapists working with transgender clients also must have a good deal of knowledge about the requirements of the standards of care and about specific medical interventions. While many gender variant people already have acquired information through the internet, younger clients, and especially parents, often need a great deal of psychoeducation. In this regard, sex therapists may have an advantage over their nonsex therapy trained peers; sex therapists are used to coordinating care with medical practitioners and to acquiring specific medical knowledge to help their clients. In addition, clinicians and their supervisors need to be open to be advocates for their clients. Therapists, and sometimes supervisors, will need to be willing to sign legal documents for their clients, allowing them, for example, to change gender and name data on driver's licenses or passports; to write "carry letters," still needed in some states to avoid criminal charges of "impersonating the opposite sex"; and, for younger clients, to intervene with school systems around "bathroom issues," name and pronoun use, and bullying (D'Augelli, Grossman, & Starks, 2006; Roberts, Rosario, Corliss, Koenen, & Bryn Austin, 2012; Toomey, Ryan, & Diaz, 2010).

Work with transgender clients often involves work with their families, directly by including them in session, or indirectly by helping clients educate their families and deal with potentially negative reactions (Grossman, D'Augelli, Howell, & Hubbard, 2005; Ryan, Huebner, Diaz, & Sanchez, 2009). Older clients may need help with spouses and children, or with aging parents. Family work is absolutely crucial for adolescents and younger children: there is research indicating that parental approval drastically reduces the risk of suicide in younger clients (Grossman et al., 2005; Ryan et al., 2009), and that accepting families can buffer and reduce the negative effects of bullying (D'Augelli et al., 2006). Therefore, some training in family systems is very helpful for a supervisor.

Appropriate interventions for transgender clients differ widely by age group, just as treatment of depression in a 40-year-old is vastly different from treatment of depression in an 8-year-old. Many trans-affirmative therapists work with adults and older adolescents. Working with pre-pubertal children, in particular, is different from working with teens and older, not only because treatment may require child-specific techniques like play therapy, but also because gender identity is much more fluid and ambiguous in younger kids (Malpas, 2011). Consequently, a supervisor who can help supervisees with pre-adolescent clients needs to be versed in techniques like play therapy specifically appropriate for children. At the Institute for Personal Growth (IPG), where transgender clients vary in age from 3 years to over 70, some supervisors oversee therapists with adolescent and older clients, while other supervisors only train supervisees who work with children.

Therapists working with adolescent and older clients also need to be in sync with the transgender community at large, and consequently so do their supervisors. The historical oppression of trans people by mental health practitioners has left some in this community with an inherent suspicion of therapists. Understanding that, and taking pains to use the language and terms that are current, will help instill trust in clients. For example, it is considered "politically incorrect" to refer to the surgeries transforming genitalia as "sex change operations." It is now called "gender affirming surgery" or "gender confirmation surgery." The clinician who uses the "old" term will immediately be pegged by many clients as "out of touch" and "unresponsive."

Finally, supervisors who clinically engage with persons who identify as transgender need to be extremely attuned to new information in the field. Because these interventions have only been in use in the United States for a short time, there is still a great deal to learn, and mental health practitioners need updated knowledge even though they themselves will not be administering the medical care (Lev & Alie, 2012; Spack et al., 2012). For example, recent research suggests that puberty blockers may impair future fertility, making considerations of when to begin them salient for parents of transgender kids (Milrod, 2014).

In fact, it is particularly challenging to work with younger trans and gender nonconforming (TGNC) clients precisely because the field is changing rapidly and research is trying to catch up with changes in practice. The medical interventions that can be introduced as early as age 9 (for assigned females entering puberty) have, in many cases, potentially irreversible consequences. We do not yet know the impact of early social transition (i.e., transition for younger children in school). Parents are usually less knowledgeable than the clinician and look to therapists for an inordinate amount of direction and guidance. Thus the sense of responsibility the clinician feels can be overwhelming, and it is the supervisor's job to help the supervisee process their feelings. A well-known pioneer in the field of gender affirmative therapy for youth once said she had a recurring nightmare in which all of the transgender kids and teens she ever treated showed up on her doorstep screaming, "What were you thinking?!" Supervisors must be able to help their supervisees accept the fact that the field is young and we have incomplete outcome data. One cannot treat younger

TGNC clients without accepting the fact that we may one day consider some current interventions harmful (e.g., early use of blockers or early social transition). Working with younger trans clients in particular involves a heavier sense of responsibility than most therapists are accustomed to, and supervisors need to be able to help their supervisees cope with anxieties associated with this burden. Supervision groups can be a very effective addition to individual supervision, because supervisees often have their own needs for support and validation. There are few other clinical situations where the decisions at stake involve life-altering, irreversible medical procedures, which are being made by minors, who by their very age have not fully developed cognitively.

It is worth mentioning another challenge that is confronting therapists working with younger trans clients. As more of society learns about transgender children, some parents may jump to the conclusion that their child is trans before careful evaluation. At IPG, in recent years it has become fairly common for families of children and adolescents to self-diagnose based on incomplete information. In an effort to avoid the depression and suicidality common to trans youth, some parents have socially transitioned their young children after even a very brief period of gender dysphoria. Occasionally, adolescents who have always felt lonely and "different" will latch onto a transgender "explanation" for their woes. Once a child has socially transitioned, changing back is complicated. And adolescents who are focused on what they believe to be gender dysphoria are frequently impatient when not allowed immediate hormone treatment. Therapists of these clients find themselves in very difficult positions, and will need guidance and support from a supervisor who can remain calm in the face of pressure from clients who are making possibly reckless decisions. Because the research on transition in children and adolescents is lagging so far behind practice, group supervision is particularly helpful so that therapists can share anecdotal information and personal experience (Olson, 2016).

Skills and Techniques

Some of the skills needed for a supervisee to work with trans and gender nonconforming youth and adults have already been outlined: knowledge about medical interventions, an understanding of gender affirmative therapy, familiarity with the trans community and history of conflict with mental health practitioners, and family therapy training. Needless to say, the clinician must also be comfortable with a model that normalizes gender variance along a nonbinary continuum. For many people, thinking in gender expansive terms is uncomfortable and difficult. The clinician and their supervisor must be self-reflective, because there are many occasions where inherent biases will be challenged. For example, the first time a therapist encounters a nonbinary client who, say, may be sporting a mustache and beard, wearing a dress, and proclaiming that "they" and "their" are preferred pronouns, he or she may experience feelings of shock, confusion, and distaste that must be deconstructed, understood, and managed before the counselor can be therapeutically effective. And supervisors must be able to guide the supervisee through this process.

Clinicians and their supervisors have to be comfortable with advocacy as part of the treatment plan. Moreover, therapists need to be extremely familiar with community and online resources for transgender people. They will need to know not only how to help a client get medical treatment, but also how to guide them to such wide-ranging services as legal help, voice training, camps for trans children, and electrolysis technicians.

Before describing the interventions used in this type of treatment, it will be helpful to elaborate more on the principles of gender affirmative therapy, the modality currently accepted to be the highest standard of care. In the past, therapists working with transgender people, called "transsexuals" prior to the 1990s, assumed that their clients suffered from a mental illness created in early childhood by disordered parent–child relationships. Children were presumed to be "treatable" and the interventions included behavioral "shaping" towards gender conformity and parent training to not allow cross gender expression or behavior. Adults were assumed to be beyond "cure" and thus theoretically eligible for medical procedures. However, there were rigid criteria for this eligibility: clients had to have the right narrative ("always felt this way," "born in the wrong body"), the right sexual orientation (one that would be heterosexual post-transition), the right presentation (the stereotype of their affirmed gender, e.g., natal males desiring to transition to female had to be feminine, wear dresses and makeup) and want to utilize all available medical treatments (e.g., it was not okay to want hormones but not genital surgery).

Gender affirmative therapy, on the other hand, assumes that variations in gender presentation and gender identity are not signs of mental illness and therefore do not require treatment. Children are not encouraged to conform to their assigned gender, but rather allowed to express themselves in whatever ways feel "authentic," and parents are taught to be accepting and validating of their kids. Clinicians are asked to follow their clients' leads in exploring their gender, not prejudge what and how they should be. There is no particular narrative required: some individuals establish a clear gender identity by age 3, others in adolescence, some not until adulthood, and some people have a fluid gender identity throughout their lifetime. Moreover, since gender is nonbinary, trans people will not all want the same types of medical procedures. Some people will want every body modification possible, others will want none, still others will want only hormones, or some surgeries but not others.

In general, gender affirmative therapists assume that since gender variance is normal, the individual will find their own way to the identity and expression that suits them. The overall approach is to validate and support clients, encourage introspection and self-exploration, help them connect to others like them, and aid in developing positive support systems in family, friends, and community. The goal is never to change a client's gender identity or presentation but instead to help them achieve what is most comfortable for them while also navigating a society that may be hostile.

Aside from those general principles, the interventions and techniques used to help TGNC clients vary, primarily by age group. The approaches described below are appropriate for clients who come to therapy to explore their identity or with help navigating "coming out" or transition. Plenty of transgender clients enter psychotherapy to deal with garden-variety problems like depression, anxiety, or a relationship breakup. The interventions here are not relevant to these issues.

Clients Who Are Middle Aged or Older

Prior to the late 1990s, most clinicians never saw a transgender client below the age of 40, and most were assigned males desiring to be females. The typical client in this age group was married with children and had experienced conflict and shame about their gender identity for an entire lifetime. Most had gone through years of clandestine cross-dressing and years of "purging"—getting rid of cross gender clothes and suppressing the desire to be female. These clients are disappearing as being transgender becomes more accepted and people are coming out at increasingly younger ages. Nevertheless, therapists and their supervisors still encounter many clients like this, particularly in areas of the country between the coasts and those that are less urbanized. In fact, the therapist may be the first person to whom the client reveals their true identity. Working with these clients requires, first and foremost, helping them deal with their internalized self-hatred and shame, often solidified over many years. Many of them still struggle with their identity, because they have tried to repudiate it for so long; it may take months or years of therapy for them to own who they are, and even longer before they decide to socially/medically transition. Those who do decide to transition will frequently be rejected by spouse, family, and/or employers. Clinicians must help these clients build entirely new lives, new communities, new support systems, and sometimes new careers. Some couples counseling or family counseling may be required if and when they decide to "come out" to their spouse, children, or family members. Since many of these clients will be rejected when they come out, the therapist must be prepared to help the client resolve grief about these losses as well as grief about years lost to secrecy. It is important, if possible, to connect them with communities or groups of older transgender people; young TGNC folk often feel they have nothing in common with elders who have lived most of their lives in shame and hiding.

Supervision of therapists working with this age group will often focus on helping the supervisee deal with countertransferential feelings such as the heartache of watching families destroyed, or judgmental feelings about the often hyperfeminine presentation of their clients. Older clients regard Caitlyn Jenner as a role model. Younger ones reject Jenner as conforming to stereotypes of womanhood. Many trans people who do not come out or transition until middle or old age go through a second adolescence in their affirmed gender, and some become extremely focused on their attractiveness. Many a feminist therapist has had to struggle with negative feelings about being asked for makeup advice or needing to compliment the looks of a client in order to support their fragile ego and assuage the fear that they look ridiculous. Assigned male/affirmed female clients in this age group tend to pass less well than their younger counterparts, perhaps because the decades of trying to look masculine can't be easily shed. Occasionally the therapist may have to be the person to tell the client that they don't "pass"; clients may not have a good sense of themselves and put themselves at risk because of their inability to conceptualize how challenging the aesthetic transition might be. Friends and family may be particularly loath to break this news to a loved one.

Clients in Their Twenties and Thirties

Transgender people in their twenties and thirties are considered Millennials, and they are less likely to have spent years pretending to be comfortable with their assigned gender (Erickson-Schroth, 2014). They are less likely to be married to people who don't know they are transgender or to have children or other close family members who don't know. They are also more likely to understand the concept of a gender continuum, and indeed one reason they may come to treatment is that although they know they are trans in some way, they are not sure if they are "nonbinary" or what, if any, interventions or lifestyle changes they want. They may want help telling others that they have decided to fully transition, or guidance in how to navigate school or employers. Often, these clients come because they need a letter for hormones or surgery, and in the course of being assessed, it is discovered that they have other mental health problems. Given the amount of information available and gradual shift in public discourse, this age group of transgender people may be the easiest to treat clinically. The therapist can usually assume the person is old enough to make informed choices, and has almost always known they are transgender for years, if not decades. Because they didn't hide as much or pretend to be cisgender, the therapist isn't as likely to be watching a long-term relationship fall apart. This group of trans people is heartening to work with because the therapist can facilitate success without a lot of accompanying heartache.

Because they are the easiest to work with, they are also the least likely age group that a supervisee will need help with. If the supervisee sees adolescents and adults of all ages, the supervisor will spend the most time helping with the treatment of the next age group.

Adolescent Clients

Trans and gender nonconforming youth in early or late adolescence present special challenges for the supervisee and supervisor. In part this is because there are medical interventions available to them with potentially irreversible effects, and decisions must sometimes be made rapidly. In the early stages of physical puberty, puberty-blocking medication is approved for use in order to stop the development of the secondary sex characteristics of the young person's assigned gender.

Not only is this event often traumatic for the child, some of these sex character-istics, such as height, cannot be changed later through a medical intervention. When puberty blockers are followed by cross gender hormones, the young per-son develops as their affirmed gender, with bodies that are physically no different from cisgender peers, except of course for genitalia and internal reproductive organs. When puberty blockers are used, the child usually socially transitions to their affirmed gender for a "test" period. If, as happens sometimes, the child changes their mind, blockers can be withdrawn and the youth will mature physi-cally in the gender of their birth. If not, and if the social transition test confirms the "rightness" of the transgender assessment, cross gender hormones follow smoothly at age 16 (current SOC) or, as is happening more frequently, at age 14 (Cohen-Kettenis, Delemarre-van de Waal, & Gooren, 2008; De Vries & Cohen-Kettenis, 2012; De Vries, Steensma, Doreleijers, & Cohen-Kettenis, 2011. Puberty blockers, while extremely helpful, are not without risks; there are concerns about sterility and future surgeries, for example (Milrod, 2014).

The role of the clinician is quite significant and carries a lot of responsi-bility. Few endocrinologists will administer puberty blockers or cross gender hormones without a letter of recommendation from a mental health provider. "Informed consent" is not available for those under age 18. It is the clini-cian's job to listen to the child and try to determine if their affirmed gender is truly authentic or perhaps a manifestation of something else. If the trans identity is genuine, and if the parents agree, puberty blockers are currently the ethical treatment of choice (Cohen-Kettenis, Delemarre-van de Waal, & Gooren, 2008), despite the risks. Cross gender hormones have potentially even more serious consequences, because most of the changes they precipitate in the body are irreversible. And yet, they too are the treatment of choice for mid-adolescent trans youth (Spack et al., 2012; De Vries, Steensma, Dore-leijers, & Cohen-Kettenis, 2011). To make matters more complicated, not all transgender teens have "always" known they were transgender. For some, the realization did not come to them until the beginning of puberty, when body changes made them confront their gender identity. Even though the research indicates that young people who identify as transgender in adoles-cence rarely change their minds (Cohen-Kettenis, Delemarre-van de Waal, & Gooren, 2008), many clinicians will have doubts about a 14-year-old who says they came to their transgender identity only a year ago, when puberty began. Nevertheless, supervisors have to be able to guide these clinicians through a process to decide whether there is genuine doubt about the client's gender identity or whether the doubts represent only the clinician's caution and fear (Milrod, 2014). When the decision is about puberty blockers, where the risk of long-term consequences is low, and the intent of the medication is to give a "time out" to really solidify gender identity, the clinician should be much less reluctant to withhold a recommendation. Some have argued that withholding such a recommendation is unethical (Giordano, 2008). It can be even more difficult to evaluate requests for cross gender hormones, especially for older adolescents who are affirming a trans identity post-puberty. We have no data

on such "late bloomers," and they are hard to evaluate. A small but significant minority of older adolescents aren't transgender at all, but instead are in
the midst of an age-appropriate identity crisis complicated by emotional/psy-
chological impairment (Ehrensaft, 2016). Since late adolescents have finished
puberty, puberty blockers are not an option. But the WPATH SOC 7 allows
cross gender hormones at age 16, and adolescents usually know this and can
be quite assertive about getting a letter recommending such treatment. In
some areas of the country, the clinician can avoid the responsibility for letter-
writing by referring a young person 18 years or older to an LGBT health
center (Callen-Lorde, 2012); most such centers have been using an informed
consent model for hormones for years. But if there is no nearby center, or if
the client is 16 or 17 years old, mental health providers must provide letters to
obtain the medication. In these situations, faced with insistent demands from
a client sophisticated about transgender treatment, it can be difficult to refuse.
In situations where the therapist refuses a letter or requests that the client
wait for one, the therapist may be accused of being a "gatekeeper," and must
search hard within to determine the basis of their denial. Supervisors can be a
very strong source of support in these situations.

If it is sometimes difficult to determine a client's authentic identity if they are
teens who only came to decide they were trans in early puberty, it is even harder
with the older adolescent. If the client did not experience gender dysphoria (or
in some cases, not even gender nonconformity) in early childhood, and did not
appear to be distressed in early puberty, can they be genuinely transgender? The
answer is yes, of course: transgender people come out at all ages, but how does
one distinguish between a teen who was repressed, anxious, or extremely com-
pliant as a child (hence the absence of nonconforming behavior or dysphoric
feelings) and one who is latching on to a false identity they will eschew a year
from now? Older clients usually have identified as transgender for years before
they come to treatment, but this kind of adolescent may have identified this
way for a year or less. How does one define the WPATH criteria of a "persistent, consistent, insistent" identity? Even seasoned therapists struggle with these
cases. To make matters worse, there is now a community of "de-transitioners"—
people who transitioned and then changed their minds and transitioned back.
The average age of transition for de-transitioners was 17; the average age of
de-transition is 23 (Stella, 2017). These facts tend to scare therapists. The need
for supervision is very strong for therapists who see people in this age group.

Pre-pubertal Children

This is the most challenging age group of all for therapists working with TGNC
clients (Drescher & Pula, 2014). The available research we have, none of which
is current, suggests that a majority of children who affirm that they are the
opposite sex, or that they desire to be the opposite sex, actually give up that
trans identity by adolescence (Steensma, Biemond, De Boer, & Cohen-Kettenis,
2011; Steensma, Mcguire, Kreukels, Beekman, & Cohen-Kettenis, 2013). The

WPATH SOC recommends a "wait and see" approach with these children, and discourages early social transition. Diane Ehrensaft writes that there are three types of children who are TGNC: authentically transgender children;, proto-gay children, where gender nonconformity is linked to sexual orientation; and nonbinary and/or gender fluid children (Ehrensaft, 2016, 2011b). Ehrensaft believes that a good therapist will be able to tease out the genuinely transgender kids from the others, and promote early social transition for those children. In practice, most clinicians are not as certain they can do this as Ehrensaft is, and attempt to encourage the wait and see approach (Nealy, 2017). With this strategy, the child's gender identity is affirmed, and they are allowed cross gender expression, at least at home, but are not allowed to change names or gender pronouns, and may be discouraged from behaviors such as an assigned male wearing dresses to school. But there are problems with this strategy. Some children are so intensely dysphoric that to force them to live in their assigned sex is condemning them to years of misery, even suicidality, and risking the kind of long-range damage that can result from years of depression in childhood. Ironically, many TGNC children are bullied more if they do not transition. A feminine boy will be a completely socially normative girl if he transitions, but will probably be labeled gay and bullied if he does not. Moreover, parents may themselves push for early social transition, as it is extremely painful to see one's child depressed and unhappy. Opponents of early social transition point to research and warn against the harmful effects of transitioning children who may change their minds later. In actuality, we have little information on socially transitioned children. Follow-up studies are in their early stages (Olson, 2016), and cannot the answer the questions about children who transition back. Early clinical experience suggests that the experience is not necessarily painful for the child. For example, at IPG we have had a handful of kids who have changed their minds during the time they were on puberty blockers. One such child was Benny, an assigned male who lived an entire year as a girl while on blockers. In the summer in between grades he announced that he wanted to be a boy after all, and discontinued the medication. He switched to another school in the fall to make the change easier. While his parents and endocrinologist were distressed by this, Benny himself took it in stride. He said he did not regret living as a girl: "I wanted to be a girl since I was little; I needed a chance to try it out." Such examples may lift some of the sense of responsibility from the shoulders of clinicians. Nevertheless, most therapists working with this age group experience a lot of uncertainty about the choices made for their young clients, and the possibility of damage from early social transition. Needless to say, supervisors can be supportive by engaging in the decision-making process with their supervisees and by helping them let go of the desire to be in control of, and certain about, the direction of treatment.

Case Examples

Because clinical work with the transgender population varies so widely depending on the age group of the clients, it will be useful to give several brief case vignettes rather than one longer case study.

Arthur/Ariel, a Middle-Aged Client

Arthur, aged 47, and his wife Jessica, 45, began marriage counseling with the author because Jessica had discovered female clothing hidden in her husband's dresser. Jessica wanted to believe Arthur, who claimed he was "only a cross-dresser." After meeting with Arthur and Jessica together and separately, it was clear that Arthur was still exploring his identity and that he could potentially want some kind of feminizing body modifications, if not full transition, in the future. When Arthur revealed this to Jessica, she declared she was unable to commit to couples counseling because she was not sure she wanted to remain in the relationship. It was suggested that both receive individual therapy; Arthur remained with the author and Jessica began treatment with the author's supervisee, Kellie. As Arthur progressed in treatment, he began gradually to feel that he did want to live as a woman full-time, and Jessica decided she could not live with him if he followed that path. Jessica had some trauma in her past and was prone to mood instability; in treatment with Kellie, she swung between despair and sadness about the collapse of her marriage, and rage at Arthur, whom she blamed for ruining her life. Kellie felt torn: on one hand, she had empathy for Jessica's sense of grief and feelings of betrayal; on the other hand, she is a gender affirmative therapist and privately applauded Arthur for finally finding his authentic self. When Jessica threatened punitive legal action, which included trying to bar Arthur from seeing their only child together, Kellie had to process her own disapproval of her client's intentions in order to treat her. Fortunately, by coming to terms with her being judgmental, Kellie was able to avoid communicating it to Jessica, and was able to help Jessica see that her intended actions, while understandable, were not in the best interest of their child. Kellie's point of view—empathic to both partners—also helped her guide Jessica later on to send their child for treatment to a trans-affirmative counselor who could help the child adjust to the changes in his father and his family. Later in treatment, the author turned to her supervision group for help with a different dilemma. Arthur, now fully transitioned and living life as Ariel, was beginning to date. She placed an ad on a popular dating site seeking males, but did not reveal that she was transgender. Because she had a broad-shouldered body, still moved with the mannerisms of a male, and had a deep voice, Ariel was distinguishable as transgender to many people. But Ariel did not realize this, which is why she did not feel she needed to disclose being transgender to dates. The author felt torn between worrying for Ariel's safety and feeling that it would be cruel to tell Ariel she did not "pass." Ultimately, with the support of her supervision group, the author came to feel that Ariel's safety was more important than her feelings, and she told Ariel as gently as possible. Ariel was crushed, but soon after had an encounter where a potential date became enraged upon meeting her in person and "reading" her as trans. Ariel was grateful she had been warned this might happen, and changed her dating ads accordingly. Moreover, since this time, the author has incorporated this issue into all her supervision of therapists seeing transgender clients.

Louis, a Freshman in College

Alison is a counselor in the Midwest who obtained telephone/Skype supervision from the author. Louis was an 18-year-old college freshman who came to Alison for therapy. He asserted that he was transgender, and that he had just determined this a few months prior, towards the end of his first semester. Upon further probing, Louis revealed that his decision was triggered by repeated suggestions from his girlfriend of 3 months. Louis was quiet, sensitive, and introspective, and had no interest in stereotypically male activities like sports. Because his character and interests were unconventional for a cisgender man, his girlfriend suggested he might actually be transgender, and Louis latched on to this idea because he felt it was a good explanation for why he had always felt "different" from other guys.

The dilemma for Alison was that her training in working with transgender clients had emphasized the need to validate the affirmed gender identity of all of them. This clashed with her fear that Louis had claimed a trans identity impulsively, and her instinct to gently challenge him. This is not uncommon for cisgender therapists working with transgender clients. The specter of "gatekeeping" hangs over their heads, since most are familiar with the deplorable history of mental health's control over transgender care. Moreover, if they are conscientious, they must frequently "check in" with themselves to ferret out internalized transphobia, such as the unconscious tendency to question the authenticity of transgender clients who do not appear to conform to the cultural stereotypes of their affirmed gender. Fortunately, in this case Louis's claiming of a transgender identity had been so recent as to be less than the 6 months minimum required in DSM-5 for a diagnosis of gender dysphoria. Louis was told this and accepted it as a reason why he could not get a "letter" for hormones immediately. This gave Alison and the author time to process her reactions. Alison needed a more experienced supervisor to validate a "wait and see" approach. During the next several months, Alison was able to get Louis to think about his gender identity, with statements like "just because you may feel like a 'failed man' doesn't mean you are a woman." While Louis pondered the origins of his transgender feelings, Alison also got him to attend several peer groups for transgender people his age. Attending peer groups is highly suggested, especially for younger clients who have never had contact with the transgender community. This was an eye-opening experience for Louis, as he found that he did not particularly identify with group members, most of whom had experienced gender dysphoria from the onset of puberty or before. When Louis's relationship ended and he no longer experienced pressure from a girlfriend who was more enthusiastic about his being trans than he was, he realized that he was, in fact, not transgender, but merely an atypical man. Alison was gratified to realize that she had helped her client avoid possibly irreversible hormone treatments, and felt reassured, confident that she had been neither transphobic nor a judgmental gatekeeper.

Shane, a Transgender 15-Year-Old

Shane was the second transgender minor ever treated by the author, in 2007. The author wisely sought supervision from someone with years of experience with TGCN youth. Shane, an assigned male, had not identified as a transgender girl until the age of 13. The author had not yet encountered a young person who did not feel they were the "opposite" sex as a child, and this frightened her at the time, which was the reason for her seeking outside supervision. The author's supervisor explained that it was in fact quite common for young people to experience gender dysphoria only when puberty brought on unwanted body changes. The author was nevertheless very cautious. Shane had already finished biological puberty; she was too old for puberty blockers and too young for cross gender hormones. Despite this, Shane was referred to an endocrinologist internationally known for treating TGNC kids to be evaluated for cross gender hormones when she turned 16. The endocrinologist validated the information transmitted by the author's supervisor. Moreover, he put Shane on spironolactone, a testosterone blocker, to give her some relief from feeling male. The author encouraged Shane to socially transition, which she did at the beginning of her junior year. Only after this did the author write a letter recommending cross gender treatment. Shane was nearly 17. Moreover, the author insisted that she remain on cross gender hormones longer than the 1 year required by SOC 7. Consequently, Shane did not get a vaginoplasty until in between her first and second year of college. Shane is 5 years post-surgery and doing quite well, but the author regrets her caution. Shane might have had a better college experience if she had been allowed to get a vaginoplasty before her freshman year. Shane was quite feminine in appearance and she kept the fact that she was transgender from her college friends. As a consequence of the delay, she was not able to be sexual for that year.

Maria, a 6-Year-Old Transgender Female

Maria exemplifies the difficulties of the "wait and see" approach. Her parents brought her to IPG in the summer between kindergarten and first grade. She had been asserting her affirmed identity since the age of 4, and by the age of 6 she was quite miserable. Neil, the author's supervisee, who saw the child and her parents, was aware of the research on pre-pubertal TGNC children and made valiant efforts to delay social transition by having the parents allow and support cross gender behavior at home, where Maria wore dresses, painted her nails, and played with dolls. They committed to having Maria start the new school year without transitioning. However, on the first day of school, Maria was so distressed about her "boy clothes" and "boy name" that she refused to leave the house. After two days of this, her mother relented and let her socially transition at school. Mom did not inform Neil beforehand nor allow him any input into this decision. Although Neil was distressed by this, in supervision he was encouraged to pivot and focus on sending the message to child and parents repeatedly that it was okay for Maria to change her mind while meanwhile assuring her safety. Neil was asked to speak to the principal and teachers at school as well as parents of other children in her class. Since Neil was unfamiliar with this kind of advocacy, the author accompanied him to school where we both answered the questions from school staff and parents and allayed their concerns. Two years later, Maria is a happy well-adjusted child, but she is still given the message that she can change her mind if she wants. It remains to be seen whether Maria will maintain a trans identity into puberty and beyond. In these types of cases, it is not uncommon for parents to allow social transition even if the therapist advises against it. Indeed, at IPG children are frequently brought to us after the parents have already transitioned the child at school and within the community.

Summary

Supervision of therapists working with transgender clients is different from most other types of supervision because the treatment of transgender people is so different. In addition to knowing a great deal of specific information, including research and medical knowledge, the supervisor has to be able to help supervisees acknowledge and resolve feelings of uncertainty, especially for cases where the client is a child or adolescent. Because the practice of therapy with these clients has exceeded the research, we have only anecdotal evidence of the efficacy of many interventions. That, in combination with the fact that transgender care involves irreversible medical treatment, makes treatment of these clients often fraught with uncertainty. Transgender mental healthcare, in particular for youth, is not for the faint-hearted supervisee—or supervisor.

About the Author

Margaret Nichols, Ph.D., is a psychologist, AASECT Certified Sex Therapy Supervisor, and founder and Executive Director of the Institute for Personal Growth, a psychotherapy organization in New Jersey specializing in sex therapy and other clinical work with the sex and gender diverse community. She is an international speaker on LGBTQ issues and author of many articles and papers on LGBTQ sexuality, transgender youth, and kink and consensual non-monogamy. She is currently involved in a project to develop a certification program for clinicians working with transgender clients.

References

American Psychiatric Association. (2013). *Diagnostic and statistical manual of mental disorders: DSM-5*. Washington, DC: Author.
Bayer, R. (1981). *Homosexuality and American psychiatry*. New York: Basic Books.

Beemyn, G. (2014). U.S. history. In L. Erickson-Schroth (Ed.), *TransBodies trans selves: A resource for the transgender community*. New York: Oxford University Press.

Callen-Lorde. (2012). *Protocols for the provision of cross-gender hormone therapy*. Retrieved from http://tmeltzer.com/assets/callen lorde-revised-protocols.pdf

Cohen-Kettenis, P.T., Delemarre-van de Waal, H.A., & Gooren, L.J.G. (2008). The treatment of adolescent transsexuals: Changing insights. *Journal of Sexual Medicine, 5*, 1892–1897.

Coleman, E., Bockting, W., Botzer, M., Cohen-Kettenis, P., DeCuypere, G., Feldman, A., & Zucker, K. (2011). Standards of care for the health of transsexual, transgender, and gender non-conforming people, version 7. *International Journal of Transgenderism, 13*(4), 165–232.

D'augelli, A.R., Grossman, A.H., & Starks, M.T. (2006). Childhood gender atypicality, victimization, and PTSD among lesbian, gay, and bisexual youth. *Journal of Interpersonal Violence, 21*(11), 1462–1482.

De Vries, A.L., & Cohen-Kettenis, P.T. (2012). Clinical management of dysphoria in children and adolescents: The Dutch approach. *Journal of Homosexuality, 59*(3), 301–320.

De Vries, A.L., Steensma, T.D., Doreleijers, T.A., & Cohen-Kettenis, P.T. (2011). Puberty suppression in adolescents with gender identity disorder: A prospective follow-up study. *Journal of Sexual Medicine, 8*(8), 2276–2283.

Drescher, J., & Pula, J. (2014). Ethical issues raised by the treatment of gender-variant prepubescent children. *Hastings Cent Report, 44*(Suppl. 4), S17–22.

Ehrensaft, D. (2011a). Boys will be girls, girls will be boys. *Psychoanalytic Psychology, 28*(4), 528–548.

Ehrensaft, D. (2011b). *Gender born, gender made: Raising healthy gender-nonconforming children*. New York: Experiment.

Ehrensaft, D. (2016). *The gender creative child: Pathways for nurturing and supporting children who live outside gender boxes*. New York: Experiment.

Erickson-Schroth, L. (2014). *Trans bodies, trans selves: A resource for the transgender community*. New York: Oxford University Press.

Flores, A.R., Herman, J.L., Gates, G., & Brown, T.N.T. (2016). *How many adults identify as transgender in the United States?* Los Angeles, CA: Williams Institute.

Giordano, S. (2008). Lives in a chiaroscuro: Should we suspend the puberty of children with gender identity disorder? *Journal of Medical Ethics, 34*, 580–584.

Grossman, A., D'Augelli, A., Howell, T.J., & Hubbard, S. (2005). Parents' reactions to transgender youths' gender nonconforming expression and identity. *Journal of Gay & Lesbian Social Services, 18*(1), 3–16.

Herman, J.L., Flores, A.R., Brown, T.N.T., Wilson, B.D.M., & Conron, K.J. (2017). *Age of individuals who identify as transgender in the United States*. Los Angeles, CA: Williams Institute.

Hidalgo, M.A., Ehrensaft, D., Tishelman, A.C., Clark, L.F., Garofalo, R., Rosenthal, S.M., . . . Olson, J. (2013). The gender affirmative model: What we know and what we aim to learn. *Human Development, 56*, 285–290.

ICD-11 Beta Site. *Gender incongruence*. Retrieved May 1, 2015, from http://apps.who.int/classifications/icd11/browse/f/en#/http://id.who.int/icd/entity/411470068

Lev, A. I. (2005). Disordering gender identity: Gender identity disorder in the DSM-IV-TR. In D. Karasic & J. Dresher (Eds.), *Sexual and gender diagnoses of the diagnostic and statistical manual (DSM): A reevaluation* (pp. 35–69). Binghamton, NY: Hawthorn Press.

Lev, A. I., & Alie, L. (2012). Transgender and gender nonconforming children and youth: Developing culturally competent systems of care. In S. K. Fisher, J. M. Poirier, & G. M. Blau (Eds.), *Improving emotional and behavioral outcomes for LGBT youth: A guide for professionals*. Baltimore, MD: Brookes.

Malpas, J. (2011). Between pink and blue: A multi-dimensional family approach to gender nonconforming children and their families. *Family Process, 50*(4), 453–470.

Menvielle, E. (2012). A comprehensive program for children with gender variant behaviors and gender identity disorders. *Journal of Homosexuality, 59*(3), 357–368.

Milrod, C. (2014). How young is too young: Ethical concerns in genital surgery of the transgender MTF adolescent. *Journal of Sexual Medicine, 11*(2), 338–346.

Nealy, E. C. (2017). *Transgender children and youth: Cultivating pride and joy with families in transition*. New York: W. W. Norton.

Nichols, M. (2014). Therapy with LGBTQ clients. In I. Binik & K. Hall (Eds.), *Principles and practice of sex therapy* (5th ed., pp. 309–333). New York: Guilford Press.

Olson, K. R. (2016). Prepubescent transgender children: What we do and do not know. *Journal of the American Academy of Child and Adolescent Psychiatry, 55*, 155–156.

Roberts, A., Rosario, M., Corliss, H., Koenen, K., & Bryn Austin, S. (2012). Childhood gender nonconformity: A risk indicator for childhood abuse and posttraumatic stress in youth. *Pediatrics, 410–417.*

Ryan, C., Huebner, D., Diaz, R. M., & Sanchez, J. (2009). Family rejection as a predictor of negative health outcomes in White and Latino lesbian, gay, and bisexual young adults. *Pediatrics, 12*(3), 346–352.

Spack, N. P., Edwards-Leeper, L., Feldman, H. A., Leibowitz, S., Mandel, F., & Diamond, D. A. (2012). Children and adolescents with gender identity disorder referred to a pediatric medical center. *Pediatrics, 129*(3), 418–425.

Steensma, T. D., Biemond, R., De Boer, F., & Cohen-Kettenis, P. T. (2011). Desisting and persisting gender dysphoria after childhood: A qualitative follow-up study. *Clinical Child Psychology Psychiatry, 16*(4), 499–516.

Steensma, T. D., Mcguire, J. K., Kreukels, B. P., Beekman, A. J., & Cohen-Kettenis, P. T. (2013). Factors associated with desistance and persistence of childhood gender dysphoria: A quantitative follow-up study. *Journal of the American Academy of Child and Adolescent Psychiatry, 52*(6), 582–590.

Stella, C. (Producer). (2017). *Why I detransitioned and what I want medical providers to know* [YouTube video]. Retrieved from https://youtube.com/watch?v=Q3-r7ttcw6c&t=2s

Stryker, S. (2008). *Transgender history*. Berkeley, CA: Seal Press.

Toomey, R., Ryan, C., & Diaz, R. M. (2010). Gender-nonconforming lesbian, gay, bisexual, and transgender youth: School victimization and young psychosocial adjustment. *Developmental Psychology, 46*(6), 1580–1589.

Wilchins, R. (2014). The start of trans activism, 1994–1995. In L. Erickson-Schrouth (Ed.), *Trans bodies trans selves: A resource for the transgender community* (pp. 525–527). New York: Oxford University Press.

13 Supervision of Therapists Who Address Out of Control Sexual Behavior

Richard Siegel

Abstract

Perhaps one of the most contentious issues within the field of sex therapy today is the debate over the legitimacy of the concept of "sex addiction." This is usually discussed in the context of relationship crisis, particularly when one partner (typically the male in a heterosexual relationship) is "busted" engaging in some sexual behavior or fantasy that is deemed unacceptable by their partner. This is further fueled in great part by popular media, particularly when someone of note has their private sexual desires, fantasies, or behavior made public by a hurt and horrified partner. While not always meaning to be judgmental, a number of mental health professionals are quick to apply a pathological (and often shaming) label to such behaviors as far-ranging as masturbation, viewing pornography or erotic material, engaging in kink, paraphilic play, or even extramarital affairs. Invariably, that label is sex addiction. This chapter presents an argument for why supervisors should encourage sexological approaches to working with individuals and couples presenting with out of control sexual behavior (OCSB), over an addictionological one, which risks making the presenting crisis the "new permanent" with labels that affect couple dynamics in unhealthy and utterly unsexy ways.

Keywords

sex therapy supervision, out of control sexual behavior, OCSB, sex addiction, porn addiction, sexological approaches

Perhaps one of the most contentious issues within the field of sex therapy today is the debate over the legitimacy of the concept of "sex addiction." Many among the larger psychotherapy community—social workers, clinical psychologists, marriage and family therapists, psychiatrists, and counselors of all stripe—have been taken in by a concerted effort by a segment of the addiction treatment field to apply an arbitrary standard as to what constitutes "appropriate sexual behavior." This is usually discussed in the context of relationship crisis, particularly when one partner (usually the male in a heterosexual relationship) is "busted" engaging in some sexual behavior or fantasy that is deemed by their partner to be too lurid, kinky, "freaky," or even too frequent. This is further fueled in great part by popular media, particularly when someone of note has their private sexual desires, fantasies, or behavior made public by a hurt and horrified partner. One would be hard-pressed to argue the fact that salacious stories about famous people are fodder, like no other, for the popular media. Whereas in the past such behavior might have been viewed as sinful or immoral, it is now seen as more of a disease. While not always meaning to be judgmental, a number of mental health professionals are quick to apply a pathological (and often shaming) label to such behaviors as far-ranging as masturbation, viewing pornography or erotic material, engaging in kink, paraphilic play, or even extramarital affairs. Invariably, that label is *sex addiction.*

In many parts of the United States, where religious conservatism still dictates social and sexual mores, it is still common to see both professional and lay groups regard problematic sexual behaviors as moral or spiritual failures. There persists a general consensus that sexual behavior is biblically defined, with any and all behavior that is not heterosexual, penile–vaginal intercourse with a married spouse considered to be a transgression. Hence, we see even greater levels of fear, guilt, and shame related to sexual temptation and a general "erotophobia" that seemingly welcomes a pathological characterization. It becomes expedient, then, to apply labels like sex addiction or porn addiction as a way of mitigating the consequences of such spiritual and moral failure. In some of these groups, the intolerance of sexual variance extends to sexual orientation and gender minorities and, in some places, further extends to state-supported assumptions of criminal deviance and predatory risk (e.g., public bathrooms and transgender individuals). Unfortunately, there are those in a number of professional circles that are easily drawn into these political and emotionally charged contentions. It cannot be underestimated how powerfully social and political influences can affect the therapeutic zeitgeist in a way that these notions are accepted as scientific and medical "fact," even in the complete absence of any validating data. Cultural histories across the globe bear this out.

A significant factor that contributes to the degree to which professional perspectives about what constitutes problematic sexual behavior can be influenced by cultural trends is the fact that, as noted elsewhere in this text, very few psychology, counseling, and medical training programs offer any substantive sexuality education (Wiederman & Sansone, 1999). The practice of sex therapy remains controversial in some circles and, like sexuality education, is still approached with ambivalence in social, religious, and educational systems. The approach to sex therapy aims to understand the psychological, biological, pharmacological, relational, and contextual aspects of sexual problems (Leiblum, 2006), which may require a broad-based academic and training foundation (discussed in Chapter 1). Unfortunately, rather than sharing the view of sexuality as an integral part of life, there are entire disciplines that seemingly avoid and/or disregard such a fundamentally essential aspect of human existence and experience.

There seems no other explanation than avoidance, as a result of discomfort, to explain the conspicuous lack of training in sexuality for most medical and mental health professionals (McKeal, 2004; Pappas & Thurlow, 2014). It is somewhat heartening that there is a growing awareness among many practitioners of the overlap and complementary interaction between the fields of substance abuse treatment and clinical sexology and of the need for healthy sexual development in those who are dealing with addiction (Braun-Harvey, 2009; James, 2012; Fawcett, 2015; Pappas & Thurlow, 2014). Although the need for this integrated treatment is being recognized, it is not being widely implemented at the rehabilitative and therapeutic levels. Medical doctors, mental health practitioners, addiction specialists, nurses, and group leaders in addiction treatment centers do not have training in clinical sexology and are seldom qualified to address sexual dysfunction at the social level in treatment settings (Robinson, Bockting, Simon Rosser, Miner & Coleman, 2002; McKeal, 2004; Siegel, 2016).

Sex therapists and sexual medicine practitioners are aware that often there is a biological basis for many sexual dysfunctions, with alcohol and other drug abuse often playing major roles in the development of such problems. Clinicians in the substance abuse field are gaining an increasing awareness that sexual dysfunction and relationship concerns are significant contributors both to the initiation of a substance abuse problem and in the relapse of clients in treatment. However, few addiction professionals ever have or receive any training in sexuality, nor do many programs have a sex therapist on-site or on call. All too often, when confronted with this deficiency, center administrators and clinical directors are quick to defend it by arguing that it requires specialty training and is outside substance-abuse treatment focus. This is quite ironic given that there is no shortage of therapists receiving thousands of hours of specialty training in such things as Eye Movement Desensitization and Reprocessing (EMDR), emotionally focused therapy, Imago therapy, music and/or art therapy, and even equine therapy—which, incidentally, is six times more likely to be offered in drug and alcohol treatment programs than sexuality education or sex therapy (Siegel, 2016). Both primary addiction therapists and group facilitators working in chemical dependency treatment centers are qualified to begin discussions, individually and in groups, to assess the sexual-social experiences and possible problems of those in recovery and assess the need for further therapeutic interventions. But with very few exceptions, they simply do not ask those questions. In this author's own survey research of present and former residential treatment patients, 62% reported receiving the message that sex during early recovery is dangerous and leads to relapse; 60% heard that addicts can suffer from co-occurring disorders of drug addiction and sex addiction; 76% were told that relationships and sex should be avoided for the first year of recovery; but yet 16% reported hearing any message at all relating to sexual health being an important part of recovery from their addiction (Siegel, 2016).

As was discussed in the introduction, the editors share a philosophy about supervision best illustrated by the familiar image of the "rubber hitting the road," as symbolic of where one's academic knowledge is forged into a therapeutic style, "road-tested," as it were, in the therapy office. Sadly, extending the metaphor to the topic of sex addiction conjures images of that road littered with debris. Sex therapists all across the country report having couples and individuals come to them after unsuccessful and often painful, absurdly expensive treatment in residential sex addiction treatment centers, from thera-pists utterly untrained in the conceptualization and management of sexual disorders and dysfunctions. What seems to constitute sex addiction therapy is too often heavy on the addiction component but light on the sex component.

Things are no better in the outpatient arena, even in private practices. The fact remains that most psychologists, social workers, and mental health counselors receive little to no sexuality education or training in their graduate programs. Chapter contributor Tammy Nelson has said, regarding supervising therapists: "I tell them to ask in the first session, 'When was the last time you had sex, and how was it?' We're talking about couples here. Why would you not talk about sex? I tell them, 'If you're not talking about sex, you're perpetuating the idea that they shouldn't be, and that just won't help'" (Sohn, 2015).

The irony is inescapable that even marriage and family therapists—despite sex being implied right in their title (why people usually get married and how they come to have families!) are woefully untrained in sexuality. Throughout his entire professional career, this sex therapist has heard marriage and family therapists (MFTs) consistently say that "if you work on the communication, the sex will take care of itself." And they inevitably admitted that they knew it was not true. It seems to fit, then, to use the analogy of it being like a plumber that does not work on toilets! None would disagree that any professional who has an issue or is uncomfortable with something so essential and at the core of their profession should receive more training in order to become comfortable. If that is not possible, perhaps another choice of profession would be warranted. By and large, marriage and family therapists do not "go there," often avoiding direct discussions of sexual desire and behavior altogether. (Of course, there are so many wonderful MFTs that do, such as chapter authors in this volume like sex therapy pioneer Gina Ogden and the hugely influential Neil Cannon and Tina Shermer Sellers.) A label of sex addiction easily becomes a go-to characteri-zation and a seemingly appropriate way to continue to avoid such discussions.

At the core of the debate over whether or not sexual behavior can be labeled an addiction lies the issue of control. The addiction view utilizes a disease model to characterize out of control sexual behavior and, like with chemi-cal addictions, afflicted individuals are unable to stop the behavior despite repeated attempts to do so. Proponents of this view often frame this explana-tion with the clinical pathologies of either compulsive or impulsive disorders, yet reserve the term "addiction" as being much more significant and qualita-tively different than either (Siegel, 2015).

Others, over the past few years, have adopted a sort of "potatoe/po-tah-toe" position that we're simply arguing over semantics: "you call it compulsiv-ity, I call it addiction, but at the end of the day we're doing the same thing." Stephanie Carnes, president of the International Institute for Trauma and Addiction Professionals (IITAP), a company that provides training and materi-als to addiction professionals, believes that "although AASECT does not agree sex addiction exists, they do agree that 'out of control sexual behavior' exists; so as stated in my statement, there is disagreement on the nomenclature" (Carnes et al., 2012). She also asserts that there is definitive neurobiological and social science evidence supporting the legitimacy of sex addiction, further declaring "all major professional organizations in the field of sexual health agree sex addiction exists." Nicole Prause, noted neuroscientist and sexological researcher, counters with this observation:

> the division between profiteering therapists with no science training searching to interpret neuroscience data differently than the actual scientists themselves interpret it has been a long-standing strategy to promote pathology to reel in paying patients. Of course, debating "nomenclature" also shows a basic misunderstanding of science, and [Dr. Carnes's] explicit claim that "all major professional organizations in the field of sexual health agree sex addiction exists" remains false.
>
> (N. Prause, personal communication, January 8, 2018)

In fact, the list of the leading professional organizations in the field of sexual health that have presented position statements in opposition to the concept of sex addiction now includes AASECT, the Society for the Scientific Study of Sexuality (SSSS), the Center for Positive Sexuality (CPS), the National Coalition for Sexual Freedom (NCSF), the Alternative Sexualities Health Research Alliance (ASHRA), and perhaps most notably, the Association for the Treatment of Sexual Abusers (ATSA)—notable mostly because a major criticism of the sex addiction model is often failing to make a distinction between consensual and nonconsensual behaviors when brandishing the "sex addict" label). ATSA released a statement in November 2017, which included these passages:

> ATSA supports the need for people who are having difficulty controlling their sexual behavior in different contexts to seek treatment. We know from research and experience that treatment can significantly reduce the likelihood of future sexual offending and prevent future victimization. We are pleased to see that many of the individuals who have been reported for sexual offending are, indeed, seeking treatment. We know that treatment works and can be a necessary step toward reform.

What keeps getting lost in the recent coverage of this issue, however, is that most of the behaviors being discussed are, in fact, nonconsensual and are likely not the result of sexual addiction, which is controversial as a diagnosis. Nonconsensual sexual activity is sexual abuse. Treatment for sexual addiction generally will not address the factors that lead people to sexually abuse others (ATSA, 2017, p. 1).

Another profound statement was issued in November of 2017, as a joint statement from three of these sexual health organizations, CPS, NCSF and ASHRA, which includes this passage in their joint position statement:

> Use of the term "addiction" to describe frequent sexual behavior and/or pornography viewing is not valid and maybe misleading and sometimes

harmful to clients. Helping professionals can effectively help clients who may be struggling with various sexual issues or problems by working from a positive sexuality perspective that utilizes multidisciplinary scholarship; applies high quality empirical research and critical analysis; and prioritizes sexual rights, diversity, and acceptance of a wide range of sexual interests, behaviors and identities.

(CPS, TASHRA, & NCSF, 2017)

The disagreements between addictionological and sexological approaches to treating problematic sexual behavior (PSB) are far from semantic; they are ideological and practical. The difference in how to treat behavior that is considered a disease and how to treat behavior that is considered symptomatic of underlying issues is immense. Moreover, attempting to treat behavior as a disease, with some vague conception of underlying brain dysfunction or mysterious neurotransmitter dysregulation, is not only clinically immeasurable, but also not likely to yield tangible results (Prause & Pfaus, 2015; Prause, Janssen, Georgiadis, Finn & Pfaus, 2017). If we see the behavior instead as an attempt to mitigate some underlying driver, like anxiety, we have an opportunity to establish a clear focus by exploring the source of that anxiety. For many, spending significant amounts of time viewing pornography and erotic material may be a form of "medicating" a range of interpersonal issues, from boredom to relationship problems to trauma. When sexual behaviors are used as a coping mechanism in this way, it will invariably fail to be "used" successfully (Siegel, 2015). We would do well to remind supervisees not to be in such a rush to pathologize these behaviors and immediately view the offended partner as the victim. As Levine and Troiden (1988) pointed out in their pivotal article, "The Myth of Sexual Compulsivity," so-called sexual and pornography addictions are not clinical entities, but rather represent learned patterns of behavior that have been historically stigmatized by dominant social institutions. Let's face it: we have a long history in the United States of pathologizing any sexual behavior that is not heterosexual, monogamous, partner-oriented, and that fits well within Judeo-Christian constraints.

It is important to note that conceptualizing it as simply a nomenclature issue is as much a mistake as shutting down the diagnostic process in favor of accepting a fictitious "diagnosis." Any of the excellent reviews of the history of sex addiction (Ley, 2012; Reay, Attwood, & Gooder, 2013; Moser, 2013; Braun-Harvey & Vigorito, 2015; Derbyshire & Grant, 2015; Garcia et al., 2016) describe centuries of attempts to moralize and/or pathologize sexuality. As David Ley writes in his seminal work, *The Myth of Sex Addiction*:

> there are an incredible number of overlapping concepts and terms that are used interchangeably in the literature around sexual addiction . . . [including] *hypersexuality, nymphomania, satyriasis, Don Juanism, erotomania, hypereroticism, hyperlibido, hyperasthenia, sexual compulsivity, perversion,*

> *dysregulated sexuality, hyperphilia, pseudohypersexuality, sexual addiction, sexual disorder not otherwise specified,* and *atypical impulse control disorder.*
> (Ley, 2012)

Sex therapy supervision involving cases of OCSB or PSB can be thoroughly rewarding, both with individuals and with couples. Would-be sex therapists are encouraged to assess the presenting problem(s), including the history of the presenting problem, before jumping into "psychodynamic underpinnings," trauma histories, or "attachment problems," which are often the tip-off to a therapist's assumption of psychopathology. In this way, so much rich, diagnostic information can be mined about the current crisis, as well as the state of the relationship, which can be useful for treatment planning that aims to put the presenting crisis "in the rearview mirror" and help the patient or couple move forward toward a sexually healthier vision of their future. Most importantly, the work can begin immediately, as the couple is being guided out of the acute crisis that brought them to therapy—not after 90 days in a sex addiction rehabilitation facility (or for as long as insurance will reimburse), 6 months of "shame reduction" and "understanding addiction" work, a year of "sexual sobriety" with a "celibacy contract," and 3 to 5 years of "learning about healthy sexuality in the 12-Step context." It should also be noted that in the Carnes' *30-Task CBT Sex Addiction Treatment Model*, addressing sex and sexuality ranks 29th (Carnes, 1990).

While it may seem inappropriate to some for a textbook on sex therapy supervision to draw the proverbial line in the sand, since, as this book has pointed out in chapter after chapter, there are many ways of approaching sex therapy, from a variety of classical and innovative directions and theoretical orientations within psychotherapy and today's rapid integration of sex therapy and sexual medicine. Nevertheless, it must be said that the clear trend being observed by the author and his mentors, colleagues, and fellow sex therapists among all of the leading and most respected sexological organizations in the country, is that the seemingly endless debate, raging on for now over 30 years, about whether there even exists such a thing as "sex addiction" seems to be finally coming to clarity. The near universal consensus is that sexual behavior problems, even those that feel to be "out of control" or compulsive, are best treated from a sex-positive, sexual health–based approach over an "addictionological" one. And that today, even the public is beginning to recognize that a questionable diagnosis and downright dubious treatment model do not adequately address the just as seemingly endless epidemic of sexual harassment, abuse, and assault, and a relentlessly sex-phobic and therefore inevitably sexually unhealthy culture.

As has been said throughout this volume, in several different ways, "all roads lead to Rome" when one is endeavoring to take a sex-positive and sexual health–informed approach to helping individuals and couples feel more connected. That is vitally important when couples need to feel in control of the myriad sexual concerns that fall under the broad banner of "problematic sexual behavior." What is crucial, however, is that a therapist's theoretical orientation must frame their approaches to these sexual problems in a "sexological" rather than an "addictionological" context. This seems to be the surest way to avoid any potential shaming of patients by conceptualizing their sexuality as in any way broken, diseased, "mis-wired," "dysregulated," or as evidence of any moral failing. A sexological approach, by definition, seeks to start any therapeutic process from a place of acceptance of our sexuality as a core part of who and what we are as human beings, and with the desire to help others find their own vision of sexual health. It is simply too oxymoronic to use rhetoric of a "sex-positive disease model," as does every addictionological approach.

Atlanta-based psychotherapist Bill Herring has been an inspiring exception to most of the criticisms leveled against the sex addiction industry in this chapter. Herring is a member of SASH (the Society for the Advancement of Sexual Health, formerly known as the National Council on Sexual Addiction and Compulsivity) and is the rare CSAT (Certified Sex Addiction Therapist) who has sought extensive training in sex therapy, and has been working tirelessly to bring a greater sex-positivity to his organization's historically sex-negative views and founding beliefs. Herring noticed the growing use of the term "problematic sexual behavior" as a sign that more professionals from various sexuality fields (read: both sides of the debate) were attempting to "describe negatively experienced chronic sexual behavior patterns in a way that transcended specific theoretical orientations or treatment methodologies," but noticed that the phrase remained poorly and arbitrarily defined, and "often has seemed to serve essentially as a substitute for 'sex addiction,' with little clear distinction beyond that mere stylistic gesture" (Herring, 2016, p. 1).

Herring, motivated by a desire to help his clearly troubled patients, struggling with sexual behaviors wreaking havoc in their lives, but also frustrated by watching years of political bickering and infighting between sexuality professionals, formulated a remarkable framework for categorizing chronic, problematic sexual behavior that does not assess any specific types or frequencies of sexual practices as inherently problematic. Instead, sexual behavior patterns are considered problematic when they are associated with one or more of the following five categories: ongoing commitment violations, values conflicts, diminished control, negative consequences, and violations of sexual responsibility (Herring, 2017). As he explains,

> this framework provides the foundation for developing models to help such people without requiring diagnoses, labels or even the establishment of individual pathology. Since it provides a conceptual foundation for the creation of assistance protocols for sexual behavior patterns that are problematic but not necessarily pathological, a diagnostic label indicative of individual pathology is not a necessary condition to access formalized professional help in reducing, controlling or illuminating some problematic form of sexual behavior.

(Herring, 2017, p. 243)

In 2015, Doug Braun-Harvey and Michael Vigorito published *Treating Out of Control Sexual Behavior: Rethinking Sex Addiction,* which most of the current leaders in sex therapy thought to be the proverbial game changer. In a similar spirit of rising above the fray, they offered an innovative sexual health psychotherapy treatment approach for men experiencing sexual lives beyond their control. "Out of control sexual behavior" (OCSB) is defined as a sexual health problem in which consensual sexual urges, thoughts, or behaviors feel out of control. As opposed to a clinical disorder, OCSB is framed as a behavioral problem within the normal range of sexual expression (Braun-Harvey & Vigorito, 2015, p. 57).

As with the dozens of other historical and proposed terms for problematic sexual behavior, the authors concede that OCSB, even in its attempt to avoid labels, is a label; further, it is one that requires explanation: "out of control" ought not be taken literally,[1] or to imply, as does "addiction," that behavior is outside of a person's ability to exercise control (such exceptions in the literature are traumatic brain injury or dopaminergic side effects from anti-Parkinson's medications, wherein reports are seen of sudden onset, uncontrollable sexual urges or impulses).

OCSB treatment matches individual and group therapy interventions with current motivational interviewing and readiness-for-change research. Further, their approach emphasizes the clinician's ethical responsibility to provide the most effective treatment while protecting clients' sexual rights and welcoming sexual diversity, and which is foundationally grown out of a vision of sexual health. By conceptualizing OCSB as a sexual health behavior problem rather than an addiction or psychosexual disorder, "it enables sexual health principles to serve as the framework to envision and guide men's sexual behavior change" (Braun-Harvey & Vigorito, 2015, p. 31).

This groundbreaking book should be considered mandatory reading for sex therapy supervisors and supervisees working with patients or couples presenting with OCSB. As the authors describe, the purpose of their book—truly a new paradigm shift—is to provide clinicians a resource "for establishing . . . a psychotherapy relationship with men wanting to change and improve their sexual health" (Braun-Harvey & Vigorito, 2015, p. xii). As with Herring's framework, there are no labels put on any particular behaviors and no presumptions of pathology are held. The kernel of Braun-Harvey and Vigorito's model is the power in what only seems like a simple question: "What is your vision of sexual health?" (Consider how much more easily most people might answer questions about their physical health, fitness, nutrition, etc.). Again, a diligent, differential diagnostic process is critical. Bill Herring summarizes succinctly with a list of possible etiologies, acknowledging the extraordinary diversity of situations from which trouble may emerge:

- It could be a manifestation of a concurrent mental illness (such as a bipolar disorder or narcissistic personality disorder).
- It could be related to other medical conditions (such as hypersexual behavior resulting from Parkinson's medication).

- It could reflect a person's core nature (such as a closeted homosexual or bisexual person engaging in same-sex behavior).
- It could represent a trauma re-enactment.
- It could be a fetish that is troublesome to a person.
- It could represent a relative deficit in a person's moral code ("it's OK if nobody knows").
- It could represent a relative deficit in a person's reflective and predictive ability ("I never really thought about the consequences").
- It could represent in undo cultural influence on sexual behavior choices ("Real men need lots of sex").

(Herring, 2017, p. 246)

These and so many other possibilities offer sex therapists a trove of insight into individuals who present as feeling out of control with their sexual behavior. Couples who present in crisis because of the discovery of one partner's solo sexual fantasies or masturbation need, above all else, redirection away from focusing on sexual acts and toward their meaning in envisioning sexuality in the context of the relationship.

> Many of the symptoms that are wrongly defined as sex addiction are actually signs of a sexual-relational structure that is not working: mismatched sex drives or interests between partners, masturbation/porn phobia, or just plain old hating sex; or they are survival strategies to bring about dialogue and change in the system.
>
> (Donaghue, 2017)

As has been pointed out in several places throughout this volume, it is not possible to provide a "one size fits all" model for sex therapy supervision, no less a step-by-step manual. The theme emphasizes the idea that sex therapy supervision is as much an art as a nascent science, with little in the way of a body of research to guide it. However, it is hoped that the collective wisdom and experience of several thought leaders in the field will serve as a foundation for those beginning to craft their own style as a supervisor, to in turn hone the skills of budding sex therapists. What follows are the thoughts and experiences of this supervisor over the course of the past 25 years as a sexuality educator, sex therapist, and supervisor, on how to best approach cases dealing with out of control sexual behavior.

It's Not About Blaming the Partner

While there is little research on the topic, there are numerous anecdotes and patient reports describing previous (usually unsuccessful) therapy experiences. These anecdotal reports reveal a common thread, one often shared by sex therapists and psychotherapists in conversations among themselves, where the most repeated theme is *blame the partner*.

More often than not, these relationship crises are born out of value conflicts and a lack of communication/agreement with respect to religion, morality, and sexual behavior. This can also be seen in the conflicts that are created in the self-diagnosing of sex or porn addiction: one partner accuses, the other defends. The accusing/blaming partner is likely to be holding on tightly to their view with a sense of righteous indignation and an unwillingness to reframe their sense of victimization. Because of this tightly held view, there is often a predictable pushback against any attempts by a therapist to normalize whatever particular sexual behavior(s) precipitated the current crisis (i.e., "the Bust"). This is followed by just as predictable an outcome of that crisis, if not prevented as soon as possible. If not redirected, there can be an immediate shift in the relationship dynamic, moving from lovers and/or partners to a punishing parent and contrite child. This can sometimes happen in the moment of discovery, wherein the shocked and angry "parent" catches the humiliated "child" engaging in "that kind of behavior" (usually perceived as disgusting or perverse) or "acting out."

In living up to those new roles, it seems natural that "Mommy" would, metaphorically if not literally, drag her misbehaving or disgusting "child" into therapy by the ear, demand that the therapist "fix him" and storm out the door. More than likely, the "busted" will show up for therapy alone, racked with guilt and shame; at the angry behest of their partner, as penance to get out of the proverbial doghouse. It could be any or all of the above. As has been especially prominent in the media, more people with identified sexual behavior problems have been seeking a "sex addict" label as a means of trying to convince their partner that they are sick, thus garnering their partner's sympathy, not their anger.

Offended partners often feel angry, disgusted, horrified, or stunned. They may be feeling like their partner, whom they thought they knew, now seems like a stranger. While these feelings of the partner certainly need to be acknowledged and respected, it is critical in these situations that the partner be encouraged to stay or join the therapy from the start. Of course, that typically means having to "put out fires" and provide tremendous support to both partners as the couple is brought out of the crisis that brought them in to therapy. Often this naturally involves a good deal of venting and therapists being tested on their abilities to mediate and teach couples to "fight fair." But the therapist must remain steadfast in their belief that whatever the issue may be, it is a couple's issue and is best treated by the couple, as a couple. The alternative, sending the identified "addict" to an individual therapist "to work on their addiction" and the partner to his or her own individual therapist to cope with being a partner of an addict, only portends the cementing of that decidedly unsexy, nonerotic relationship dynamic.

It is also important to assess the couples' current and past sexual status as soon as possible in the treatment process. This in itself may carry the risk of fanning the flames of blame (e.g., "if we had sex more often, I wouldn't have to . . ."). Naturally, a therapist, particularly a sex therapist supervisee, would have to be guided to gently navigate what could be highly volatile emotions and threatened defenses. Potential countertransference, in the form of taking sides or commiserating with a partner who feels like everything they thought was true may now be perceived to be a lie, must be vigilantly watched for and avoided. Again, a sex therapist should feel obliged to remain neutral, to remind the couple that they are lovers and, if they are committed to remaining in the relationship, guide them to redefine sexuality for that relationship. The core of this work is to recognize each partner's numerous symbolic sexual meanings and the lifetimes of often rigid scripts about "shoulds and shouldn'ts" in sex and relationships.

This also requires that the therapist remain diagnostically curious, using the couple's sexual status (or lack thereof, as the case often is) and the identified sexual problems as always symptomatic—never the disease (or necessarily even a disease at all). While it certainly would be easier, and often feels like meeting the patient where they or their protesting partner is, the experience of dozens of sex therapists has reiterated that there is little benefit to the health of the couple in "going with the pop culture flow" and cutting off that diagnostic investigation with the simplistic summation, "because you're an addict." To paraphrase Braun-Harvey and Vigorito, it's akin to a patient walking into an oncologist's office and saying, "I have cancer," and the oncologist saying, "well, let's start the chemo!" One would hope a thorough assessment and differential diagnosis were completed before any treatment begins, avoiding what Braun-Harvey famously refers to as "premature evaluation" (Braun-Harvey & Vigorito, 2015, p. 55).

It should be noted that for some, encouraging such focus on the relationship rather than diagnosing a sexual pathology in one partner may set the stage for the exchanges of blame. It is also not helpful to stay rigidly wed to the idea that "it must be the relationship."

As Esther Perel points out in *The State of Affairs*:

> The idea that infidelity can happen in the absence of serious marital problems is hard to accept. Our culture does not believe in no-fault affairs. So, when we can't blame the relationship, we tend to blame the individual instead. The clinical literature is rife with typologies for cheaters—as if character always trumps circumstance. Psychological jargon has replaced religious cant, and sin has been eclipsed by pathology.
>
> (p. 153)

She later goes on to say, "it's easier to label than to delve" (Perel, 2017, p. 153). How true that is! But supervisors must be vigilant to make sure their supervisees always remain open to the reality that for every couple that presents in the sometimes still-smoldering aftermath of a discovered infidelity, there are at least two realities in the room: the reality of the betrayal of the "cheater" and all the anger and pain that they likely experience, and the reality of the "cheater," who may have been searching desperately for some meaning, or some feeling at all, after experiencing the loss or symbolic death of a moribund, sexless, lonely marriage. "Having a disease that offers some sort of redemption is very appealing for people whose only other choice is to be a pervert" (Braun-Harvey & Vigorito, 2015, p. 56). Isn't it ironic, then, that choosing a disease label instead of exploring relationship dynamics and the wondrous and powerful intricacies of sexuality is, in fact, blaming the partner?

As stated earlier, the problem with the sex addiction approach is the philosophical belief, though clinical error, that the symptom is the disease. This invariably leads to a premature "diagnosis" that tends to take the current crisis and freeze it into a "new permanent": the offending partner is labeled a "sex addict" and the partner embraces the label "partner of a sex addict"—now and forever. Reay et al. wrote in "Inventing Sex: The Short History of Sex Addiction" (2013):

> Unlike most claimed medical disorders, self-diagnosis is an important strand of sex addiction. Many sex addicts are either self-defined or labeled as such by offended partners or loved ones. "Does your partner spend an inordinate amount of time thinking about sex? Has your relationship been damaged by his sexual activities? Are there times when his sexual urges, thoughts or images seem to control him?" If so, he—or she—may not be necessarily an un-trustworthy cad but an addict in need of psychiatric help.
>
> (p. 7)

One of the most harmful aspects of the sex addiction approach is that this "treatment model" reinforces the worst fears of a couple in crisis. The crisis that brought them into therapy, which has seriously threatened the *lover* dynamic of their relationship, is cemented by a characterization that confirms the fear that the "addict's" sexuality is somehow broken or untrustable. Worst of all, this approach will significantly increase the likelihood that the couple will never be lovers again.

This further complicates sex therapy supervision with cases involving reported or assumed OCSB because the sex therapist often has to begin their work by undoing the work of previous therapists. These are usually CSATs who, as mentioned before, typically lack training in sexuality or hold any type of certification in sex therapy. Consequently, they do not possess the understanding or ability to appropriately assess and/or diagnose sexual disorders.

This supervisor has seen the diagnosis of "sex addiction" or "porn addiction" put couples into that unsexy, parent/child dynamic so often over the past two decades, that the classic approach to psychotherapy called transactional analysis (TA) consistently comes to mind. TA was introduced by Eric Berne in his book, *Transactional Analysis in Psychotherapy* (1961), and it quickly became an early pop psychology staple (even more so following publication of his subsequent book, *Games People Play*, in 1964). In developing this approach to psychoanalysis, Berne observed Freud's foundational theory of personality, described by the "competing drives" of the id (irrational and emotional), the ego (rational), and the superego (moral). As stated on the Berne estate website:

> perhaps Freud's greatest contribution (and the one that influenced Berne) was the fact that the human personality is multi-faceted. Regardless of

the classification or name given to a particular area of personality (id, superego, etc.), each individual possesses factions that frequently collide with each other. And it is these collisions and interactions between these personality factions that manifest themselves as an individual's thoughts, feelings, and behaviors. Thus, under Freud's theories, an individual's behavior can be understood by analyzing and understanding his/her three factions.

(www.ericberne.com, 2015)

It was Berne's belief, however, that Freud's descriptions proposed "concepts . . . [and not] phenomenological realities" (Berne, 1961, p. 4). He ultimately defined "ego states" differently—as parent, adult, and child—and argued that while Freud's ego states were unobservable and theoretical, his were confirmable through actual observation of the behavior (Berne, 1961). Of course, the basis of TA's application to work with couples was the observation of *transactions*, or communications, that were either complementary (e.g., Adult → Adult or Adult → Actual child) or crossed (e.g., one person is attempting to communicate Adult → Adult, but their partner is responding Child → Parent).

Particularly in the context of this chapter, it is quite easy to see how Berne's TA can be modified to working with couples presenting in these various dilemmas known, collectively, as "sex addiction" (with the contemporaneous guilt, shame, and embarrassment that are predictably in tow). One need not get too psychodynamic with the symbolisms; a here-and-now, cognitive-behavioral approach is sufficient to use the symbolic parent, adult, and child conceptualizations to help couples identify from which ego states they are interacting, before, and during their current crisis. The sex therapy "twist" that supervisors can remind their supervisees to remind their couples is that people are not *supposed* to feel erotic attraction to their parent or their child, so if that is how one is behaving in the relationship, no one should be surprised if the couple is no longer sexually and erotically connected. In fact, it's a rather typical response to an abnormal relationship dynamic for two adults who are supposed to be lovers. So if a mother of two is heard complaining about her three kids because she feels overwhelmed with the burdens of parenting and maintaining the home while her husband drinks beer with his work buddies until dinnertime and then lies in front of the TV every night, it is easy to imagine that these can be serious turn-offs and lead to subsequent rejection of any attempt to initiate sexual activity—whether out of anger, sadness, resentment, injustice, or all of the above.

Add to this dynamic the oft-mentioned "bust": getting caught masturbating, looking at porn, getting caught going to massage parlors, prostitutes, paramours, and so forth. It's simply not the role of a partner to "bust" their partner—that's the role of an angry parent. From this supervisor's experience, it is imperative to help the couple break out of a parent/child dynamic and back into an adult/adult dynamic as quickly as possible if there is to be hope of saving the relationship and re-establishing a loving and erotic sex-life. Any "buy in" to these pop-culture trends of knee-jerk labeling people as "addicts" and "partner of addicts" risks preventing that realignment from ever happening. More often than not, the dynamic morphs from parent/child to "cop/suspect" or "warden/convict." No matter how much it is considered an important part of family involvement in addiction therapy, no wife who has installed "internet nanny" software to track her husband's web browsing, or uses smartphone GPS apps to track her husband, will again see him as a lover in this dynamic. By the same token, no husband who was made to feel humiliated, emasculated and shamed; oftentimes "outed" to his children, extended family, boss, co-workers, and law-enforcement will likely struggle to feel like an adult, much less a lover, coming home from work and being interrogated with questions like, "Did you masturbate today? Did you look at porn? Let me see your phone!"

Two adults, choosing to share their lives together as intimate partners, embark on a journey of discovery about themselves and each other. Of course, sometimes those discoveries are made in unplanned and jarringly surprising ways, like accidentally walking in on a partner self-pleasuring or coming across a hidden "stash" of the accouterments of a particular kink or fetish. Sometimes, the impact that discovery has on the discoverer's perceived realities and threatened values can push them immediately into parent mode; angry, judgmental, punitive. Ultimately, the likelihood of this becoming the "new permanent" or something the couple moves past and grows through might depend largely on the bias of the therapist they call.

It's Not About the Porn!

Another foundational piece that is essential on which to successfully build a framework for helping couples get past the crisis of "discovering a porn addiction" involves the recognition that we, as a culture (particularly in the United States), need to simply grow up and admit that the oft-used euphemism "looking at porn" really—and exclusively—refers to masturbation. Much of the conflict of such a high-distress couple presenting with the "crisis" resulting from the discovery of one's partner enjoying solo pleasuring to online erotica can be mitigated by simply acknowledging that self-pleasuring is considered normal, healthy behavior and is not necessarily an indictment of one's partner or the relationship. Masturbation is a natural, not abhorrent, behavior. This simple awareness, in and of itself, can do much to provide clarity and understanding to the situation. Such hackneyed euphemisms only serve to distance the individual from the real issue/behavior and prevents both partners from clearly seeing what may be going on. It might be worth noting that sexual euphemisms are often humorously ironic. *Looking at porn?* One's eyes are often closed during much of self-pleasuring activity, even when using erotic imagery to fuel their fantasies. A similar irony can be found in the even more overused euphemism, *sleeping together.* One can't help chuckle when hearing, in response to the question "did you sleep together?" "no, we didn't get any sleep at all! We were having sex all night!" (one can also include the common phrase, "sexually active," prompting the classic sex educators' joke, "no, I'm not sexually active, I usually just lie there!").

Immediately reframing the issue as being about our most basic sexuality (and natural role masturbation plays in that), rather than demonizing porn, is powerfully effective in (a) not reinforcing the cultural obsession with porn and it being the root of all evil, and (b) keeping the focus on the dynamics of the couple and their sexual relationship. It affords wonderful opportunities for the couple to discuss their own and each other's sexuality—often for the first time in their relationship, possibly in their lives and, now, with a brutal honesty they've likely been hiding from for a long time. Sex therapy supervisors must ensure that their supervisees are comfortable enough, not only in guiding a couple through their crisis, but in making that shift to the role of educator, and moving the discussion away from arguments over pornography (and the multitude of symbolism porn represents that each is likely defending) and back toward sex—solo and partnered, private and shared. Rather than framing it in crisis, it should be framed as an opportunity to better understand each other's desires and expectations in order to improve the relationship. It is also an opportunity to reveal some underlying issues that either or both partners may not be aware of or may quietly be struggling with. Intimacy issues, recurring obsessive fantasies, conditioned association between gratification and isolation, and avoidant behavior are just some of the underlying issues that can be addressed if they are brought to light. It is also important to work with both partners on ways to manage and redirect (when necessary) those behaviors in a way that empowers them, eschewing the troubling assertion in virtually all recovery programs that the problematic behavior is uncontrollable and, therefore, requires a lifelong vigilance to ensure they do not "relapse." From a relationship perspective, it would be virtually impossible to maintain a level of trust and acceptance of one's partner if one continues to be vigilant in expecting the next betrayal.

Supervisees also need guidance in navigating a likely onslaught of arguments that sex addiction proponents, and spurned partners alike, often make: that porn is addictive and changes brains; that it is a sign of a significant psychosexual disorder; that it means their partner is no longer attracted to them; that it is the reason for all the problems in their relationship (ironically, since in most cases, the behavior had been unknown until revealed). Unfortunately, many partners buy into the pop-culture phenomenon that is "porn addiction" often present with a laundry list of evidentiary factors to "prove" their partner's disease and that their brains are changed because of it. A common assertion put forth by proponents of sex addiction states that the chemical actions in the brain during sexual activity are the same as the chemical activity involved in alcohol and drug use. They, therefore, claim that both sexual activity and substance abuse share reward and reinforcement mechanisms that produce the "craving" and "addictive" behaviors. This assertion is flawed on several levels, not the least of which is that it is based on drawing conclusions from brain scan imaging that are devoid of any real interpretive foundation; a "leap of faith," so to speak. Furthermore, it is somewhat of a stretch to equate the neurophysiological mechanisms which underlie chemical dependency, tolerance, and withdrawal with the underlying mechanisms of what is most often compulsive or anxiety-reducing behaviors like gambling, shopping, sex, and other so-called "process addictions" (Siegel & Siegel, 2007, 2011; Prause, Steele, Staley, Sabatinelli & Proudfit, in press).

It is also quite likely that angry partners with extremely negative views and prejudices about pornography can be openly hostile to a sex therapist that does not immediately "take their side" and support their own assertions about porn use. Some will even go so far as to characterize the therapist's sex- and porn-positivity as evidence of *their* own "perversion." Couples presenting with issues related to a partner's discovered use of erotic material most often fall into a victim–perpetrator narrative, which then evolves into a kind of parent–child dynamic where the offended partner demands contrition and a reason to trust before letting their partner out of the proverbial doghouse.

As was previously noted, it is a troubling state of affairs that a significant proportion of today's psychotherapy and mental health communities are seemingly abdicating their diagnostic responsibility and simply accepting the sex- or porn-addiction "diagnosis" upon presentation and at the patient's or partner's word, while automatically siding with the partner as a "collateral victim" of this purported disease. It should also be noted that, once again, the more that porn is demonized in society, the more dangerous a path we embark upon. Again, failing to learn from history's lessons and those of our sex-positive advances, erotophobes and religious zealots have been re-energized to use either pseudo-science or outright charlatanism to justify their continued religious-masquerading-as-political crusades. As of this writing, six US states—Utah, South Dakota, Virginia, Tennessee, Florida, and Pennsylvania—have either already passed or are considering proposed legislation to declare pornography the number one public health crisis! (National Conference of State Legislatures, 2016). Not gun violence, AIDS, or climate change; it is porn. Even the president's declaration on the opioid epidemic only warranted a "public health emergency" status, far lower in status than a crisis, but governors are lining up to utilize the full resources of their offices to battle porn addiction.

Sen. Mae Beavers, a Republican member of the Tennessee Senate, filed a resolution to declare porn a public health crisis in 2017, stating that porn use among youth "leads to low self-esteem and eating disorders, an increase in problematic sexual activity at younger ages, and an increased desire to engage in risky sexual behaviors." It goes further with such baseless and ludicrous claims, adding that pornography "treats women and children as objects" and sensationalizes rape culture and sex trafficking as well as "lessening the desire in young men to marry and propagates infidelity."

According to the Baptist Press (2017), Jay Dennis, founder of the One Million Men anti-pornography ministry, declared that the states' measures are a valuable victory in communicating porn's harm. "The fact that states are beginning to recognize pornography as a public health hazard, underscores what the Bible has been clear upon—sexual sin is destructive not only spiritually, but also emotionally and physically," said Dennis, who recently retired as pastor of First Baptist Church at the Mall in Lakeland, Florida. "Identifying pornography as a public health hazard presents factual information to those outside of Christianity that this is not just a spiritual battle, it is a health issue facing every person." Dennis encourages pastors to educate their churches on the dangers of porn, which he believes feeds sexual sin including human trafficking. This is not confined to Dennis and his group, however. There is a widespread and growing coalition of religious groups in the United States, known as the Porn is a Public Health Crisis Movement, and it appears to also be growing in its influence on politicians and public decision makers. It should also be a note of interest that those states with the highest rates of restrictive religiosity (like Utah) are the states where guilt and the subsequent panic over porn use is the highest. What is regarded as "porn addiction" by many is merely a religiously based experience of guilt over some perceived violation of religious tenets or laws regarding sexual behavior (i.e., nonheterosexual, non-penile-vaginal sexual behaviors are defined as *sodomy*).

What must it say, then, about the therapists and supervisors who undoubtedly advised Senator Beavers or to those that practice in the state where the legal values about sexuality lead to policy which presumes to dictate the sexual mores of the state—and, by extension, its citizens—and which are based on overly simplistic and arbitrarily moralistic beliefs rather than science and professional consensus?

Another common accusation leveled against sex therapists is that they are so accepting of porn, and so "rejecting of the reality of porn addiction" (Carnes, 2017) that they normalize or rationalize porn use and, as a result, minimize the suffering of "untold millions" who feel their porn use is addictive or out of control. To begin, not accepting a fatuous diagnosis that has failed to demonstrate any scientific validity in over 30 years is not "rejecting a reality." Furthermore, no good therapist would dismiss or minimize presenting complaints of their patients, particularly one in distress. And no supervisor should allow a supervisee to be dismissive, even if out of the desire to ease a patient's anxiety, as with the previously used example of a patient who presents feeling "unable to control" due to a monthly masturbation "habit." Again, what is essential is to explore the anxiety that is behind the presentation, as well as, of course, the precipitating factors that brought the patient to therapy. (It has been said, as possibly reflective of the relational aspect of these so-called porn problems, that "no one is a porn addict until they're busted.")

Now imagine a young man on his honeymoon, so racked with insecurity and anxiety about sexual performance that he would make an excuse to leave the couple's hotel room or lock himself in the bathroom to masturbate to porn on his smartphone. Whether a therapist would characterize this as "porn addiction" or "severe anxiety disorder" would certainly influence the type of intervention provided. Again, trends being what they are, a great many would be eager to diagnose PIED—"porn-induced erectile dysfunction"—which, despite earning itself an acronym, is entirely fabricated and has no place in the clinical language of licensed professionals. Using such clinical-sounding, but fictitious, terminology is exactly the kind of reinforcing, iatrogenic harm that can be done by uninformed therapists.

Clearly, that is not the typical presentation to sex therapists' offices. They are far more likely to be men that have been in long-term relationships, though even that concept seems more relative than ever. There is a body of research indicating that the famous "seven-year itch," a psychological and pop-media term that suggests that happiness in a relationship declines after the seventh year of marriage, is now closer to 4 years (Kurdek, 1999; Dalton, 2000). Of course, many of these men also complain of a diminished or absent sex life or, like so many couples, complain that sex is routine, perfunctory, or obligatory. Sometimes there is a sexual dysfunction present, perhaps one that predates the relationship (lifelong) or one that occurred at some point along the way (acquired), that led to increasing avoidance of partnered sexual activity. It is also well established that a primary sexual dysfunction in one partner can lead to a secondary dysfunction in the other and, thus, more avoidance. Well-respected sex therapists and psychologists Stan Althof and Barry McCarthy have written extensively on secondary partner dysfunction (Althof & Needle, 2016) and low- or no-sex marriages (McCarthy & McCarthy, 2003, 2014).

For those men who present complaining of masturbating compulsively, several times a day, and reporting that they feel unable to stop, a sexological approach has proven far more effective than an abstinence-based or addiction approach. Even a sex therapy approach that parallels more "old-school" cognitive-behavior psychotherapy techniques is shown to be more effective. For example, many sex therapy students and supervisees notice how often the step-by-step nature of many sensate focus techniques, particularly with such dysfunctions as vaginismus[2] in women or the inability to orgasm with a partner, resemble traditional systematic desensitization treatment for phobias. For these "addicted" men, sex therapists can guide them through a sort of "sensate focus for one" and be instructed to have solo sensual dates, during which time they can use guided masturbation techniques to re-form new patterns of mindfulness, enhance their genital and overall sensitivity to erotic touch, expand the repertoire of their sexual fantasies, and improve their ability to "log on" to more sexy thoughts in their mind as they decrease their perceived dependence on outside imagery for fantasy "fodder." In other words, by using a step-by-step method, the masturbation can be uncoupled from the porn, a crucial first step in beginning to look therapeutically at why and how masturbation became the obviously "go-to" anxiety reducer.

Another important and extremely helpful adjunct to this step-by-step disconnecting of masturbation from porn, for men, is the encouragement and training to both enhance their sensitivity and expand their masturbatory repertoire. In the words of this supervisor's supervisor, the late Dr. Susan Lee, a Helen Kaplan–trained sex therapist and extraordinary supervisor, that she loved to remind her students and patients alike: it is all about friction plus fantasy! An unavoidable reality for most people, however, is that the need for both increases as we age. For most adolescents, the fantasy part seems a given. For adolescent boys, the pressure of clothing may be all the friction necessary! Another reality for most people, not just men, is that orgasm is often easier to achieve and more intense alone than with a partner (in a 20-year career, this sex therapist has treated numerous cases of delayed or completely inhibited ejaculation in men but, in every case, it was when with a partner. It is extremely rare to hear of a man presenting with "I have never ejaculated"). For most men, masturbatory "styles" typically emerge in adolescence and remain fairly unchanged into adulthood, presumably finding what works and sticking with it to provide maximum friction. Together with the high-intensity arousal of endless, on-demand porn available online and the ability to completely lose oneself into "porn world," it is easy to see how easy it is! Bring in a partner, and of course, the level of self-conscious arousal is likely to decrease as performance anxieties and expectations rise.[3] Furthermore, that unique, often idiosyncratic masturbation style that produces the friction a particular man may be accustomed to from masturbating may not be reproducible by any mouth, vagina, or anus in the world!

Men who feel that their porn use has desensitized them to partnered sex (or, again, believe they have been stricken with the fictitious "porn-induced erectile dysfunction") should be instructed to follow the sage advice of renowned sex columnist and newly published sex researcher, Dan Savage, who has long advised adolescent boys to "mix it up" when they masturbate (e.g., overhand/underhand grip, right-handed, left-handed, with lube, without lube, even with condoms[4]) in order to make sure they and their penises remain responsive to a wider variety of stimuli. In addition, many men have had success, following this same step-by-step logic, by using sleeve-type sex toys such as the "Fleshlight," a device that looks like an ordinary flashlight but, instead, has a latex mouth, vagina, or anus at the end.

If a man is partnered, supervisors can guide the sex therapist in integrating the one partner's "solo work" with the couple's sex therapy (for this supervisor, typically modified sensate focus-type behavioral assignments, or "sensual dates," but trying to reconnect the couple intimately again as soon as possible), ultimately bringing these now parallel tracks into one, wherein the individual "practice" has become incorporated into the couple's sensual dates and increasingly erotic "homework assignments." A willing and involved partner can be the most valuable therapeutic tool and can help the effectiveness of the work immeasurably.

When supervising therapists working with couples for whom masturbation is prohibited, typically for orthodox religious reasons, and the discovered masturbation "addiction" is what has presented for therapy, there will naturally be resistance to the idea of "guided masturbation" or that masturbation can be "therapeutically necessary." Of course, that should be respected. However, a little "psycho-education" can go a long way in teaching a couple about sexual pleasuring not being limited to penile–vaginal intercourse, that masturbation implies a solo act, and that however they pleasure themselves and each other together is sex, not masturbation. So, the same type of behavioral assignments can be done by the couple together—in the best-case scenarios, the partner's anger has since dissolved into a desire to participate and the sex therapy assignment itself can be a huge step toward healing the hurt, rekindling the affection, and reconnecting them intimately. Also, in many cases, sex therapists are fortunate enough to align with clergy in their communities (a rich source of referrals for many!) to whom they can refer a couple for what is often referred to as "special dispensation"—a religious blessing, or permission, to use exercises that involve self-pleasuring (e.g., an Orthodox Jewish man referred to his rabbi for permission to practice "stop/start" to get over his rapid ejaculation that was affecting the couple's ability to conceive).

It is also beyond the scope of this chapter to wander into the foray of decades of arguments over the differences between erotica and pornography, who gets to decide obscenity laws, or what is or is not acceptable fantasy material—be it accessed via the internet, "old-school" magazines, or Harlequin romance novels. But it is this supervisor's intent to encourage sex therapists to continue to steer their clients away from focusing on porn or erotic material as the cause of the couple's problem and, instead, to see an opportunity for the couple to grow together, both intimately and sexually.

Working With Patients "in Recovery"

Naturally, therapists are most often encouraged to "meet the client where they are" (barring severe psychopathology). Surely, most would agree that it is rarely prudent to argue with our patients and clients. It would be ludicrous to respond to a patient who says, "I'm a sex addict," with an answer like, "no you're not, there is no such thing!" or "I don't believe in that!" While this may be just arrogance and countertransference on the part of the therapist, it may actually arise more out of a genuine desire to normalize the patient's behavior and decrease the shame they may assume the patient or client is experiencing by identifying as a "sex addict."

What would be useful diagnostically would be to ask the patient *why* he or she identifies as a sex addict and, specifically, about the behavior(s) presumably being used as evidence or "symptoms" of their self-diagnosed "disease."[5] Of course, it would also be helpful to know if the label was, in fact, self-diagnosed or imposed by a spouse or partner, a parent, a boss, or an iatrogenically harmful therapist. As with any differential diagnosis, the therapist should have their "sex detective" hat on (Perelman & Grill, 2013) to ascertain the nature of the reported problem, be it any of the "usual suspects" of compulsive masturbation, visiting of porn sites or strip clubs, soliciting sex workers, a revealed (voluntarily or involuntarily) sexual interest in kink or any type of paraphilia, or garden-variety affairs and infidelities.

Regardless, supervisors should encourage their supervisees to position themselves as allies and advocates for their clients' choices (at least at first, until a comfortable rapport allows for more of a challenge of certain rigid beliefs), rather than present as contrarian to their conclusions about addiction, language choice, and choice to participate in a 12-Step fellowship. In other words, sex therapists can reassure patients who are somehow affiliated with "sex addiction recovery" that sex therapy can be seen as an important adjunct to their recovery plan. This is true regardless of whether they are already entrenched or merely considering participating in a recovery community, consider themselves "sexually sober," or "working a program." (It is helpful to also include a reminder that 12-Step fellowships may be helpful support systems, but they are just that—support groups are not treatment for their sexual issues.)

There are a number of criticisms leveled against 12-Step programs as a foundation for recovery from any issue. Most of these criticisms address to what often seems to be a cult-like adherence to an insular life by many "in the program," a reliance on slogans and catchphrases that constitute much of 12-Step parlance, and debates about 12-Step culture's inherent religiosity and conservative Christian roots. These criticisms notwithstanding, for the moment, it is important for therapists working with self-identified "recovering sex addicts" to have a thorough and working knowledge of that culture. While we would certainly want to be the best allies for our patients and clients, it is crucial to understand that even in the relative uniformity of the more than fifty 12-Step fellowships in existence today, and the near-universal replication of the original 12 steps of Alcoholics Anonymous (with the obvious exception of replacing "alcohol" with whichever substance or behavior one is claiming their "powerlessness" over), when it comes to groups for "sex addiction," there are no fewer than seven fellowships (five for "addicts" and two for partners, or "codependents," of addicts or "co-addicts"). All of these programs utilize the same 12-Step tenets of AA, but they differ in their approach to how they define "sex addiction" or even what constitutes sobriety and relapse. Sex Addicts Anonymous (SAA), Sex and Love Addicts Anonymous (SLAA), Sexual Compulsives Anonymous (SCA), Sexual Recovery Anonymous (SRA), and Sexaholics Anonymous (SA) all treat the same "disease," with (supposedly) the same tools; but quite differently. There is also a fellowship called Recovering Couples Anonymous (RCA), who have adapted the first step of AA to state, "We admitted we are powerless over our relationship, and our lives became unmanageable together" (RCA, 1991, 2001)—a veritable smorgasbord of possibilities for any relationship therapist before sex is even mentioned!

To clarify some of these differences, official fellowship descriptions will be referenced. As summarized in the literature from Sex Addicts Anonymous:

> Our goal when entering the SAA program is abstinence from one or more specific sexual behaviors. But unlike programs for recovering alcoholics or drug addicts, Sex Addicts Anonymous does not have a universal definition of abstinence. Most of us have no desire to stop being sexual altogether. It is not sex in and of itself that causes us problems, but the addiction to certain sexual behaviors. In SAA we will be better able to determine what

behavior is addictive and what is healthy. However, the fellowship does not dictate to its members what is and isn't addictive sexual behavior. Instead we have found that it is necessary for each member to define his or her own abstinence.

(SAA, 2007)

SLAA focuses on both "sex and love addiction," which is defined as:

any sexual or emotional act, no matter what its initial impulse may be, which leads to loss of control over rate, frequency, or duration of its occurrence or recurrence, resulting in spiritual, mental, physical, emotional, and moral destruction of oneself and others.

(SLAA, 1997)

SLAA defines "sobriety" in terms of complete abstinence from one's self-identified "bottom-line" behaviors. Examples of bottom line behaviors might include sexual or romantic activity outside the scope of monogamous relationships, anonymous or casual sex, compulsive avoidance of intimacy or emotional attachment, one-night stands, compulsive masturbation, obsessive fantasy, compulsive attraction to unavailable or abusive partners, and a wide variety of addictive sexual, romantic, or avoidant behaviors.

As stated on its website, "SLAA is open to anyone who knows or thinks they have a problem with sex addiction, love addiction, romantic obsession, co-dependent relationships, fantasy addiction and/or sexual, social and emotional anorexia" (SLAA, 1997). In the view of some practitioners, there are people who are purported to have a sexual addiction, which is expressed through a variety of behaviors such as visiting strip clubs, soliciting sex workers, visiting internet porn sites, and so forth, but fit the definition of "sexual anorexic" in that they seem to lack the ability to have a relationship of a sexual nature beyond a paid-for or anonymous experience. The person is not regarded as being averse to sex but, rather, to intimacy (Carnes, 1997; Katehakis, 2010). The use of such clinical-sounding parlance, at least to the lay public, belies the fact that there is simply no clinical validity to any of these concepts. As was noted earlier, licensed clinicians, legally and ethically bound to their profession's ethics, should not be allowed to simply make up dreadful-sounding pseudo-diagnoses to justify what amounts to an arbitrary belief.

In SCA (Sexual Compulsives Anonymous),

Members are encouraged to develop their own sexual recovery plan, and to define sexual sobriety for themselves. We are not here to repress our God-given sexuality, but to learn how to express it in ways that will not make unreasonable demands on our time and energy, place us in legal jeopardy—or endanger our mental, physical or spiritual health.

(SCA, 2001)

It is noteworthy that SCA was originally formed to primarily serve gay and bisexual men, undoubtedly due to the clearly heterosexist definition of a "normal" relationship and the homophobic "broad brush" that often equated homosexual sex with not only addiction, but with dozens of historically judged acts of perversion or paraphilia. SCA now welcomes all sexual orientations and an increasing number of women and heterosexual men are currently attending their meetings (Herring, 2017).

In Sexual Recovery Anonymous, sexual sobriety is defined as "the release from all compulsive and destructive sexual behaviors. We have found through our experience that sobriety includes freedom from masturbation and sex outside a committed relationship" (SRA, 2010). SRA was originally formed by members of Sexaholics Anonymous (SA) who broke away from the group because of its narrow, restrictive definition of sobriety. SRA also defines sobriety in terms of specific practices, although it is not as restrictive as SA (Herring, 2017).

Perhaps the most disconcerting 12-Step support group for "sex addiction" is Sexaholics Anonymous (SA). According to their literature, "any form of sex with one's self or with partners other than the [heterosexual] spouse is progressively addictive and destructive." Some fundamental, underlying tenets of SA underscore how restrictive (if not regressive) the program can be. For example, SA describes more of an addiction to lustful desires that to actual sexual behavior. Furthermore, SA is the only group that defines "sexual sobriety" in terms of specific sexual behaviors, narrowly defining the only appropriate context for sexual behavior as being with one's spouse. The SA literature specifically defines "spouse" as either a heterosexual man or woman to which one is legally married. It is further asserted that anyone outside a heterosexual marriage is expected to remain celibate.

COSA is a recovery program for family or friends whose lives have been affected by someone else's compulsive sexual behavior. According to the group's website,

> the material is what will be used in COSA literature as the "official version," with the understanding that individual COSA groups have the right to "take what you like and leave the rest." Each COSA member may choose to define him/herself as a codependent of sexual addiction, as a co-sex addict, or simply as a member of COSA, according to his or her own personal experience and conscience.
>
> (COSA, 2007, 2018)

COSA members are encouraged to "define your own abstinence," not engage in masturbation or self-pleasuring in any form, and to "resist temptations of lust." This institutionalized erotophobic and sex-negative view runs counter to the philosophy and core values inherent in sex therapy and presents an obstacle to introducing a view of sexual health and positive sexual growth and development in recovery communities. This, in turn, makes it virtually impossible to move from viewing sex through a lens of fear and suspicion to appreciating the powerful ally that a sexually healthy treatment focus can be in strengthening relationships and reducing one's reliance on distressing or undesired sexual outlets.

Still another confounding piece to the problem inherent in 12-Step approaches to treating what should be referred to as "out of control sexual behavior" (OCSB), and one of particular relevance to sex therapy supervisors, is the culture within most 12-Step recovery communities. Since the development of the "Minnesota Model" in the 1950s and the unlikely alliance between psychiatric treatment and 12-Step involvement that it espoused (AA had been historically adversarial to psychiatry), in addition to the development of the 28-day residential treatment model for alcoholism and chemical dependency, it has come to be expected and accepted that part of the treatment team will be made up of nonprofessional also-recovering staff, trained around the principles of Alcoholics Anonymous. Over the decades, this has become cemented into treatment center culture, such that universally, treatment centers employ what this supervisor has referred to as "paid sponsors"—staff that are largely unschooled and untrained in counseling skills or group facilitation but are "credentialed" to work there by virtue of the self-assessed and self-professed "strength of their recovery." The fact that these untrained professionals are the staff that are actually facilitating the majority of the groups that addicts in recovery centers attend every day is problematic. Most "addicts" in residential treatment settings see their primary therapist no more often than they would an outpatient, private practice therapist: one hour per week. There is an obvious risk to both the effectiveness of treatment and the welfare of the client, particularly in the case of the staff member who "drank the Kool-Aid," to borrow a phrase, and is mired in 12-Step slogans and platitudes that continue to keep a patient stuck in a cycle of shame and failure; being told day in and day out that "it works if you work it" and "you are just not working your program hard enough." This is typically accompanied by "you are not hitting your knees and praying," "you are not turning your will over to God," or "you are taking it back." We should be hard-pressed, as sexuality and sexual health professionals, to accept this as a viable therapeutic perspective.

Not only is this clearly not clinically helpful (it can be argued that as "therapeutic treatment" it is ethically dubious), but sadly, when so culturally entrenched, it often flows upward, and many treatment centers now commonly employ primary therapists—licensed clinicians—who also identify as "recovering addicts" and are entrenched in this 12-Step philosophy. For many years, the present author has referred to these professionals as "two-hatters"—those individuals who aspire to be helping professionals by day and are recovering addicts by night . . . or at least, off the clock. Not surprisingly, the skill level needed to successfully keep those two parts of themselves "well-boundaried" varies greatly and often presents as countertransference or counselor bias.

This volume has two excellent chapters on dealing with both conservative Christian guilt and countertransference. But additionally, supervision with therapists working in addiction treatment settings may present unique challenges with both. The present author has had a number of supervisees, both sex therapy supervisees and pre-licensed counselor interns, who found themselves in a seeming tug-of-war, wherein their on-site supervisor (typically the clinical director or a primary therapist) had actively discouraged them from enacting appropriate psychotherapeutic interventions, or even lines of inquiry, that went beyond the typical addiction-treatment approach and were often met with such justifications as, "we don't have them that long; we don't want to 'open them up!'"

Oftentimes the level of countertransference with respect to anything even *remotely* sexual has led to the highly unusual situation, quite common for the author of this chapter, of a treatment center either sending a residential patient to an outpatient sex therapist or bringing the sex therapist into the treatment center to act as co-therapist. This is most commonly motivated by the same knee-jerk response from the therapist—*or even the entire treatment team*—that they are "outside their wheelhouse" whenever issues relating to sex or sexuality arise, as discussed earlier in this chapter.

Supervision of sex therapists working in addiction settings often requires a particular level of advocacy for the supervisee, who can most likely expect some resistance to their looking for opportunities to work with patients on sexual issues, particularly in residential or partial hospitalization program (PHP) settings. As Doug Braun-Harvey noted in his first book, *Sexual Health in Drug and Alcohol Treatment* (a must-read for every would-be sex therapist working in a treatment setting):

> It seems when the sexuality of drug addicts or alcoholics is mentioned, the notion that this sexuality could only be of clinical pertinence if it is a co-occurring sexual addiction is so automatic that it is unconsciously assumed. It is only when I slowly describe the purpose and function of sexual health relapse prevention that people turn away from their automatic sex-addict framework and open their minds to a health-based framework for discussing sex in recovery. A vision for sexual health as a relapse prevention skill is yet to become a common one within drug and alcohol treatment—nor will it without many other drug and alcohol treatment specialists, sexologists, therapists, researchers, grantees, and government funding on board. We will all need to work together to improve the lives of the men and women currently entering treatment with high sex/drug-linked addiction patterns.
>
> (Braun-Harvey, 2009, p. 12)

Sadly, after almost a decade since that prescient observation was made, the treatment center industry has yet to make the shift toward widespread incorporation of sexual health programming and sex therapy into "addiction treatment," despite research supporting the expressed desire of patients to discuss sexuality and treatment centers' continued failure to do so (Siegel, 2016) and the effectiveness in strengthening treatment outcomes and reducing relapse rates (Braun-Harvey, 2009).

Nevertheless, supervisors would be well advised to discuss these issues when supervising "two-hatters" and be mindful of the importance of exploring a variety of conceptualizations of "addiction." One should also be extra vigilant of avoiding not just the countertransference trap of becoming their patients' "recovery coach" or paid sponsor, but the potential for iatrogenic harm from perpetuating the dogmatic and clinically flawed view of addiction as lifelong and incurable, especially when being applied to a person's sexuality.

The wise and truly 12-Step-informed sex therapist will partner with their patients "in recovery" or who identify as members of 12-Step fellowships and constantly remind them of the programs' underlying promise of being "happy, joyous and free" and living a life in balance. Perhaps most importantly, in sexual health. They would certainly not see themselves as part of a collective effort to remain hypervigilant of "relapse behavior," mistrustful of sexual self-confidence as a sign of "denial," or reticent to believe that a distressing event or problematic sexual behavior can indeed be put in one's past.

Sex Addiction to Justify Infidelity

If ever there was a clinical presentation begging for someone to call "shenanigans" on, this would be it. The claim of an overwhelming and uncontrollable urge to engage in so volitional an act as having an extrarelational affair is eminently challengeable and sex therapy supervisors should encourage a firm resolve in their supervisees to make that challenge. As with much of the current discussion of sexual harassment by men in positions of power, what is much more obviously explained by a sheer sense of entitlement, an adolescent desire to "have one's cake and eat it too," or having a narcissistic personality does not stand up to any reasonable symptomology of an addictive disorder. Extrarelational affairs, whether with one or multiple partners, do not meet the criteria for any of the diagnostic categories that define DSM-listed labels of abuse or dependency, unless the behavior is accompanied by distressing behavior and distressing thoughts, which does not seem to occur with infidelity (Grubbs, Stauner, Exline, Pargament & Lindberg, 2015; Johnson, 2017).

Another favored allegory used to shed light on these situations is the classic "Strange Case of Dr. Jekyll and Mr. Hyde." We all possess the potential for an internal struggle between good and evil, between dignified reserve and wild abandon; we often fail to acknowledge that for all the struggle, for all the battles between our devils and our angels,[6] it is the volitional choice to "drink the potion" and act on our particular urges. Examining a sexual episode forensically, one can identify a series of volitional choices leading up to what this supervisor refers to as the "screw it" moment; the moment the individual makes the decision to act (one can easily envision the devil on one shoulder, yelling "do it!" in one ear and then running over to kick the angel off the other shoulder). A common illustration is a man who leaves his home for a "quick release" sexual encounter, such as those procured at a massage parlor or from a sex worker. There can usually be some ritual identified, perhaps a lie concocted for the partner and dozens of minute-to-minute decisions, from grabbing the car keys to unlocking the car door and getting in; opening the garage door, backing out of the driveway, putting the car in drive and driving away; making arrangements to meet and going to a specific place for that meeting, and so forth. Each one of these moments represents an opportunity to make a different choice: to put the keys down, to put the car back and park, to go back in the house and do something different to "fill that hole"—perhaps exercise, perhaps a put-off chore, perhaps even approaching his partner romantically.

Like the cognitive-behavioral therapy techniques that addiction treatments often employ, a person can practice "observing themselves" better, checking in with their mood and physical feelings and learn to notice any familiar feelings of restlessness or anxiety that precede the thought to "step out"—what many recovering addicts and alcoholics referred to as the "empty hole that seeks to be filled."

It is worth repeating that supervisees approach these cases as couples' cases and to adopt a sexological approach. While couples work following infidelity is obviously critical, sex therapists are often reminded that the so-called pure sex therapy case is often more a luxury for the classroom but, in the therapy room, we must be psychotherapists first. One's biases may bring about an understandable enthusiasm but it is entirely possible to bring in sex therapy too soon. Supervisees must develop the judgment and "feel" for when to steer a couple toward healing their sexual relationship; after anger and betrayal issues are addressed and, again, after the initial "fires" have been put out. Chapter author Tammy Nelson brilliantly addresses guiding supervisees through these waters in Chapter 7. Katherine Ellin also discusses the nuances of couples work utilizing transference and countertransference in Chapter 8. And, of course, Stephanie Buehler in Chapter 6 covers the critical ethics and supervision challenges that may arise from separating couples in therapy in order to see each partner individually, without slipping into the role of moderator or referee, and the special importance of supervisors guiding their supervisees through the potential pitfalls of being a "secret-keeper." Yet another potential "mine field," particularly for a couple after a crisis, is that of the difference between "secrecy" and "privacy." It can be among the most difficult conversations to have and often the most challenging to the values of both patients or clients and therapists alike.

It might be a lot to expect that people would feel like even discussing sex, no less having sex, with someone they are feeling angry at and/or hurt by. "Make-up sex" hardly seems relevant (though sometimes quite hot, is rarely as effective in resolving conflict than how it is depicted in most romantic comedies), angry sex (the so-called grudge fuck), or letting the cheated on have their own affair to "even the score" can only worsen an already bad situation. However, reminding a couple that they are together for a reason, ideally because they are lovers (or at least were) and not roommates, siblings, or platonic "soulmates." Also, a reminder that anger does not mean hate can go far in starting to heal (i.e., remembering that you can be angry at someone you love and still love them).

Esther Perel's latest book, *The State of Affairs: Rethinking Infidelity*, and Tammy Nelson's *The New Monogamy: Redefining Your Relationship After Infidelity* both provide exceptional perspective for helping couples past the crisis of an affair. Perel presents a comparison between a "typically European" versus a "typically American" response by the "cheated on" after many affairs. In the former, the response is more likely to be one of "well, what does this affair mean for us?" This allows for a wealth of valuable discussion from a mature, adult perspective and invites many helpful follow-up questions, like "would you rather be with that other person or with me?"; "are we done or do we want to fix this?"; and, perhaps most helpful and meaningful, "how did our relationship get to this point?" Many coming from this perspective see infidelity as a "bump in the road" and an opportunity to enhance and improve the relationship.

Conversely, the typically American response says, "how could you do this to me?" This inevitably turns the crisis into a morality play, further justifying the anger and intensifying the sense of betrayal with outrage. It also will likely justify the change in roles, as "Mommy" often becomes the cop, the detective, and the warden all at once. As was discussed earlier in this chapter, it is clear to see the perfectly natural way this relationship dynamic shift can simply kill the erotic connection between people, even when they insist that they still love one another deeply.

Threatening to tip this already precarious situation into doom, one or both members of the couple may prefer the less painful path: to label rather than to delve. A therapist may actually be unknowingly colluding and abetting the couple's avoidance (hopefully, it is not the therapist's avoidance!) by going along with the sex-addict label, either at the insistence of the transgressor, who is looking for that "Get Out of Jail Free" card, or the partner, who is looking to be relieved of the burden of having to question everything about their reality and can find comfort in believing the family has been stricken with a disease not unlike like cancer or diabetes. Perel acknowledges feeling compelled to mention this sex addiction debate even in her book about infidelity because of the strength of this new wave of this "*malady du jour,*" as she refers to it in *The State of Affairs*, of cheaters seeking to blame their disease for their dalliances. She acknowledges that "whatever we call it, sexually compulsive behavior is a real issue for many people and both they and their loved ones suffer tremendous pain as a consequence. Lives, reputations, and families have been destroyed by it" (Perel, 2017, p. 212). She also concedes, as do respected researchers and sex therapists like Stan Althof, that for many people, being able to name their behavior with some disease diagnosis can initially be a positive step, helping to assuage the shame that may be keeping them from getting the help they may desperately need. Nonetheless, Perel pointedly observes, "even if we call it a disease, it hasn't lost its stigma." To that end, she describes the moms that struggle to tell their children that they are leaving their father because he is a sex addict, "whereas she wouldn't have faced the same mortification over an alcoholic spouse" (Perel, 2017, p. 212).

Infidelity can have a devastating effect on a relationship. Although some people find it difficult to move past their sense of hurt and betrayal, dealing with infidelity can be the opportunity for partners to really talk about the relationship and their expectations, in a way that they may never have before, and come out of this crisis stronger and more connected to each other. It is important, however, for supervisees to ensure that they avoid some of the common pitfalls involved in working with couples such as enmeshment, triangulation, and unintentional collusion. The therapist must be cognizant of the fact that both partners are coming in with their own narrative, often holding tightly and defensively to it, without favoring one story over the other. In accomplishing this, the supervisee will be better able to work with the couple on creating a new narrative, one that both partners create together, that allows them to continue forging a future together that is gratifying and satisfying to both. The end of a chapter does not have to be the end of the story.

About the Author

Richard Siegel, Ph.D., LMHC, CST, is the Director of Modern Sex Therapy Institutes, a postgraduate continuing education institute that trains sex therapists and sexual medicine specialists at multiple sites throughout the country. He is a Florida-licensed mental health counselor and board-certified sex therapist, and is certified by the American Association of Sexuality Educators, Counselors and Therapists (AASECT) as a sex therapist and supervisor. He has a rich experiential background, including over 20 years working in sexuality education and addiction treatment, teaching on college campuses, and maintaining a private sex therapy practice. He was an early champion for the integration of sexual health into addiction treatment, having conducted hundreds of groups at dozens of treatment centers in South Florida and nationally since the 1990s. Dr. Siegel's dissertation research is titled *Sexuality Issues in Addiction, Treatment and Recovery*.

Notes

1 A classic joke, appearing in a dozen variations all over the internet, tells of a doctor coming into the examining room, holding his patient's chart, and with a look of concern, tells his male patient, "Look, you've got to stop masturbating," to which the patient asks, "Why, Doc?" And the doctor says, "So I can examine you!" It can be said with certainty that virtually all men who are saying, "I can't stop," are doing so in a therapist's office, fully clothed, having left their homes, driven to the therapist's office, perhaps sat in a waiting room, and sat through their session, without once engaging in whatever it is they're claiming they can't stop.
2 This involuntary spasm or "lock down" of the vaginal introital muscles has now been subsumed under the DSM-5 diagnosis, "genito-pelvic pain/penetration disorder."
3 Patients should be reminded often that anxiety causes adrenaline to be released, which is a powerful stimulant, and is known to be an erection killer.
4 Safer sex skills for future partnered sex are not a bad thing for adolescent boys to practice, either!
5 As has been mentioned several times throughout this book, the larger fields of psychotherapy, including social work, mental health counseling, clinical psychology, and, ironically, even marriage and family therapy, most often either

under-address or ignore sex outright in the training of their professionals. Therefore, it is always essential that supervisors inculcate in their supervisees the comfort and competence to take a thorough sexual history, including psycho-sexual development throughout the life stages, masturbatory status and current sexual status.

6 Another always helpful illustration for recognizing difficulties with impulse control, and fascinating fodder for therapy to wonder why the devils, or id impulses, are also so instant and insistent, and that it takes patience for the angels, that superego "conscience," to show up before acting, well, impulsively!

References

Althof, S. E., & Needle, R. B. (2016). It takes two to tango: Evaluation and treatment of sexual dysfunction in the couple. In L. Lipshultz, A. Pastuszak, A. Goldstein, A. Giraldi & M. Perelman (Eds.), *Management of sexual dysfunction in men and women* (pp. 351–356). New York: Springer. https://doi.org/10.1007/978-1-4939-3100-2_31

Althof, S. E., McCabe, M. P., Assalian, P., Leiblum, S., Chevert-Measson, M., Simonelli, C., et al. (2010). Psychological and interpersonal dimensions of sexual function and dysfunction. In F. Montorsi, R. Basson, G. Adaikan, E. Becher, A. Clayton, A., F. Giuliano . . . I. Sharlip, I. (Eds.), *Sexual medicine. Sexual dysfunctions in men and women* (pp. 121–181). Paris: Health Publication.

Association for the Treatment of Sexual Abusers (ATSA). (2017, November 16). Statement about sexual addiction, sexual abuse, and effective treatment. Retrieved from http://www.atsa.com/Public/Office/Media/2017_11_15_Media_statement_re_sexual_addiction_and_sexual_abuse.pdf

Berne, E. (1961). *Transactional analysis in psychotherapy.* New York: Grove Press.

Braun-Harvey, D. (2009). *Sexual health in drug and alcohol treatment: Group facilitator's manual.* New York: Springer.

Braun-Harvey, D., & Vigorito, M. A. (2015). *Treating out of control sexual behavior: Rethinking sex addiction.* New York: Springer.

Carnes, P. J. (1990). Tasks of sex addiction recovery. Retrieved from https://strengtheningmarriage.com/wp-content/uploads/2012/11/DOCS-Tasks_of_-Sex_Addiction_Recovery_Carnes.pdf

Carnes, P. J., Green, B. A., Merlo, L. J., Polles, A., Carnes, S., & Gold, M. S. (2012). PATHOS: A brief screening application for assessing sexual addiction. *Journal of Addiction Medicine, 6*(1), 29–34. https://doi.org/10.1097/ADM.0b013e3182251a28

Carnes, P. (1997). *Sexual anorexia: Overcoming sexual self-hatred.* Center City, MMN: Hazelden.

Carnes, S. (2017). Commentary from ICD-11 Beta Draft Foundation. Retrieved from http://id.who.int/icd/entity/1630268048

COSA Retrieved March 28, 2015, from https://www.cosa-recovery.org/

CPS, TASHRA, & NCSF. (2017). Addiction to sex and/or pornography: A position statement from the Center for Positive Sexuality (CPS), The Alternative Sexualities Health Research Alliance (TASHRA), and the National Coalition for Sexual Freedom (NCSF). *Journal of Positive Sexuality, 3*(3), 40–43.

Dalton, A. (2000, January). The ties that unbind. Retrieved from www.psychologytoday.com/us/articles/200001/the-ties-unbind

Derbyshire, K. L., & Grant, J. E. (2015). Compulsive sexual behavior: A review of the literature. *Journal of Behavior and Addiction, 4*(2), 37–43.

Donaghue, C. (2017). *Is sex addiction just an excuse for bad behavior?* Retrieved from www.thefix.com/sex-addiction-just-excuse-bad-behavior

Fawcett, D. M. (2015). *Lust, men and meth: A gay man's guide to sex and recovery.* Wilton Manors, FL: Healing Path Press.

Garcia, F. D., Assumpção, A. A., Malloy-Diniz, L., De Freitas, A. A.C., Delavenne, H., & Thibaut, F. (2016). A comprehensive review of psychotherapeutic treatment of sexual addiction. *Journal of Groups in Addiction & Recovery, 11*(1), 59–71.

Grubbs, J. B., Stauner, N., Exline, J. J., Pargament, K. I., & Lindberg, M. J. (2015). Perceived addiction to internet pornography and psychological distress: Examining relationships concurrently and over time. *Psychology of Addictive Behaviors, 29*(4), 1056–1067. https://doi.org/10.1037/adb0000114

Herring, B. (2017). A framework for categorizing chronically problematic sexual behavior. *Sexual Addiction & Compulsivity, 24*(4), 242–247. https://doi.org/10.1080/10720162.2017.1394947

James, R. L. (2012). *Sexuality and addiction: Making connections, enhancing recovery.* Santa Barbara, CA: ABC-CLIO.

Johnson, S. A. (2017). Sexual addiction or simply cheating? *Journal of Forensic Research, 8*(1), 368–372. https://doi.org/10.4172/2157-7145.1000368

Katehakis, A. (2010). *Erotic intelligence: Igniting hot, healthy sex while in recovery from sex addiction.* Deerfield Beach, FL: HCI.

Kurdek, L. A. (1999). The nature and predictors of the trajectory of change in marital quality for husbands and wives over the first 10 years of marriage. *Development Psychology, 5,* 1283–1296.

Leiblum, S. R. (Ed.). (2006). *Principles and practice of sex therapy.* New York: Guilford Press.

Levine, M. P., & Troiden, R. R. (1988). The myth of sexual compulsivity. *Journal of Sex Research, 25*(3), 347–363.

Ley, D. (2012). *The myth of sex addiction.* Lanham, MD: Rowman & Littlefield.

McCarthy, B. W., & McCarthy, E. (2003). *Rekindling desire.* New York: Routledge.

McCarthy, B. W., & McCarthy, E. (2014). *Therapy with men after sixty: A challenging life phase.* New York: Routledge.

McKeal, P. L. (2004). *Using American sex therapy techniques to train medical students, physicians, health care workers and mental health workers: A training manual* (Unpublished doctoral dissertation). American Academy of Clinical Sexologists, Orlando, FL.

Moser, C. (2013). Hypersexual disorder: Searching for clarity. *Sexual Addiction & Compulsivity, 20*(1–2), 48–58.

National Conference of State Legislatures. (2016, December 21). *State policies on sex education in schools.* Retrieved from www.ncsl.org/research/health/state-policies-on-sex-education-in-schools.aspx#2

Pappas, T. W. and Thurlow, R. (2014). Is human sexuality training important for a drug & alcohol therapist? *Advances in Addiction and Recovery (Summer 2014) 2*(2). Retrieved from www.naadac.org/assets/1959/aar_summer2014?web.pdf

Perel, E. (2017). *The state of affairs: Rethinking infidelity.* New York: HarperCollins.

Perelman, M. E., & Grill, E. A. (2013). The role of sex therapy for male infertility. Chapter 25 in Section 8, Sexual Disorders, in M. Goldstein & P. N. Schlegel (Eds.), Surgical and medical management of male infertility. Cambridge: Cambridge University Press.

Prause, N., Janssen, E., Georgiadis, J., Finn, P., & Pfaus, J. (2017). Data do not support sex as addictive. *Lancet Psychiatry, 4*(12), 899.

Prause, N., & Pfaus, J. (2015). Viewing sexual stimuli associated with greater sexual responsiveness, not erectile dysfunction. *Sexual Medicine, 3*(2), 90–98.

Prause, N., Steele, V. R., Staley, C., Sabatinelli, D., & Proudfit, G. H. (in press). Modulation of late positive potentials by sexual images in problem users and controls inconsistent with "porn addiction." *Biological Psychology.*

RCA - Recovering Couples Anonymous (1991, 2011). *The twelve steps of RCA.* World Service Organization for Recovering Couples Anonymous, Inc. Retrieved on March 26, 2015, from http://recovering-couples.org/webdocs/program/12steps.pdf

Reay, B., Attwood, N., & Gooder, C. (2013). Inventing sex: The short history of sex addiction. *Sexuality & Culture, 17*(1), 1–19.

Robinson, B. E., Bockting, W. O., Simon Rosser, B. R., Miner, M., & Coleman, E. (2002). The sexual health model: Application of a sexological approach to HIV prevention. *Health Education Research, 17*(1), 43–57.

SA – Sexaholics Anonymous (1997, 2018). *What is a sexaholic and what is sexual sobriety?* Retrieved March 26, 2018, from https://www.sa.org/sexaholic/

SAA - Sex Addicts Anonymous (2007). *Three Circles - Defining Sexual Sobriety In SAA.* International Service Organization of SAA. Retrieved on March 26, 2015, from https://saa-recovery.org/literature/three-circles-defining-sexual-sobriety-in-saa/

SCA - Sexual Compulsives Anonymous (2001). *Twelve steps of SCA.* International Service Organization of Sexual Compulsives Anonymous. Retrieved March 26, 2015 from https://sca-recovery.org/WP/recovery-program/steps/

Siegel, L. A. (2015). Sex addiction: Not a useful concept. In P. Whelehan & A. Bolin (Editors in Chief), *Encyclopedia of human sexuality.* New York: John Wiley & Sons.

Siegel, L. A., & Siegel, R. M. (2007). Sex addiction: Recovering from a shady concept. In W. J. Taverner (Ed.), *Taking sides: Clashing views on controversial issues in human sexuality.* New York: McGraw-Hill/Dushkin.

Siegel, L. A., & Siegel, R. M. (2011). Sex addiction: Semantics or science? In W. J. Taverner & R. W. McKee (Eds.). *Taking sides: Clashing views in human sexuality.* New York: McGraw-Hill.

Siegel, R. M. (2016). *Sexuality issues in addiction, treatment and recovery.* Orlando, FL: American Academy of Clinical Sexologists.

SLAA - Sex and Love Addicts Anonymous (1997, 2018). *40 Questions for Self Diagnosis.* The Augustine Fellowship, SLAA, Fellowship-Wide Services, Inc. Retrieved March 23, 2015 from https://slaafws.org/download/core-files/The_40_Questions_of_SLAA.pdf

Sohn, A. (2015, July 1). First comes sex talk with these renegades of couples' therapy. *New York Times.* Retrieved from www.nytimes.com/2015/07/05/fashion/first-comes-sex-talk-with-these-renegades-of-couples-therapy.html

SRA – Sexual Recovery Anonymous (2010). *Our purpose.* Sexual Recovery Anonymous World Wide Services, Inc. Retrieved March 28, 2015, from http://sexualrecovery.org/about.html

Wiederman, M. W., & Sansone, R. A. (1999). Sexuality training for professional psychologists: A national survey of training directors of doctoral programs and predoctoral internships. *Professional Psychology: Research and Practice, 30*(3), 312–317. https:// doi.org/10.1037/0735-7028.30.3.312

14 Supervision Issues in Working With Conservative Christian Clients

Tina Schermer Sellers

Abstract

Many clinical supervisees find themselves unprepared for treating conservative Christian clients. Such clients often view their bodies with suspicion or sexual shame, reflecting a common pattern through much of Christian history. Judeo-Christian tradition, however, actually provides rich affirmations of the body, including sexual desire, although such concepts have been neglected in Christian teaching at large over the last two millennia. "M.E.S.S.," a Model for Erasing Sexual Shame, is a fourfold process for helping conservative Christian clients rediscover their heritage's affirmation of sexual desire: "Frame" helps clients become educated about their bodies and desires; "Name" guides clients to tell their own stories of experiencing or overcoming religious sexual shame; "Claim" helps clients to celebrate their bodies creatively and intentionally; and "Aim" prompts clients to imagine how they can experience a life free from religious sexual shame. In a case study, a supervisee guides a married couple through the M.E.S.S. model.

Keywords

religious sexual shame, sexuality, clinical supervision, conservative Christianity, desire

One of the challenges that inexperienced clinical supervisees face is in helping their clients to integrate their spiritual selves with their sexual selves, especially if a given client's religious upbringing is foreign to the therapist. The act of mentoring fledgling counselors presents its own set of challenges for supervisors as well, as they watch emergent therapists flounder their way through the spiritual landscapes of clients whose faith subculture and religious vocabulary can be completely foreign to the supervisee. This is especially true with conservative religions that have historically treated the body and its desires with suspicion, often thwarting the generational transmission of any knowledge that might have guided the client in how to live as a sexual being in his or her relationships and daily life.

I. Introduction to the Type of Supervision: Learning to Treat Conservative Christian Clients

This supervision chapter provides direction for experienced therapists to work with their supervisees when they encounter some conservative Christians. Sometimes it is difficult to serve individuals clinically whose sexuality can be marked by sexual fear, dysfunction, isolation, pain, unhappiness, ignorance, and/or compulsion, as is often the case for clients who are conservative Christians or who used to be. Oftentimes, there seems to be a collision between the power of their erotic yearnings on the one hand and a long history of body-suspicion in their conservative Christian backgrounds on the other. This chapter offers context for supervisors to understand the sociopolitical history that shaped some of the sex-negative religious landscape among many conservative Christians, informing what came to be understood by many Christian clients as "truth" about God, the body, the other gender, and sexuality. This discussion will provide an alternative, sex-positive yet thoroughly Judeo-Christian narrative, based in ancient Hebrew writing, that can be shared with clients to reveal the elegant biopsychosocial-sexual and spiritual design in the human body for connection and pleasure, as it was acutely understood by ancient Hebrew people.

This discussion will explore an operational definition of sexual shame, along with an evidence-based model for healing that has been used by the author in clinical practice and with supervisees for over a decade. This four-step model, as will be shown, is recursive in nature, as each layer of sexual shame reveals a new step of the work needed below it. Finally, the chapter will conclude with some of the touch and nontouch intimacy practices that the author has given to supervisees for assigning to their conservative Christian clients as homework during the therapeutic process. These healing and intimacy practices help to shed light on the impact of religious sexual shame on what is often a client's underlying sense of worthlessness, and how that shame is wreaking havoc on their relationships with their partners, with themselves, and with their God. As clients try these practices with their partners, they and their therapists often begin to see an integration of their spiritual self with their sexual self, along with a simultaneous healing of the mind/body split. Therapists, as will be shown, can help clients understand that these two elements of human life (mind and body) aren't nearly the mutual contradictions that pop culture and the Christian church's history have often assumed them to be, and that in fact, they go hand in hand.

II. Distinct Features and Challenges

In North America, many conservative elements of Christianity have kept sexuality and spirituality separate for centuries, often rigidly so. Thankfully, the "purity" movement, one of the more ascetic and toxic eras in sexual ethics in the last 100 years, seems to be waning. But like so many conservative Christians born after 1977, who hit their adolescence just as the purity movement hit in 1992 (Barbee, 2014), many people are still struggling to find a way to reconcile their sexual desires with the religious elements of their lives. Prior to this time, during the late 1960s and through the 1970s, there had been a relatively brief sex-positive moment in Christian culture known as the "Jesus Movement," which in many ways paralleled the openness of second-wave feminism. But how did Christianity become sex-negative over the length of its history, since Christians in general believe that God created the body as good?

Throughout Christian history, the relationship between those in power inside the Christian church and those in political leadership has been close, going back to Constantine in the fourth century CE. During this time, socio-political trends involving threats to those in power have often yielded fear-induced acetic movements, led by various elements of the Christian church. The most recent of these has been the purity movement (Schermer-Sellers, 2014), which emerged in the conservative American church in the early 1990s in the wake of the ascent of the Moral Majority and the Religious Right to political power in the 1980s. Those groups' rise had been in direct response to some Christians' perceived threat from second-wave feminism, the economic downturn of the 1980s, and the civil rights/desegregation movement (Balmer, 2014). But this history, born out of patriarchy and the dualism of the mind–body split, is not endemic to Judeo-Christian core teachings.

Jewish scripture and ancient Hebrew mystic writing, as this chapter will show, contain treasure troves of sex-positive and erotic writings, revealing a sex- and body-positive God. These ideas are echoed in the ministry of Jesus, whom we see demonstrating mutuality, showing a deep love and respect for women, children, and the marginalized, and telling many stories and parables that involve an appreciation for the giving and receiving of love and healing—the sensual.[1] However, the unfolding of the Christian religion over the next four centuries following the death of Jesus, followed by the establishment of the formal church by Constantine in the fourth century, sterilized the ancient sex-positive Hebrew stories, and separated Jesus's use of and comfort with the body from the development of the Christian faith. Upon close historical examination, it is evident that the sex-positive ethics in much Jewish writing was not brought forward and instituted in the development of the Christian church, nor was a Jesus-based, "Christian" sexual ethic developed (Schermer Sellers, 2017).

Most Christians are unaware that much of their ancestral history on the Abrahamic line is sex-positive, or that the Old Testament contains stories and ancient Jewish mystic tales of a God who calls them beloved and seeks for them to live abundantly. Most have not had the book of the Song of Songs (or Song of Solomon), a book of erotica in the Biblical canon, exposited for them in their Christian education or worship settings. Many first-century rabbis spoke of the Song of Songs as the most sacred book of the Torah and referred to the need for the remaining canon to serve the purposes of the Song of Songs. It was explained that the Song of Songs, in demonstrating the erotic longing of two lovers, gives us a picture of how deeply God loves and longs for his people.

One of the discoveries in the Hebrew sexual ethic was the Vow of Onah. This vow, taken by men at the time of marriage, was taught to both men and women as they grew up. Each of the guidelines was oriented in a positive way, describing what to do, not what to refrain from doing. Here is an example:

- All forms of sexual enjoyment are recognized and valued, if desired by both partners.
- Sex is a woman's right, not a man's. He is to be sure that she experiences pleasure, closeness, and joy.
- The purpose of all sexual touch is to reinforce the loving bond over the lifespan. (The idea that the elderly aren't sexual was unheard of in the Torah.)
- Sexual touch is to be celebrated in joy, not in anger or disinterest, when drunk, or in self-interest.
- Sex is not seen as shameful, sinful, or obscene.
- Sexual enjoyment is recommended in times when procreation is impossible.
- Making love involves being mindful of the body, mind, soul, and spirit of one's partner (Schermer Sellers, 2017).

Another ancient Hebrew story involved the cherubim over the Ark of the Covenant inside the Holy of Holies, the most sacred area of the Jewish Temple. Only the rabbi could enter the Holy of Holies, and then only on the Day of Atonement after very careful, elaborate preparation. The cherubim, said to be the vehicle through which Moses was able to hear the divine voice, were arranged over the Ark of the Covenant on two staffs, in a particular arrangement that depicted an aspect of God. They were thought to have an amount of life in them and were said to turn toward each other when Israel followed God's commandments, turning away from each other when Israel sinned. While there were gold cherubim in each rebuilding of the Temple and Tabernacle (the mobile tent that the Hebrews used before the first Temple was built), the dimensions, depictions, and positions of the cherubim varied. Some were open-winged, in mutual protection of the Ark; some were seated in sexual embrace overtop of it. The explanations for this appear in many places across Hebrew literature, though they are often vague.

Moshe Idel, a leading Jewish scholar, has written that the nature of the intertwining cherubs functions as a metaphor of the divine eros that God has for his people. When the last temple was destroyed in 72 CE, the role of the cherubs as a dwelling place for the presence of God was believed to be preserved through the sexual union when a couple prepared to enter their sacred lovemaking space (at home, perhaps) with the same kind of intention and preparation as a priest entering the Holy of Holies (Idel, 2005).

Circumstances have changed considerably since those Hebrew understandings of eros developed thousands of years ago, such that today clinicians are treating the effects of religious sexual shame—a far cry from the sex-positivity of the ancient Hebrews. Recently, the author of a grounded theory study developed the first operational definition of sexual shame (Clark, 2017). Like a patient who gets a long-awaited diagnosis after living with their symptoms for years, having a clear operational definition of sexual shame removed the opacity of a phenomenon that many in the Christian church had only been able to sense intuitively before that time but hadn't been able to name. The definition states:

> Sexual shame is a visceral feeling of humiliation and disgust toward one's own body and identity as a sexual being and a belief of being abnormal and inferior; this feeling can be internalized but also manifests in interpersonal relationships having a negative impact on trust, communication, and physical and emotional intimacy. Sexual shame develops across the lifespan in interactions with interpersonal relationships, one's culture and society, and subsequent critical self-appraisal. Furthermore, sexual shame reflects a vulnerability and a distrust of one's own ability to make decisions related to safety and autonomy in sexual relationships.
>
> (Clark, 2017, p. 87)

This definition becomes very important when helping supervisees to have a baseline vocabulary for interacting with their religiously shamed clients. When people from religious homes and those impacted by abstinence education are not provided comprehensive sex education from safe and loving adults who do not shame their curiosity and desire to learn, they absorb large quantities of sexual shame. This shame goes on to interrupt their sexual development and can short-circuit their ability to experience intimacy and attachment. For these reasons, it is imperative that supervisees know how to assess and then treat clients.

III. Skill Set of Supervisee: A New Treatment Model

The author's method for working with supervisees who are treating conservative Christian clients is similar to the PLISSIT model, in that it builds upon itself and fills in the blanks left by a society heavily influenced by Christianity, one that has failed to educate and nurture healthy sexual development. The four-step process described below deconstructs the damaging messages that clients may have absorbed from cultural influences, including some of the conservative religious experiences they may have had, along with Western culture's commodification of sexuality. The model also serves as a supplement for the Christian subculture's dearth of good sex education, which mirrors patterns in the wider culture as well.

The four stages in this treatment process are not linear, but circular. The process enables supervisees to reflect upon the narrative of shame as a tightly woven tapestry wrapped around the heart and mind. The supervisee, acting as the therapist, will facilitate the unwrapping, thread by thread, in a "circular" fashion—moving through the steps as many times as it takes to see progress and healing. Sometimes, to free a thread, the client must set down one thread and pick up another, working with that one for a while before going back to the first one. That's normal, but it's best for a clinician just to follow the threads patiently, one by one, and to take as much time as is necessary. As the therapist walks through these four steps with a client, it's also important that the therapist remember that the precise order is not nearly as important as that they follow each of the steps at some point.

IV. Techniques: Erasing the M.E.S.S. (Model for Erasing Sexual Shame)

FRAME—Build a Framework of Sexual Knowledge

Sometimes, the best thing to teach supervisees is to help their clients build a framework for accurate education about sex and the body. Using the PLISSIT model, it is important for clients to know that they are not alone in their desire to be heard with compassion. They also need to be given permission to seek out accurate information about human sexual functioning and the wide range of sexual behavior, and permission to challenge ideas that have not made sense to them. Permission is the first structural element of our framework.

The *Frame* process provides permission both to explore and to access information—to build a framework. In this process, supervisees guide their clients by giving them instructive information about arousal cycles, safe sex, and sexually transmitted infections (STIs), along with how to deepen connection through spiritual intimacy or other forms of sexual exploration. Supervisees should be encouraged to be mindful of their own parallel processes: Have they done their own spiritual/sexual exploration? Have they asked themselves all the questions they are now asking their clients? Are they staying clear about where their own selfhood begins and ends, and where their client's self begins and ends?

The framing process continues with the client's exploration into their own pleasure, identifying how, where, and in what way their own body likes to be touched, and noticing how their feelings, thoughts, and desires respond to various kinds of physical contact. Supervisees should invite their clients to see their whole, integrated body as a miracle—unique unto itself, utterly unlike anyone else's—and to see themselves as the expert of their unique and special body.

Another aspect of framing is to help supervisees guide their clients in an exploration of gender and power messages in our culture. The emergent therapists should be coached to invite their clients to watch documentaries such as

Miss Representation (Newsom, 2011) and *The Mask You Live In* by the Representation Project (Newsom, 2015), perhaps viewing the films with friends and following up by discussing social and cultural pressures as well as how to protect and support each other. If a supervisee is working with a female client, the clinician might invite the client to explore the framing process by role-playing how to stand up for oneself. If a supervisee has a male client who needs permission to expand his emotional life, it might be helpful to role-play how he can best be protective with the women he cares for, or how to get support in accessing and expressing his emotional wisdom. In framing, clients can be invited to explore intimate relationships by reading books like Resnick's *The Heart of Desire* (2012), McCarthy and McCarthy's *Sexual Awareness* (2012), or Johnson's *Love Sense* (2013), or by listening to *Men, Women, and Worthiness* by Brené Brown (2012).

NAME—Name and Share Your Story

If a client's sexual story has been shrouded in secrecy, ignorance, trauma, fear, or shame, the supervisee will need to help them understand how important it will be for them to find a safe tribe of compassionate, loving, and empathetic people who can bear witness as they name, identify, and bring image to their own story. At first, the supervisee will be a witness to the story. This is a critical role in the healing process, but it is essential that the tribe be extended beyond just the therapist. This is a kind of "walkabout," a meandering process that may take some time to develop fully as clients learn to speak new narratives about themselves to those around them. Sexual shame cannot live in the presence of love, and it begins to fade in the absence of judgment, which is why the naming process in itself can bring healing to clients over time with patience and deliberate attention, even though it may take a while.

It is difficult for a person to grow up in a culture as sexually silent, ignorant, and confused as ours and not absorb heaps of shame along the way, and unless someone intervenes and helps to alter this reality for them, the shame might otherwise be permanent. Adding an element of specifically *religious* condemnation and judgment to the mix only compounds the issue and can cause the shame to adhere to a client even harder. It is important for supervisees to understand how toxic this sense of shame can be for their clients, and for clients to know that nothing is wrong with them—that they are, in the words of the Bible, "fearfully and wonderfully made" (Ps. 139:14 [NRSV]). They deserve to have their story heard, and for grace and knowledge to be given them when it is.

If a supervisee's client has an inner circle of friends they trust to begin this process of sharing, the supervisee should help them to begin a practice of storytelling. The client should be encouraged to invite some friends together for the purpose of naming (storytelling about) their own battles with or liberation from sexual shame. The client will need to be coached to set some initial parameters and boundaries—confidentiality, for example—so that the group can talk together in safety. Groups can talk in person if they are close, or by video chatting if they live far away—whatever is convenient and facilitates the process of sharing openly. As long as loving and compassionate witnesses are able to hear the client's story and share their own in an atmosphere of acceptance and grace, it will usually be enough: the clients will be invited into an environment where they can practice the naming process. Therapists may even want to run a group therapy session devoted to the naming process, or to offer a weekend retreat focused on story-healing. These ideas can be discussed between the experienced clinician and his or her supervisee during the supervision process.

CLAIM—Claim and Celebrate the Body

One of the topics worth discussing with supervisees is how much of marketing culture is aimed toward getting people to disapprove of their bodies or appearances so that they'll spend more money in search of being "good enough." But part of the job of supervisors is to help supervisees, and in turn their clients, to shed light on the fact that life is too short *not* to appreciate the deep beauty of their own uniqueness, and the legitimacy of their human desire to be seen, known, loved, and accepted. These realities are theirs to *claim*, and to live boldly and loudly every day.

Supervisors can invite therapists under their care to encourage their clients to make "gratitude lists" of things they like about their bodies or their eroticism, or to write affirmations of various aspects of themselves on paper. Therapists should invite clients to locate the places on their bodies where they feel joy, gratitude, or love—and to live "from" these places. If a client is focused in one particular area, for example the genitals only, the supervisor can invite the therapist to think about how to expand the vocabulary of sensual curiosity. Female clients, for example, could be invited to go to an all-women's spa for a day and to observe how women of all shapes and sizes let themselves be pampered; following this, the clients could be invited to share the ways that those women seemed comfortable living "from" various places on their body, such as savoring the feeling of a back massage or the aroma of an essential oil in the air. Clients could then be invited to compare and contrast what they think their own sensual preferences are, and how they compare and contrast to what they saw other women experiencing at the spa. Another place where this kind of self-discovery can be accomplished, both for women and for men, is at clothing-optional beaches. In such settings, clients can experience not being objectified, often for the very first time in their lives.

If neither of these experiences sound comfortable for a supervisee to imagine for their client, they might choose another alternative: finding someone currently in their sixth or seventh decade of life who feels especially comfortable in his or her skin, and interviewing that person about how he or she got to that level of peace about his or her physical self.

As supervisors, experienced therapists can invite those they oversee to coach couples toward exploring sensual pleasure and play, learning over time to seek out the "inner child" in each of them, discovering their body again and the joy it can bring. Clinicians under supervision can invite their clients to befriend and inhabit the *power* in sexual arousal, learning to savor and enjoy something they are often conditioned to fear through religion and tradition, and to harness it for deep, loving pleasure with the one they care for. In this kind of sensual play, there should be no goal other than fun and pleasure with their partner.

Supervisees should also pay attention to see if clients have places in their bodies that feel tight or hurt, and to help them learn to listen deeply to the "story" within them that might be triggering those feelings. If they feel guilt or shame when they experience pleasure, supervisees should help them learn to sit *with* those feelings and to identify the messages that invited the original shame. Supervisees should be guided to help them claim a new story around the gift of pleasure, one that says, "This is okay, this is beautiful, this is the way God created me—*this is me*." The author often suggests to her supervisees that this may best be done through having clients read and then discuss a book like Emily Nagoski's *Come as You Are* (2015) or some other book that can guide clients in discovering pleasure. Supervisees should be invited to help clients learn to give themselves whatever amount of love and grace is needed for any hardship or pain they have suffered; clients also need to know that they have permission to heal and to find whatever help and support they need for this part of their journey. Many people, including many conservative Christians, will have to be clearly invited to the idea that they're allowed to explore these things at all. The author has found it helpful to counsel in a group setting so that support and stories can be shared between clients and couples, to help them to see that they're not alone. Regardless of how the supervisee proceeds with the claiming process, the goal is to help clients to own that their bodies are good gifts, and to enjoy the powerful sensations that they experience when they are aroused by their partner.

AIM—Aim to Live a New Sexual Legacy

Many supervisees who work with clients shrouded in religious sexual shame may find that their clients' sexual stories, prior to their work in therapy, were constructed for them by others, often without their permission or awareness, and certainly without a sense of self-ownership. In the Aim step, supervisees need to come to understand how important it is to hand the "pen and paper" back to their clients, inviting them to begin actively writing *their* story of sexuality and intimacy in any way that will bring *them* joy, fulfillment, and satisfaction. This is an active process and can be an enlightening discussion with supervisees. Framing deals with the present, what the human body *does*. Claiming and naming deal with the past—where one has *been*, the good and bad. In aiming, supervisees help their clients to look toward the future, helping them to see that from this point forward, it will be *their* story that prevails, and no one else's. In this step, supervisees invite their clients to consider what their values, their hopes, and their desires are, and they help them aim to write their sexual story in a new way with an eye to what they want the future to look like for themselves.

Some of the questions that supervisees might consider asking their clients may include:

- "What is the legacy you want to live into?"
- "What is the story you want to share with the children in your life?"
- "When has sexual touch been most spiritual, satisfying, and meaningful for you, and how can this be cultivated even further?"
- "What resources are available that can expand your integration of body, mind, soul, and spirit as you develop your sexual repertoire?"
- "When will you know you are ready for varying degrees of vulnerability with your partner?"

Above all, therapists should invite their clients to focus on this question: "What story do you want to write that will honor the beautiful, unique gift that is the sensual, powerful *you*?"

As supervisees help their clients erase the M.E.S.S. of sexual shame by weaving these four healing threads (Frame: get education; Name: tell their story; Claim: own their body; and Aim: write a new legacy) they will gain more sexual, emotional, relational, and spiritual intelligence with each pass of the four-part cycle. They'll also strengthen a community of loving, compassionate, like-minded others, each discovering the power and beauty in the gift of pleasure and the exquisite liberation that comes from crafting their own authentic sexual legacy. Supervisors will see their supervisees grow in cultural competence as they see profound transformation take place in their clients. As supervisees help clients to live boldly and unapologetically into the gift of their sexuality in ways that allow them to feel seen, known, loved, and accepted, throwing off generations of ignorance and shame along the way, they may start to notice their clients having more delight around sexual issues, rather than fear. Clients who are parents, for example, may start reacting to their 4-year-old children's naked antics around the house with laughter and delight, rather than a fear or concern.

Case Study

Sydney

Sydney is a 35-year-old family therapist who has been licensed for about five years. She has completed about one-third of her client contact and supervision hours toward AASECT[2] certification. Sydney presents the following case in group supervision:

> John and Jamie had been married for 13 years. Both were Christians and had grown up in conservative Christian homes. They

had three children: two boys, ages 6 and 9, and a girl, age 11. They presented for therapy with the wife complaining of long-standing low sexual desire and a recent disclosure to John that she felt that they had "never actually made love, just had sex."

In the first session, John said that since the first day of their marriage, Jamie had not emotionally equated sex with intimacy or love. John also disclosed that he had not felt that he had fully understood all the issues of intimacy outside of sex that were important to Jamie. John told Sydney that for most of their relationship so far, when they did have sex, Jamie had felt objectified, and if they did not have sex, John had felt irritable and unfulfilled, and a sense of distance from Jamie.

Sydney conducted individual sex histories and learned that John's family, while very conservative, *had* provided limited sex education growing up, albeit with a strong proviso to wait to have sex until marriage. John had used pornography in high school and college and had felt very guilty about it. He had been involved in a Christian youth group at his church throughout those years as well, and he described several instances of having talked to a youth director during his teenage years about his "porn habit." He'd had limited premarital sexual experimentation prior to meeting Jamie in college, but had been a virgin when they got married at 22.

Jamie had also grown up in a very conservative Christian home, but hers had been silent and shaming about anything having to do with sex or sexuality. She could not remember any expressed affection between her parents, and she recalled having been yelled at by her mother for touching herself in the bathtub when she had been about four years old. Jamie remembered her parents as having been guarded about sex, and she distinctly recalled thinking that anything about the naked body must be horrible, disgusting, and bad.

Jamie, too, had been involved in a youth group in high school and college. She'd had a very painful premarital sexual relationship in college, one that she had kept secret from her peers and the people at church for fear of being judged and ostracized. In that relationship, Jamie had been bullied, and her boyfriend had ultimately coerced her to be sexual. She had felt trapped for a long time, not knowing whom she could talk to, internally condemning herself for being a fraud. For years, she had believed that she deserved the abuse she was receiving, as punishment for violating God's plan for her life.

As a married couple, Jamie and John, along with their kids, were actively involved in their church, and faith was still a significant part of their life. John and Jamie each described themselves as having a reasonable marriage, but they each recognized that their lack of "real" emotional and sexual connection was unsustainable, and they both wanted to do something about it. They just had no idea how.

Jamie said that sex just wasn't something she ever remembered enjoying, except perhaps when the relationship had been young and things had been exciting. But when Sydney asked more questions, she discovered that Jamie was actually referring to a time in their relationship prior to their marriage and their first intercourse, when their intimacy had involved other forms of sexual touch and still had a kind of "forbidden" overtone for each of them. When Sydney asked about their sexual relationship after marriage, she noticed that the account almost instantly devolved into a story of a transactional, obligatory dance for the two of them. Jamie experienced John as "expecting it" on a regular basis, and John experienced Jamie as "reluctant." Other forms of intimate touch had seemed to disappear altogether. Children, it should be noted, had come within two years of their being married.

Sydney, the supervisee, grew up in a nonreligious home and describes herself as a humanist and feminist. She found it difficult to understand how Jamie could feel so responsible for the abuse she suffered in college, and she struggled against wanting to feel anger on Jamie's behalf for the injustice she had experienced both from this boyfriend and from the church. Sydney could also feel her own frustration with the sense of sexual entitlement John seemed to have, and that Jamie seemed to feel obligated to give him what he wanted. These ideas were foreign to Sydney, as she hadn't been exposed to the conservative Christian subculture that had been home for Jamie and John since birth. It seemed to her that Jamie had no sense that she had a right to her own voice or pleasure, or even to know her own body. She knew that she couldn't unbalance the system by taking Jamie's side, but she could feel a desire to try anyway.

Sydney's initial instinct was to do emotion-focused therapy (EFT), dealing with the attachment dance of Jamie's emotional distancing and John's emotional pursuit. Sydney reasoned that over time, she could interrupt their emotional dance and eventually introduce sensate activities, taking intercourse off the table for a while.

266 Tina Schermer Sellers

In supervision, the author worked instead to raise Sydney's cultural competency by providing some of the cultural history that put in perspective the patriarchal ideas that were supporting the sexual and gender naïveté that Jamie and John carried with them, along with John's sense of sexual entitlement and Jamie's sense of powerlessness. Through supervision, Sydney came to understand the dissonance in how church doctrine, as it related to sexual ethics and the human body, did not actually align with the ministry of Jesus, or the core values of God, which many Christians desire to understand and follow. Sydney learned that with many Christian clients, having these ideas pointed out to them has the effect of opening the clients up, loosening the double-bind they often feel, and freeing them to listen to the wisdom that is within them.

Sydney was encouraged to read the author's book *Sex, God, and the Conservative Church* (Schermer Sellers, 2017) in order to get a broad overview of the culture in which John and Jamie had been raised. Sydney was guided as to how to introduce the sex-positive stories that were likely new to both of her clients, and the difference that knowing these stories might make for them. In particular, the author and Sydney deconstructed the Vow of Onah and how it might rebalance the entitlement dance. Sydney was also asked to talk about how she would apply the model of Frame, Name, Claim, and Aim in John and Jamie's case, and the books that she might have them read together as a start to their sex education. Sydney decided to begin with *Sex, God, and the Conservative Church* (Schermer Sellers, 2017), which she had just read herself, and Emily Nagoski's book *Come as You Are* (2015).

At about five months into their couples work together, Jamie wrote an email to Sydney, in which she said:

> I am working through a lot of my preconceived notions of sex, which has been amazing. Seriously, sex for Christian wives is a freaking minefield! All the messed-up messages we receive, along with the awful teaching, is just doing so many of us in! It's been a really freeing season, unearthing all of those harmful ideas, and I feel like I have my voice back to ask for what I like and enjoy in sex, like I'm allowed again to say what I don't enjoy. John and I have cleared the table, so to speak, of every idea, expectation, and obligation that we have brought to each other

for sex, including what wives "should" do and what wives "should" like and so much more. I've learned that I actually have a say, and that John and I are to co-create our sex lives for ourselves! I've learned that it doesn't matter if most wives give oral sex: if I don't enjoy it or if I feel demeaned, I don't have to do it, and that's okay. I've learned to make my pleasure and enjoyment a priority again and not just to make it about my husband's "needs." God designed sex with me in mind, too! I feel like I've had so many light bulb moments and that Dr. Sellers' book has been a huge part of that!

No Small Thing

There is a great deal for therapists of all backgrounds to learn while in graduate school, but we tend, at large, to have received precious little training, if any, in the areas of sexuality and spirituality. For many of us, we have had to pursue familiarization with religious sexual shame on our own, *after* we have finished our first graduate degree. Yet our clients come to us biopsychosocial, spiritual and sexual beings, and they assume, reasonably but too often incorrectly, that we are trained in how to handle the dynamics of their cultural backgrounds. That's why it's crucial, for the sake of our clients, that therapists take the time to be comprehensively trained, adding sex therapy and spiritual intimacy to our skills in individual, couples, and family therapy. To be aware of one's own biases around religion and sexuality is also of paramount help to those clients who have been long silenced and who have received suboptimal care from medical and psychotherapeutic providers. Reading books like *Sexual Shame: An Urgent Call to Healing* (McClintock, 2001); *Real Intimacy: A Couple's Guide to Healthy, Genuine Sexuality* (Hodson, Worthington, & Harrison, 2012); and even the author's own *Sex, God, and the Conservative Church: Erasing Shame from Sexual Intimacy* (Schermer Sellers, 2017), and providing sound supervision to therapists treating the clients who were impacted by years of undereducation around sexuality, is critical. These practices will allow the supervisor, and thus the emergent therapist, not to take a bifurcated stance of all-or-nothing, good or bad in regard to human sexuality or even Judeo-Christian heritage itself, but rather to understand the historical and religious context of how and why Christian culture came to suspect the body. Using the four-part therapeutic model in this chapter will offer something of substance to the therapist and client who want to keep nuanced portions of their spirituality intact while affirming that the body is, and always has been, a thing of worth and beauty, and not something simply to be suspect or to fear.

About the Author

Tina Schermer Sellers has had a distinguished career as a marriage and family therapist, medical family therapist, and certified sex therapist. She also serves as a supervisor, professor, researcher, author, and speaker. She has won numerous awards and been featured on radio, TV, and podcasts. She is founder and Medical Director of the Northwest Institute on Intimacy, and she founded the community group ThankGodForSex.org. She is in her third decade as an Associate Professor in the School of Psychology, Family, and Community at Seattle Pacific University, where she teaches courses in marriage and family therapy, medical family therapy, and sex therapy.

Notes

1 See, for example, Matt. 18:6, 10; 25:31–46; 27:55–56, 61; 28:1, 8–10; Mark 9:37, 42; 16:15; Luke 2:10–11, 36–38; 7:11–17, 36–50; 13:10–17; 14:12–14; 17:2; John 8:1–11.
2 AASECT is the American Association of Sexuality Educators, Counselors and Therapists, the primary credentialing body for sex therapists in the United States.

References

Balmer, R. (2014). The real origins of the religious right. *Politico*. Retrieved June 29, 2017, from www.politico.com/magazine/story/2014/05/religious-right-real-origins-107133

Barbee, A. (2014). Naked and ashamed: Evangelical women and purity culture. *Other Journal: An Intersection of Theology & Culture*. Retrieved from https://the otherjournal.com/2014/03/03/naked-and-ashamed-women-and-evangelical-purity-culture/

Brown, B. (2012). *Men, women and worthiness: The experience of shame and the power of being enough* [Audiobook]. Louisville, CO: Sounds True.

Clark, N. (2017). *The etiology and phenomenology of sexual shame: A grounded theory study* (Doctoral dissertation). Retrieved from Seattle Pacific University Digital Commons: http://digitalcommons.spu.edu/cgi/viewcontent.cgi?article=1024&context=cpy_etd

Hodson, K. B., Worthington, A. B., & Harrison, T. G. (2012). *Real intimacy: A couple's guide to healthy, genuine sexuality*. Springville, UT: CFI.

Idel, M. (2005). *Kabbalah and eros*. New Haven, CT: Yale University Press.

Johnson, S. (2013). *Love sense: The revolutionary new science of romantic relationships*. Boston, MA: Little, Brown.

McCarthy, B., & McCarthy, E. (2012). *Sexual awareness: Your guide to healthy couple sexuality* (5th ed.). New York: Routledge.

McClintock, K. A. (2001). *Sexual shame: An urgent call to healing*. Minneapolis, MN: Fortress.

Nagoski, E. (2015). *Come as you are: The surprising new science that will transform your sex life*. New York: Simon & Schuster.

Newsom, J. S. (Director). (2011). *Miss representation* [Motion Picture]. Representation Project, U.S.A.

Newsom, J. S. (Director). (2015). *The mask you live in* [Motion Picture]. Representation Project, U.S.A.

Resnick, S. (2012). *The heart of desire: Keys to the pleasure of love.* Hoboken, NJ: John Wiley & Sons.

Schermer-Sellers, T. (2014). How the "Christian" purity movement causes symptoms of sexual abuse. *MindBodyNetwork.* Retrieved June 29, 2017, from http://mindbodynetwork.com/article/how-the-christian-purity-movement-causes-symptoms-of-sexual-abuse

Schermer Sellers, T. (2017). *Sex, God, and the conservative Church: Erasing shame from sexual intimacy.* New York: Routledge.

15 Creating Empathic Collaboration in Sex Therapy Supervision

The Four-Dimensional Wheel as a Practical Approach for Supervisors, Therapists, and Clients

Gina Ogden

Abstract

Guidance for recognizing and teaching empathic collaboration is detailed in supervisory manuals for psychologists, marriage and family therapists, and other health professionals; this chapter is the first to address this guidance for sex therapy supervisors. This chapter identifies eight key teachable elements for practicing the focused, multilevel attention that sets the stage for empathy and collaboration in sex therapy supervision and with clients: creating safe space, clarifying intentions, setting clear boundaries, engaging rather than diagnosing and treating, establishing a language of trust, modeling flexibility, acknowledging physical presence, recognizing countertransference issues when they arise, and understanding when empathy is contraindicated as a therapeutic strategy. The author's 4-Dimensional Wheel approach for sex therapy provides a practical model for empathic collaboration with both supervisees and clients. The dimensions of the Wheel invite clients to explore the contexts of their issues and their lives, physical, emotional, mental, and spiritual; the core dynamics of the 4-D approach engage clients through ritual, movement, and concretizing abstract concepts. Two case studies demonstrate how the 4-D Wheel can function as a clinical and supervisory GPS for supervisors, therapists, and clients.

Keywords

Empathy, Collaboration, 4-D Wheel, Countertransference, Therapeutic Presence, Integrative Sex Therapy

> **em·pa·thy**: the psychological identification with or vicarious experiencing of the feelings, thoughts, or attitudes of another. The imaginative ascribing to an object, as a natural object or work of art, feelings or attitudes present in oneself.
>
> (www.dictionary.com)

It is widely recognized by mental health practitioners that effective sex therapy supervision requires expertise in a full range of knowledge areas regarding the kinds of challenges clients may present. These areas include the DSM dysfunctions, gender and relationship concerns, anatomic and medical issues, cultural and racial diversities, behaviors such as BDSM, pornography use, and more. Along with ethical and protective practices such as confidentiality and boundary setting, these knowledge areas form the major guidelines for certification as a sex therapist, which is prerequisite for certification as a sex therapy supervisor as indicated by the American Association of Sex Educators, Counselors and Therapists. But not yet detailed are requirements or even suggestions about how sex therapy supervisors might relate and collaborate empathically with their supervisees or guide supervisees to practice the skills for the focused, multilevel attention that sets the stage for shared energetic resonance with their clients—aligning with how it feels to live their lives, walk in their shoes.

The concept of empathic collaboration is difficult to articulate because of its intangible nature, ephemeral, and dependent on variable personalities and circumstances. Nonetheless, empathy between practitioners and patients is documented as a crucial aspect of healing in medicine (e.g., Kaptchuk, 2002; Razzaghi & Afshar, 2016) and psychotherapy (Brown, 2016; Goleman, 1995, Porges, 2017, Siegel, 2010). Skills involved for teaching empathy are spelled out in supervisory manuals for psychologists, marriage and family therapists (MFTs), and other health professionals as vital to the overall therapeutic process (e.g., Zur, 2006). It is past time to establish empathic collaboration as a core competency required for sex therapy supervisors, with practical guidelines that can be transmitted both in person and over remote platforms such as telephone and Skype. This chapter introduces The Four-Dimensional Wheel approach (4-D approach) as a tested model for teaching and practicing the basic elements of empathic collaboration. Examples later in the chapter demonstrate how the 4-D approach can be used in conjunction with other methods to expand the supervision experience for all involved: supervisors, supervisees, and clients.

Key Teachable Elements of Empathy in Sex Therapy Supervision

The following are key elements that can be transmitted by sex therapy supervisors to supervisees, ideally through modeling them in the course of supervision, even when supervision takes place via telephone, Skype, or other platforms:

1. Creating safe space that allows clients and supervisees to feel heard, validated, and open to creative therapeutic responses (e.g., Batson, 2011; Graham, 2013; Porges, 2011).
2. Regularly clarifying intentions, goals, and parameters of supervision and therapy. This means continual checking in with supervisees and clients to update what they want and need, rather than making assumptions, deciding for them, or sticking to prescribed protocols (e.g., Allione, 2008; Watson & Greenberg, 2011).
3. Engaging collaboratively with supervisees rather than simply instructing them. This models how supervisees might encourage clients to explore

the full spectrum of their own issues, rather than simply diagnosing and treating their dysfunctions (e.g., Chasin, 1974; Corey, 2010; P. Ogden & Fisher, 2015; P. Ogden & Minton, 2006; Satir, 1983).

4. Forming a common language of understanding with supervisees and clients that emanates from shared organizing principles and that forges mutual trust (e.g., Barnett et al., 2014; Capra, 1984; Eisler, 1995).

5. Modeling a depth and flexibility of therapeutic presence—that is, the poise, self-assurance, and quality of being that projects the authenticity of who we are, not just what we say, and allows clients and supervisees to feel cared about and in competent professional hands. This might include judicious use of therapist self-disclosure to help clients feel less isolated on their path to wholeness (e.g., Conrad, 2014; Miro-Quesada & Coffin, 2014; Wegela, 2010).

6. Acknowledging physical presence, such as posture, eye contact, and touch as motivating factors in some therapeutic situations and negotiating if, when, and how to express these for the well-being of clients (e.g., Scurlock-Durana, 2010; Van der Kolk, 2015).

7. Demonstrating differences between empathic collaboration and conscious or unconscious overinvolvement with clients and supervisees—whether this takes the form of attraction, repulsion, fear, competitiveness, rescue missions, "countertransference" or other (e.g., Fincke, 2017).

8. Discerning when open-hearted empathy is contraindicated regarding a particular client or supervisee or situation, and developing abilities to project a presence that more appropriately fits (e.g., G. Ogden, 2017, p. 23).

What Is the 4-D Approach? And How Is It Practical for Transmitting Empathic Collaboration?

The 4-D approach is an integrative, embodied, active process that serves as an organizing principle to guide supervisors to guide supervisees to elicit from their clients enough detail and nuance so they can "experience their feelings, thoughts, and attitudes," that is, empathize with them for the purpose of helping them move beyond the issues that limit them and move toward their goals.

At the heart of the 4-D approach is the Four-Dimensional Wheel of Sexual Experience, which provides a graphic representation of four aspects of the sexual issues clients present in sex therapy: their physical sensations, mental or cognitive constructs, emotional feelings, and spiritual connections and meanings (Figure 15.1). This 4-D template offers supervisors a visual, systematic model to remind supervisees to help clients differentiate mindfully among the complex components of issues such as love, intimacy, desire, pain, dysfunction, and many more—with opportunities for reducing assumptions, increasing understanding and empathic connection, and inviting collaboration between clients and therapists.

The diagram of the Wheel can be used in a variety of ways: on paper to illustrate the 4-D concept to clients or supervisees, on the floor to invite clients or supervisees to get out of their chairs and actively explore the four dimensions,

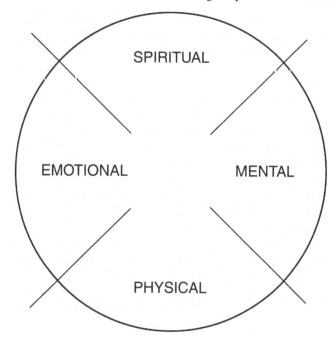

Figure 15.1 The Four-Dimensional Wheel of Sexual Experience (4-D Wheel)

or in the mind of the therapist or supervisor, to use as an organizing checklist or therapeutic GPS.

To amplify opportunities for eliciting complex information, each dimension in the Wheel implies a continuum of positive and negative components and experiences. Positive components and experiences of each dimension include a full range of coherence, excitement, pleasure, and joy. Negative components and experiences of each dimension include a full range of incoherence, dysfunction, pain, and despair. Contexts, identities, and personality attributes vary with each client and situation, and may be further complexified for supervisors by responses of supervisees.

Although distinguishing between positive and negative may seem broad, even simplistic, constant awareness of the continuum can be a crucial and centering practice for supervision. It provides opportunities for curiosity and collaborative interaction. It fuels hope, which, among its other attributes, is a prime component of the placebo effect, where clients shift spontaneously from fear and pain to an expectation of healing and health, a state that can change neurochemistry as well as belief systems (Kaptchuk, 2002). While the inevitable focus of supervision is on our supervisees' responses to their clients' problems and dysfunctions, we need also to help supervisees look beyond pathology in the interest of helping clients gain enough perspective to move beyond a painful past and present toward a future in which their lives will be richer, happier, more sexually satisfying. Humanistic psychology pioneer Abraham Maslow articulated this notion of nonduality in the mid-1950s in describing his hierarchy of needs: "Only by fully appreciating this dialectic between sickness and health can we help to tip the balance in favor of health" (Maslow, 1959, p. 135).

The process of guiding both supervisees and clients to develop the awareness to inhabit the spaces along the continuum of positive and negative offers a further arena for empathic relationship: teachable supervisory moments about what clients want from sex therapy as distinct from what supervisees may project onto clients. Often, this means acknowledging their choices between yes and no—to sex, to life, to therapy. Therapeutic applications of the yes–no response are reflected in techniques often used in conjunction with sex therapy, such as Eye Movement Desensitization and Reprocessing (EMDR) (Shapiro, 1997, 2012), brainspotting (Grand, 2013), and somatic movement (P. Ogden & Minton, 2006; P. Ogden & Fisher, 2015; Scurlock-Durana, 2010; Van der Kolk, 2015), especially in cases where trauma is involved.

Also implicit in all interactions on the Wheel are the various dimensions of time, which invite clients to explore the ages and stages of their experiences—physical, emotional, cognitive, and spiritual. Here, the Wheel becomes a vehicle for time-shifting: allowing clients to step into past, present, or future and locate themselves there fully enough to sense and feel and remember the essence of their particular experience before they bring these awarenesses back with them to the present. "Re-Membering" (G. Ogden, 2017, pp. 61–76) is a unique 4-D strategy to focus intensive attention on sexual and relational issues that may be impossible to reach by cognitive methods alone. These issues may include deeply ingrained states of dislocation, disconnection, disbelief, and dis-ease—what Fritz Perls, father of Gestalt therapy, called "the gap between the now and the then" (Perls, 1992).

This strategy of stepping consciously back and forth in time can clarify both the therapeutic and supervisory process (as in the example with Mike, later in this chapter). As a result of holding space for clients to explore the Wheel in this way, supervisees can learn to know their client's responses in such detail that they can offer a literal answer to a supervisor's question: "Where is that client coming from?"

Viewed as a whole, the four dimensions of the Wheel constitute a complex and fluid template that invites clients to fully explore the contexts of their issues and their lives. This kind of exploration opens a luminous window into these issues and lives, which can be fertile material for all concerned: clients, therapists, and their supervisors.

The 4-D Core Dynamics

While the template of the Wheel provides the structure, the moving force behind the 4-D approach is powered by the core dynamics. These include: creating safe space, initiating positive rituals, inviting movement, and concretizing abstract concepts. These core dynamics create innovative and collaborative conditions in which supervisors can interact empathically with their supervisees, and supervisees can interact empathically with their clients.

Creating and holding safe space involves establishing a physical and energetic arena in which therapists can acknowledge clients' pain and dysfunction while also encouraging them to expand their options for pleasure, desire, and intimacy. Such space is ideally clear, comfortable, confidential, protected from intrusion, and focused absolutely on the clients' well-being. According to Porges (2017), therapeutic safety is more than removal of threat. Rather, it is a felt sense that opens paths to relationship and connection, thus optimizing empathic collaboration. Such safety is essential to the feelings of hope that characterize the placebo effect (Kaptchuk, 2002). As a supervisory issue, creating and holding safe space begins with, or may be enhanced by, modeling from the supervisor (Graham, 2013).

Therapeutic ritual can be an integral part of creating safe and potent space for sex therapy and for setting the stage for empathic collaboration. Such ritual may include specific activities for clearing, relaxation, mindfulness, and focus (e.g., Allione, 2008; Kaptchuk, 2002; Miro-Quesada & Coffin, 2014; Wegela, 2010). Or it may be as simple and organic as usual and repeated ways of opening sessions, greeting clients, and so forth (e.g., Conrad, 2014; G. Ogden, 2013, 2017; Satir, 1983). However, it is used, ritual can clear the way to empathic collaboration by establishing the kind of trust that comes with fulfilled positive expectation. Further, creating new rituals constitutes tangible ways for clients to risk practicing new routines to replace habits that no longer serve them. As a supervisory issue, creating ritual also begins with modeling by the supervisor.

Movement is an embodied way for clients to expand their stories—positive and negative; past, present, and future. Inviting empathic to get out of their chairs so that they can physically explore their issues in each dimension of the 4-D Wheel engages their body's intelligence, allowing more information than if they remain seated, describing their issues in conventional talk-therapy mode (G. Ogden, 2008, 2013, 2017). Further, this kind of movement allows therapists to note and resonate to body language, expanding information and widening their sphere of empathic resonance beyond purely cognitive thinking or even emotional feeling (e.g., P. Ogden & Fisher, 2015; Van der Kolk, 2015).

Concretizing abstract concepts by working with tangible objects is a creative opportunity for clients to bring to life significant events that inform their sexual experience—much in the spirit of art therapy, where clients concretize their thoughts and emotions through painting, or of psychodrama, where clients act out a life story with words and gestures. As a core dynamic in the 4-D approach, supervisees are guided to ask clients to choose tangible objects that represent certain aspects of their sexual stories—typically an aspect they want to keep and expand, and an aspect they want to release and move beyond. As an example, one woman brought in a ripe mango to represent the juicy lushness she felt with her lover, and a black rock to represent the heaviness and terror of the childhood summers of sexual abuse she suffered in the idyllic family cabin by the lake.

Whatever the chosen objects, they engage clients in doing their own work, bring to light extraordinary complexities of information, and offer active ways to engage empathic understanding from therapist, partner, whoever is in the room—a special advantage for couples communication. At the same time, clients experience taking charge of these objects as they move them back and forth to different quadrants of the Wheel—body, mind, heart, and spirit. The process of concretizing lasts beyond the session; clients take their objects home, where these objects can continue to act as teachers (G. Ogden, 2013, 2017).

Together with the template of the Wheel, the 4-D core dynamics go far beyond the diagnosis-and-treatment model of sex therapy and the core-knowledge-area model of sex therapy supervision.

For supervisors, the 4-D approach can amplify the quality of supervision by providing supervisees with multiple ways to elicit information from clients and to report information to supervisors—through embodiment, differentiation, body language, and more. For instance, attention to the core dynamics can help supervisees discover, acknowledge, and bring into focus intersectional and contextual issues such as gender variance, sexual orientation, partnership choices, racial distinctions, cultural differences, abuse histories, and much more. And while the 4-D approach looks beyond prescriptive methods, both supervisors and therapists can incorporate any of these, if and as they are relevant for clients.

The Science and Neuroscience of the 4-D Wheel

Underscoring scientific and neuroscientific bases for the 4-D approach assures supervisees that they can explain the 4-D Wheel to clients who need technical clarification as distinct from the relational and abstract properties of the Wheel.

The 4-D approach is evidence-based, as it emerged directly from sex survey research (Irvine, 1990; G. Ogden, 2002, 2006a, 2006b, 2007, 2009, 2015; Reich, 1973/1942), and is grounded in holistic principles and systems theory (Bateson, 2000; Capra, 1984; Csikszentmihalyi, 2008), along with family process (Bowen, 1993; Napier & Whitaker, 1977; Satir, 1983), cultural anthropology (Eisler, 1987, 1995), cross-cultural perspectives on religion (Beatty-Jung, Hunt & Balikrishnan, 2001; Three Initiates, 2008), and somatic movement (Conrad, 2014; P. Ogden & Fisher, 2015; Scurlock-Durana, 2010). The 4-D approach to sex therapy and sex therapy supervision encompasses the widest possible range of cultural and relational dynamics, including historical influences, religion, epigenetics, and the evocative effects of the stories the body tells. In all instances, using the 4-D approach presupposes contemporary ethical and boundary guidelines such as those specified by AASECT, APA (2010), and other associations for professional development.

Equally influential in conceptualizing the Wheel have been spiritual practices that transcend therapeutic logic—what transpersonal psychiatrist Carl Jung referred to as "the irrational facts of experience" (Jung, 1970, p. 105). These include sacred geometry (e.g., Lawlor, 1982), which is implicit in the template of the 4-D Wheel, and practices from shamanic healing, such as meditative journeys and use of power objects, which are time-honored practices for expanding awareness beyond ordinary boundaries (e.g., Allione, 2008; Ingerman, 2006; Miro-Quesada & Coffin, 2014).

The 4-D Wheel approach is affirmed by current findings on the neuroscience of psychotherapy and sex therapy (Carter & Porges, 2013; Peciña et al., 2015). The template of the Wheel demonstrates the diagnostic and therapeutic power of differentiation, which "mindsight" pioneer Daniel Siegel places at the center of the quest for interpersonal integration (Siegel, 2010); mirror neurons are part of what he refers to as "the neurobiology of WE" (Siegel, 2010, p. 210). Research in brain plasticity (Graham, 2013) and in the neurobiology of orgasm (Komisaruk, Beyer-Flores, & Whipple, 2006) affirm that our brains are interactive and that we are hard-wired for spontaneous shifts in consciousness.

Movement between positive and negative components of each quadrant of the Wheel triggers bilateral stimulation, activation of both brain hemispheres (Omaha, 2004). The neuronal basis for the movement between yes and no is expressed in polyvagal theory (Porges, 2011), which tracks separate paths to the fight/flight response and to the response for social engagement and pleasure. The yes–no response underlies the sex therapy of optimal sexual function, as evidenced by the dual control (brake-and-accelerator) model of sexual response, pioneered by Janssen and Bancroft (2007) and popularized by Nagoski (2015).

Skill Sets of Supervisees

Supervisees of varying skill sets can use the 4-D approach to assess clients' issues and also deepen the process of sex therapy. Because the approach is both client centered and collaborative, supervisees can—and should—integrate 4-D with any therapeutic skills they already possess, from cognitive, behavioral, analytical, and relational, to techniques for relieving physical pain and dysfunction. The Neuro Update edition of *Expanding the Practice of Sex Therapy* connects the 4-D approach with the evidence-based realm of neuroscience (G. Ogden, 2018).

For supervisees who are experienced therapists but new to sex therapy, such as MFTs and social workers, the 4-D approach offers permission to let go of the need to be an expert in every sexual trend and behavior. The template of the Wheel allows them to invite clients to express differentiated details of their own sexual stories, where a major job of the supervisee is to hold space, listen with care, and question intelligently—as if they are entering a new land with their clients as their guides. For supervisees who are conversant with sexual issues but not current with the ever-changing advances in the sex field, the Wheel provides a nonjudgmental forum for clients to express updated information concerning issues such as intersectionality, cultural competency, microaggressions, affairs, nonbinary language, kink, gender fluidity, and more. For sex therapists who have received much of their training via online courses or academic institutions that undervalue experiential training, the core dynamics of movement, ritual, and concretizing may serve as on-the-job practice in somatic awareness.

"Walking the Wheel" has proven especially effective when the course of therapy feels stuck. Supervisors can suggest that supervisees invite clients to explore each quadrant along with their representative objects. This combination often unlocks dynamics that may have been in place for years—a factor most probably of engaging the clients as co-creators (note the example of "Neera," below). When countertransference is an issue, supervisors can ask supervisees to explore the Wheel to revisit their own responses to a particular case, even if only to mentally review their sensations, feelings, thoughts, and meanings (note the example of "Mike," below).

In short, the 4-D approach can serve as effective supervisory shorthand for a range of skill sets. How each supervisor chooses to use it depends on the receptivity of the supervisees and the issues presented by their clients. Outcomes of 4-D supervision have been reported as increased flexibility, trust in intuition, and above all, willingness to listen to clients closely and with compassion instead of having to have all the answers (G. Ogden, 2013, 2017, 2018). Feedback from this author's practice suggests that the 4-D approach may change supervisors and therapists as well as clients.

Three Crucial Caveats:

1. Using the 4-D approach in sex therapy supervision need not exclude other approaches. In fact, the 4-D approach is integrative, meaning that all of the skills and techniques that already work for supervisors and their supervisees can (and should) be incorporated into the 4-D approach. For instance, if a supervisor's preferred mode of therapy is medical, he/she will adapt the Wheel to clients who seek medical consultation; true also for cognitive-behavioral approaches, mindfulness, somatic work, and many more.
2. Supervisors need to experience the 4-D Wheel themselves before practicing it with supervisees.
3. Using the Wheel does not appeal to everyone. It is essential for supervisors to assess sensitively the approaches that work with their particular supervisees, and/or adapt their approaches to interest their supervisees (G. Ogden, 2013, 2017, 2018).

The examples below focuses on an experienced practitioner who is new to sex therapy:

Case Study

Danna: Discovering the Wheel Through Cultural Expansion: A Report From a 4-D Supervisor

The supervisee, Danna, a PhD-level psychologist and clinical fellow, had 16 years of therapy experience through agencies and private practice, and was now pursuing sex therapy certification. She opted for 4-D supervision after attending a training with a 4-D clinical supervisor.

Danna's client was Neera, a 42-year-old cis-gendered married woman who with her husband had immigrated in their mid-twenties to the United States from southern India. Referred to Danna by a local gynecologist, Neera's presenting problems were low sexual desire and vaginal pain on intercourse, conditions she said had been ongoing for many years.

Danna had expressed two points of anxiety about working with Neera: (1) this was her first case involving a specific sexual dysfunction and (2) she was unfamiliar with Indian culture and the issues that might affect therapy. Danna's supervisor reassured her that she did not have to know everything, suggested that she ground herself in the 4-D template and core dynamics, and reminded her that basic to the 4-D approach (and all good therapy) is curiosity: the freedom to ask clarifying questions. With Neera, as with every other client, Danna could regard herself as a traveler in a new land. Neera would be her guide on significant parts of the journey.

What Danna Learned During the Initial Session With Neera

Danna's premonitions about culture proved true. Deeply ingrained inhibitions about privacy along with an absolute belief in the intercourse model of sex had prevented Neera and her husband from seeking therapy as a couple. About a year earlier, Neera had secretly consulted a sex therapist because of increasing vaginal pain and lack of desire for any kind of physical intimacy with her husband. In a one-time consultation, she had been advised to use K-Y Jelly as lubrication, and had been assigned sensate focus exercises to practice with her husband. Although the lubrication helped at first, Neera continued to experience both pain and low desire. She reported to Danna that she had never asked her husband to engage in the sensate focus exercises, because her trip to the doctor had been secret, and because she knew her husband believed intercourse was the only acceptable way to have sex.

During this first session, Danna used her familiarity with the 4-D approach to hold impeccable space for Neera to relate her story. She prompted her with questions about her physical, emotional, mental, and spiritual responses, and listened respectfully without pushing to suggest change. With the Wheel template in mind, she tracked her perceptions of Neera's body language (tense), emotional affect (anxious, deferential, and at times disarmingly hopeful), mental attitude (smart and perceptive, but mostly hesitant), and spiritual energy (highly developed, longing for connection). At the end of the session, Danna shared some of her observations of Neera, asking her if they matched her own perceptions (yes). She then asked if Neera had felt safe sharing her story (yes) and invited Neera to make another appointment.

Two Weeks Later: Danna's Second Session With Neera

Before Neera's second session, the supervisor suggested that Danna show Neera a diagram of the Wheel as a visual aid to illustrate how sexual experience is multifaceted and interconnected. The supervisor explained that seeing the diagram and understanding her vaginal pain as part of a larger picture might encourage Neera to begin to explore the origins of her pain—perhaps residing in her relationship with her husband—and herself.

But in the session, the results were more immediate. As soon as Neera saw the Wheel, she pointed to the emotional quadrant and began to cry. Danna reported holding space again, this time for Neera to express her depths of feeling. As Neera sobbed, Danna pointed to the quadrants of the Wheel and gently encouraged her to imagine that the pain she felt in her body might be related to her emotional feelings that had poured out so spontaneously. Moreover, that her body's pain might be related to cultural messages about sex that she had internalized, and also to the deep meanings that sex and intimacy hold for her life.

Danna continued her narrative until Neera's sobbing cleared and she looked at Danna and nodded. Per supervisory suggestions, Danna then indicated how Neera could use the Wheel as a kind of map, so that she would be able to relate her physical pain to factors beyond intercourse, or even physical stimulation.

Once it was apparent that Neera understood the critical concept of interconnectedness, Danna placed the diagram of the Wheel on the floor of her office and invited Neera to stand up and speak briefly from each of the four quadrants. She modeled to Neera how she could move into each space and use simple, declarative "I" statements to differentiate aspects of her experience of low desire and vaginal pain—"just to see what would happen if you allowed yourself to speak." Neera began in the physical quadrant, then progressed to emotional, mental and spiritual. Her statements appear in Figure 15.2.

The statements Neera offered provided two breakthroughs for the therapy. First, they allowed both Neera and Danna to form cogent reference points and language for Neera's extremely complex story which was about to emerge. Equally important, getting out of her chair and stepping into the Wheel activated a flood of body intelligence for Neera, which seemingly overrode the cultural inhibitions against speaking about sex. Emotions underlying her story poured out in a torrent—offering far more information than in traditional sex history-taking, and for Neera, proving to be therapeutic.

**(4) "I want to reconnect
with my husband—
he means so much to me!"**

**(2) "I feel closed
and numb."**

**(3) "I'm a failure
as a woman
and a wife."**

(1) "I hurt so much!"

Figure 15.2 Neera's "I" Statements Regarding Her Low Desire and Vaginal Pain Organized via Quadrants of the 4-D Wheel

Neera's story centered on the stillbirth, 13 years ago, of her fifth child—a son that she and her husband had long awaited. Neera and her husband had never mourned the death. Her husband's major response had been anger towards the doctor, for whom he blamed the baby's death and Neera's ensuing hysterectomy that prevented her from becoming pregnant again. Neera felt like a failure. In fact, she *was* a failure by the cultural standards she and her husband lived by. Attempts at sexual intercourse between Neera and her husband were now infrequent, embarrassing, painful, and unsatisfying. Neera feared he would leave her for another woman who would give him what he wanted. She would have no way of supporting herself in the United States. If Neera returned to her extended family in India, she would be an outcast.

Danna quickly grasped Neera's grief and terror along with the cultural quandary. She chose not to enter deeper into details of Neera's story, understanding that Neera would not be attending regular sessions because her husband disapproved. Rather, she gave Neera a handout of the Wheel so that she could review how she had just experienced connecting her body, mind, emotions, and spirit. She also encouraged Neera to show the Wheel to her husband, and gave her a printed page of neuroscientific affirmations for using the Wheel, so that Neera could underscore her own truths and vulnerabilities with evidence-based information her husband might be inclined to value more, or at least differently. Finally, Danna gave Neera a referral to a pelvic floor therapist who understood the integrative value of the Wheel. She encouraged Neera to return when she was able, to let her know how things were progressing.

Neera returned in 2 months for a final session to report that the pelvic floor sessions were relieving her pain. She said she had showed her husband a copy of the Wheel and that he listened with interest to her experiences. The result was that she and her husband were finally able to express their grief together and have what she described as "heart-to-heart meetings" about all that the death of their baby son meant to them both—and about the closeness they both desired. She no longer feared he would leave her. Danna expressed gratitude that Neera had done such heart-centered work, and left the door open for her to return whenever she wished.

Discussion

Danna's story illustrates how the Wheel can be an effective aid for both supervisees and clients, even with clients who can tolerate only a few sessions, or in settings where only brief counseling may be possible.

For Neera, the supervisory suggestion to address all four quadrants of her presenting issue apparently offered her enough information to seek solutions on her own. In other cases, exploring all the quadrants can function as an effective diagnostic indicator for more intensive therapy or possibly a referral to another practitioner with specific skills in sex therapy, relationship therapy, trauma therapy, spiritual counseling, or more.

For Danna a main learning was that she could use the Wheel to acquire a great deal of client information in a short time, and she has incorporated the Wheel diagram into her toolkit for taking a comprehensive sex history and for helping clients who find themselves mired in stuck places. Importantly to the 4-D supervisory process, the experience with Neera illustrated for Danna how both the differentiation implicit in the Wheel and the core dynamic of movement can inspire clients to define and refine their own issues, tell their own stories, and interrupt stories of blame and self-blame—in short, to take responsibility for themselves. Danna revaluated the cognitive-behavioral process of diagnosing and treatment which had characterized her former training. She learned that using the Wheel in judicious ways relieved her of having to know all the answers—and of the lurking fear that she could never know enough. She took from this 4-D supervision perhaps the first great lesson of therapeutic presence and therapeutic empathy: hold safe space, listen deeply, and trust yourself, your client, and the process.

Case Study

Mike: Countertransference and Concretizing

"Why can't I get Arnold to move out of his head and into his body?" Karin's supervisee Mike posed this question in some frustration. Mike and Karin had experienced seven sessions of one-on-one telephone supervision together, and had already addressed his tendency to intellectualize, and also to take responsibility for his clients attaining their goals. So when he posed this question, it was evident to Karin that the "headiness" might have as much to do with Mike as with Arnold.

Like Danna, Mike's basic training had been cognitive-behavioral therapy (CBT). His approach to sex therapy was intelligent and straightforward. A self-described autodidact, he tended to find rational purpose for most behaviors in the universe. When asked why he opted for 4-D supervision, he answered, "I'm intrigued because I so totally don't understand the part about spirituality." He also related that he had had two prior "supervisors from hell" (disorganized, autocratic, and blaming), and Karin quickly learned that his ego could be easily bruised by anything he interpreted as criticism. Like many supervisees, Mike was better able to learn through a creative challenge than through direct confrontation.

Karin understood that intrinsic to the art of sex therapy supervision is the balance between delivering didactic information, offering suggestions, and allowing supervisees to make discoveries on their own. In Mike's case, he was smart, well-read, and could effectively debate any client (and supervisor). The issue was how to guide him to inhabit a larger worldview to help him invite his clients to do the same. The Wheel offered a concrete vehicle for expanding Mike's awareness as a therapist.

Not wanting to invite resistance, Karin decided not to name the issue between Mike and Arnold as countertransference. Rather, she posed the issue as a 4-D question she hoped would be a teaching opportunity with double yield: it would allow Mike to name his countertransference for himself and at the same time demonstrate for Mike a method of using the Wheel as a diagnostic tool—whether or not he had room in his intellectual universe for the concept of spirituality.

Karin initiated a simple 4-D "walk" around the Wheel during their next phone supervision session. The dialogue went like this:

> "Mike, I hear your frustration and wonder if it would be helpful for you to step into the Wheel to explore your question. First, imagine the Wheel." ("Got it.") "Now say one word or phrase in

each quadrant and see what happens. You can use the quadrants in any order. I won't comment until you've addressed all
four quadrants."

4) "The meaning I make of what I've just said is:
If you want a client to change, sometimes it's
important to notice yourself…"

1) "I'm pissed off that I can't
figure out how to get
Arnold out of his head."

2) "OK, duh! 'figure it out'–I spend
most of my time in my own head
so of course that's the behavior
I'm modeling for Arnold."

3) "Stopping to breathe and step into
my body feels grounding. But it also feels
scary in terms of being a therapist—I always
think I should know more than my clients."

Mike began in the emotional quadrant, then moved to mental, then
physical, then summed up his experience in spiritual: Here is what
he said:

As a result of his 2-minute experience on the Wheel, Mike was able
to make a full-spectrum connection on his own: that it was he who
escaped to his head as well as his client; that to help Arnold move out
of his head and into his body, Mike would have to move into his own
body first. The results in Mike's work with Arnold were almost instant.
Mike not only learned a valuable lesson, but instantly gained a tool he
could use when he felt stuck with clients in the future.

The Wheel technique used with Mike looks similar to the one
Danna used with her client, Neera. The truth is, what works for clients
also works for supervisees. A major difference of course, is that with
supervisees it is never *therapy*, it is an *awareness exercise* coupled
with skill-training.

Concretizing Abstract Constructs

A further 4-D intervention arose for Karin in response to her supervisory query about what Arnold actually wanted from engaging in sex
therapy. Arnold had presented with "gender confusion," what he called
"unwillingness to ascribe to macho male norms" and also major fears
about the unknown effects of taking hormones.

So far therapy had consisted of intellectual repartee between Arnold and Mike, taking place only in the mental quadrant. To help therapy move to more dynamic levels, Karin suggested that Mike ask Arnold to bring in tangible objects to concretize his ideas of "gender confusion" (G. Ogden, 2013, 2017). To represent the macho traits he despised, Arnold brought a mean-looking "Suicide Squad" action figure. To represent the possibilities he hoped for his future, Arnold brought a crystal bowl of water, which he described as transparent, fluid, and connected with nature.

Working directly with the action figure and the bowl of water consumed the better part of the next 5 months—as both Arnold and Mike focused on exploring each of these objects in the context of the Wheel. They shifted the therapy from talking heads to a body-and-soul-searching gender journey for Arnold, following his relationship with both macho-ness and fluidity: "rage at the patriarchy, dressing in drag, all of it."

For Mike, entering into therapy at these levels of deep revelation and feeling represented a life-changing commitment to being more compassionate and empathetic as a therapist. He found he was able to remain focused with Arnold, wherever Arnold needed to go. When Arnold reached back in time to relive the sexual abuse with his father and brothers, Mike held space, affirming the pain and betrayal and using the Wheel quadrants to guide Arnold back into the here and now, body, mid, heart, and spirit. When Arnold practiced walking in high heels, Mike offered balance exercises and acknowledged Arnold's "tottering" and need to rehearse more before going public. When Arnold revealed subtle bullying from his gender queer peers to come out as queer, Mike guided him to use the Wheel to chart his own reactions and make his own decisions as to how to respond. Together, Mike and Arnold struggled over what pronouns fit Arnold's phases of gender nonconformity. At this writing they have not come to a final conclusion.

For Karin, both 4-D suggestions not only transformed the supervision, but also led to a learning experience in gender-transitioning, which became a productive collaboration from which Arnold benefited.

Discussion

Karin's 4-D supervision with Mike is a reminder of three basic tenets of supervision:

1. Paying attention to one's self is crucial for therapists, not only to forestall countertransference issues, but also to develop empathy.

Paying attention hones the ability to use one's self as a tuning fork for clients' issues.

2. Collaboration with clients to assert themselves in their own behalf can be transformative for therapists and supervisors as well as clients.

3. In sex therapy supervision, the ultimate beneficiary is the client of the supervisee.

In closing, using the 4-D Wheel is safe, embodied, moving, collaborative, integrative, inspiring, and often surprising (G. Ogden, 2013, 2017). As an approach for supervisors, it can be relevant to a full range of sexual diversities and can be adapted to any phase of therapy, from history-taking and assessment to deep healing work. Supervisors can use it in conjunction with any other supervision models they already know.

Nuances of 4-D practice extend well beyond brief counseling, countertransference issues, and the scope of this chapter. The 4-D core dynamics include how to develop therapeutic presence, clear the energy of both supervisees and clients, and hold safe space for clients' stories. Innovative 4-D applications include how to help clients concretize abstract concepts such as desire and intimacy, and how to create deepening practices and initiate rituals for addressing and healing a range of issues, from abuse and trauma to compulsivity and affairs.

Questions for Supervisors to Consider

Choice Points—When Do You Use the 4-D Approach?

- Do your supervisees struggle with clients who are "resistant" or "noncompliant"?
- Do your supervisees tend to lose clients after the first few sessions?
- Do your supervisees see couples who cannot relate to each other with empathy or compassion?
- Do you ever find your supervisees working harder than their clients (or a particular client)?
- Do you see this their issue or the client's issue?
- Do your supervisees ever feel stuck with their clients?
- Do you ever feel stuck knowing how to help a supervisee?
- Do your supervisees ever feel they don't know enough to help their clients?
- Do you ever feel you don't know enough to help your supervisee?
- Do your supervisees ever feel perplexed about obtaining more information about a client (such as cultural differences, or desires for sexual practices they are unfamiliar with)?

- Are you clear about helping your supervisees focus on the client, not only the diagnosis?
- Are you clear about holding (and modeling how to hold) impeccably safe space?
- Are you clear about what it means to listen closely and without judgment?
- Can you describe your own meanings of empathic collaboration in therapy?

About the Author

Gina Ogden, Ph.D., LMFT, is an award-winning sex therapist, supervisor, researcher, and founder of the 4-D Network for Body, Mind, Heart, and Spirit. Her work is archived in the Kinsey Institute; her latest books are the Neuro Update edition of *Expanding the Practice of Sex Therapy* and the companion workbook *Exploring Desire and Intimacy*. www.GinaOgden.com www.4-Dnetwork.com.

References

Allione, T. (2008). *Feeding your demons: Ancient wisdom for resolving inner conflict*. Boston, MA: Little, Brown.

American Psychological Association (APA). (2010). *Manual of the American Psychological Association* (6th ed.). Washington, DC: American Psychological Association.

Beatty-Jung, P., Hunt, M., & Balikrishnan, R. (2001). *Good sex: Feminist perspectives from the world's religions*. New Brunswick, NJ: Rutgers University Press.

Barnett, E., Spruijt-Metz, D., Moyers, T. B., Smith, C., Rohrbach, L., Sun, P., & Sussman, S. (2014, December). Bi-directional relationships between client and counselor speech: The importance of reframing. *Psychology of Addictive Behavior, 28*(4), 1212–1219.

Bateson, G. (2000). *Steps to an ecology of mind* (Rev. ed.). Chicago, IL: University of Chicago Press.

Batson, C. D. (2011). These things called empathy: Eight related but distinct phenomena. In W. Ickes & J. Decety (Eds.), *The social neuroscience of empathy*. Cambridge, MA: MIT Press.

Bowen, M. (1993). *Family therapy in clinical practice*. New York: Jason Aronson.

Brown, L. S. (2016). *Supervision essentials for the feminist psychotherapy model of supervision*. Washington, DC: American Psychological Association.

Capra, F. (1984). *The turning point: Science, society, and the rising culture*. New York: Bantam.

Carter, C. S., & Porges, S. W. (2013). The biochemistry of love: An oxytocin hypothesis. *EMBO Reports, 14*(1), 12–16. Retrieved from http://doi.org/10.1038/embor.2012.191

Chasin, R. (1974, October 12). Personal communication, Family Therapy Symposium.

Csikszentmihalyi, M. (2008). *Flow: The psychology of optimal experience*. New York: HarperCollins.

Conrad, E. (2007). *Life on land: The story of Continuum*. Berkeley, CA: North Atlantic Books.

Corey, G. (2010). *Clinical supervision in the helping professions: A practical guide*. Alexandria, VA: American Counseling Association.

Eisler, R. (1987). *The chalice and the blade: Our history, our future*. New York: HarperCollins.

Eisler, R. (1995). *Sacred pleasure: Sex, myth, and the politics of the body*. New York: HarperCollins.

Fincke, G. (2017, April 20). Personal communication.

Graham, L. (2013). *Bouncing back: Re-wiring your brain for maximum resilience and well-being*. Novato, CA: New World Library.

Grand, D. (2013). *Brainspotting: The revolutionary new therapy for rapid and effective change*. Louisville, CO: Sounds True.

Goleman, D. (1995). *Emotional intelligence: Why it can matter more than I.Q.* New York: Bantam.

Ingerman, S. (2006). *Shamanic journeying: A beginner's guide*. Louisville, CO: Sounds True.

Irvine, I. (1990). *Disorders of desire: Sex and gender in modern American sexology*. Philadelphia, PA: Temple University Press.

Janssen, E., & Bancroft, J. (2007). The dual control model: The role of sexual inhibition and excitation in sexual arousal and behavior. In E. Janssen (Ed.), *The psychophysiology of sex*. Bloomington: Indiana University Press.

Jung, C. G. (1970). Civilization in transition. In *The collected works of Carl G. Jung. I* (Vol. 10). New York: Bollingen.

Kaptchuk, T. J. (2002). The placebo effect in alternative medicine: Can the performance of a healing ritual have clinical significance? *Annals of Internal Medicine, 136*(11), 817–825.

Komisaruk, B., Beyer-Flores, C., & Whipple, B. (2006). *The science of orgasm*. Baltimore, MD: Johns Hopkins University Press.

Lawlor, R. (1982). *Sacred geometry. Philosophy and practice*. London: Thames and Hudson.

Maslow, A. (1959). *Toward a psychology of being*. New York: John Wiley & Sons.

Miro-Quesada, O., & Coffin, B. G. (2014). *Lessons in courage: Peruvian shamanic wisdom for everyday life*. Faber, VA: Rainbow Ridge.

Nagoski, E. (2015). *Come as you are: The surprising new science that will transform your sex life*. New York: Simon and Schuster.

Napier, A., & Whitaker, C. (1977). *The family crucible: The intense experience of family therapy*. New York: HarperCollins.

Ogden, G. (2002). *Sexuality and spirituality in women's relationships: Preliminary results of an exploratory survey* (Working Paper 405). Wellesley, MA: Wellesley College Center for Research on Women.

Ogden, G. (2006a). *The heart and soul of sex: Keys to the sexual mysteries*. Boston, MA: Trumpeter.

Ogden, G. (2006b). The spiritual dimensions of sexual health: Broadening clinical perspectives of women's sexual desire. In M. Tepper & A. Owens (Eds.), *Sexual health* (Vol. 4, pp. 131–153). Englewood Cliffs, NJ: Praeger.

Ogden, G. (2007). *Women who love sex: Ordinary women describe their paths to pleasure, intimacy, and ecstasy* (3rd ed.). Boston, MA: Trumpeter.

Ogden, G. (2008). *The return of desire: A guide to rediscovering your sexual passion*. Boston, MA: Trumpeter.

Ogden, G. (2009). It's not just a headache dear: Why some women say no to connecting sex and spirit. In A. Mahoney & O. Espin (Eds.), *Sin or salvation: Implications for psychotherapy* (pp. 105–125). New York: Routledge.

Ogden, G. (2013). *Expanding the practice of sex therapy: An integrative model for exploring desire and intimacy*. New York: Routledge.

Ogden, G. (Ed.). (2015). *Extraordinary sex therapy: Creative approaches for clinicians.* New York: Routledge.

Ogden, G. (2017). *Exploring desire and intimacy: A workbook for creative clinicians.* New York: Routledge.

Ogden, G. (2018). *Expanding the practice of sex therapy: The Neuro Update edition.* New York: Routledge.

Ogden, P., & Fisher, J. (2015). *Sensorimotor psychotherapy: Interventions for trauma and attachment.* New York: Norton.

Ogden, P., & Minton, K. (2006). *Trauma and the body: A sensorimotor approach to psychotherapy.* New York: W.W. Norton.

Omaha, J. (2004). *Psychotherapeutic interventions for emotion regulation: EMDR and bilateral stimulation for affect management.* New York: W.W. Norton.

Peciña, M., Bohnert, A.S., Sikora, M., Avery, E.T., Langenecker, S.A., Mickey, B.J., & Zubieta, J.K. (2015, November). Association between placebo-activated neural systems and antidepressant responses: Neurochemistry of placebo effects in major depression. *JAMA Psychiatry, 72*(11), 1087–1094. https://doi.org/10.1001/jamapsychiatry.2015.1335

Perls, F. (1992). *Gestalt therapy verbatim* (Rev. ed.). Gouldsboro, ME: Gestalt Journal Press.

Porges, S.W. (2011). *The polyvagal theory: Neurophysiological foundations of emotions, attachment, communication, and self-regulation.* New York: W.W. Norton.

Porges, S.W. (2017). *The pocket guide to the polyvagal theory: The transformative power of feeling safe.* New York: Norton.

Razzaghi, M.R., & Afshar, L. (2016, November 8). A conceptual model of physician-patient relationships: A qualitative study. *Journal of Medical Ethics and History of Medicine, 9,* 14.

Reich, W. (1973/1942). *The function of the orgasm* (V. Carfagno, Trans.). New York: Farrar, Strauss & Giroux.

Satir, V. (1983). *Conjoint family therapy* (3rd rev. ed.). Palo Alto, CA: Science and Behavior Books.

Scurlock-Durana, S. (2010). *Full body presence: Learning to listen to your body's wisdom.* Novato, CA: New World Library.

Shapiro, F. (1997). *EMDR: The breakthrough therapy for overcoming anxiety, stress, and trauma.* New York: Basic Books.

Shapiro, F. (2012). *EMDR: Getting past your past.* Emmaus, PA: Rodale.

Siegel, D. (2010). *Mindsight: The new science of personal transformation.* New York: Bantam.

Three Initiates. (2008). *The Kybalion: A study of the hermetic philosophy of ancient Egypt and Greece* (1st Jeremy P. Tarcher/Penguin, ed.). New York: Jeremy P. Tarcher/Penguin.

Van der Kolk, B. (2015). *The body keeps the score: Brain, mind, and body in the healing of trauma.* New York: Penguin.

Watson, J.C., & Greenberg, L. (2011). "Empathic resonance:" A neuroscience perspective. In W. Ickes & J. Decety (Eds.), *The social neuroscience of empathy.* Cambridge, MA: MIT Press.

Wegela, K.K. (2010). *The courage to be present: Buddhism, psychotherapy, and the awakening of natural wisdom.* Boston, MA: Shambhala.

Zur, O. (2006). *The complete fee-for-service private practice handbook.* Sebastopol, CA: Zur Institute for Continuing Education.

16 The Future of Sex Therapy Supervision

James C. Wadley

Abstract

The future of sex therapy supervision will be influenced by technology and continual shifts in the field. Supervisors will have to take into account how accessible they are to supervisees and begin to think differently about the manner in which supervision is conducted face-to-face or online. Mentoring, enhanced cultural competence, and self-care will become increasingly important in order to remain at pace with the growing demands of supervisees and clients. Individual and systemic adaptability continues to become a necessity for all supervisors.

Keywords

Sex therapy supervisors, face-to-face supervision, online supervision, mentoring, cultural competence, self-care, sexuality, supervisees

The future of sex therapy supervision will push supervisors and supervisees to think differently about how best to engage with one another and with clients to address difficult issues. The practice of supervision will continue to transform into becoming more specialized and convenient. It will continue to become more specialized as the needs of supervisees and clients become more nuanced and sophisticated. In addition, supervisors and supervisees will want supervision be more convenient because of time and resource constraints. Moreover, supervisees will soon want the same convenience that is offered to some clients regarding meeting times, location, and frequency. Whatever paths are taken by the field regarding supervision in the future, it should be kept in mind that the foundation of effective supervision contributes to counselor development and reaching specific knowledge and skill outcomes (Sweitzer & King, 2014). Given this, and in consideration of specialization and convenience, there are five projections for the future of sex therapy supervision identified in the following text. The projections include the development of a supervision "app" or an avatar (e.g., a virtual supervisor) for sex therapy supervision; the use of remote office space; the inclusion of mentoring in supervision; enhanced cultural competence; and frequent discussions about self-care.

Supervision Application and Avatar
for Sex Therapy Supervision

The field of sexology continues to shift and grow. The number of profession-als in the field has increased because of the demand for competent service providers has swelled over the past thirty years. The number of universities, colleges, and sexuality institutes for training sex therapists has also grown over the past forty years. The quantity of formal educational programs has risen because of growing public interest in learning more about sexual health and wellness, as well as the accessibility of sexuality information. While there has been a high influx of clinicians into the field, the number of credentialed sex therapist supervisors remains limited. For those few clinicians who serve as supervisors for the growing number of sex therapists, use of online supervi-sion, similar to the convenience of online counseling has been a successful medium (Hanley, 2009; Leibert, Archer, Munson, & York, 2006; Mallen, Vogel, Rochlen, & Day, 2005; Shaw & Shaw, 2006). Perhaps consideration should be given to developing an internet/mobile-based application devoted to supervision that would be intuitive enough to address complex questions that supervisees might have.

For example, if a supervisee has a question about a particular sexual dys-function and how its etiology may have been impacted by a combination of physiological and sociocultural issues, the therapist would be able to consult an application on a smartphone or computer for support. Maybe the appli-cation could also address countertransference by inviting the supervisee to check a number of demographic and affective domains (fear, guilt, satisfac-tion, arousal, elation, etc.) that may yield immediate feedback. Because the field has evolved over the past decade to now include the use of distance supervision via Skype, FaceTime, or other internet-based platforms, it seems likely that the profession may not be that far off from engaging in "instant supervision," which is certainly more convenient.

The convenience of clinical services has already been extended to consumers who would like to access a therapist using an app. There are companies (e.g., Talk-space and Betterhelp) that have apps that consumers can use to contact therapists "on demand," and offer opportunities to discuss concerns and issues. It seems probable that there will soon be an app devoted to supervision on demand for therapists to contact a supervisor on any day, at any time, from anywhere.

The convenience of using a smartphone app may be criticized because of the assumed lack of personal connectedness one might feel in contrast to a face-to-face supervisory session. The same criticism was offered a few dec-ades ago about the use of the internet and the ability to meet with clients from a remote location. Also, like internet-based counseling, supervisors may not be able to guarantee confidentiality through the use of apps. Depending upon the nature of what is shared or disclosed, this may be problematic. Also, Haberstroh, Duffey, Evans, Gee, and Trepal (2007) found that the greatest challenge to using online counseling was technical problems, as ever-evolving technology brings new problems with bandwidth and connectivity, and the fact that computer literacy or tech-savviness varies widely among both clinicians and clients. Practitioners need to insure alternative measures of communication are available.

Beyond the smartphone application, there will probably be the use of a computerized supervisor avatar who conducts supervision using three-dimensional virtual technology. This "virtual reality supervisor" will have a wealth of knowledge and be able to sense and respond to supervisee's concerns instantly. Using artificial intelligence, the virtual supervisor (and supervisee) would be able to detect and process issues around transference and countertransference, ethical care, and possible relevant interventions. Because of the potential of having a virtual supervisor at any given time or location, supervisees may not have to leave their homes to be a part of supervision. The possibility of having a virtual supervisor is likely not that far off in the future.

The Use of Remote Office Space

If the future of sex therapy supervision may involve the increased use of remote supervision via internet, the use of applications, or virtual supervisors, there exists the possibility that the long standing therapeutic model of office visits will continue to diminish. Therapists may choose to forego the use of office space and only see clients virtually. Therapists (and supervisors) may save significant amounts of money and bypass some of the administrative responsibilities (e.g., paying rent, utilities, housekeeping, maintenance, maintaining files, etc.) that are involved with sustaining an office. Seeing clients virtually assumes that therapists and supervisors will be technologically savvy enough to run their practices and supervision in areas that have internet or telephonic service. In most cities across the country, the use of virtual office space is growing exponentially.

Inclusion of Mentoring in Supervision

Traditionally, sex therapy and clinical supervision has involved case conceptualization and consultation where supervisors and supervisees discuss relevant theories, ethical care, and intervention options. This relationship is maintained by effective communication between the supervisor and supervisee. Communication between the supervisor and supervisee must be based upon respect and humanistic principles that include trustworthiness, genuineness, authenticity, and empathy in order to meet supervision objectives (Neukrug, 2012). Effective communication serves as a foundation for the supervisor/supervisee relationship and remains important for processing cases.

While this traditional relational model of supervision will continue to remain crucial for effective treatment, perhaps the future of supervision should become something different. The evolving demands of professionals within the fields of sexual and mental health; having knowledge about new clinical strategies; the need for cross-cultural exposure and competence; and engagement in community service and activism lend themselves to the need for supervisors to become mentors to supervisees. Over the years, a mentor has been described as a role model, advisor, advocate, guide, or supporter who is willing to share knowledge and experience in the counseling field (Roberts, 1999; American Counseling Association, 2012, p. 68). In a study completed with students in counselor educator programs, respondents indicated that mentors should be approachable, have a personal style of mentoring, be encouraging, and provide clear direction and feedback (Boswell, Wilson, Stark, & Onwuegbuzie, 2015). Mentorship of supervisees would include providing guidance, support, and encouragement to engage in professional development activities that may allow for an increased understanding and appreciation of the profession and the responsibilities associated with being a sexuality therapist and/or mental health practitioner.

The days of supervisors merely reviewing cases with supervisees have passed, and the professional relationship should include mentoring as a component for specialized growth. In the future, supervisees may require a more dynamic and fluid interaction, wherein supervisors are capable of processing cases as well as emergent professional challenges.

Enhanced Cultural Competence

Within the past few years, there have been a number of compelling national and global phenomena to emerge that are relevant and may impact supervision and the professional growth of supervisees. Some notable changes include shifting immigration policies; the emergence of xenophobia, tribalism, nationalism, and discourse around white supremacy; increased sensitivity around sexual harassment and sexual coercion (e.g., #metoo movement); and the legal recognition of same sex marriage and LGBTQAI challenges. Supervisors will need to be in tune with both domestic and international phenomena that may impact romantic relationships and sexual functioning. Multicultural competence (awareness of one's own assumptions, values, and biases; enhanced worldview of diverse clients, etc.; Sue, Arrendondo, & McDavis, 1992) and exposure will be needed in order to address a myriad of issues presented by supervisees and clients. Inviting supervisees and clients to discuss their connection and interpretation of events may contextualize some of the challenges that exist in forming and maintaining secure attachments as well as navigating sexual dysfunctions. Supervisors should be prepared to host discussions with supervisees that offer some of the systemic and sociocultural issues that foster or inhibit intimacy. The future of cultural competence may soon require supervisors to become community advocates so that they may have firsthand knowledge of societal shifts. Some supervisors complete a cultural competence course or two during graduate school but never engage in learning about other cultures and communities outside of their offices. Supervisees will want to have supervisors who understand and/or have encountered a robust set of experiences who can address a broad range of issues that may potentially serve as undercurrents to healthy sexual functioning and wellness. Supervision discussions may become more dynamic in the future as supervisors and supervisees increase their familiarity with how domestic and international issues affect individual and relational wellness.

The present and future demands that supervisors receive additional training through organizations and conferences devoted to the needs of traditionally marginalized populations (people of color, persons with disabilities, alternative sexuality communities, etc.). Professionals will have to move out of their comfort zones in order to be educated about communities who represent different backgrounds and lifestyles. The Association of Black Sexologists and Clinicians, PolyDallas Millenium, Sex Down South, Catalyst Con are just a few examples of organizations, conferences, and programs that seek to engage sexuality professionals in dialogue that are devoted to inclusivity and diversity. Supervisors should encourage their supervisees to learn more about these organizations and possibly attend at least one event every other year.

Engage in Frequent Discussions About Self-Care

Not only should supervisors engage in good self-care for themselves, but should also consistently discuss the necessity and variety of methods of self-care (exercise, proper eating, setting boundaries, spending time with family or friends, etc.) with their supervisees. Because of the value laden and emotional work done by clinicians with their clients, it is often easy to neglect one's own physical and emotional needs. The cumulative effect of listening to clients' experiences and empathizing with what is revealed in therapy may result in vicarious trauma of the therapist. Vicarious trauma or secondary stress of clinicians is a response to clients experiencing traumatic, chaotic affect, provocative images, and/or intrusive memories (Stamm, 1995; Sexton, 1999; Jenkins & Baird, 2002). These reactions by the therapist may be short- or long-term responses as a result of countertransference in working with trauma survivors (e.g., Blank, 1987; McCann & Pearlman, 1990) or those who experience some level of relational dysfunction. Clinicians may also spend significant amounts of time negotiating and managing relationships with peers and a myriad of other professionals (MacKay, 2017) and possibly engage in challenging administrative work that leaves few spaces for good self-care.

There are several studies that address the nature of "good self-care" (Bressi & Vaden, 2016; Bradley, Whisenhunt, Adamson, & Kress, 2013). Lee and Miller (2013) suggest that self-care includes the following:

> Personal self-care is defined as a process of purposeful engagement in practices that promote holistic health and well-being of the self, whereas professional self-care is understood as the process of purposeful engagement in practices that promote effective and appropriate use of self in the professional role within the context of sustaining holistic health and well-being.
>
> (p. 98)

This conceptualization of self-care suggests that the therapist or counselor must be intuitive enough to recognize that there is an imbalance between professional and personal responsibilities. Too often, supervisors and clinicians become so immersed in their work that they are unable or refuse to acknowledge the debilitating effects of neglecting self-care. Moreover, some mental health practitioners are unsure of what good self-care even consists of. Physiological maintenance includes regulation of one's body and mind through getting enough rest and sleep, eating healthy foods, immunity building through frequent exercising, engaging and maintaining healthy relationships with friends and family, and spending time participating in leisure activities or hobbies (Lee & Miller, 2013; Newell & Nelson-Gardell, 2014). Roland (2009) suggests:

> Find what helps, embrace a stress-free zone now and then (whatever that is for you), and allow time and attention to use that help. If you meditate, do that regularly. If you use self-talk, then talk away. . . . Whatever the activity—whether physical, mental, or emotional—include it in your daily routine as much as possible.
>
> (p. 66)

Therapists should also have the capacity to say "No," and be able to set time, emotional, spatial and other behavioral boundaries in order to exercise good self-care (Bressi & Vaden, 2016; Lee & Miller, 2013). This can be elusive for some, as the helping profession presents an inherent paradox and dilemma. On one hand, professionals are encouraged to assist and support those who have poor individual or relational decision making or mental health issues. On the other hand, it is assumed that therapists should be emotionally present for all clients for every session. It is this natural conundrum that should be consistently discussed between supervisor and supervisee. The future of supervision lies in this often overlooked discussion about countertransference and its relationship to good self-care.

Conclusion

The future of sex therapy supervision will require individual and systemic adaptability, agility, and flexibility. Quality supervision and treatment of clients should continue to remain the primary objective for supervisors and supervisees. Moreover, supervisors should make sure that treatment of supervisees and clients remain ethically sound in order to increase the likelihood of sexual wellness and healthy sexual functioning. The future and art of sex therapy supervision will more than likely involve an expanded template of colors and abstractions, and it is imperative for supervisors to be competent and skilled artists who are capable of using various mediums to help supervisees become better practitioners.

About the Author

James C. Wadley, Ph.D., is Associate Professor and Chair of the Counseling and Human Services Department at Lincoln University. As an AASECT Certified Sex Therapist Supervisor and licensed professional counselor, he maintains a private practice in the States of Pennsylvania and New Jersey.

He is the founding editor of the scholarly, interdisciplinary journal, the *Journal of Black Sexuality and Relationships* (University of Nebraska Press). He is also the founder and Principal of the Association of Black Sexologists and Clinicians. His professional background in human sexuality education, educational leadership, and program development has enabled him to galvanize scholars and practitioners in the field of sexology around the world.

References

American Counseling Association. (2012). ACA graduate student committee launches mentorship initiative. *Counseling Today, 54*, 68–69.

Blank, A. S. (1987). Irrational reactions to post traumatic stress disorder and Vietnam veterans. In S. M. Sonnenberg (Ed.), *The trauma of war: Stress and recovery in Vietnam veterans*. Washington, DC: American Psychiatric Press.

Boswell, J. N., Wilson, A. D., Stark, M. D., & Onwuegbuzie, A. J. (2015). The role of mentoring relationships in counseling programs. *International Journal of Mentoring and Coaching in Education, 4*(3), 168–183.

Bradley, N., Whisenhunt, J., Adamson, N., & Kress, V. (2013). Creative approaches for promoting counseling self-care. *Journal of Creativity in Mental Health, 8*, 456–469.

Bressi, S., & Vaden, E. (2016). Reconsidering self-care. *Clinical Social Work Journal, 45*(1), 33–38.

Haberstroh, S., Duffey, T., Evans, M., Gee, R., & Trepal, H. (2007). The experience of online counseling. *Journal of Mental Health Counseling, 29*(3), 269–282.

Hanley, T. (2009). The working alliance in online therapy with young people: Preliminary findings. *British Journal of Guidance and Counseling, 37*(3), 257–269.

Jenkins, S. R., & Baird, S. (2002). Secondary traumatic stress and vicarious trauma: A validation study. *Journal of Traumatic Stress, 15*(5), 423–432.

Lee, J. J., & Miller, S. E. (2013). A self care framework for social workers: Building a strong foundation for practice. *Families in Society: The Journal of Contemporary Social Services, 94*(2), 96–103.

Leibert, T., Archer, J., Jr., Munson, J., & York, G. (2006). An exploratory study of client perceptions of Internet counseling and the therapeutic alliance. *Journal of Mental Health Counseling, 28*(1), 69–83.

MacKay, L. (2017). Differentiation of self: Enhancing therapist resilience when working with relational trauma. *Australian and New Zealand Journal of Family Therapy, 38*(4), 637–656.

Mallen, M. J., Vogel, D. L., Rochlen, A. B., & Day, S. X. (2005). Online counseling: Reviewing the literature from a counseling psychology framework. *Counseling Psychologist, 33*(6), 819–871. https://doi.org/10.1177/0011000005278624

McCann, L., & Pearlman, L.A. (1990). Vicarious traumatization: A framework for understanding the psychological effects of working with victims. *Journal of Traumatic Stress, 3*(1), 131–149.

Neukrug, E. (2012). *The world of the counselor: An introduction to the counseling profession* (4th ed.). Belmont, CA: Brooks/Cole, Cengage Learning.

Newell, J.M., & Nelson-Gardell, D. (2014). A competency based approach to reaching to reaching professional self-care: An ethical consideration for social work educators. *Journal of Social Work Education, 35,* 107–116.

Roberts, A. (1999). The origin of the term mentor. *History of Education Society Bulletin, 64,* 313–329.

Roland, C. (2009). Counselor self-care: The discussion begins. *Adultspan Journal, 8*(2), 66.

Sexton, L. (1999). Vicarious traumatization of counsellors and effects on their workplaces. *British Journal of Guidance and Counselling, 27,* 393–403.

Shaw, H., & Shaw, S. (2006). Critical ethical issues in online counseling: Assessing current practices with an ethical intent checklist. *Journal of Counseling and Development, 84*(1), 41–53.

Stamm, B.H. (1995). *Secondary traumatic stress: Self-care issues for clinicians, researchers, and educators.* Lutherville, MD: Sidran Press.

Sue, D.W., Arrendondo, P., & McDavis, R.J. (1992). Multicultural competencies/standards: A call to the profession. *Journal of Counseling and Development, 70*(4), 477–486.

Sweitzer, H.F., & King, M.A. (2014). *The successful internship: Personal, professional, and civic development in experiential learning* (4th ed.). Belmont, CA: Brooks/Cole Cengage Learning.

Index

Note: *Italicized* page numbers indicate a figure on the corresponding page.